T0323292

Advances in Corporate Governance

Advances in Corporate Governance

Comparative Perspectives

Edited by
HELMUT K. ANHEIER
THEODOR BAUMS

OXFORD
UNIVERSITY PRESS

OXFORD

UNIVERSITY PRESS

Great Clarendon Street, Oxford, OX2 6DP,
United Kingdom

Oxford University Press is a department of the University of Oxford.
It furthers the University's objective of excellence in research, scholarship,
and education by publishing worldwide. Oxford is a registered trade mark of
Oxford University Press in the UK and in certain other countries

Published in the United States of America by Oxford University Press
198 Madison Avenue, New York, NY 10016, United States of America

British Library Cataloguing in Publication Data
Data available

Library of Congress Control Number: 2020935585

ISBN 978-0-19-886636-7

Printed and bound in Great Britain by
Clays Ltd, Elcograf S.p.A.

Links to third party websites are provided by Oxford in good faith and
for information only. Oxford disclaims any responsibility for the materials
contained in any third party website referenced in this work.

Preface

This is the sixth edited volume produced by the Hertie School as part of the Governance Report series, published by Oxford University Press since 2013. The annual publication series also includes a compact report and a dedicated website at www.governancereport.org with additional background information, a governance innovations database, and an extensive set of governance indicators. The Governance Report aims to provide both policy-makers and analysts with ideas, knowledge, and tools to consider and implement policies and programmes that lead to better solutions to public problems.

In previous years, the edited volume has been essentially a scholarly companion to the more policy-oriented compact report. Contributions from academic experts in the respective field have provided more in-depth analyses of issues covered therein and alternative perspectives on the compact report's main themes. This year's edited volume departs from that pattern by taking up a topic—corporate governance—that was not covered in depth in *The Governance Report 2018*, even if corporate governance failures were seen as contributing to the global financial and economic crisis that was the Report's focus. Indeed, corporate governance had begun receiving the attention of policy-makers and the wider public already in the aftermath of large-scale corporate failures such as Enron and WorldCom in the early 2000s.

For this volume, we invited experts from within and outside the Hertie School to contribute chapters extending the study of corporate governance beyond that of listed corporations in order to shed new light on the overall performance of different kinds of corporations in market economies. We examine the strengths and weaknesses of current corporate governance systems and codes, experiences across countries, and the implications these might have for understanding governance behaviour and for policy-makers.

The impetus for this volume was the award of the Hertie School's Michael Endres Prize to Professor Theodor Baums, Professor for Civil, Trade, and Business Law at the Goethe University in Frankfurt am Main, in 2017. Professor Baums, co-editor on this volume, was honoured for his contributions to the legal study of corporate governance, especially those made in his capacity as chairman of the Government Commission on Corporate

Governance that led to the German Corporate Governance Code. The prize is named for the long-time Chairperson of the Hertie Foundation, Dr Michael Endres, who was instrumental in founding the Hertie School and who has helped guide its successful development since.

In addition to the chapter authors, many people have been involved in getting the Governance Report series to print. This volume in particular would not have been produced without the work of Regina List, formerly Managing Editor of the Governance Report series, and Christoph Abels, doctoral student at the Hertie School. At Oxford University Press, we are grateful for the support and patience of Dominic Byatt and Olivia Wells.

We also wish to thank the Board of Trustees of the Hertie School for encouraging this effort, and for providing critical feedback and direction. In addition, we would like to mention the members of the Report's original International Advisory Committee: Craig Calhoun (Arizona State University), William Roberts Clark (Texas A&M), John Coatsworth (Columbia University), Ann Florini (University of Maryland), Geoffrey Garrett (University of Southern California), Mary Kaldor (London School of Economics), Edmund J. Malesky (Duke University), Henrietta Moore (University College London), Woody Powell (Stanford University), Bo Rothstein (University of Gothenburg), Shanker Satyanath (New York University), James Vreeland (Princeton University), Kent Weaver (Georgetown University), Arne Westad (Yale University), and Michael Zürn (Wissenschaftszentrum Berlin and Freie Universität Berlin).

Finally, we wish to acknowledge the support that made the Governance Report series possible provided by the Hertie Foundation, the Berggruen Institute, Evonik, and Stiftelsen Riksbankens Jubileumsfond.

Helmut K. Anheier
Berlin, January 2020

Helmut K. Anheier is Past President and Professor of Sociology at the Hertie School, initiator of the Governance Report series, and a member of the Luskin School of Public Affairs at the University of California, Los Angeles.

Contents

List of Tables and Figures

Tables

Figures

List of Tables and Figures

Tables

Figures

List of Abbreviations

AktG	Aktiengesetz (Stock Corporation Act, Germany)
BO	beneficial owner
C. com	Code de commerce (French commercial code)
Cac	Cotation Assistée en Continu (French stock market index)
CEO	chief executive officer
CIC	community interest company
CRD	Capital Requirements Directive
CSR	corporate social responsibility
DAFNE	Donors and Foundations Networks of Europe
DAX	Deutscher Aktien Index (German stock market index)
DCGK	Deutscher Corporate Governance Kodex (German Corporate Governance Code)
DSW	Deutsche Schutzvereinigung für Wertpapierbesitz e.V. (German Association for Private Investors)
EBA	European Banking Authority
ecgi	European Corporate Governance Institute
ecoDa	European Confederation of Directors' Associations
EFC	European Foundation Centre
EPA	United States Environmental Protection Agency
EU	European Union
FAANG	Facebook, Amazon, Apple, Netflix, Google
FATF	Financial Action Task Force
FCA	Financial Conduct Authority
FIGO	formal international (intergovernmental) organisation
FSA	Financial Services Authority
FTSE	Financial Times Stock Exchange
GDP	gross domestic product
GDPR	General Data Protection Regulation
GmbH	Gesellschaft mit beschränkter Haftung (limited liability company)
IACD	Integrity and Anti-Corruption Department
IIGO	informal intergovernmental organisation
ILO	International Labour Organization
IMF	International Monetary Fund
IMFC	International Monetary and Financial Committee
IO	international organisation
IPO	initial public offering

M&A	mergers and acquisitions
MiFID	Markets in Financial Instruments Directive
MNC	multinational corporation
MOC	municipal-owned enterprise
NGO	non-governmental organisation
NPO	non-profit organisation
OECD	Organisation for Economic Co-operation and Development
PCG	public corporate governance
PCGC	public corporate governance code
PRA	Prudential Regulation Authority
PRC	People's Republic of China
QCA	Quoted Companies Alliance
SA	société anonyme
SEC	United States Securities and Exchange Commission
SEFORÏS	Social Enterprises as a Force for more Inclusive and Innovative Societies
SMEs	small and medium enterprises
SOE	state-owned enterprise
SOX	Sarbanes-Oxley Act
TGI	transgovernmental initiative
UN	United Nations
UNESCO	United Nations Educational, Scientific and Cultural Organization
UNFPA	United Nations Population Fund
UNICEF	United Nations Children's Fund
WGIG	United Nations Working Group on Internet Governance
WHO	World Health Organization
WIPO	World Intellectual Property Organization
WTO	World Trade Organization

About the Contributors

Christoph M. Abels is a PhD candidate at the Hertie School in Berlin, where he studies the reach and impact of disinformation and misinformation. Christoph co-heads the programme area digital transformation and cyber security at Polis180, a grassroots think tank on foreign and European policy based in Berlin. He holds a bachelor's degree in psychology from the University of Hagen and a master's in public policy from the Hertie School.

Carl Åberg is Associate Professor at the Department of Business, Strategy, and Political Sciences at the University of South-Eastern Norway. He completed his PhD at the Chair of Management and Governance at the Witten/Herdecke University. His research interests are in the areas of corporate governance, boards of directors, strategy, digitalisation, and dynamic capabilities. Beyond his academic work, Carl has worked as a consultant in various leadership, strategy, and corporate governance projects, in both the public and private sectors.

Helmut K. Anheier is past President of the Hertie School in Berlin and Professor of Sociology. He is also a faculty member of the Luskin School of Public Affairs at UCLA. His research centres on indicator systems, social innovation, culture, civil society and philanthropy, and organisational studies. He held a Chair of Sociology at Heidelberg University and served as Academic Director of the Centre for Social Investment and Innovation. He was a senior researcher at the Johns Hopkins University's Institute for Policy Studies, and Centennial Professor at the London School of Economics and Political Science. Anheier is author of over 500 publications and received various international awards.

Theodor Baums was Director of the Institute for Banking Law at the Johann Wolfgang Goethe-University in Frankfurt/Main and a founder of the Institute for Law and Finance where he serves as a management board member. He has held numerous lectureships in Europe and the US. Areas of current scholarly interest are corporations and capital markets. He has published more than 120 books and articles on corporations and civil and antitrust law. In 2005 he was awarded the Euro Corporate Governance Quality Award by the Federal Minister of Justice, in 2006 the Grand Cross 1st Class of the Order of Merit of the Federal Republic of Germany, and in 2017 the Hertie School's Michael Endres Prize.

Thomas Biersteker is Gasteyger Professor of International Security and Director for Policy Research at the Graduate Institute, Geneva. He previously taught at Yale University, the University of Southern California, and Brown University. Author/editor of ten books and principal developer of SanctionsApp, his research focuses primarily on international relations theory, multilateral governance, and international sanctions. He received his PhD and MS from the Massachusetts Institute of Technology and his BA from the University of Chicago.

Cecilia Cannon is a researcher at the Graduate Institute of International and Development Studies, where she also lectures in the interdisciplinary master programmes and co-directs the Executive Master in International Negotiation and Policy-making. She obtained a PhD in International Relations/Political Science at the Graduate Institute and the University of Geneva. Her research focuses on the design, reform, and effectiveness of international organisations (IOs); non-state actors in international policy processes; and migration policy. Cecilia advises IOs and non-governmental organisations on their engagement with non-state actors and their governance and advocacy projects.

Iris H-Y Chiu is Professor of Corporate Law and Financial Regulation, Faculty of Laws, University College London, specialising in corporate governance, company law, banking, and investment regulation, and is Director of the UCL Centre for Ethics and Law. She has published books including *The Foundations and Future of Financial Regulation* (Routledge 2014, co-authored with Mads Andenas) and *The Legal Framework for Internal Control in Banks and Financial Institutions* (Hart Publishing 2015). She is editor of *The Law of Corporate Governance in Banks and Financial Institutions*, Executive Editor of the *European Business Law Review*, and Research Fellow, European Corporate Governance Institute.

Gemma Donnelly-Cox is Assistant Professor of Management (Organisation Theory) at Trinity Business School, Trinity College Dublin. Her research is focused on philanthropy, organisational hybridity, and organisational responses to altered conditions of support at the level of organisation, organisational field, and society. She is co-Director of the Trinity Centre for Social Innovation and has expertise in research, consulting, and management in the non-profit and philanthropic sectors.

Jonas Gabrielsson is Professor of Business Administration at Halmstad University, Sweden. He is active in the European Academy of Management (EURAM), where he is a past chair of the Corporate Governance Strategic Interest Group. His research and teaching are focused on corporate governance and control from entrepreneurship, strategic management, and organisational behaviour perspectives. He also has a general research interest in the evolution and development of entrepreneurship education, innovation and societal cooperation in universities, and the commercialisation and diffusion of new sustainable technologies.

Morten Huse is Professor of Organisation and Management at BI Norwegian Business School. He has created research streams on topics such as boards in small and medium enterprises, actual board behaviour, and women on boards. His book *Boards, Governance and Value Creation* (Cambridge University Press 2007) has become a building block for scholars and practitioners around the world. High on his present scholarly agenda is rethinking scholarly identity and contributing to making academic research meaningful. He was President of the National Association of Corporate Directors in Norway and the European Academy of Management. He is 2019–22 member of the board of American Academy of Management.

Alexandra Ioan is a researcher focusing on the development of effective civil society organisations and governance processes. She currently leads the Learning and Action Center at Ashoka. She completed her PhD in Governance at the Hertie School in Berlin and holds further degrees in communication science, public administration, and public policy from the Hertie School, the University of Bucharest, and the National School of Public Administration and Political Studies in Romania. She also conducted research at the Stanford Center on Philanthropy and Civil Society, Stanford University.

Johanna Mair is Professor of Organisation, Strategy, and Leadership at the Hertie School in Berlin and co-directs the Global Innovation for Impact Lab at the Stanford Center on Philanthropy and Civil Society. She studies how organisations address societal challenges and contribute to economic and social progress. She earned a PhD in Management from INSEAD.

Michael Meyer is Professor of Nonprofit Management at WU Vienna, where he also serves as academic director of the Competence Center for Nonprofits and Social Entrepreneurship. His current research focuses on urban civil societies, managerialism, non-profit governance, civic participation (volunteering, giving), and social entrepreneurship. His teaching and training activities concentrate on leadership, organisational behaviour, and team management.

Ulf Papenfuß is Professor for Public Management and Public Policy at the Zeppelin University Friedrichshafen. Previously, he was Junior Professor for Public Management at the University of Leipzig and research assistant at the Chair for Public Administration and Management and the Chair for Business Administration at the Helmut-Schmidt-University in Hamburg. Previously, he was an officer in the military police of the German Federal Armed Forces and studied business administration and political/administrative sciences at the Helmut-Schmidt-University. His research focuses on public corporate governance and political control of public administrations and state-owned enterprises.

Julia Redenius-Hövermann is Associate Professor of Civil and Company Law at Frankfurt School of Finance and Management. She obtained a PhD from Paris II-Assas and the 'habilitation' from the University of Frankfurt. She was admitted to the Paris and the Düsseldorf Bar Exam. Her research focuses on corporate law, comparative law, banking law, and law and economics. Her advisory activity covers requests from national and international ministries and corporate firms concerning German corporate law and corporate governance.

Daniela Stockmann is Professor of Digital Governance at the Hertie School. Her research focuses on the impact of digitalisation and its challenges for policy-makers and citizens. Her most recent research project, funded by a Starting Grant of the European Research Council, explores the impact of the technological design of social media platforms on user behaviour regarding politics. She received her PhD from the University of Michigan, Ann Arbor. Before joining the Hertie School, she was Associate Professor of Political Science at Leiden University. Her book, *Media Commercialization and Authoritarian Rule in China* (Cambridge University Press 2013), received the 2015 Goldsmith Book Prize.

Hanna Surmatz is Enabling Environment Manager at the European Foundation Centre. Prior to that she was employed by the Association of German Foundations (Bundesverband Deutscher Stiftungen) in Berlin, where she worked on foundation law issues and international matters. She studied law at the Westfälische-Wilhelms-Universität Münster, Germany and at the University of Poitiers, France. She served on the board of the European Center for Not for Profit Law (ECNL) and, since 2017, has been the representative of the philanthropic sector on the Financial Action Task Force Private Sector Consultative Forum.

Filip Wijkström is Associate Professor at the Stockholm School of Economics, Sweden, where he also serves as the Director of the Stockholm Center for Civil Society Studies. As part of an extensive and active international network of scholars, he has a broad interest in civil society organising and comparative studies. Recent research interests include institutional fields, intermediary organisations, organisational hybridity, transnational studies, and governance. Empirically his interests embrace non-profit and voluntary sector organisations engaged in welfare, religion, advocacy, philanthropy, urban development, and education.

Miriam Wolf's research revolves around social innovation, social entrepreneurship, sustainability, new forms of organising, and organisations pursuing social and/or environmental goals. She holds an MA in Social and Cultural Anthropology from the Ludwig-Maximilians-Universität Munich, a Master in Sustainable Resource Management from the Technische Universität Munich, and a PhD in Organisational Theory and Innovation Policy at Leeds University Business School. She was a post-doctoral researcher at the Hertie School and worked at the Institute for Management and Social Policy at the Zürcher Hochschule für Angewandte Wissenschaft in Zürich.

1

Corporate Governance in Comparative Perspective

Helmut K. Anheier and Christoph M. Abels

The governance of the modern corporation is broadly understood as the mechanisms, relations, and processes for balancing the interests of stakeholders. It spells out the rules and procedures for decision-making, accountability and transparency, and distributional rights. More specifically, the governance structure of a corporation stipulates the distribution of rights and responsibilities among stakeholders, including owners, shareholders, debtholders, boards, managers, employees, customers, and regulators among others. Corporate governance thus provides the framework in which corporate objectives are set, the means of attaining them, the kind of performance monitoring required, and which roles different actors play in these aspects.

Large-scale corporate failures like Enron, WorldCom, and Arthur Andersen in the early 2000s, and the collapse or near-collapse of major financial institutions during the global financial crisis of 2008–9 in particular (e.g., Lehman Brothers, Bear Stearns, AIG in the United States, Northern Rock and the Royal Bank of Scotland Group in the United Kingdom, HSH-Nordbank and Commerzbank in Germany, and ABM-Amro in the Netherlands), brought the issue of corporate governance to the attention of policy-makers and the wider public.

How could such major institutions fail? While there were specific reasons in each case, one general answer was regulation, or the lack of adequate regulation of how corporations are run, especially in terms of financial decision-making, expertise, and oversight. Many of the regulations introduced in response to failures and crises have focused on financial matters and the role of finance in listed corporations generally. Such legislative action was spearheaded in the US and is most clearly expressed in the Sarbanes-Oxley Act of 2002 and the Dodd-Frank Wall Street Reform and Consumer Protection Act of 2010.

Helmut K. Anheier and Christoph M. Abels, *Corporate Governance in Comparative Perspective* In: *Advances in Corporate Governance: Comparative Perspectives.* Edited by: Helmut K. Anheier and Theodor Baums, Oxford University Press (2020). © Hertie School.
DOI: 10.1093/oso/9780198866367.003.0001

Next to legislative action, some countries had already introduced corporate governance codes. Such codes are a form of soft law, and are statements of principles, expectations, and good practice. In 1978, the US Business Roundtable was the first to publish such guidelines. However, the 1992 Cadbury Report in the UK (Cadbury 1992) and various Organisation for Economic Co-operation and Development (OECD) (1999, 2004) reports elevated the issue to the international level, which resulted in the formulation of general corporate governance principles in several key fields: the rights and equitable treatment of shareholders; the interests of other stakeholders such as government and the community-at-large; the role and responsibilities of the board; integrity and ethical behaviour; and disclosure and transparency.

The OECD corporate governance principles themselves rest on the tenet of 'comply or explain': if actual corporate behaviour is not in accordance with any of the principles, the corporation is obliged to explain the reasons for it. This tenet has become the cornerstone of governance codes generally, and as of 2020, the great majority of countries with a corporate governance code adhere to the 'comply or explain' tenet, and only very few treat such codes as binding and close to hard law (OECD 2017).

The OECD Corporate Governance Principles were first issued in 2004 and were updated and revised as a joint G20/OECD statement in 2015 (OECD 2015a). Since then versions of the OECD corporate governance code have spread to over 90 countries (Cuomo, Mallin, and Zattoni 2016; OECD 2017). Corporate governance has become a combination of hard and soft law and a more proactive than reactive field of policy-making in three arenas: the OECD, the G20, and the European Union (EU) (see OECD 2017).

The EU, however, represents a special case: corporate governance across member states is very diverse, reflecting different legal systems and corporate law traditions as well as varieties of capitalism and democracy. In 2003, also in view of the expansion of the EU to include ten new member states, and thereby creating the world's largest single market, the European Commission took initiative and issued COM (2003) 284 (European Commission 2003, 2012) under the title 'Modernising Company Law and Enhancing Corporate Governance in the European Union—A Plan to Move Forward'. The Communication was less of a statement of principles than an action plan to improve corporate governance practice in three general areas: enhancing corporate governance disclosure, strengthening shareholders' rights, and modernising the board of directors.

In one of the first systematic studies of national corporate governance codes in twenty-seven EU member states to date, Kubíček, Štamfestová, and Strouhal (2016) expanded initial research by Hermes, Postma, and Zivkov (2006, 2007) and found a significant strengthening of the quality of governance codes and compliance with them since the mid-2000s. What is more, they also observed a greater tendency towards convergence with international best practices, although major differences remain in terms of basic legal frameworks of corporate law and security, preferences for binding versus recommended provisions, and the kind of custodians or agencies in charge of corporate governance codes and their implementation (OECD 2017).

In addition, a veritable 'cottage industry' of corporate governance indicators and rankings has developed and provides relevant information to the burgeoning markets of economic performance statistics. Examples include academic measures like the G and E indices that measure takeover defences (Bebchuk, Cohen, and Ferrell 2009; Bhagat and Bolton 2008), the Gov-Score as an index that combines external and internal governance provisions (Brown and Caylor 2006), and commercially offered indicators such as MSCI ESG Governance Metrics as well as Standard and Poor's Corporate Governance Score. Although these various indicators of corporate governance have been developed and widely spread, there is an ongoing debate about the validity of what is being measured and at what unit of analysis (Black et al. 2017). Additionally, the direction of causality remains unclear: does firm performance require corporations to adopt particular governance practices or do these practices enable a certain level of firm performance (Aguilera and Desender 2012)? Some authors even argue that there is no consistent relationship between governance ratings and firm performance, as effective corporate governance regimes are dependent on context and firm-specific circumstances (Bhagat, Bolton, and Romano 2007). Whatever their methodological and statistical soundness, such indicators and rankings create media and public attention, and thereby at least indirectly support greater transparency.

More than a decade after the massive failures in the governance of financial corporations, and with continued governance failures in other parts of the economy since then, including the 2020 Wirecard scandal, it nonetheless seems that the combined efforts of international bodies (OECD, the G20, the EU, also the World Bank and the International Monetary Fund) and their national counterparts in governments, regulatory agencies, and corporate boardrooms are paying off. Yet many questions remain: what are the strengths and weaknesses of current corporate governance systems and codes? What have been the experiences across countries? And, finally, what implications for understanding governance behaviour and for policy-makers and regulators come to mind?

Corporate governance, however, is not only a matter of listed corporations. There are other kinds of corporations as well, even though they have received less attention as regulatory and norm-setting action focused on larger stock corporations and financial institutions in particular. Other corporate forms are not only more numerous *in toto*, they also represent a significant share of the economy. For example, as of 2018–9, Germany has 324 listed corporations at its main stock exchange in Frankfurt, over 720,000 limited liability companies, nearly 23,000 foundations, and 600,000 non-profit associations. In 2018, the US counted a total of 4,397 listed corporations (World Bank 2019) and more than 30 million small and medium-sized enterprises (US Small Business Administration 2018). In 2015, 1.56 million non-profit organisations were listed with the US Internal Revenue Service, of which more than one million were classified as public charities, including 86,203 foundations (McKeever 2018), In addition, there are public agencies, international organisations as well as national, regional, and local administrative bodies—a form diversity that applies to all countries.

Therefore, extending the study of corporate governance beyond that of listed corporations sheds new light on the overall performance of corporations in market economies. These include small to medium-sized corporations such as limited liability companies, non-profit organisations and philanthropic foundations, public corporations and public–private partnerships, social enterprises and cooperatives, international organisations, and corporations in cyberspace. In this sense, the present volume adds a comparative perspective to the study of corporate governance: across countries and across corporate form.

Throughout, we will keep a keen interest in theory and conceptual models. The standard reference is, of course, principal–agent theory as introduced by Jensen and Meckling (1976), based on theories of the firm and problems of information asymmetry in markets. Since its initial formulation, economic theory based on the principal–agent model has advanced considerably. Williamson (1988) introduced transaction costs considerations and the impact of asset specificity on corporate governance, and Voorn, van Genugten, and van Thiel (2019) expanded the model to multiple stakeholders and hence multiple contracts and their inherent information asymmetries. Davis, Schoorman, and Donaldson (1997) challenge the assumptions underlying principal–agent models and introduce instead a stewardship theory that assumes that agents or managers as stewards will place higher value on compliance and cooperation than on self-serving behaviour and defection.

Specifically, we will address the following questions across the various corporate forms covered in this volume:

- What is the applicability and usefulness of the various theoretical approaches for understanding governance behaviour?
- How does corporate governance differ across organisational forms?
- What implications for policy-makers, regulators, and corporate leaders come to mind?

The structure of this volume is as follows: Chapter 2 provides an overview of key conceptual and policy-related issues in the field of corporate governance. It first introduces the concept of corporate governance and reviews developments in the context of the global financial crisis of 2008–9. The chapter further discusses two internal control mechanisms, i.e., independent directors and board diversity, and then examines the relevance of corporate social responsibility and stakeholder-oriented approaches to corporate governance. The chapter also sheds light on the governance of technology companies, which have become an increasingly significant factor in many economies, as they seem to involve specific governance challenges.

Chapter 3 deals with two sets of major questions in the field of corporate governance codes that have emerged since the early 2000s in particular. First, what is the intended and actual reach or scope of such codes? Could and should all regulations of a listed company's life be explicitly codified in law? Or can a clear line be drawn between a code on the one hand and statutory provisions on the other? The second set of questions refers to a critical element of most codes: whether a majority or even all outside directors or members of a supervisory board should be 'independent', and with what implications for corporate governance.

Compared to most other listed corporations, financial corporations are different in terms of structure and operation, as Chapter 4 points out. The chapter asks whether the application of shareholder-centred corporate governance standards is indeed inadequate for financial corporations and discusses the role of regulation (i.e. board responsibilities, shareholder roles and rights, aspects of internal control, and the like). The chapter makes a case for a distinct corporate governance regime for financial corporations.

Chapter 5 acknowledges the different regulatory environment of small and medium enterprises (SMEs) and reviews codes that have been developed to establish guidelines for good corporate governance practices for these types of firms. The chapter points out that theories and models of corporate governance developed for large, and typically listed, corporations have limitations for understanding SME governance. Instead, the chapter proposes the extended team production approach as a potentially useful theoretical model for understanding corporate governance in SMEs.

Do corporate governance principles apply to public benefit foundations, considering the specific structure of philanthropic foundations as asset-based and purpose-driven organisations without owners and shareholders? Chapter 6 suggests that the corporate governance discourse needs adaptation for public benefit foundations since they have to consider both 'internal' and 'external' governance mechanisms, such as reporting regulations, external audits, and state oversight. Using a comparative perspective, the chapter reviews the rules of public benefit foundations as tools to safeguard the will of the founder and the statutory public benefit purpose. It also takes stock of current hard and soft laws and points to potential future trends and their implications.

Chapter 7 discusses the governance of non-profit organisations (NPOs), provides an overview of the development of the governance concept as it relates to NPOs, examines different constituencies and stakeholders whose interests should be balanced and integrated in organisational decision-making, and addresses theoretical positions of governance. The chapter provides a brief outline of various models of good governance in the field of non-profits and offers perspectives on emerging issues.

Like NPOs, social enterprises pursue a social mission, but more so than NPOs through the use of market mechanisms. Chapter 8 suggests that basic agency theories may fall short in understanding the governance of social enterprises. Multiple stakeholders—funders, beneficiaries, donors, and clients—typically act as principals. The specific challenges implied in pursuing multiple goals simultaneously and being accountable to multiple stakeholders make such entities prone to mission drift—losing sight of their social mission or downwards accountabilities, while focusing too much on profit generation or upwards accountability to stakeholders such as capital providers.

Public corporate governance is addressed in Chapter 9. It presents the theoretical and conceptual basics of governance of public corporations, mainly state-owned enterprises, before outlining the challenges addressed in empirical studies. The chapter also examines the Guidelines on Corporate Governance of State-Owned Enterprises by the OECD (2015b) and the diffusion of public corporate governance codes with a focus on the German public sector, reflecting on the crucial differences between, and potentials of, public corporate governance codes across different countries.

Chapter 10 examines the ways and means through which international organisations are governed. It initially focuses on the three parties that constitute their governance—member states (the legislative branch), secretariats (the executive branch), and executive boards (that advise member states and oversee the secretariat's work). Examining accountability mechanisms that have been put in place, it includes examples of mismanagement, corruption, and failed programmes. It also considers design features such as mandate, financing, rule-making, and engagement with non-state actors. Finally, the chapter reflects on some of the contemporary challenges international organisations are facing and describes different ways in which they are adapting and reforming.

The governance of social media corporations is the focus of Chapter 11, which provides an overview of the tension between the public and commercial rationales built into social media platforms, and their implications for corporate governance in cyberspace. Over time, the trend has been away from self-regulation towards a strengthening of national-level and EU-level regulations, that is, from soft to hard law. The chapter points out that industry-specific approaches towards governing social media have, however, not relied on insights from corporate governance in dealing with the challenge of how to combine public and commercial interests.

Chapter 12 then turns to behavioural economics and its application in assessing and understanding corporate governance. The chapter points out several key insights that can be gained from behavioural economics and how these could inform corporate law and governance codes. Specifically, the chapter depicts where hindsight biases, peer-group effects, groupthink, and denial effects have come into or could come into effect in German, French, and UK corporate law.

These chapters offer rich descriptions and analyses of corporate governance for a wider range of corporate forms than is the case in much of the literature, which mostly concentrates on large, listed corporations and tends to neglect other private corporate forms as well as public corporations. What is more, the chapters do so from cross-national and interdisciplinary perspectives. The results and implications for corporate governance research and policy are then assessed in a final Chapter 13.

References

Aguilera, R. V. and Desender, K. A. (2012). 'Challenges in the Measuring of Comparative Corporate Governance: A Review of the Main Indices', in C. Wang, D. Ketchen, and D. Bergh (eds.), *West Meets East: Building Theoretical Bridges*. Bingley: Emerald Publishing, 289–322.

Bebchuk, L., Cohen, A., and Ferrell, A. (2009). 'What Matters in Corporate Governance', *Review of Financial Studies*, 22(2): 783–827. https://doi.org/10.1093/rfs/hhn099

Bhagat, S. and Bolton, B. (2008). 'Corporate Governance and Firm Performance', *Journal of Corporate Finance*, 14(3): 257–73. https://doi.org/10.1016/j.jcorpfin.2008.03.006

Bhagat, S., Bolton, B., and Romano, R. (2007). 'The Promise and Peril of Corporate Governance Indices', ECGI Working Paper Series in Law (Vol. 108). Working paper #: 089/2007. Brussels: European Corporate Governance Institute (ECGI).

Black, B., de Carvalho, A. G., Khanna, V., Kim, W., and Yurtoglu, B. (2017). 'Corporate Governance Indices and Construct Validity', *Corporate Governance: An International Review*, 25(6), 397–410. https://doi.org/10.1111/corg.12215

Brown, L. D. and Caylor, M. L. (2006). 'Corporate Governance and Firm Valuation', *Journal of Accounting and Public Policy*, 25(4): 409–34. https://doi.org/10.1016/j.jaccpubpol.2006.05.005

Cadbury, A. (1992). *Cadbury Committee Report: The Financial Aspects of Corporate Governance*. London: Gee.

Cuomo, F., Mallin, C., and Zattoni, A. (2016). 'Corporate Governance Codes: A Review and Research Agenda', *Corporate Governance: An International Review*, 24(3): 222–41. https://doi.org/10.1111/corg.12148

Davis, J. H., Schoorman, F. D., and Donaldson, L. (1997). 'Toward a Stewardship Theory of Management', *The Academy of Management Review*, 22(1): 20. https://doi.org/10.2307/259223

European Commission (2003). *Modernising Company Law and Enhancing Corporate Governance in the European Union: A Plan to Move Forward*. Retrieved from https://eur-lex.europa.eu/legal-content/EN/TXT/PDF/?uri=CELEX:52003DC0284&from=EN (accessed 23 August 2019).

European Commission (2012). *European Company Law and Corporate Governance—A Modern Legal Framework for more Engaged Shareholders and Sustainable Companies*. Retrieved from https://eur-lex.europa.eu/legal-content/EN/ALL/?uri=CELEX%3A52012DC0740 (accessed 23 August 2019).

Hermes, N., Postma, T. J. B. M., and Zivkov, O. (2006). 'Corporate Governance Codes in the European Union: Are They Driven by External or Domestic Forces?', *International Journal of Managerial Finance*, 2(4): 280–301. https://doi.org/10.1108/17439130610705490

Hermes, N., Postma, T. J. B. M., and Zivkov, O. (2007). 'Corporate Governance Codes and Their Contents: An Analysis of Eastern European Codes', *Journal of East European Management Studies*, 12(1): 53–74.

Jensen, M. C. and Meckling, H. (1976). 'Theory of the Firm: Managerial Behavior, Agency Costs and Ownership Structure', *Journal of Financial Economics*, 3: 305–60.

Kubíček, A., Štamfestová, P., and Strouhal, J. (2016). 'Cross-Country Analysis of Corporate Governance Codes in the European Union', *Economics & Sociology*, 9(2): 319–37. https://doi.org/10.14254/2071-789X.2016/9-2/22

McKeever, B. (2018). 'The Nonprofit Sector in Brief 2018'. Retrieved from https://nccs.urban.org/publication/nonprofit-sector-brief-2018 (accessed 23 August 2019).

OECD (1999). *OECD Principles of Corporate Governance*. Paris: OECD Publishing.

OECD (2004). *OECD Principles of Corporate Governance 2004*. Paris: OECD Publishing. https://doi.org/10.1787/9789264015999-en

OECD (2015a). *G20/OECD Principles of Corporate Governance 2015*. Paris: OECD Publishing. https://doi.org/10.1787/9789264236882-en

OECD (2015b). *Guidelines on Corporate Governance of State-Owned Enterprises*. Paris: OECD Publishing.

OECD (2017). *OECD Corporate Governance Fact Book (2017)*. Paris: OECD Publishing.

US Small Business Administration (2018). '2018 Small Business Profile: United States'. Retrieved from https://www.sba.gov/sites/default/files/advocacy/2018-Small-Business-Profiles-US.pdf (accessed 23 August 2019).

Voorn, B., van Genugten, M., and van Thiel, S. (2019). 'Multiple Principals, Multiple Problems: Implications for Effective Governance and a Research Agenda for Joint Service Delivery', *Public Administration*. https://doi.org/10.1111/padm.12587

Williamson, O. E. (1988). 'Corporate Finance and Corporate Governance', *The Journal of Finance*, 43(3): 567–91.

World Bank (2019). Listed domestic companies, total. Retrieved from https://data.worldbank.org/indicator/CM.MKT.LDOM.NO?locations=US (accessed 23 August 2019).

2

Corporate Governance:
What Are the Issues?

Helmut K. Anheier and Christoph M. Abels

In the most general sense, corporate governance is concerned with the behavioural consequences when ownership and management of a corporation are separate. Effross (2013: 1) pointedly summarises the core issues when stating that: 'corporate governance is about "who gets what, when, and how"'. More specifically, corporate governance is about balancing the interests of directors, officers, shareholders, and other stakeholders affected by corporate decisions and behaviours. Corporate governance deals with 'power and influence over decision making within the corporation' (Aguilera and Jackson 2010: 487). More broadly, Lord Cadbury (Foreword in Iskander and Chamlou 2000: vi) views corporate governance as concerned 'with holding the balance between economic and social goals and between individual and economic goals'.

How this balance is interpreted, however, depends on the understanding of corporate governance in the first place. Narrowly understood, corporate governance becomes a means to minimise risks resulting from principal–agent problems. If understood in a broader sense, corporate governance takes into account the risks of other stakeholders as well, and can even extend to aspects of corporate social responsibility (CSR) more widely, thereby linking corporate and societal goals. The underlying models that inform these variations differ as well: principal–agent models stress the primacy of the shareholders, while models concerned with stakeholders extend the responsibility of a corporation to more diverse set of interests.

Related to a narrow and broad understanding of corporate governance are primarily economic versus managerial perspectives (Aguilera and Jackson 2010). For the former, agency theory is the prime example, with the assumptions of microeconomics providing the basis (Dalton et al. 2007). Managerial views start from the stewardship approach introduced by Davis, Schoorman,

Helmut K. Anheier and Christoph M. Abels, *Corporate Governance: What Are the Issues?* In: *Advances in Corporate Governance: Comparative Perspectives.* Edited by: Helmut K. Anheier and Theodor Baums, Oxford University Press (2020).
© Hertie School.
DOI: 10.1093/oso/9780198866367.003.0002

and Donaldson (1997), which uses a different set of assumptions, in particular a preference for contract compliance rather than self-serving behaviour.

Let's look at agency theory first. It assumes that the separation of ownership and management entails inherent problems since the interests of both parties are not necessarily aligned (Fama and Jensen 1983; Jensen and Meckling 1976). These problems have to be mitigated by monitoring the management and aligning their behaviour with shareholders' interests. However, this monitoring is costly, since shareholders only have imperfect information, and dispersed ownership can cause free-rider problems, which reduce incentives to exercise rights.

To control managerial behaviour, and thereby cope with the agency problem, Dalton et al. (2007) identify three approaches: first, the independence approach, which requires governing boards to be independent of management; second, the equity approach, which gives managers some degree of ownership through equity, with the objective of achieving greater alignment of their interests with those of the principals; and third, the discipline or market control approach, whereby management with primarily self-serving motivations ultimately expose the corporation to acquisition, which would put their own positions in jeopardy.

Agency theory has a major limitation: it does not account for relationships beyond the principal–agent dyad. Both actors are assumed to have no outside relationships that might influence their behaviour—the agent's loyalty is entirely devoted to the principal, while the principal allocates all available resources to the agent. Additionally, agency models often assume long-term relationships in which either party is locked in given positions (Hoskisson et al. 2013).

These assumptions, however, do not reflect the increasing complexity and diversity in the corporate world. As Hoskisson et al. (2013) point out, private equity funds, hedge funds, and venture capital firms operate as principals in those firms in which they have invested and simultaneously act as agents to those who have provided them with the necessary resources. Accordingly, the authors distinguish between agent-owners, i.e., principals in the traditional sense, ultimate principals, i.e., investors spreading their capital such as institutional investors, and agents, i.e., corporations owned by investors holding equity. Furthermore, corporations with social objectives, such as philanthropic foundations, social enterprises, and non-profit organisations, have multiple principals they have to serve (see Surmatz and Mair, Wolf, and Ioan, in this volume).

In stewardship theory, managers are not seen as being only driven by self-interest; rather, they wish to reach the organisation's objectives (Davis,

Schoorman, and Donaldson 1997). As Davis and colleagues (1997: 24) argue, 'The steward places higher values on cooperation than defection.' Therefore, stewardship theory highlights motivations beyond economic incentives and stresses the roles of values and purpose. Valuing cooperation also highlights the relevance of corporate culture and management models that focus on cooperation instead of top-down leadership. Stewardship theory therefore must be viewed in the light of a specific corporate culture and a certain type of leadership style.

Overall, agency theory is a good starting point as it addresses the essence of the problem that led to the development of corporate governance: the division of owners and managers of a firm. However, as companies are increasingly scrutinised for their role in society, agency theory is increasingly too narrow to handle multiple stakeholders. As a result, agency theory is less well equipped to inform the governance of organisations and corporations other than listed companies. Hybrid organisations, such as social enterprises, do not have a single principal, nor do hedge funds have only one agent. Accordingly, other theoretical approaches, like stewardship theory, could provide a better frame to discuss corporate governance. Understanding corporate governance as the art of determining 'who gets what, when and how' highlights the importance of asking what is meant by 'who'.

Shareholder Primacy and Corporate Social Responsibility

Corporate governance is about agency problems caused by the division of ownership and control. The underlying rationale is primarily informed by shareholder primacy, which states that corporations exist to generate profits for their shareholders (Berle and Means 1968). Milton Friedman (1970) famously argued that social responsibility is harming free societies. By demanding socially responsible business operations, businesses are promoting views that demonise profits as 'wicked' and 'immoral' and subsequently encourage regulation by external forces. For Friedman (1970), 'there is only one social responsibility of business—to use its resources and engage in activities designed to increase its profits so long as it stays within the rules of the game, which is to say, engages in open and free competition without deception or fraud.'

Shareholder primacy is not without criticism. Stout (2013) argues that for most of the twentieth century, corporate executives and directors understood themselves to be stewards of their companies, serving more than just equity investors, but also various stakeholders and society as a whole. Yet, this 'managerialist' philosophy was replaced by shareholder primacy and the rise of neoclassical economics, which assumes that agency cost problems are efficiently solved with a focus on shareholder value.

Stout (2013) casts serious doubt over the efficiency of shareholder primacy for corporate performance. Returns on investment for shareholders remained flat during the 'lost decade' of 2000–9, while corporations became more shareholder-centric and, therefore, more attractive to investors. Moreover, the number of corporations listed on United States exchanges declined from 8,823 to 5,401 between 1997 and 2008, which seems inconsistent with the shareholder primacy concept dominant at that time. Beyond this general critique, shareholder primacy is also criticised from a CSR perspective, highlighting the absence of environmental or social considerations. The 'triple bottom line' of social, environmental, and economic sustainability seems to find greater resonance among stakeholders, including institutional investors (Filatotchev and Stahl 2015).

In contrast to a shareholder-centric approach, a stakeholder approach takes a more holistic perspective on corporate governance. Fundamentally, it is based on the idea that a company has more stakeholders than just executives, directors, and shareholders. The approach states that corporate managers should work for the interests of all stakeholders and include them in the governance process. The concept took off in the 1980s with the release of Freeman's (1984) seminal book *Strategic Management: A Stakeholder Approach*, which embedded the concept in management scholarship and management practice (Mitchell, Agle, and Wood 1997). Freeman (1984: 46) defines stakeholders as 'any group or individual who can affect or is affected by the achievement of the organization's objectives'.

Donaldson and Preston (1995) argue that stakeholder theory is essentially managerial: managers are to address the legitimate interests of relevant stakeholders when setting objectives and policies, establishing organisational structures and procedures, and making decisions case by case. However, with different implications than shareholder-centric models, the theory is also normative. It assumes that the interests of stakeholders are of intrinsic value, in the sense that every stakeholder merits its own consideration in view of their interests, and that these may not necessarily benefit shareholders.

CSR is an expression of stakeholder approaches and has become more important in the context of multinational corporations (MNCs) in particular. While CSR was for a long time seen primarily as a responsibility in the home countries of such corporations, it is increasingly relevant across constituencies and jurisdictions. For example, MNCs operating global supply chains have environmental, economic, and social impacts in multiple countries (Andersen and Skjoett-Larsen 2009). Next to manufacturing MNCs, software and technology companies face CSR-related problems as well. Facebook, for example, was criticised for its role in the ongoing genocide of the Rohingya minority in Myanmar (Stecklow 2018). The company was castigated for allowing hate speech and fake news to flourish on its platform, which encouraged violence against the Muslim community. This is particularly problematic in Myanmar, where Facebook is a dominant source of information (Mclaughlin 2018).

Including CSR in corporate strategy and endorsing a stakeholder approach raises questions about best practices. Filatotchev and Stahl (2015) provide a framework for MNCs based on centralisation and localisation. In this framework, MNCs need to decide whether their CSR approach is globally coordinated by headquarters (global CSR approach), driven by responsiveness to local needs (local CSR approach), or a combination of both (transnational CSR approach). The authors endorse the transnational approach, demanding that corporations develop global strategies but simultaneously allow executives of local subsidiaries to adjust the global strategy to local circumstances and needs. When adopting the transnational approach, MNCs would need to align their corporate governance regime accordingly. According to the authors, control mechanisms should be based not on financial indicators, but on strategic ones, promoting a growing market share as well as legitimacy and local stakeholder support, which favours a long-term orientation instead of short-term financial gains. Additionally, management should be incentivised based on the triple bottom line, thereby also making them accountable to a more diverse body of stakeholders. Risk management systems should include both economic as well as social factors. Finally, Filatotchev and Stahl (2015) recommend that the board be made more diverse, with institutionalised stakeholder representation, including a stakeholder relations committee.

Looking at corporate governance through the lens of CSR shows the limitations of the shareholder primacy approach. Serving the narrow interests of those financially invested in a company ignores the firm's broader role in society: achieving economic sustainability is no longer seen as the only responsibility a company has. Indicating a shift away from shareholder primacy, chief executive officers (CEOs) of leading US corporations have recently started to acknowledge their responsibility beyond mere shareholder value (Gelles and Yaffe-Bellany 2019). For this broader understanding of corporate governance, enlarging the 'who' in Effross's (2013) definition, stakeholder theory can provide a suitable analytic framework. Accordingly, corporate governance codes, one of the main policy instruments in the field, have to adapt to the changing demands of an increasingly interconnected world and reflect changing societal understandings as to the responsibilities of the corporation as well.

Corporate Governance Codes

Corporate governance approaches are closely linked to the development of corporate governance codes, which themselves are often a response to corporate scandals rather than proactive and precautionary thinking among policy-makers or businesses. These codes define standards of good practice on issues such as board independence, remuneration, accountability to shareholders, and the like. In 1978, the US Business Roundtable issued the first such guidelines, followed by Hong Kong Stock Exchange's Code of Best Practice, Listing Rules in 1989 (Aguilera and Cuervo-Cazurra 2009). Three years later, in 1992, the Cadbury Committee Report, *The Financial Aspects of Corporate Governance*, was published in the UK, following the 1990 British recession and a series of prominent corporate failures (Aguilera and Cuervo-Cazurra 2004).

The Cadbury Report proposed 'properly constituted boards, separation of the functions of chairman and of chief executives, audit committees, vigilant shareholders and auditing systems which provide full and timely disclosure' (Cadbury 1992: 53) as central to good corporate governance. Accordingly, the Report defined a Code of Best Practice that set standards concerning boards, non-executive and executive directors, as well as controlling and reporting guidelines. The Cadbury Report attracted much interest from other countries and, with the OECD taking a lead role from the 1990s onward, triggered the development of corporate governance codes across the world.

Another major development that drew the attention of the general public, regulators, and scholars alike to the field of corporate governance unfolded during the corporate scandals of the early 2000s. In 2000, Enron, a US energy company, was named the most innovative corporation by *Fortune* magazine's survey of Most Admired Companies (Stein 2000). It was Enron's sixth consecutive award, being the most innovative company since 1995 (McLean and Elkind 2006). However, within one year Enron's stock price dropped to nearly zero, and eventually the corporation filed for bankruptcy on 2 December 2001 (Healy and Palepu 2003). The company had used a variety of fraudulent accounting practices to inflate their earnings, while actually losing money. Enron's external auditors, Arthur Andersen, was blamed for not recognising the company's problems while earning $25 million in audit and $27 million in accounting fees (Healy and Palepu 2003).

Less than a year later, on 21 July 2002, WorldCom, a telecommunications company, filed for bankruptcy after what was until the Lehman Brothers collapse in 2008 the largest filing in US history. WorldCom conducted fraud valued at more than $9 billion through false or unsupported accounting entries (Beresford, Katzenbach, and Rogers 2003). The main causes of these corporate scandals were seen as a bias towards short-term stock price gains over the company's well-being and its long-term profitability (Mitchell 2001), and the capture of external auditors like Arthur Andersen.

In the increasingly politicised climate in the wake of these two major scandals that questioned existing approaches to corporate governance, lawmakers hurried to adopt the Sarbanes-Oxley Act (SOX) of 2002 (see Effross 2013). The Act was a significant change in US legal precedence relating to corporate governance: it meant a transition from a regulatory approach consisting primarily of disclosure requirements to a substantive corporate governance oversight mandate given to the US Securities and Exchange Commission (SEC), formerly a domain of state-level corporate law (Romano 2005). The Act included measures to require independent audit committees, restrict corporations' purchases of non-auditing services from their auditors, prohibit corporate loans to officers, and require executive certification of financial statements.

With SOX having received a mixed reception, the next reminder for the importance of good corporate governance came with the global financial crisis of 2008–9. So clear was the failure of corporate governance that some critics even called it 'corporate apocalypse' (Caulkin 2013). The day Lehman Brothers filed for bankruptcy, on 15 September 2008, the *Wall Street Journal* asked 'Where Was Lehman's Board?' (Berman 2008). In the article, the *Journal* stressed that 'a group of 10 people [...] carried the health of the world's financial system on their shoulders [...]', out of which only one person had knowledge of current market developments, the rest substantially lacked financial expertise or acquired theirs during another era, not comparable to the requirements of modern finance. If SOX intended to improve the financial expertise of corporate boards, it did not succeed in time to prevent the 2008–9 financial crisis.

Whether corporate governance failures alone led to the financial crisis is nonetheless disputed (see below). While some explicitly blame dysfunctional monitoring of excessive risk-taking (Kirkpatrick 2009), others argue that, although corporate governance failed in the sense that the system did not prevent a loss for shareholders, other aspects such as termination of CEO contracts and reining in executive pay worked out well, as largely intended by SOX. Yet there is one major exception: financial corporations. For these corporations, the governance regulations required by SOX failed (Cheffins 2009). Hopt (2017: 439) in that respect states, 'The corporate governance of financial institutions is very special compared to the general corporate governance of corporations.' This special status is based on banks' overall importance for the economy, e.g. by offering access to a payment system and managing risk, and the macroeconomic tasks they fulfil. Compared to other corporations, banks operate with a comparatively limited capitalisation, while also being vulnerable to bank runs, which can result in macroeconomic problems.[1] This tight link between financial institutions and the rest of the economy requires special and stricter regulation, as the global financial crisis clearly showed.

More recent corporate scandals emphasise the continued relevance of good corporate governance. In September 2015, the US Environmental Protection Agency (EPA) informed Volkswagen about its violation of the Clean Air Act. The EPA found software in Volkswagen diesel engines that deceived US regulators by reducing nitrogen oxide emissions under test conditions (The Economist 2015). Armour (2016), discussing the governance implications of this scandal, points out that the monitoring of software developers should become a central aspect of risk management approaches.

Software-related issues are also at the centre of Facebook's data security breaches. In most cases, these breaches were at least partly caused by insufficient risk management. Corporate governance failures are also to blame. As with other big tech companies, Facebook lacks an independent chairperson, since Mark Zuckerberg is both CEO and board chair. Additionally, as one commentator claimed, Facebook's board is rather ineffective in monitoring the company's management (Brown 2018).

What the Volkswagen and Facebook scandals suggest is that corporate governance principles and practices must adapt to changes and new challenges. The drivers of these changes can be technical, e.g. new software or financial instruments, or otherwise. In some cases, these drivers lead to information asymmetries and rearrangements in corporate power structures. Emerging groups of experts can accumulate asset specificity and shield their knowledge from principal as well as agent control, thus making self-serving behaviour

---

[1] As seen in the case of investment bank Bear Stearns, which on 11 March 2008 was subject to a major bank run that ended in Bear Stearns filing for bankruptcy three days later (Sidel et al. 2008). Due to the bank's substantial relevance to the economy, government intervention was necessary, which, in an unprecedented move, led the Federal Reserve to finance Bear Stearns' toxic assets worth $30 billion (Mishkin 2011).

more likely. Further, rapidly growing companies and founder-controlled companies can have governance structures unsuited to adequate risk management. In other words, corporate governance is an evolving system.

The legal environment is evolving, too, as circumstances change. As Baums (in this volume) describes, the right way to regulate corporations is constantly debated among legal experts as well. Fundamentally, either corporations can be bound by statutory law, which forces them to comply, or desired corporate behaviour can be recommended by corporate governance codices, which are not legally binding. Many such codices contain 'comply or explain' requirements by which non-conformity with the recommendations of the code have to be declared. Statutory law is typically used when non-compliance is incompatible with the public interest or carries high risks. Then again, company-specific circumstances can also make it necessary to use a more flexible regulatory approach, for which comply or explain can be the right choice.

The history of corporate governance codes and their development—from the Cadbury Report to SOX—shows that corporate governance arrangements have often been driven by scandals that made further developments necessary. In many cases, responses have only been tailored to listed corporations— although other corporate forms such as SMEs and social enterprises could equally benefit from proper corporate governance regimes as well. Beyond the limited scope of many codes, the underlying shareholder primacy model has created its own problems, as illustrated by the global financial crisis.

Enter the Global Financial Crisis

If corporate governance systems evolve in response to changing and changed conditions, what has been the impact of the global financial crisis and the attention it placed on corporate behaviour, especially in financial institutions? The answer seems clear, and according to Ferrarini (2017), key official policy documents issued after 2008 highlight that corporate governance failures in financial institutions contributed significantly to the crisis. The High-Level Group on Financial Supervision in the EU even declared corporate governance 'one of the most important failures of the present crisis' (de Larosière et al. 2009: 29). The group's report identifies a problematic incentive structure that led financial corporations to value short-term gains over long-term profits and encouraged extensive risk-taking. In many cases, these developments resulted from governmental action, i.e. by implementing accounting rules that 'were systemically biased towards short-term performance' (de Larosière et al. 2009: 30). This view is supported by Bebchuk et al. (2010), who argue that compensation arrangements created excessive risk-taking incentives for executives.

Additionally, de Larosière et al. (2009) argue that board members failed to control management, partly due to an insufficient understanding of the risks associated with the new and complex financial problems, as well as the aggregate risk exposure of their institutions. An OECD report attributed the financial crisis 'to an important extent [...] to failures and weaknesses in corporate governance arrangements' (Kirkpatrick 2009: 2). Particularly problematic was the failure of corporate governance to prevent financial institutions from excessive risk-taking—a situation caused by failing risk management systems due to inappropriate corporate governance procedures. A Green Paper by the European Commission also identifies disproportionate risk-taking by financial institutions, again evoked by ineffective risk management, as an important factor that contributed to the financial crisis (EC 2010).

However, as mentioned above, this line of argumentation that makes failing corporate governance largely responsible for the financial crisis is contested and is seen as too simplistic in diminishing the perhaps equally important role policy-makers played. Hopt (2017) agrees with the various EU and OECD reports in that the financial crisis highlighted major deficits of the corporate governance of banks, especially in the areas of risk management. In particular, he points to a lack of qualification and experience of board members and senior management, bank structures that made the implementation of a coherent corporate governance policy across parent and subsidiary companies difficult to achieve, perverse incentives that encouraged managers to take high long-term risks for short-term gains, and failures in disclosure and transparency, especially in multinational settings (Hopt 2013). Yet, while acknowledging these deficiencies, Hopt (2013) contends that the majority view in the literature assigns much more weight to factors beyond corporate governance as causes of the financial crisis. He states that policy-makers acknowledged these factors well before the crisis, and accordingly enacted many regulatory and supervisory reforms that extend far beyond the scope of corporate governance to 'capital, liquidity, systemic risk, more competences for the banking supervisory agencies, restrictions on certain transactions and products, and last but not least rescue and insolvency, among others' (Hopt 2013: 15).

Another aspect relates to a bank's ownership structures: shareholding by lower-level managers increases the likelihood of a default as it creates a moral hazard problem, encouraging them to take more risk (Berger, Imbierowicz, and Rauch 2014). According to Hopt (2017), this can be seen as an indication that regular corporate governance practices are not suitable for financial institutions and might even have adverse effects. Similarly, Chiu (in this volume) questions the appropriateness of shareholder primacy as a basis for corporate governance of financial institutions, as it might undermine certain public interest goals. Ferrarini (2017: 8) argues, after having reviewed several studies on bank performance during the crisis, that 'almost paradoxically, [...] "good governance" simply led managers to engage in more risky activities'. By contrast Berger et al. (2014) primarily highlight the negative impact of CEO shareholding on a bank's return on equity. This is at least partly due to strong alignments of boards with shareholder interests, meaning shareholder wealth maximisation (Aebi, Sabato, and Schmid 2012). This is why Hopt (2017) argues in favour of a special 'creditor governance' tailored to banks that consider the interests of debtholders and depositors, even before those of shareholders.

To understand Hopt's proposal, let's compare it to the shareholder-centric model. A shareholder-centred approach to corporate governance, as prevalent in the UK and US for example, focuses on value creation for a company's shareholders, or in this case, the bank's shareholders. Yet, as we have seen above, financial institutions' responsibilities go far beyond their shareholders. In particular, these institutions have to take care of the money provided by depositors. A traditional shareholder primacy model, however, cannot account for both relationships, as pointed out by multiple agency theory (Hoskisson et al. 2013). Thus, Hopt (2017) argues that shareholder primacy does not reflect the complexity of financial institutions and their accountability to multiple stakeholders. To identify appropriate governance mechanisms, other models have to be applied. Hopt's proposal of a creditor governance, which juxtaposes two groups of stakeholders, shareholders and depositors, could be more suitable for the governance of financial institutions.

The financial crisis suggests two insights. First, over the medium to longer term, the shareholder primacy model does not guarantee that shareholder values actually increase, even if the necessary corporate governance mechanisms are correctly implemented. Second, effective corporate governance depends on corporate form and purpose. For financial institutions, traditional corporate governance arrangements did not achieve the intended goals. Even worse, it enabled behaviour which ultimately hurt the shareholders' interests— and the economy as a whole.

Thus, it is debatable whether the crucial role of financial institutions in the economy can be met without the broader view of corporate governance that takes into account more than just shareholders. Hopt's (2017) suggestion to adopt a stakeholder model that includes depositors deserves consideration. Yet, especially given the increasing demand for CSR, this proposal might not reach far enough. Although financial institutions are unlike other corporations, there is no a priori reason to assume that other corporate forms might not also require modified shareholder models. SMEs, social enterprises, philanthropic foundations, and certainly also public agencies are different from listed corporations. However, corporate governance regimes are largely based on listed corporations as the default and are designed accordingly. In other words, like Hopt (2017) did for financial corporations, we should question the appropriateness of standard governance mechanisms for other forms as well.

Corporate Governance Mechanisms

Corporate governance comprises internal and external mechanisms for efficient decision-making within the company (Cuervo 2002). Internal mechanisms include independent directors, the composition of the board of directors, as well as executive remuneration. The market for corporate control as well as competition are examples of external corporate governance mechanisms. Here we look first at the three internal mechanisms and then at the market for corporate control to illustrate external mechanisms.

Independent Directors

In general, there are three different types of directors: executive directors, who are part of the executive team and by definition dependent; non-executive independent directors, i.e. those who do not belong to the executive team and are without ties to the firm; and non-executive dependent directors, with ties to the firm. The idea of independent directors, which first came to policymakers' attention in the 1990s in the UK, was adopted as a fundamental corporate governance principle in the European Union in the early 2000s. The term independent director is also often used to describe directors that do not belong to a company's executive team and lack personal ties with the firm or the management (Hsu and Wu 2014), hence avoiding any conflict between duty and self-interest when monitoring the management (Dalton et al. 2007).

The rationale behind using independent directors was to install directors from outside the company to act as 'professional referees who stimulate and oversee the competition among the firm's top management' (Fama 1980: 293–4). The performance of these outside directors is, as Fama states, then monitored by the market, which disciplines low-performing outside directors through competition of other outsiders willing to replace them on the board. Both the European Model Company Act (2015) and the OECD Principles of Corporate Governance (2015) recommend assigning important oversight tasks to independent board members (Baum 2016).

Empirically, however, the effect of independent board members on firm performance remains unclear (Adams, Hermalin, and Weisbach 2010; Dalton et al. 2007; Fogel, Ma, and Morck 2015). An initial study on the relationship of non-independent and independent board directors (insiders vs outsiders) to firm performance by Jensen and Meckling (1976) suggests that a higher number of outsiders increases firm performance. Since this initial study, the accumulated evidence does not generally support the suggested positive impact of independent directors (Baum 2016). A meta-analysis by Dalton et al. (1998) found no systematic relationship. Findings from another analysis by Deutsch (2005: 440) also did not lend 'support to the widespread belief within the business community that a board with a higher percentage of outside directors is a better guardian of shareholders' interests'.[2] Results from a study by Gay and Denning (2014) even found that an increase of independent directors reduced stock returns. Hsu and Wu (2014) show that corporations with a greater share of non-executive dependent directors relative to executive and independent directors are less likely to fail.

Fogel et al. (2015) provide empirical evidence partly in favour of independent directors. Their findings suggest that powerful independent directors, broadly speaking those with strong and numerous connections to other directors and top executives of US listed companies, can increase shareholder value. Powerful independent directors can protect shareholders' interest by deterring CEOs from engaging in potentially value-destroying decisions, such as economically unsound merger bids. These directors can also force out underperforming CEOs and discourage earnings manipulation. Additionally, such well-connected independent directors are more likely to link CEO pay to actual performance. If the majority of the board's directors are legally independent and powerful, the whole board is considered to be a powerful independent board. However, these effects do not hold for independent directors lacking a strong social network.

---

[2] More broadly, it should be noted that serving shareholder interests is not synonymous with good governance, as the financial crisis has made clear.

In light of these mixed findings, seeing independent directors as a way to cope with agency problems and increase firm value seems largely unfounded. The result is partly due to the assumptions articulated by agency theory: driven by self-interest, executive directors need to be monitored by directors without ties to the company, who, by definition, lack this self-interest. This, however, ignores the individual contributions of independent directors beyond their monitoring role—an implicit shift from agency to resource dependence theory.[3] Furthermore, independent directors as a governance tool might not be suitable for every type of corporation. Banks, for example, performed worse during the financial crisis when their boards had a larger share of independent directors (Erkens, Hung, and Matos 2012). In the end, it is not only about being independent, but about bringing the right skills and expertise to the board.

Board Composition and Member Diversity

Next to directors' independence, board diversity has become a key issue, also in the public eye. For example, in 2013, Twitter Inc. was criticised when the public filing ahead of its IPO revealed that its board included not a single female director (Miller 2013). Six years later at the time of writing, the company had two females among the eight total directors. In 2018, Lagarde (2018) published an IMF blog discussing the tenth anniversary of the global financial crisis, stating, 'If it had been Lehman Sisters rather than Lehman Brothers, the world might look different today.'

Although increasing the share of female directors has become an issue in many societies, evidence on firm performance is mixed (Terjesen, Sealy, and Singh 2009). However, this is partly caused by difficulties in the research process, such as endogeneity problems related to board composition, board selection, and financial performance (Simpson, Carter, and D'Souza 2010). Another aspect that might explain the absence of a relationship can be found in assimilation processes. Although Rose (2007: 411) did not find any evidence of a link between female board representation and firm performance in a Danish sample, he argues that this might be caused by female directors assimilating to the behaviour of the traditional 'old boys' club', thereby suppressing any

---

[3] Resource dependence theory highlights the relevance of a corporation's external relations to ensure its survival and autonomy. First articulated by Pfeffer and Salancik (1978), the theory especially sheds light on aspects of power, which is seen as a determining factor of a company's ability to autonomously pursue its own strategic goals.

attributes that might distinguish themselves from the rest of the board. Rose stresses that this assimilation might be the only way to gain access to the boardroom, a circumstance that might bury any performance gain under encrusted corporate culture. Yet, some studies support the notion of a positive link. Erhardt, Werbel, and Shrader (2003), for example, found a positive association between board diversity more generally and return on investment as well as return on assets. Furthermore, while Simpson, Carter, and D'Souza (2010) did not find empirical evidence for a causal relationship between board diversity and financial performance, they also did not find a negative relationship, which, if they had, would provide evidence against more diverse boards.

Although the evidence concerning hard financial performance is inconclusive, descriptive indicators provide some support for initiatives to increase the number of women on corporate boards. Boards with female directors substantially differ from male-only boards in their approach to strategy measurement and implementation. Of boards with at least three women, 74 per cent identify criteria for strategy measurement and 94 per cent monitor strategy implementation, compared to 45 per cent and 66 per cent of all-male boards, respectively (Brown et al. 2002). Moreover, boards with two or more women review five or more non-financial performance measures, compared to 2.5 for male boards. More diverse boards are also more likely to use an executive and a strategic planning committee, thereby actively shaping the organisation's strategic direction. Brown et al. (2002: 5) conclude that 'boards with more women surpass all-male boards in their attention to audit and risk oversight and control', whereas Sila et al. (2016) could not find any evidence for an association between gender diversity on boards and risk-taking. Thus, the evidence on the impact of gender diversity on risk management remains inconclusive.

Beyond gender diversity, educational diversity is another issue to consider. Some evidence suggests that educational background does not affect corporate performance. Rose (2007) argues that board responsibility does not make any specialised education necessary. Board members only need to understand the information provided by the managing directors. This, however, does not hold for financial institutions. As Adams (2012) points out, banks with directors lacking the necessary financial expertise to understand the inner workings of the bank have performed worse than other banks with experienced directors during the financial crisis. Therefore, the effect of educational backgrounds on the performance of a firm might differ depending on the corporate form. Policy-makers addressing board diversity need to be aware of this context dependence.

Executive Remuneration

Executive compensation is among the most controversial issues in the area of corporate governance—among scholars and policy-makers as well as the general public. Many corporations see themselves involved in discussions around increasing inequality that in many cases also target the compensation of corporate executives and other board members. Often, these discussions highlight the discrepancy between employee salaries and compensation of companies' chief executives. The US is a prominent example. With the implementation of the 2010 Dodd-Frank Wall Street Reform and Consumer Protection Act (Dodd-Frank Act), corporations have to disclose the ratio of a median employee's salary to the company's chief executive (Securities and Exchange Commission 2017a). The rule is intended to allow shareholders to assess a company's compensation practices. While the SEC is primarily addressing investors, the annual publication of executive-to-median-employee pay ratios also sparks public controversy about the inequality these ratios point out. In 2018, the *New York Times* highlighted the 'growing gap between the C-Suite and the typical employee', with a median pay ratio across all 160 companies that disclosed compensation practices of 275 to 1 (Gelles 2018), meaning that the median employee has to work 275 years for the CEO's annual compensation. Equity-based compensation has further increased income inequality in the US, according to analysts like Useem (2019).

For agency theory, linking executive's compensation to the wealth of the shareholders is a reasonable approach. This is often done in the form of performance-based equity: performance-vesting stock and performance shares (Edmans, Gabaix, and Jenter 2017). Under performance-vesting stock, the executive receives a fixed number of shares after a certain period if performance goals are fulfilled and the executive remains with the company. With performance shares, the executive receives a variable number of shares depending on his or her performance after a certain period. Edmans et al. (2017) point out that besides equity incentives, many executives also participate in bonus plans, by which a bonus payment is a function of one or more performance measures, such as sales or earnings per share, a particularly common metric. This, however, only reflects a company's short-term performance and is also rather easily manipulated. As a Reuter's report has highlighted, share buybacks can be used by executives to reach performance goals, as they increase the share price without substantially increasing firm performance (Brettell, Gaffen, and Rhode 2015). In the eight days after a corporation has announced a buyback, executives sell more than five times the amount of stock they sell in the days before the buyback (Jackson 2018). As SEC Commissioner Jackson describes it, 'Executives capture the benefit of the short-term stock-price pop created by the buyback announcement.' Accordingly, although agency theory suggests giving executives stock to align their interests with shareholder's interests, share buybacks have undermined this mechanism, thereby invalidating the agency approach. Beyond that, CEOs can extract further rent by trying to make themselves irreplaceable, as discussed by Williamson (2002) in the context of the asset-specificity problem.

Excessive executive compensation is not the only issue: compensation can also be too low and unattractive. For two-tier systems, common in Germany and Switzerland, associations, corporate governance experts, and former supervisory board members highlight the need for an attractive salary for non-executive board members. The chairman of the German Corporate Governance Code commission, Rolf Nonnenmacher, argued in 2018 that supervisory board members in Germany are 'heavily underpaid' for the workload and responsibility they bear, which will make it much more difficult in the future to attract the right people (Neuscheler 2018).

This problem has already led to a prominent case: German industrial firm Thyssen-Krupp was unable to find an agreement with its designated supervisory board chairman, a former Daimler Chief Financial Officer, who was unwilling to accept a remuneration of more than €200,000 annually—a comparatively low figure in the German corporate landscape (Deutsche Bank supervisory board chairman Paul Achleitner receives around €800,000). To address this problem, former Deutsche Bank supervisory board chairman Jürgen Fitschen has proposed to untie compensation from the company's current business development and share prices. The German Association for Private Investors (Deutsche Schutzvereinigung für Wertpapierbesitz e.V., DSW) even argued to move to a fixed salary system (Benner-Heinacher, Hölz, and Kurz 2018). The DSW points out that supervisory board chairs are especially challenged in times of crisis, with often multiple meetings a year. This workload would not be reflected in a performance-based compensation system.

Market for Corporate Control

According to Manne (1965), a necessary precondition for the efficient operation of capitalist economies is an active market for corporate control. It enables successful management teams to take over control of large amounts of resources. If a company operates in a way that does not maximise shareholders' wealth—where management behaviour has led to a decline in stock prices—it will be taken over and its managers be replaced by more shareholder-friendly ones (Allen and Gale 1998). Depending on whether a bid is accepted by the target's board, a takeover is considered friendly or hostile (Weir 2013). The market for corporate control is considered to be the main external governance mechanism in the US and UK.

Does the market for corporate control serve as an effective corporate governance tool? Based on a literature review, Aguilera et al. (2015) argue that although the market might be able to discipline managers, it can also create subsequent problems. Empirical evidence suggests that in the long run, shareholder wealth is reduced by takeovers (Moeller, Schlingemann, and Stulz 2005; Tuch and O'Sullivan 2007). Aguilera et al. (2015) argue that these negative effects are caused by information asymmetries between target corporation and investor or acquiring corporation, which makes target evaluation difficult, as well as anti-takeover measures by the target company. However, whether a rejection of a bid by the board is indeed against shareholder interests is unclear. Rejecting a bid could also be seen as a strategy to increase the company's value, and thereby the wealth of the target company's shareholders (Weir 2013).

Corporate Governance in Technology Companies

As mentioned earlier, founder-controlled tech companies pose a new challenge for corporate governance. These companies, such as Facebook, Google, and Amazon, are often managed by founder-CEOs who successfully created a globally operating corporation built on their long-term vision.

Taken together, the five US tech companies known as FAANG (Facebook, Amazon, Apple, Netflix, and Google) came to be worth more than the entire FTSE 100, also exceeding the value of Germany's DAX and the French Cac 40 combined (Fletcher 2018). But these companies are not only powerful due to their economic force; the services they provide are deeply embedded in the lives of many people, who use services like Facebook or Google on a daily basis. With an influence like this, corporate stewards must be especially aware of their societal impact and accordingly need to implement a governance regime that strives to achieve the aim articulated by Lord Cadbury to 'align as nearly as possible the interests of individuals, corporations, and society' (Iskander and Chamlou 2000: vi). Yet, taking corporate scandals as a proxy for failed corporate governance, some of these companies need to improve their approaches.

Dual-class Stock Structures

A prominent characteristic of technology corporations today is a specific share structure that keeps voting rights in the hands of the founders. When Snap Inc., the company responsible for the smartphone messaging application Snapchat, filed its initial public offering (IPO) on 2 February 2017, the company intended to offer shares of non-voting Class A common stock. Besides this class, Snap Inc. had two other classes of stock: Class B common stock, with its shares entitled to one vote, and Class C common stock, with ten votes per share. Even before the IPO, each of the two founders of Snap Inc., Evan Spiegel and Robert Murphy, held 44.3 per cent of voting power (Securities and Exchange Commission 2017c). Their collective voting power increased further with the IPO. When corporate executives hold the majority of votes, without stockholders being able to overrule their decisions, external corporate governance mechanisms like the market for corporate control are rendered ineffective.

IPOs with unequal voting structures, usually referred to as dual-class structures, are not uncommon among US tech companies (Tallarita 2018). In these structures, effective control of corporate executives by public shareholders is largely limited since investors do not acquire enough voting rights to exercise their monitoring and controlling functions. Another prominent example for this dual-class structure is Facebook Inc., which offered a class with one vote per share and another with ten votes per share (Securities and Exchange Commission 2012). With this structure, Mr Zuckerberg effectively held 56.9 per cent of voting power before the public offering. These developments were not without criticism. As Tallarita (2018) points out, policy-makers, corporate governance consultants, and institutional investors, among others, have expressed their concern, but have done little about it so far.

Tallarita (2018) describes three hypotheses (Efficient Private Benefits Hypothesis, Entrepreneurial Hypothesis, and Inefficient Entrenchment Hypothesis) that provide rationales for the implementation of a dual-class structure. The Efficient Private Benefits Hypothesis states that an unequal voting arrangement is beneficial as it maximises value for shareholders, controllers, and executives. Investors are aware of the increased agency costs due to their limited controlling capabilities but are compensated by a discounted stock. An important aspect in the decision to establish a dual-class structure is furthermore that pre-IPO owners receive benefits that are not shared with public shareholders. As Tallarita points out, this can be seen in the social recognition gained from being the controlling shareholder of a company or access to exclusive social relationships and opportunities. These benefits are especially pronounced for the founder, for whom these benefits are relevant as the marginal utility of a higher firm value is comparatively small, in particular if the founder is already wealthy, in relation to the perceived psychological advantages of staying in control of their own firm.

The Entrepreneurial Hypothesis argues that for entrepreneurs who want to pursue their particular vision, a dual-class structure protects them from being replaced by shareholders who disagree with this vision or lose their patience in the light of poor corporate performance. The premise that this inoculation against market pressure increases the company's value and compensates for the higher agency costs caused by the dual-class structure finds some support in the US, where capital markets became focused on short-term gains instead of a long-term orientation (Bushman 1998; Coffee and Palia 2016; Martin 2015). These developments were recognised by corporate America as well: Larry Fink, Chairman and CEO of BlackRock, demanded in his 2018 letter to CEOs that they focus on long-term value creation (Fink 2018). For technology companies, this short-termism poses an especially severe problem, as R&D investments are typically long-term oriented and are therefore associated with a higher risk for the firm and its shareholders (Tallarita 2018). Both Google in a letter to prospective IPO investors (Securities and Exchange Commission 2004) and Facebook in a statement against a stockholder proposal that would have created a stock structure with equal voting rights (Securities and Exchange Commission 2017b) used arguments focused on the protection of their founder's long-term vision for the companies.

Tallarita (2018) names a third rationale, the Inefficient Entrenchment Hypothesis, that is used to argue in favour of a dual-class stock. In this case, IPO investors systematically underestimate the agency costs caused by the unequal distribution of voting rights. When investors are aware of net agency costs but underestimate the effect to a sufficient extent, the controlling stockholder might benefit from the adoption of a dual-class stock even if the reduction in firm value is higher than the private benefits.

Using data from a US stock exchange on all single-class and dual-class IPOs between January 2012 and February 2017, Tallarita (2018) finds evidence that supports the notion that a dual-class structure is adopted to extract private benefits. He furthermore finds a positive correlation between the presence of a founder-CEO and the adoption of a dual-class structure, while this structure is negatively correlated with the share of equity owned by venture capital and private equity investors. However, no evidence supports the idea of protection of managers against market pressure.

The Problem with External Control Mechanisms

In the case of Facebook, another important aspect emerges: the company's impact on institutions and democracy in a broader sense. With the scandal around Cambridge Analytica and Facebook users' impact on different elections around the world, an approach focused primarily on increasing shareholder value ignores the corporation's broader role in society. With 2.27 billion monthly active users, the company has a global reach that is probably unparalleled (Facebook 2018). Yet, generously said, the company's leadership does not seem to have taken full account of its power and societal impact and the consequences thereof. Facebook's behaviour affects public goods in various ways. In 2016, for example, Facebook intended to launch Internet.org in India, a website which was to serve as an application interface allowing users to avail of different services, such as weather information, Bing (Microsoft's search engine), and Wikipedia, essentially free of charge since any use of Internet.org would not draw on a user's paid data volume (Vaidhyanathan 2018). The website was launched in cooperation with a mobile company. However, in February 2016, India's Telecommunication Regulatory Authority decided that Facebook's initiative violated network neutrality, the idea that all content providers are treated equally by digital services. Although Facebook's intent was reportedly to provide internet access to poor communities, its approach violates the broader public good of network neutrality.

This case demonstrates the risks of having a dual-class stock structure and a founder-CEO controlled company. Given the frequency of large-scale scandals such as the ones described, it is likely that shareholders holding equal voting power would have stepped in and replaced Zuckerberg as the company's chief executive. In some cases, as with Internet.org, it has been government agencies that acted and sought to regulate the company or CEO. Specialised agencies such as India's Telecommunication Regulatory Authority and the SEC in the US can provide an external control of corporate behaviour.

Yet, such controls do not (yet) exist for more hard-to-grasp problems often faced by providers of social media platforms (Facebook, Twitter, YouTube, and others), such as services being used to spread disinformation and hate speech. As Stockmann (in this volume) points out, most social media corporations choose and have been allowed to regulate themselves. Yet, Facebook's frequent involvement in scandals brings into question the effectiveness of this approach (Lapowsky 2018).

Social media platforms are, however, not the only companies with large societal responsibilities. Companies such as Amazon and Netflix have collected vast amounts of customer data that need to be protected against security breaches. Hackers gaining access to addresses, credit card numbers, and also everyday habits can impact people's everyday lives. This is not an abstract problem. The World Economic Forum names data fraud or theft as one of the ten most likely risks (World Economic Forum 2018).

Policy-makers need to take back control and exercise their oversight mandate. This, however, is not an easy task. Some countries have started to implement laws, such as the German Network Enforcement Act, to cope with these phenomena. But laws have to be thoughtfully crafted to avoid side effects that might otherwise infringe fundamental rights (Holznagel 2017). The complexity of tech companies' operations is another challenge for policy-makers, as illustrated by Mr Zuckerberg's appearance before the European Parliament, where many members of the European Parliament appeared to struggle to understand Facebook's business model.

Taken together, tech companies pose a challenge to current corporate governance approaches, as their ownership structure inhibits some external and internal control mechanisms, and other mechanisms are often incapable of effectively regulating these complex corporations. Economically powerful companies, such as FAANG, have taken on great importance for societies across the world. To secure proper accountability mechanisms, policy-makers need to develop new governance approaches that allow for effective internal and external control.

Lessons from Europe: Germany's Co-determination

It is not entirely surprising that these developments have mostly been related to US-based tech companies, given the country's rather negative views of stakeholder involvement, which have only recently started to change (Gelles and Yaffe-Bellany 2019). Other countries, however, have followed a different path in this respect.

A prominent example for the involvement of stakeholders on corporate boards is Germany. The country's Co-determination Act of 1976 guarantees workers' participation 'in the economic planning and decision-making of a company' (Federal Ministry of Labour and Social Affairs 2019: 4). The degree of employee participation is tied to company size. For companies with more than 2,000 employees, the supervisory board must consist of an equal share of employee and shareholder representatives. In practice shareholders have a slight advantage in decision-making, as the chairperson is most often a shareholder representative and can serve as a tiebreaker. For companies between 501 and 2,000 employees, one-third of the supervisory board has to consist of employee representatives. Employee representatives are either directly elected by the employees or through delegates, depending on the number of employees in the corporation. On the level of the executive board, co-determination provides a labour relations director, who is primarily concerned with 'personnel and employee welfare matters' (Federal Ministry of Labour and Social Affairs 2019: 12). The labour relations director has the same status as other executive board members. Although other countries such as the Netherlands and Luxembourg have co-determination laws in place as well, Germany's regulation is the most far-reaching (Kraft, Stank, and Dewenter 2011).

The impact of this arrangement on economic measures of corporate success has been extensively discussed. Fauver and Fuerst (2006) provide evidence that employee representation can increase firm efficiency and market value. They argue that the relationship between employee representation and firm value follows an inverted U-shape: the corporation increasingly benefits from including employee representatives on their boards up to a certain point and is likely to benefit less beyond that. In their view, this optimal point is likely below 50 per cent, in line with an analysis made by Gorton and Schmid (2004: 895) who find that 'corporations with equal representation trade at a discount of 31 per cent compared with corporations that are subject to one-third representation on the supervisory board.' According to Gorton and Schmid, this reduced stock price is caused by employee representatives using their voting power to maintain high staffing levels and, thereby, an extensive payroll. In contrast, moderate levels of representation can increase communication between top-level management and employees, improving the board's decision-making (Fauver and Fuerst 2006). Especially in coordination-requiring industries, such as transportation, pharmaceuticals, and manufacturing, employee representation can provide an advantage, according to Fauver and Fuerst. Employee representation is also associated with higher spending on R&D (Kraft et al. 2011). Based on empirical evidence, Kraft et al. conclude that investments in research might be considered by employees as an approach to long-term job protection.

Germany's Co-Determination Act provides an illustrative example of the benefits of including employees on corporate boards. Although problems might occur in some situations if representation leads to excessive staffing, overall evidence points to a predominance of the Act's benefits. It also indicates that different industries and corporate characteristics (e.g. workforce size) might demand a specific legal framework—in contrast to a one-size-fits-all approach to corporate governance.

Conclusion

For a long time, 'shareholders' and 'value' were the definitive answers to the 'who' and the 'what' of corporate governance. Increasing the wealth of its shareholders was the company's prime concern; Friedman (1970) famously denied any social responsibility of corporations. Yet, this shareholder primacy approach to corporate governance has drawn considerable criticism. Initiatives that stress the triple bottom line of environmental, economic, and social sustainability of corporate behaviour, as poignantly formulated by the CSR approach, do not accept a mere focus on economic aspects of corporate performance. Nevertheless, shareholder primacy has its merits, as it makes clear that even without operative control of the company, the owners should still benefit from their investment. Together with agency theory, shareholder primacy has been at the centre of corporate governance regimes for almost fifty years. Nevertheless, we see that it has become necessary to rethink how corporate governance is approached.

As a result, we identify three major issues that are crucial for further developing corporate governance. First, shareholder primacy is unfit to inform a modern take on corporate governance and does not reflect societal commitments to social and environmental sustainability. In September 2019, 181 US CEOs expressed this commitment by signing a Statement on the Purpose of a Corporation that extends corporate responsibility beyond the shareholder (Gelles and Yaffe-Bellany 2019). Accordingly, theoretical approaches to corporate governance need to reflect this evolving understanding. Stakeholder theory can provide a starting point for this.

Second, policy-makers and scholars need to acknowledge the diversity of corporate forms and the necessity of tailoring corporate governance mechanisms to the respective form. A one-size-fits-all approach does not reflect the complexity of the corporate world—and can have devastating consequences, as illustrated by the global financial crisis. Although it is clear that corporate governance is primarily informed by the needs of listed corporations, the following chapters in this volume will illustrate the variety of corporate forms and the benefits a fitting governance regime can bring to them. Unlike agency theory, stakeholder theory can help to develop corporate governance codes for various corporate forms. Especially technology companies have to be analysed through the lens of stakeholder theory, as their conflicting commercial and public rationales demand a broader understanding of corporate governance (Stockmann, in this volume).

And finally, empirical evidence needs to be taken into account when developing corporate governance codes. As shown above, some common corporate governance mechanisms lack the necessary evidence that would justify their enshrinement in governance codes. Yet, policy-makers continue to prescribe these mechanisms as ways to deal with agency problems, as illustrated in the case of independent directors. In some contexts, the limited empirical understanding can even lead to unintended or opposite effects, e.g. when independent directors lack the necessary experience to deal with the complexity of financial institutions. This example also shows the relevance of taking account of insights from the social sciences in the development of corporate governance: Redenius-Hövermann (in this volume) makes the case for including findings from behavioural economics in soft corporate law.

Overall, corporate governance is evolving, and finding the best models is an ongoing task as economic, societal, and environmental challenges continue to arise. Such models must take better and more systematic account of the significant differences across corporate forms, countries, and regions.

References

Adams, R. B. (2012). 'Governance and the Financial Crisis', *International Review of Finance*, 12(1): 7–38. https://doi.org/10.1111/j.1468-2443.2011.01147.x

Adams, R. B., Hermalin, B. E., and Weisbach, M. S. (2010). 'The Role of Boards of Directors in Corporate Governance: A Conceptual Framework and Survey', *Journal of Economic Literature*, 48(1): 58–107. https://doi.org/10.1257/jel.48.1.58

Aebi, V., Sabato, G., and Schmid, M. (2012). 'Risk management, corporate governance, and bank performance in the financial crisis', *Journal of Banking & Finance*, 36(12): 3213–26.

Aguilera, R. V. and Cuervo-Cazurra, A. (2004). 'Codes of Good Governance Worldwide: What is the Trigger?', *Organization Studies*, 25(3): 415–43. https://doi.org/10.1177/0170840604040669

Aguilera, R. V. and Cuervo-Cazurra, A. (2009). 'Codes of Good Governance', *Corporate Governance: An International Review*, 17(3): 376–87. https://doi.org/10.1111/j.1467-8683.2009.00737.x

Aguilera, R. V., Desender, K., Bednar, M. K., and Lee, J. H. (2015). 'Connecting the Dots: Bringing External Corporate Governance into the Corporate Governance Puzzle', *Academy of Management Annals*, 9(1): 483–573. https://doi.org/10.108 0/19416520.2015.1024503

Aguilera, R. V. and Jackson, G. (2010). 'Comparative and International Corporate Governance', *Academy of Management Annals*, 4(1): 485–556. https://doi.org/1 0.1080/19416520.2010.495525

Allen, F. and Gale, D. (1998). *Corporate Governance and Competition, Center for Financial Institutions Working Papers*. Philadelphia, PA: Wharton School.

Andersen, M. and Skjoett-Larsen, T. (2009). 'Corporate Social Responsibility in Global Supply Chains', *Supply Chain Management: An International Journal*, 14(2): 75–86. https://doi.org/10.1108/13598540910941948

Armour, J. (2016). 'Volkswagen's Emissions Scandal: Lessons for Corporate Governance? (Part 2)', Oxford Faculty of Law Blog, 17 May. Retrieved from https://www.law.ox.ac.uk/business-law-blog/blog/2016/05/volkswagen's-emissions-scandal-lessons-corporate-governance-part-1 (accessed 29 August 2018).

Baum, H. (2016). 'The Rise of the Independent Director: A Historical and Comparative Perspective', Max Planck Private Law Research Paper Series No. 16/20. Hamburg: Max Planck Institute for Comparative and International Private Law. Retrieved from https://ssrn.com/abstract=2814978 (accessed 2 September 2018).

Bebchuk, L. A., Cohen, A., and Spamann, H. (2009). 'The Wages of Failure: Executive Compensation at Bear Stearns and Lehman 2000–2008', ECGI Finance Working Paper No. 287/2010. Brussels: European Corporate Governance Institute (ECGI).

Benner-Heinacher, J., Hölz, C., and Kurz, J. (2018). Pressekonferenz: DSW-Aufsichtsratsstudie 2018, Press conference: DSW-Supervisory Board Study 2018. Retrieved from https://www.dsw-info.de/presse/archiv-pressekonferenzen/pressekonferenzen-2018/dsw-aufsichtsratsstudie-2018/ (accessed 5 January 2019).

Beresford, R. D., Katzenbach, N. deB., and Rogers Jr, C. B. (2003). *Report of Investigation by the Special Investigative Committee of the Board of Directors of WorldCom, Inc.* Washington, DC: US Securities and Exchange Commission. Retrieved from https://www.sec.gov/Archives/edgar/data/723527/000093176303001862/dex991.htm (accessed 24 August 2018).

Berger, A. N., Imbierowicz, B., and Rauch, C. (2014). 'The Roles of Corporate Governance in Bank Failures During the Recent Financial Crisis', *Journal of Money, Credit and Banking*, 48(4): 729–70.

Berle, A. A. and Means, G. C. (1968). *The Modern Corporation and Private Property*. New York, NY: Harvest Books.

Berman, D. K. (2008). 'Where Was Lehman's Board?', *The Wall Street Journal*, 15 September. Retrieved from https://blogs.wsj.com/deals/2008/09/15/where-was-lehmans-board/ (accessed 24 August 2018).

Brettell, K., Gaffen, D., and Rhode, D. (2015). 'Stock Buybacks Enrich the Bosses Even When Business Sags', *Reuters*, 10 December. Retrieved from https://www.reuters.com/investigates/special-report/usa-buybacks-pay/ (accessed 24 August 2018).

Brown, D. A. H., Brown, D. L., and Anastasopoulos, V. (2002). *Women on Boards Not Just the Right Thing...But the 'Bright' Thing. The Conference Board of Canada*. Ottawa, ON: The Conference Board of Canada. Retrieved from https://utsc.utoronto.ca/~phanira/WebResearchMethods/women-bod&fp-conferenceboard.pdf (accessed 25 August 2018).

Brown, G. (2018). 'Facebook's Light Approach to Corporate Governance', LSE Business Review Blog, 1 May. Retrieved from https://blogs.lse.ac.uk/business-review/2018/05/01/facebooks-light-approach-to-corporate-governance/ (accessed 28 August 2018).

Bushman, R. M. (1998). 'The Influence of Institutional Investors on Myopic R&D Investment Behavior', *The Accounting Review*, 73(3): 305–33.

Cadbury, A. (1992). *Cadbury Committee Report: The Financial Aspects of Corporate Governance*. London: Gee.

Caulkin, S. (2013). 'Corporate Apocalypse', *Management Today*, 1 January. Retrieved from https://www.managementtoday.co.uk/corporate-apocalypse/article/870435 (accessed 23 August 2018).

Cheffins, B. R. (2009). 'Did Corporate Governance "Fail" During the 2008 Stock Market Meltdown? The Case of the S&P 500', ECGI Working Paper Series in Law No. 124. Brussels: European Corporate Governance Institute (ECGI).

Coffee, J. C. and Palia, D. (2016). 'The Wolf at the Door: The Impact of Hedge Fund Activism on Corporate Governance', Columbia Law and Economics Working Paper No. 521. New York, NY: Columbia Law School.

Cuervo, A. (2002). 'Corporate Governance Mechanisms: A Plea for Less Code of Good Governance and More Market Control', *Corporate Governance: An International Review*, 10(2): 84–93. https://doi.org/10.1111/1467-8683.00272

Dalton, D. R., Daily, C. M., Ellstrand, A. E., and Johnson, J. L. (1998). 'Meta-analytic Reviews of Board Composition, Leadership Structure, and Financial Performance', *Strategic Management Journal*, 19(3): 269–90.

Dalton, D. R., Hitt, M. A., Certo, S. T., and Dalton, C. M. (2007). 'The Fundamental Agency Problem and Its Mitigation', *The Academy of Management Annals*, 1(1): 1–64. https://doi.org/10.1080/078559806

Davis, J. H., Schoorman, F. D., and Donaldson, L. (1997). 'Toward a Stewardship Theory of Management', *The Academy of Management Review*, 22(1): 20–47. https://doi.org/10.2307/259223

de Larosière, J., Balcerowicz, L., Issing, O., Masera, R., McCarthy, C., Nyberg, L.,... Ruding, O. (2009). *The High-Level Group on Financial Supervision in the EU*. Brussels: European Commission.

Deutsch, Y. (2005). 'The Impact of Board Composition on Firms' Critical Decisions: A Meta-Analytic Review', *Journal of Management*, 31(3): 424–44. https://doi.org/10.1177/0149206304272185

Donaldson, T. and Preston, L. E. (1995). 'Stakeholder Theory: Concepts, Evidence, Corporations and its Implications', *Management*, 20(1): 65–91. https://doi.org/10.2307/258887

Edmans, A., Gabaix, X., and Jenter, D. (2017). 'Executive Compensation: A Survey of Theory and Evidence', in B. E. Hermalin and M. S. Weisbach (eds.), *The Handbook of the Economics of Corporate Governance*. Amsterdam: North Holland, 383–539.

Effross, W. A. (2013). *Corporate Governance: Principles and Practices* (2nd ed.). New York: Wolters Kluwer Law & Business.

Erhardt, N. L., Werbel, J. D., and Shrader, C. B. (2003). 'Board of Director Diversity and Firm Financial Performance', *Corporate Governance*, 11(2): 102–111. https://doi.org/10.1111/1467-8683.00011

Erkens, D. H., Hung, M., and Matos, P. (2012). 'Corporate Governance in the 2007–2008 Financial Crisis: Evidence from Financial Institutions Worldwide', *Journal of Corporate Finance*, 18(2): 389–411. https://doi.org/10.1016/j.jcorpfin.2012.01.005

European Commission (2010). *Green Paper: Corporate Governance in Financial Institutions and Remuneration Policies*. Retrieved from https://op.europa.eu/en/publication-detail/-/publication/1788e830-b050-447c-8214-77ed51b13241 (accessed 30 March 2020).

Facebook (2018). Company Info. Retrieved from https://newsroom.fb.com/company-info/ (accessed 29 December 2018).

Fama, E. F. (1980). 'Agency Problems and the Theory of the Firm', *Journal of Political Economy*, 88(2): 288–307. https://doi.org/10.1086/260866

Fama, E. F. and Jensen, M. C. (1983). 'Separation of Ownership and Control', *The Journal of Law & Economics*, 26(2): 301–25.

Fauver, L. and Fuerst, M. E. (2006). 'Does Good Corporate Governance Include Employee Representation? Evidence from German Corporate Boards', *Journal of Financial Economics*, 82(3): 673–710. https://doi.org/10.1016/j.jfineco.2005.10.005

Federal Ministry of Labour and Social Affairs (2019). *Co-determination 2019*. Berlin: Federal Ministry of Labour and Social Affairs.

Ferrarini, G. (2017). 'Understanding the Role of Corporate Governance in Financial Institutions: A Research Agenda', Law Working Paper No. 347. Brussels: European Corporate Governance Institute (ECGI).

Filatotchev, I. and Stahl, G. K. (2015). 'Towards Transnational CSR: Corporate Social Responsibility Approaches and Governance Solutions for Multinational Corporations', *Organizational Dynamics*, 44(2): 121–9. https://doi.org/10.1016/j.orgdyn.2015.02.006

Fink, L. (2018). 'Larry Fink's Annual Letter to CEOs: A Sense of Purpose', BlackRock. Retrieved from https://www.blackrock.com/corporate/investor-relations/larry-fink-ceo-letter (accessed 8 January 2019).

Fletcher, N. (2018). 'Faang-tastic Five: Can US Tech Giants Continue Their Stellar Rise?', *The Guardian*, 29 June. Retrieved from https://www.theguardian.com/business/2018/jun/29/faanga-us-tech-giants-facebook-amazon-apple-netflix-google (accessed 25 August 2018).

Fogel, K., Ma, L., and Morck, R. (2015). 'Powerful Independent Directors', Finance Working Paper No. 19809. Cambridge, MA: National Bureau of Economic Research.

Freeman, R. E. (1984). *Strategic Management: A Stakeholder Approach*. Boston: Pitman.

Friedman, M. (1970). 'The Social Responsibility of Business Is to Increase its Profits', *The New York Times Magazine*, 13 September. Retrieved from http://umich.edu/~thecore/doc/Friedman.pdf (accessed 29 August 2018).

Gay, S. and Denning, C. (2014). 'Corporate Governance Principal-Agent Problem: The Equity Cost of Independent Directors', Working paper. Chicago: University of Chicago.

Gelles, D. (2018). 'Want to Make Money Like a C.E.O.? Work for 275 Years', *The New York Times*, 25 May. Retrieved from https://www.nytimes.com/2018/05/25/business/highest-paid-ceos-2017.html?module=inline (accessed 28 August 2018).

Gelles, D. and Yaffe-Bellany, D. (2019). 'Shareholder Value Is No Longer Everything, Top C.E.O.s Say', *The New York Times*, 19 August. Retrieved from https://www.nytimes.com/2019/08/19/business/business-roundtable-ceos-corporations.html?action=click&module=RelatedLinks&pgtype=Article (accessed 30 August 2018).

Gorton, G. and Schmid, F. A. (2004). 'Capital, Labor, and the Firm: A Study of German Codetermination', *Journal of the European Economic Association*, 2(5): 863–905. https://doi.org/10.1162/1542476042782260

Healy, P. M. and Palepu, K. G. (2003). 'The Fall of Enron', *Journal of Economic Perspectives*, 17(2): 3–26. https://doi.org/10.1257/089533003765888403

Holznagel, B. (2017). *Legal Review of the Draft Law on Better Law Enforcement in Social Networks*. Vienna: Organization for Security and Co-Operation in Europe.

Hopt, K. J. (2013). 'Better Governance of Financial Institutions', Law Working Paper No. 207. Brussels: European Corporate Governance Institute (ECGI).

Hopt, K. J. (2017). 'Corporate Governance von Finanzinstituten', *Zeitschrift für Unternehmens- und Gesellschaftsrecht*, 46(4): 438–459. https://doi.org/10.1515/zgr-2017-0018

Hoskisson, R. E., Arthurs, J. D., White, R. E., and Wyatt, C. (2013). *Multiple Agency Theory: An Emerging Perspective on Corporate Governance.* Oxford: Oxford University Press.

Hsu, H. H. and Wu, C. Y. H. (2014). 'Board Composition, Grey Directors and Corporate Failure in the UK', *British Accounting Review*, 46(3): 215–27. https://doi.org/10.1016/j.bar.2013.12.002

Iskander, M. R. and Chamlou, N. (2000). *Corporate Governance Overview: A Framework for Implementation.* Washington, DC: The World Bank Group.

Jackson Jr, R. J. (2018). 'Stock Buybacks and Corporate Cashouts', speech at the Center for American Progress, 18 June. Washington, DC: U.S. Securities and Exchange Commission. Retrieved from https://www.sec.gov/news/speech/speech-jackson-061118 (accessed 22 January 2019).

Jensen, M. C. and Meckling, H. (1976). 'Theory of the Firm: Managerial Behavior, Agency Costs and Ownership Structure', *Journal of Financial Economics*, 3: 305–60.

Kirkpatrick, G. (2009). 'The Corporate Governance Lessons from the Financial Crisis', *OECD Journal: Financial Market Trends*, (1): 61–87. https://doi.org/10.1787/fmt-v2009-art3-en

Kraft, K., Stank, J., and Dewenter, R. (2011). 'Co-determination and Innovation', *Cambridge Journal of Economics*, 35(1): 145–72. https://doi.org/10.1093/cje/bep080

Lagarde, C. (2018). 'Ten Years After Lehman—Lessons Learned and Challenges Ahead', International Monetary Fund Blog, 5 September. Retrieved from https://blogs.imf.org/2018/09/05/ten-years-after-lehman-lessons-learned-and-challenges-ahead/ (10 November 2018).

Lapowsky, I. (2018). 'The 21 (and Counting) Biggest Facebook Scandals of 2018', *Wired*, 28 August. Retrieved from https://www.wired.com/story/facebook-scandals-2018/ (accessed 29 January 2019).

Manne, H. G. (1965). 'Mergers and the Market for Corporate Control', *Journal of Political Economy*, 73(2): 110–20.

Martin, R. L. (2015). 'Yes, Short-Termism Really Is a Problem', *Harvard Business Review*, 9 October. Retrieved from https://hbr.org/2015/10/yes-short-termism-really-is-a-problem (accessed 23 August 2018).

Mclaughlin, T. (2018). 'How Facebook's Rise Fueled Chaos and Confusion in Myanmar', *Wired*, 6 July. Retrieved from https://www.wired.com/story/how-facebooks-rise-fueled-chaos-and-confusion-in-myanmar/ (accessed 7 June 2018).

McLean, B. and Elkind, P. (2006). 'The Guiltiest Guys in the Room', *CNN*, 29 May. Retrieved from https://money.cnn.com/2006/05/29/news/enron_guiltyest/ (accessed 29 August 2018).

Miller, C. C. (2013). 'Curtain Is Rising on a Tech Premiere with (as Usual) a Mostly Male Cast', *The New York Times*, 5 October. Retrieved from https://www.nytimes.com/2013/10/05/technology/as-tech-start-ups-surge-ahead-women-seem-to-be-left-behind.html (accessed 27 August 2018).

Mishkin, F. S. (2011). 'Over the Cliff: From the Subprime to the Global Financial Crisis', *Journal of Economic Perspectives*, 25(1): 49–70. https://doi.org/10.1257/jep.25.1.49

Mitchell, L. E. (2001). *Corporate Irresponsibility: America's Newest Export*. New Haven: Yale University Press.

Mitchell, R. K., Agle, B. R., and Wood, D. J. (1997). 'Toward a Theory of Stakeholder Identification and Salience: Defining the Principle of Who and What Really Counts', *Academy of Management Review*, 22(4): 853–86.

Moeller, S. B., Schlingemann, F. P., and Stulz, R. M. (2005). 'Wealth Destruction on a Massive Scale? A Study of Acquiring-firm Returns in the Recent Merger Wave', *Journal of Finance*, 60(2): 757–82. https://doi.org/10.1111/j.1540-6261.2005.00745.x

Neuscheler, T. (2018). 'Die Aufsichtsratschefs in Deutschland sind heftig unterbezahlt', *Frankurter Allgemeine Zeitung*, 30 November. Retrieved from https://www.faz.net/aktuell/wirtschaft/unternehmen/die-aufsichtsratschefs-sind-heftig-unterbezahlt-15916682.html (accessed January 30 2019).

Pfeffer, J. and Salancik, G. R. (1978). *The External Control of Organizations: A Resource Dependence Perspective*. New York, N.Y.: Harper & Row.

Romano, R. (2005). 'The Sarbanes-Oxley Act and the Making of Quack Corporate Governance', *Yale Law Journal*, 114: 1523–611. https://doi.org/10.2139/ssrn.596101

Rose, C. (2007). 'Does Female Board Representation Influence Firm Performance? The Danish Evidence', *Corporate Governance: An International Review*, 15(2): 404–13. https://doi.org/10.1111/j.1467-8683.2007.00570.x

Securities and Exchange Commission (2004). *Google Inc. Form S-1 Registration Statement*. Washington, DC: U.S. Securities and Exchange Commission.

Securities and Exchange Commission (2012). *Facebook Inc. Form S-1 Registration Statement*. Washington, DC: U.S. Securities and Exchange Commission.

Securities and Exchange Commission (2017a). *Commission Guidance on Pay Ratio Disclosure*. Washington, DC: U.S. Securities and Exchange Commission.

Securities and Exchange Commission (2017b). *Facebook Inc.—Notice of Annual Meeting of Stockholders*. Washington, DC: U.S. Securities and Exchange Commission.

Securities and Exchange Commission (2017c). *Snap Inc. Form S-1 Registration Statement*. Washington, DC: U.S. Securities and Exchange Commission.

Sidel, R., Ip, G., Phillips, M. M., and Kelly, K. (2008). 'The Week That Shook Wall Street: Inside the Demise of Bear Stearns', *The Wall Street Journal*, 18 March. Retrieved from https://www.wsj.com/articles/SB120580966534444395 (accessed 28 August 2018).

Sila, V., Gonzalez, A., and Hagendorff, J. (2016). 'Women on Board: Does Boardroom Gender Diversity Affect Firm Risk?', *Journal of Corporate Finance*, 36: 26–53. https://doi.org/10.1016/j.jcorpfin.2015.10.003

Simpson, W. G., Carter, D. A., and D'Souza, F. (2010). 'What Do We Know About Women on Boards?', *Journal of Applied Finance*, 20(2): 27–39. https://doi.org/10.1093/humupd/dmu065

Stecklow, S. (2018). 'Why Facebook Is Losing the War on Hate Speech in Myanmar', *Forbes*, 15 August. Retrieved from https://www.reuters.com/investigates/special-report/myanmar-facebook-hate/ (accessed 2 September 2018).

Stein, N. (2000). 'The World's Most Admired Companies: How Do You Make the Most Admired List? Innovate, Innovate, Innovate', *Fortune*, 2 October. Retrieved from http://archive.fortune.com/magazines/fortune/fortune_archive/2000/10/02/288448/index.htm (accessed 23 August 2018).

Stout, L. A. (2013). 'The Toxic Side Effects of Shareholder Primacy', *University of Pennsylvania Law Review*, 161(7): 2003–23. Retrieved from https://www.jstor.org/stable/23527857

Tallarita, R. (2018). 'High Tech, Low Voice: Dual-Class IPOs in the Technology Industry', Economics and Business Fellows Discussion Paper Series No. 77. Cambridge, MA: Harvard Law School.

Terjesen, S., Sealy, R., and Singh, V. (2009). 'Women Directors on Corporate Boards: A Review and Research Agenda', *Corporate Governance: An International Review*, 17(3): 320–37. https://doi.org/10.1111/j.1467-8683.2009.00742.x

The Economist (2015). 'A Mucky Business', *The Economist*, 26 September. Retrieved from http://www.economist.com/news/briefing/21667918-systematic-fraud-worlds-biggest-carmaker-threatens-engulf-entire-industry-and (accessed 23 August 2018).

Tuch, C. and O'Sullivan, N. (2007). 'The Impact of Acquisitions on Firm Performance: A Review of the Evidence', *International Journal of Management Reviews*, 9(2): 141–70. https://doi.org/10.1111/j.1468-2370.2007.00206.x

Useem, J. (2019). 'The Stock-Buyback Swindle', *The Atlantic*, 26 July. Retrieved from https://www.theatlantic.com/magazine/archive/2019/08/the-stock-buyback-swindle/592774/ (accessed 2 September 2019).

Vaidhyanathan, S. (2018). *Anti-social Media: How Facebook Disconnects Us and Undermines Democracy*. New York, NY: Oxford University Press.

Weir, C. (2013). 'The Market for Corporate Control', in D. M. Wright, D. S. Siegel, K. Keasey, and I. Filatotchev (eds.), *The Oxford Handbook of Corporate Governance*. Oxford: Oxford University Press. https://doi.org/10.1093/oxfor dhb/9780199642007.013.0015

Williamson, O. E. (2002). 'The Theory of the Firm as Governance Structure: From Choice to Contract', *Journal of Economic Perspectives*, 16(3): 171–95. https://doi.org/10.1257/089533002760278776

World Economic Forum (2018). *The Global Risks Report 2018*. Cologny/Geneva: World Economic Forum.

3

Listed Companies: Regulatory Tools and Current Reform Issues

Theodor Baums

Following the British example (Committee on the Financial Aspects of Corporate Governance 1992), legislatures of the member states of the European Union (EU) and—with the remarkable exception of the United States—have introduced a code of best practices in listed companies.[1] These codes have been revised regularly in order to adapt them to changes in the domestic or international regulatory environment or to the expectations of global investors and other stakeholders.[2]

There exist still marked differences between these codes. These differences relate to the bodies which develop such codes—is it a committee set up by the state, the stock exchange, the chamber of commerce, or some other organisation of business firms? They also relate to the content of the codes and to the various techniques by which these codes assure that their provisions are being considered and taken into account by the addressees.

Two questions in this regard are of particular interest, and a unanimous answer to them has not yet been found. Both topics are important, and the provisions in the codes relating to them vary widely. 'Advances in Corporate Governance', as in the title of this volume, does not mean that these fundamental questions have been answered and settled in a convincing way.

The first question concerns the appropriate role of a code as an 'instrument of self-regulation' in its relation to the provisions of the respective statutory public law. What is the realm of a code? Could and should all regulations of a listed company's life, if at all necessary or recommendable, be left to a code, or can a

---

[1] Details on such codes around the world are available online from the European Corporate Governance Institute (ecgi) (https://ecgi.global/content/codes). On the US, where such codes have not been formally legislated at the federal level, see American Law Institute (1994).

[2] Comparative analyses can be found in Autorité des Marchés Financiers (2016) and Allen & Overy (2017).

Theodor Baums, *Listed Companies: Regulatory Tools and Current Reform Issues* In: *Advances in Corporate Governance: Comparative Perspectives.* Edited by: Helmut K. Anheier and Theodor Baums, Oxford University Press (2020).
© Hertie School.
DOI: 10.1093/oso/9780198866367.003.0003

clear line be drawn between a code on the one hand and statutory provisions (including their interpretation and rulings by the courts) on the other?

The second question which will be addressed in this chapter refers to one critical element in most codes, that a part of, a majority, or even all outside directors or members of a supervisory board should be 'independent'. A comparative look at the codes shows that they vary widely in this regard. What is the rationale behind this requirement? A closer examination will show that one has to differentiate between independence from the incumbent management and the company on the one hand and independence from a controlling shareholder on the other. This necessary differentiation allows for better acceptance of such recommendations in codes.

Statute and Code

Codes of best practice for companies supplement the provisions of the statutory public law on companies of a specific legislature. That is one of the explanations for the wide variation in the content of such codes. For example, as British company law contains fewer mandatory provisions for public and, among them, for listed companies than does the German Stock Corporation Act (*Aktiengesetz*), the space and the need for supplementary principles and recommendations for good corporate governance is greater in the United Kingdom. But if one puts this difference between jurisdictions *de lege lata* aside, it is unclear which role the legislature should play with regard to corporate governance and which matters should be included in a corporate governance code. This question is the subject of this section. It takes the German situation as an example, but the issue is relevant for all jurisdictions with a code for listed companies which face these two levels of regulation (cf. also most recently Döll (2018), with a comparison of the British and German systems).

Corporate governance in publicly listed companies is determined first and foremost by statutory requirements. The dichotomy between management board and supervisory board in the governance structure of a German stock company, the co-determination on the part of employees as members of the supervisory board, and the fundamental duties of members of the management and supervisory board are codified in the mandatory provisions of the Stock Corporation Act, the Commercial Code, and the Co-determination Act. These rules are laid down by the German legislature. The enacted provisions are compulsory in the context at issue here, unless a deviation from the rules by private rule-making has been explicitly permitted (Stock Corporation Act, § 23, para. 5).

How can a corporate governance code be differentiated from a statute? From a formal point of view, a code can be distinguished obviously by the fact that the code is not enacted by the legislature but, for example as in Germany, formulated by a commission of experts, the Regierungskommission Deutscher Corporate Governance Kodex (Code Commission), set up for this purpose. The Stock Corporation Act lends support to the German Corporate Governance Code by obligating the management board and the supervisory board of a company to explain whether they complied with the recommendations of the code (Aktiengesetz/Stock Corporation Act, § 161). This does not make the recommendations legally binding, but it establishes the requirement of a legally mandated declaration of conformity or non-conformity ('comply or explain').

Differentiation between the content of a code and of a statute is more difficult: which regulations are better included in a corporate governance code and which are reserved for legal rules? Company practitioners and the financial press often erroneously believe that Germany's Code Commission acts as a surrogate legislator, asserting that the legislature essentially decided not to interfere in the area of corporate governance. Legislative measures in this area, in particular on disclosure and the appropriateness of executive compensation, were wrongly understood to have undermined the competence of the Code Commission. This assumption misrepresents the proper role of a code.

First, it has to be noted that the legislature can at any time generally or on a case-by-case basis reverse the 'self-commitment' which it created by establishing the German Code Commission and instructing the Commission to create a non-legislative code of conduct. The legislature is free to enact legal, dispositive, or mandatory rules for corporate governance and to limit the leeway of the Code Commission with respect to a particular question. As an example, after the German Corporate Governance Code had been introduced, the legislature enacted a cooling-off period for members of a company's management board before they can be elected to the supervisory board (Aktiengesetz/Stock Corporation Act, § 100, para. 2, no. 4). One does not have to agree with this rule. However, the legislature saw it differently and was of the opinion that the regulation of the question should not be left to the Code Commission, especially after two Commission chairs failed to comply with the recommended cooling-off period which had already been included in the Code. The legislature therefore clearly retains the legislative prerogative even with regard to corporate governance matters: the Code Commission is only authorised to issue corporate governance recommendations insofar and as long as the legislature does not use its legislative powers to enact rules for this area.

Second, another limit to the power of the German Code Commission is the fact that the Code—except to the extent that it reproduces the text of the law—only makes and may only make recommendations on how to act (see Stock Corporation Act, § 161, para. 1). This means that all matters of company law, co-determination law, and commercial law that are not addressed to the company bodies and are not meant to influence or control their behaviour in one way or the other are reserved for statutory regulation. One can think here of formal requirements, rules on jurisdiction, and similar matters. A closer look reveals that this limitation of the permissible content of a corporate governance code does not extend as far as it might seem at first. Substantive legal rules can often be phrased as behavioural guidelines for the company bodies and can therefore take the form of code recommendations.

Third, corporate governance codes for listed companies are mostly directed at and limited to recommendations for the company's organs (governing boards and their members). In the German case, this is even determined by the Stock Corporation Act, which states that only the management board and the supervisory board may be addressees of a code recommendation (see Aktiengesetz/Stock Corporation Act, § 161, para. 1). However, corporate governance in a publicly listed company is shaped by numerous additional actors. They include, first and foremost, the shareholders: private investors, majority shareholders, institutional investors, and activist shareholders. They can exercise their individual rights as shareholders and possibly also exert de facto influence on the company's organs, and they can influence the company collectively by amending the articles of association or by adopting other resolutions. Nonetheless, shareholders are not addressees of the German Code in either function.

The same applies to proxy advisors, auditors, remuneration consultants, and—in co-determined companies—employees entitled to vote, none of which are addressees of the German Code. If this were to be changed, for example, by including recommendations for auditors or institutional investors in the code, the Stock Corporation Act (§ 161 AktG) would have to be amended. In this regard, it should be mentioned however that the German Code utilises a trick in some places: instead of directly addressing the auditor who is out of its reach, it makes recommendations for the management board to contractually obligate the auditor to comply with the recommendations (cf. German Corporate Governance Code/DCGK, sec. 7.2.3, paras. 1 & 2; see also DCGK, sec. 7.2.1., paras. 1 & 2).

Fourth, with regard to codes of conduct for the management board and the supervisory board, when should the legislature act and when is the code better suited to regulate the subject? A corporate governance rule must be enacted by statute if public interest requires a mandatory rule without deviation, in particular when the enforcement of a provision presupposes a publicly enforceable sanction. Vice versa, a regulation should be included in a corporate governance code if these considerations are not relevant and if atypical, company-specific circumstances demand the flexibility of the 'comply or explain' mechanism. Once again, it should be emphasised that the legislature is free to enact statutory rules in cases that fall into the second category.

Here are two examples for this. According to section 5.3.2 of the German Corporate Governance Code, the supervisory board *shall* establish an audit committee that addresses, *inter alia*, the monitoring of the accounting, the risk management system, and the audit. 'Shall' means that it is not mandatory and that a deviation from the recommendation is permissible. Without doubt, the work of the audit committee is of enormous importance, and one would expect a mandatory rule. That the German legislature has not opted for a mandatory rule in spite of this can be explained by the special circumstances surrounding companies with only three members on the supervisory board. In these cases, the establishment of an audit committee would be nitpicking with regard to formal requirements because the membership of the audit committee would be identical to the membership of the supervisory board. The company-specific circumstances of companies with only three supervisory board members require that no separate audit committee be established and that the full supervisory board take on that committee's duties. Atypical, company-specific circumstances require the flexibility of the 'comply or explain' mechanism. Public interest might require that the usual tasks of the audit committee are performed, but it does not require that small stock corporations explicitly establish such a committee for this purpose; the tasks can be performed by the full supervisory board.

A counterexample can be provided by the duty to disclose an individual management board member's remuneration in the financial statement (Handelsgesetzbuch/Commercial Code § 285, no. 9, § 314, para. 1, no. 6). Atypical, company-specific circumstances that would dictate a deviation from the duty to disclose that information to shareholders and the capital market do not exist. Disclosure requirements of publicly listed companies are therefore generally better suited for a statute than a code based on the 'comply or explain' principle. Hence, the German legislature has determined that public interest demands a statutory rule in this respect. The legislature's action came after it was revealed that the previously applicable disclosure recommendation of the German Corporate Governance Code had not been complied with on a widespread basis, prompting allegations that non-compliance was based on collusion.

To recapitulate, the relationship between statute and German Corporate Governance Code and between legislature and Code Commission, as enacted by the legislature in § 161 of the German Stock Corporation Act, can be summarised as follows:

- The legislature has without doubt the legislative prerogative also with regard to corporate governance. The Code Commission is authorised to make corporate governance recommendations only insofar and as long as the legislature has not used its competence to adopt legislation in this area.
- The Code—except to the extent that it reproduces the text of the law— only makes recommendations on how to act. The Code does not contain rules regarding the formation or structure of the company and other provisions that do not require actions of the board(s) or refer to the behaviour of the board members. All aspects of company law, co-determination law, and commercial law that do not address the company bodies and that are not meant to influence their behaviour one way or another are reserved for statutory regulation.
- In the German context only the management and the supervisory board and their members may be addressees of Code recommendations. Other actors that influence or may influence the corporate governance of a publicly listed company cannot. This applies to shareholders as well as their proxy advisors, the auditor, the remuneration consultant, and—in co-determined companies—the employees entitled to vote. To the extent that a change of that situation is desirable and wanted (for example, inclusion of recommendations for auditors or institutional investors), the Stock Corporation Act (§ 161) would have to be amended.
- A corporate governance rule must be enacted by statute if public interest requires a mandatory rule without deviation. On the other hand, a regulation should be included in the Corporate Governance Code if these considerations are not relevant and if atypical, company-specific circumstances demand the flexibility of the 'comply or explain' mechanism.

Independence of Outside Directors and Supervisory Board Members

A second point of discussion both on the national and on the international level is the meaning and in particular the appropriate number of independent members of the (supervisory) board. Frequently one finds the recommendation that the board should have an appropriate number of independent members, sometimes even the majority of the outside directors, or at least the members of subcommittees like the audit committee or the remuneration committee should be independent.[3] The German Code envisages a balanced approach which, however, has been occasionally misinterpreted by practitioners and the scholarly literature on that topic (for more details, see Baums 2016: 697–706). The reform which is currently underway (cf. Nonnenmacher 2018), following the reforms of the Dutch and UK codes, should clarify this.

Every supervisory board of a publicly listed company should include an appropriate number of independent members. This is provided for in the German Corporate Governance Code (DCGK, sec. 5.4.2, sentence 1). The question of whether a company has an 'appropriate number' has to be answered differently depending on whether it means being independent of the management board and the relevant company or being independent of a controlling shareholder or being independent of a major competitor of the corporation.

With regard to a co-determined supervisory board with parity representation, for example, all shareholder representatives should be independent of the management board, of the company that it governs, and of the affiliated companies. This rule does not apply however to independence from the controlling shareholder (if one exists, as is often the case in Continental European companies and in German listed companies; cf. the comparative studies in Barca and Becht 2001). The Code recommends that '[t]he Supervisory Board shall include what it considers to be an appropriate number of independent members, thereby taking into account the shareholder structure' (DCGK, sec. 5.4.2, sentence 1).

'Taking into account' means that the minority shareholders, i.e. the 'external' investors in a publicly listed company dominated by a controlling shareholder, should be given the guarantee that not all members of the supervisory board

---

[3] For the national level cf. the ecgi website (https://ecgi.global/content/codes); for the EU level cf. European Commission (2005).

that are chosen by majority voting are 'dependent' on the controlling share-holder. On the one hand, the German Corporate Governance Code does not want to curtail the incentives that the controlling shareholders have to control their companies by requiring them to only or for the most part choose super-visory board members that are 'independent' of them. On the other hand, when a controlling shareholder exists, it is understandably recommended that the needs of the minority shareholders be taken into account by choosing supervisory board members that are independent of the controlling shareholder.

In this regard the independence postulate is intended to compensate for the majority principle: the larger the investment quota of the controlling shareholders, i.e. the larger their percentage of shares owned, the more they can demand that the supervisory board seats reserved for shareholders are filled with people they trust and have personal links with. The requirement of independence from the controlling shareholder is a correlate of the majority principle according to which the controlling shareholder is able to push through all candidates for the board irrespective of the fact that the minority has also contributed to the company's capital and is exposed to the same risks as the controlling shareholder.

Conclusion

This chapter has looked at two areas of the current debate surrounding cor-porate governance codes as instruments of regulation for listed companies. First, the relationship between statutory legislation and codes has been discussed. A corporate governance rule must be enacted by statute if public interest requires a mandatory rule without deviation, in particular when the enforcement of a provision presupposes a publicly enforceable sanction. A regulation should be included in the corporate governance code if these considerations are not relevant (which means that public interest does not require a mandatory rule without deviation) and atypical, company-specific circumstances demand the flexibility of the 'comply or explain' mechanism.

The second area examined is the independence requirement in codes for listed companies. In order to determine whether a company has independent supervisory board members (in the one-tier model, outside directors), two dif-ferent perspectives need to be considered. The appropriate number of board members that are independent of the management board and of the company governed by it, on the one hand, and the appropriate number of supervisory board members that are independent of the controlling shareholder, on the other hand, have to be determined separately. The two numbers need not necessarily match.

References

Allen and Overy (2017). *Corporate Governance: Comparative Study.* Antwerp/ Brussels: Allen & Overy.

American Law Institute (1994). *Principles of Corporate Governance,* 2 vols, Philadelphia: American Law Institute.

Autorité des Marchés Financiers (2016). *Comparative Study: Corporate Governance Codes in 10 European Countries.* Paris: Autorité des Marchés Financiers.

Barca, F. and Becht, M. (eds.) (2001). *The Control of Corporate Europe.* Oxford: Oxford University Press.

Baums, T. (2016). 'Unabhängige Aufsichtsratsmitglieder', *Zeitschrift für das gesamte Handelsrecht und Wirtschaftsrecht (ZHR),* 180: 697–706.

Committee on the Financial Aspects of Corporate Governance (1992). *Report of the Committee on the Financial Aspects of Corporate Governance.* London: Gee and Co. Ltd.

Döll, M. (2018). *Aktienrecht und Codes of Best Practice.* Berlin: Duncker & Humblot.

European Commission (2005). 'Commission Recommendation of 15 February 2005 on the role of non-executive or supervisory directors of listed companies and on the committees of the (supervisory) board (2005/162/EC)', *Official Journal of the European Union,* L 52/51.

Nonnenmacher, R. (2018). 'Corporate Governance im Spannungsfeld von Investorenerwartungen und Kodexreform', *WPg—Die Wirtschaftsprüfung,* 11: 709–12.

4

Corporate Governance of Financial Corporations

Iris H-Y Chiu

After the global financial crisis of 2007–9, a wave of regulatory reform was introduced for banks at the international, European Union (EU), and national (United Kingdom) levels. One aspect of such reforms was the regulation of financial corporations' corporate governance in certain areas, as part of an expanded scope of microprudential regulation. These reforms add a qualitative dimension to the chiefly quantitative paradigm of microprudential regulation which deals with banks' prudent risk management.

Conventional standards in corporate governance apply to the banking sector as part of the corporate sector generally in the form of securities markets rules or 'soft law' such as codes of corporate governance adopted in the EU and in international capital markets (see Baums, Ch. 3 in this volume). Regulatory law on financial sector corporate governance is of a different nature, as it is targeted at the framework and organisation of bank risk management for financial stability objectives, instead of shareholder accountability objectives upheld in conventional corporate governance standards. Hence, Cheffins (2009) observed that adherence to conventional corporate governance standards had little relevance to preventing the corporate disasters experienced by the banks embroiled in the global financial crisis.

The role of regulation in financial corporations' corporate governance introduces a new dimension in corporate governance that is not dominated by private organisational perspectives or the primacy of securities markets, although it cannot be said that there is no tension between market-based corporate governance standards and regulatory standards. The corporate governance of corporations is highly shaped by the political economy traditions of the jurisdictions in which companies are incorporated (Gordon and Roe 2010), but regulatory governance attempts to introduce common denominators in the interest of prudential management, a matter of universal interest.

Iris H-Y Chiu, *Corporate Governance of Financial Corporations* In: *Advances in Corporate Governance: Comparative Perspectives*. Edited by: Helmut K. Anheier and Theodor Baums, Oxford University Press (2020).
© Hertie School.
DOI: 10.1093/oso/9780198866367.003.0004

Avgouleas and Cullen (2014) advocate less focus on regulatory reforms in corporate governance because even if there were flaws in the failed banks' corporate governance adherence, these were not considered to be determinative of their disasters. This perspective could resolve the tensions between regulatory standards and market-based corporate governance standards which now concurrently apply to listed financial institutions. On the other hand, most policy-makers and regulators have taken an integrated perspective, determined to address weaknesses in various aspects of corporate governance through both regulation and market-based governance. This is because even if corporate governance factors were not causal, their contributive effect was significant and perhaps reinforced poor risk management (Walker 2009; Basel Committee on Banking Supervision 2010; OECD 2009).

The first part of this chapter considers why financial corporations' corporate governance should be treated differently from that of the general corporate sector. Corporate governance standards for the general corporate sector are based on the well-accepted agency theory of corporate governance. This part also examines whether the agency theory of corporate governance is too narrow an approach for understanding financial institution corporate governance. Further, as there is public interest served by the financial sector which underpins financial regulation, the application of shareholder-centred corporate governance standards to financial corporations may be inappropriate. The following section considers the role of regulation as moderating certain corporate governance applications and critically discusses whether this has addressed all the issues highlighted in the prior section. This section thus discusses key features of regulation in the EU in respect of financial corporations' corporate governance in terms of boards, shareholders' roles, internal control, financial sector remuneration, individual responsibility, and liability regimes (introduced in the UK only). The final section offers brief concluding remarks on why the corporate governance regulatory regime for financial corporations is likely unique.

Why Corporate Governance in Financial Corporations Is Different

Corporate governance in Anglo-American literature is often understood as a private contractarian phenomenon (Moore and Petrin 2017: Ch. 2; Easterbrook and Fischel 1991) aimed at resolving the agency problem between shareholders, whose financial capital commitment to companies is open-ended, and directors, whose management powers may allow them to benefit themselves and injure shareholders' investment interests (Jensen and Meckling 1976; Armour, Hansmann, and Kraakman 2017). Hence, the general understanding of corporate governance is its private and incentive-based nature derived from the structure of the company's capital. In this way, corporate governance is about how well directors and managers are monitored and disciplined to exercise their powers over corporate assets appropriately in order to ensure that the interests of financial capital are not adversely affected. This is realised through the allocation of powers in company law in favour of shareholders as well as the financial discipline of shareholder primacy upon directors. The predominantly 'private' nature of corporate governance in Anglo-American jurisdictions may arguably be contrasted with other jurisdictions where corporate governance may reflect social bargains, such as co-determination in Germany and a few other European jurisdictions (Hall and Soskice 2001). However, it is also arguable that the 'varieties of capitalism' shaping different jurisdictions' corporate governance traditions vary in terms of reflecting the range and balance of constituents represented in corporate governance, but still essentially culminate in systems of private contractarianism within a corporate structure.

In the UK, as key constituents in corporate governance because they provide long-term financial capital, shareholders are (a) the subjects of directors' accountability,[1] (b) the organ to exercise key powers in certain aspects of decision-making in the company,[2] and (c) the constituents whose capital return interests should form the basis for corporate management.[3] Securities

---

[1] S172, Companies Act 2006 explicitly provides that directors' duties are to promote the long-term success of the company for the benefit of the members as a whole. This has come to be coined as 'enlightened shareholder value', a long-termist and more inclusive perspective for corporate performance, but revolving around shareholders. But most commentators are of the view that the focus on 'shareholder value' will unlikely introduce any revolutionary move in directors' conduct towards stakeholders, see e.g. Davies (2005), Williams (2012), Keay (2007), and Lynch (2012).

[2] Such key aspects include the appointment and removal of directors (s168, Companies Act 2006); the power to approve of certain transactions such as loans and guarantees or substantial transactions to directors, long-term incentive arrangements, and payments for loss of office (s188ff); the power to ratify directors' breaches of duties or defaults (s239); the power to direct management in a specific matter by special resolution (Art 4, The Companies (Model Articles) Regulations 2008); and a power to approve (or otherwise) directors' remuneration packages on a three-yearly basis (s439A). Shareholders also have extensive powers to determine capital restructuring, such as approval of capital reduction or redemption of shares (s641ff, 659); and are the key organ to determine if a takeover of the company is approved (Armour, Deakin and Konzelmann 2003).

[3] Shareholders are treated by economists as 'residual claimants', meaning that their supply of capital to the company is under an open-ended arrangement which renders them liable to be ultimate losers if the company should fail. The 'residual claimant' status of the shareholders therefore requires protection so that managers do not abuse the privilege of being in control of the use and application of capital. See Alchian and Demsetz (1972).

markets regulation also protects shareholders' interests by ensuring regular accountability and, increasingly, the imposition of corporate governance standards as part of listing conditions, in order to maintain the attractiveness of securities markets for investor confidence (Zingales 2009; La Porta, Lopez-de-Silanes, and Shleifer 2006). Further, it is often the case that debtholders may also have rights in the governance and financial discipline of companies,[4] such as in appointing bank nominee directors, ensuring regular accountability and reporting, and enforcing certain financial covenants and collateral. Even in other jurisdictions of greater stakeholder orientation, shareholders' rights and accountability to them remain paramount, largely because of international competition and the integration of global securities markets (La Porta et al. 2006).

Compared to most other companies in the listed sector, listed financial corporations are financed in a different structure, and it may be argued that conventional corporate governance standards do not quite capture the corresponding complexity and therefore inadequately provide governance rights and roles linked to financial capital provision (Deakin 2011). In particular, banks are financed to a large extent by deposits, but depositors often only have a contractual right of demand for return of their deposit and no other governance or stakeholder rights (House of Lords 1848). This phenomenon is common for financial corporations across different corporate governance traditions.

Banks and many financial corporations also generate significant amounts of funding from borrowing in institutional funding markets, often on a short-term basis, using the financial assets they hold as collateral (Singh 2014). These borrowing transactions are structured as 'repos' i.e. the sale and repurchase of securities assets which act as collateral in fact. Repo transactions are subject to private contractual pricing, such as 'haircuts' on the value of collateral used to support the borrowing, and are carried out by all financial institutions vis-à-vis each other including banks, investment banks, prime brokers, hedge funds, pension funds, and collective investment funds in general (Committee on the Global Financial System 2010). These financial counterparties have a keen stake in each other's prudent risk management, but they only have contractual means of discipline and recourse to collateral. As such borrowing is short-term, there is usually no consideration of protection in terms of governance aspects. Often such external and contractual means of discipline are not ideal, as financial counterparties may need to enforce

[4] The 'proprietary' rights of debtholders are discussed in parts in Armour and Whincop (2007).

against collateral when default risks have materialised, and such enforcement is usually in a downward and turbulent market, exacerbating the mutual financial damage done to each other.[5]

Conventional corporate governance standards that value shareholder primacy do not reflect banks' complex financing arrangements (Ciancelli and Reyes Gonzalez 2000). However, even in corporate governance traditions with stakeholder inclusion such as those that support co-determination, the main group of non-shareholder constituents included is employees, and so these traditions also do not cater for banks' complex financing arrangements. A number of commentators point out that shareholders 'free-ride' on the complex financing structures for banks and prefer banks to take high levels of risk in order to maximise shareholder returns. In terms of empirical research in relation to the banks stricken in the global financial crisis of 2007–9, Beltratti and Stultz (2009) find that banks with shareholder-friendly boards were correlated with worse financial performance. This result is consistent with Gropp and Köhler's (2010) and Westman's (2010) findings that shareholder-aligned boards—either because of the operation of a better shareholder rights protection legal regime or due to the presence of a controlling shareholder—led their banks into larger losses during the crisis. The results indicate that the risks taken, consistent with shareholders' preferences, have generally been greater and the materialisation of risks leading to losses more extensive. Shareholder alignment could occur in financial institutions with dispersed and concentrated ownership. Erkens, Hung, and Matos (2012) find that dispersed institutional shareholders exhibit higher risk-taking preferences and their influence on boards has not been salutary in the financial crisis: banks with institutional shareholders have recorded greater losses and worse stock performance. However, according to Boubaker, Nguyen, and Rouatbi (2012), banks with multiple large owners exhibit high risk-taking behaviour too.

There is a case for regarding the private nature of corporate governance, whether subjecting the management of financial corporations to the discipline of shareholders in securities markets or other contractarian forms of corporate governance, as not providing an adequate framework for disciplining management in relation to the public interest in the safety of financial corporations. This is because private incentives such as shareholder primacy form the basis for skewed priorities for bank management and could cause management to neglect the other financing contributors who are not accounted for in the conventional corporate governance framework. Regulatory intervention

---

[5] On the 'run' risk in markets, see Jackson (2013) and Financial Stability Board (2015).

is a means to provide certain correcting balances to incentives for management, but regulatory intervention does not curtail shareholders' powers, roles, or influence in banks. This may be due to the need to ensure that banks are able to access equity financing cost-effectively. Furthermore, reforms in prudential and bail-in legislation[6] impose on banks the obligation to raise extra levels of equity capital. These regulatory reforms intend to put shareholders more at risk in order to shape their influence on bank management. Further regulatory reforms intervene directly in bank management in order to enforce prudent risk management on the part of managers, as discussed later in this chapter.

The discussion now turns the focus on the regulation of financial institution corporate governance that is premised upon meeting certain public interest objectives such as financial stability. The context of the regulatory reforms lies in the global financial crisis of 2007–9. In the wake of the crisis, it is opined that excessive levels of risk-taking (Erkens, Hung, and Matos 2012; Ramirez 2009)[7] coupled with poor risk management[8] at banks culminated in the failure of a number of financial institutions (Brunnermeier et al. 2009; Sabato 2009; Mikes 2008; Blommestein, Hoogduin, and Peeters 2009; Crouhy 2010: 283; Sheedy 2010: 301; Partnoy 2011). The Basel Committee on Banking Supervision (2010: para. 15) is of the view that '[s]upervisors have a keen interest in sound corporate governance as it is an essential element in the safe and sound functioning of a bank and may adversely affect the bank's risk profile if not implemented effectively.' The risk and control culture at failed institutions has now come under scrutiny and the role of corporate governance has been called into question.[9] Regulatory reforms affecting corporate governance may be seen to be targeted ultimately at the public interest of financial stability (Kokkinis 2018) and have developed the qualitative side of microprudential regulation.

Regulation of Corporate Governance Aspects

The regulation of various corporate governance aspects at financial corporations is premised on meeting the public interest objective of financial stability.

---

[6] Basel III Accord, as implemented by the CRD IV Regulation 2013, and bail-in provisions in the Recovery and Resolution Directive 2014/59/EU.

[7] But what is 'excessive' is difficult to pinpoint, as Miller (2010) points out that taking low but severe risks could turn out to be 'excessive' and not calculated after all, and Okamoto and Edwards (2010) warn that it is impossible to define what is socially optimal risk-taking for banks.

[8] Poor risk management at firms has been argued to be an important contributing factor to firm failure and financial instability (Brunnermeier et al. 2009; Kirkpatrick 2009; Murphy 2011).

[9] For policy implementation, the key documents are Walker (2009), Basel Committee on Banking Supervision (2010), and OECD (2009).

Corporations' governance structures may affect levels of risk-taking and risk management, hence policy-makers see a need to align such structures and organisational incentives with the public interest objective of microprudential stability (Malloy 2003). The purpose is not only to prevent financial corporations from failing as such, but to prevent systemic consequences that may result from their failure. Individual failures can result in stresses for their counterparties, and in a highly interconnected financial world, as can be seen from the example of repo markets above, a cascading effect of failure can hit other financial institutions connected with a failed institution (Schwarcz 2008). Further, individual failures may also 'spook' markets and result in wider episodes of turbulent confidence and instability in markets.

Such regulatory reforms are not made in order to reflect the different and complex funding structures of financial corporations, and hence they do not include an expanded scope of governance 'actors' or 'rights'. Instead, key aspects within the financial corporation are required to be structured in such a way so as to ensure that the public interest objective of prudential risk management is not undermined. Such required changes do not disturb fundamental corporate governance frameworks such as the norm of shareholder primacy that is supported by Anglo-American capital markets. The regulatory aspects exist alongside the market-based rules for corporate governance, and an obvious tension is the failure of regulatory standards to address any perverse incentives that corporate governance traditions such as shareholder primacy may exert upon the board.

Soft Law on Shareholders' Roles

The UK Prudential Regulation Authority (PRA) is keen to enrol shareholders in the governance landscape to act as gatekeepers in risk management supervision of financial corporations. The Walker Review (Walker 2009) suggests that shareholder engagement is relevant to corporate governance reforms in financial corporations in the wider interest of risk management and financial stability. The Review is of the view that shareholder monitoring should take on a character of 'stewardship', viz.:

> The potentially highly influential position of significant holders of stock in listed companies is a major ingredient in the market-based capitalist system which needs to earn and to be accorded an at least *implicit social legitimacy*.

As counterpart to the obligation of the board to the institutional shareholders, this implicit legitimacy can be acquired by at least the larger fund manager through assumption of a reciprocal obligation involving attentiveness to the performance of investee companies over a long as well as a short-term horizon. On this view, those who have significant rights of ownership and enjoy the very material advantage of limited liability should see these as complemented by *a duty of stewardship. This is a view that would be shared by the public, as well as those employees and suppliers* who are less well-placed than an institutional shareholder to diversify their exposure to the management and performance risk of a limited liability company.

(Walker 2009: para. 5.7; emphasis added)

The role of shareholders as monitors in the risk management of financial corporations, providing a form of co-governance, is an idea that is embraced at many policy-making levels in the UK. However, it may be argued that shareholder primacy does not help in improving prudential risk management. Empirical research tends to suggest that shareholder incentives are aligned with excessive risk-taking (Deakin 2011; Mülbert 2009). Hence, looking to shareholders to provide a form of governance could be fundamentally flawed.

Arguably, policy-makers in the UK are not endorsing shareholder primacy as such, but 'shareholder stewardship'. Hence, policy-makers are nudging shareholders towards a form of engagement and responsibility that promotes the long-term viability of the financial corporation and not their short-termist tendencies that may be deleterious to the financial corporation. This may suggest that shareholders are enrolled in their corporate governance roles only insofar as they subscribe to the notion of 'stewardship'.

The UK Stewardship Code (FRC 2020) was first rolled out in 2010 in response to the Walker Review to apply to institutional shareholders on a 'comply or explain' basis.[10] The Code applies to all institutions' investee companies, whether financial corporations or otherwise. The key notions in 'stewardship' seem to be long-termism and taking a more holistic view of the well-being and performance of the company. Principles 9–11 of the Code require that, as a matter of stewardship, institutional shareholders should 'monitor' their investee companies. Such monitoring includes seeking to be satisfied that corporate governance arrangements are robust, carrying out meetings with company directors and/or the chairman of the board, maintaining records of such

---

[10] See Baums, Ch. 3 in this volume, on how the 'comply or explain' mechanism is applied in the German Corporate Governance Code.

meetings, considering the use of voting power, and attending general meetings. Monitoring also includes the 'escalation' of shareholder engagement by, for example, intensifying meetings with board members, making public statements, and even requisitioning general meetings, where it is appropriate to do so to protect and enhance shareholder value. Monitoring is couched in terms of protecting and 'enhancing' shareholder value. In this sense, it may be argued that the monitoring called for by the Code is an outworking of private interest, reaffirming the well-accepted private corporate governance role of shareholders in the agency paradigm. So does 'stewardship' imply an active shareholders' role in monitoring investee financial institutions for prudent risk management? Although stewardship policies are to be publicly disclosed, stewardship reporting is private in nature, as institutional investors account to their beneficiaries only, according to Code Principles 9–11.

The principles in the UK Stewardship Code do not seem to couch shareholder monitoring in terms of specific interests such as the safety and soundness of financial corporations. The Code provides a template for legitimate shareholder behaviour without articulating whether such behaviour is to be rooted in wider common interests. The framing of stewardship has not fundamentally changed shareholders' behaviour, and the private and incentive-based nature of their corporate governance roles cannot for certain be said to be aligned with the objectives of public interest for financial corporations. The UK's position on nudging shareholders towards stewardship reinforces shareholder primacy as the fundamental tenet of listed companies' corporate governance whether in relation to financial corporations or otherwise. The failure to address potentially adverse effects of shareholder primacy continues to be a glaring gap in the UK.

The discussion now turns to enumerating the regulatory reforms in board composition and responsibilities, internal control structures, individual liability and responsibility, and remuneration. It may be argued that as regulatory reforms have now made prescriptive inroads into organisational and governance issues in financial corporations, there is less room for adverse influences resulting from shareholder primacy to affect risk management at financial corporations. To an extent boards, senior management, and internal control staff have all become reoriented towards the public interest objective of financial stability. But shareholder primacy is likely to continue affecting strategic decision-making. The potential tensions for a financial corporation between catering to shareholder preferences and meeting public interest objectives should not be ignored.

Regulating Boards

The functions of the board of regulated credit institutions[11] and investment firms[12] in the EU are articulated to include (a) the overall responsibility for strategic objectives, risk strategy, and internal governance; (b) the responsibility to ensure integrity in accounting and financial reporting; (c) the responsibility to ensure compliance with laws and regulations; (d) the oversight of disclosure and communications in the firm; (e) the responsibility to provide effective oversight of senior management; and (f) periodic review of all governance arrangements. These explicit board responsibilities are now transposed in the UK in the PRA Rulebook, *General Organisational Requirements: Management Body* (para. 5.1).

It is to be noted that risk governance has now been raised in profile to sit alongside the board's usual role in strategic management, and this reflects the public interest in the prudential management of banks.[13] Boards in the pre-crisis years have been roundly criticised because they did not prioritise the monitoring of risk-taking and management (Govindarajan 2011; Hopt 2013; Larcker and Tayan 2011: Ch. 6). In particular, a board risk committee is to be set up for banks of sufficient size, scale, and complexity. The risk committee has the responsibilities of identifying, measuring, and reporting all material risks in the firm, advising the management body on overall risk appetite and strategy, and overseeing the strategy's implementation.[14] Further, the board is explicitly mandated to ensure regulatory compliance. In this way, the regulatory prescriptions for board responsibilities now infuse elements of public interest and are not merely framed towards being accountable to shareholders.

Board Composition

Certain aspects of board composition are now prescribed in EU legislation,[15] and transposed into UK law by the PRA.[16] First, board members are to be assessed for suitability for their appointment 'as a whole' (EBA and ESMA 2016). This means that individual qualities, skills, and experience are looked at in order to ascertain fit for the board as a whole. Board members need to possess certain personal qualities: 'sufficiently good repute', 'integrity', and

---

[11] CRD IV Directive, Art 88(1).

[12] MiFID (Markets in Financial Instruments Directive) II, Art 9 contains similar provisions on oversight of effective and prudent management and the board's responsibility to set an appropriate remuneration policy.

[13] CRD IV Directive, Art 76.   [14] PRA Rulebook, Risk Control at 3.1ff.

[15] CRD IV Directive, Art 91(7); MiFID II 2014, Art 45(4)ff for market operators.

[16] PRA Rulebook, *General Organisational Requirements: Management Body* at para 5.2.

'independence of mind'.[17] Next, board members need to possess sufficient knowledge, skills, and experience for their capacities on the board. A number of commentators opine that the lack of board competence or expertise has been correlated with failures and adverse performance at banks and financial institutions.[18]

Qualifications of Board Members

There is however no general prescription provided in EU or UK legislation as to what qualifications in terms of financial expertise may be required for bank board members, except in relation to the audit and risk committees. The PRA requires that at least one member of the audit committee have accounting expertise, and all the members of the audit committee must have competence in relation to the sector in which the financial firm is operating.[19] Further, all members of the risk committee are required to have relevant knowledge, skills, and expertise to fully understand and oversee the firm's risk strategy and risk appetite.[20] EU legislation and the Basel Committee's standards support an overall notion of a balanced board, comprising a diverse but balanced slate of skills, knowledge, and expertise. The Capital Requirements Directive (CRD) 2013 transposed by the PRA envisages boards to be populated with members drawing from a 'broad range of experience',[21] while the Basel Committee (2015: Principle 2) emphasises a range of skills and expertise too. The Basel Committee sees the diversity and balance of skills and expertise as necessary so that different views and critical discussion can be promoted on the board. Hence the need to ensure a diverse and balanced board may run counter to the perceived need for prescribing qualifications.

Board Committees

The nomination, remuneration, and audit committees of the board are also subject to an extent of regulatory prescription. The PRA requires that a bank that is 'significant' institute a nomination committee of the board. The

---

[17] CRD IV Directive, Art 91(7) and PRA Rulebook, *General Organisational Requirements: Management Body* at para 5.2.

[18] For example, Hau and Thum's (2009) empirical study finds correlations between the lack of financial expertise and experience on the part of supervisory boards in German financial institutions and larger losses suffered by those institutions in the global financial crisis. Note however that Mehran, Morrison, and Shapiro (2012) warn that directors with financial expertise and experience may also favour greater risk-taking and hence could exacerbate risk-taking tendencies in banks and financial institutions.

[19] PRA Rulebook, *Audit Committee* at para 2.2.   [20] PRA Rulebook, *Risk Control*, at para 3.1.

[21] CRD IV Directive 2013 at Art 91(1); PRA Rulebook, *General Organisational Requirements: Management Body* at para 5.2.

nomination committee, which must be composed fully of non-executive members, has the responsibility to recruit persons adhering to the earlier discussed criteria for appointment to the board and a continuing role to ensure that directors' skills, expertise, and experience are assessed in order to meet the needs of the corporation. The committee also has an ongoing role in guaranteeing that the board dynamics remain healthy for discussion and decision-making.[22]

The PRA stipulates that all banks must have an audit committee on the board whose members must be non-executive and a majority of them independent in terms of formal independence.[23] If the bank is 'significant', then all the members of the audit committee must be independent.[24] The responsibilities of the audit committee are prescribed, and key aspects[25] include oversight of the financial reporting mechanisms within the bank in order to comply with statutory audit and reporting requirements, oversight of the bank's internal control functions, systems, and processes, and responsibility for appointment and review of tenure of the external auditor. These responsibilities are by and large endorsed by the Basel Committee (2015: Principle 3).

Next, a bank which is significant in terms of size and internal organisation and in relation to the nature, scope, and complexity of its activities must establish a remuneration committee in order to determine remuneration policies that are consistent with the bank's capital, liquidity, and funding risk profiles.[26] This is consistent with the earlier recommendations (30 and 35) of the Walker Review (Walker 2009) and has been transposed into the UK under 'Remuneration' (para. 7.4) within the PRA Rulebook. The remuneration committee, which must comprise a chair and members who are non-executive, is responsible for ensuring that bank remuneration policies are consistent with sound risk management and take into account the interests of shareholders, stakeholders, and the public. The emphasis on remuneration being aligned with sound risk management is designed to meet public interest in banks' prudent risk-taking.

Regulating Internal Control

Since the global financial crisis of 2007–9, regulators first uncovered excessive risk-taking behaviour at banks, followed by misconduct such as mis-selling

---

[22] See also EBA Suitability Guidelines 2016 at sections 21, 22.
[23] PRA Rulebook, *Audit Committee* at para 2.2.   [24] Above.
[25] Above and see EBA Guidelines 2016 at section 5.5.   [26] Art 95, CRD IV Directive 2013.

(Sabato 2009; Mikes 2008; Blommestein et al. 2009; Crouhy 2010; Sheedy 2010; Partnoy 2011).[27] Policy-makers have thus become sceptical of banks' ability to institute sound organisational governance in order to manage prudential and conduct risks adequately. Regulatory reforms have now been introduced to enhance internal control at banks, so that these control functions are mandated to perform a gatekeeping function for risky or poor conduct. The European Banking Authority (EBA) (2017) regards 'internal control' as comprising three lines of defence: the compliance, risk management, and internal audit functions.

Regulators have now taken the step of directly prescribing how the internal control functions in banks and financial institutions, i.e. the compliance, risk management, and internal audit departments, should be structured, assigned, and governed, as argued in Chiu (2015). First, the three functions are to be protected in their independence so that they may be able to objectively gate-keep the financial institution from wrongdoing. The tenure, accountability, and career progression of personnel performing these tasks should be separate from business interests. The accountability of the three functions lies directly with the board of directors and not with the chief executive officers so that their independence may not be compromised.

Next, the three functions are to be headed by sufficiently senior officers such that they are not intimidated by senior executives who represent business interests. In particular, the institution of the chief risk officer[28] was recommended after the Walker Review (Walker 2009). The three functions are to be assured adequate resources and empowerment such as access to firm-wide information in order to carry out their roles, some of which are now explicitly prescribed so that financial institutions cannot marginalise the three functions from key business decisions. For example the risk management function must be consulted for marketing of new products and work with the compliance function in this regard (EBA 2017).

Regulatory prescriptions now intervene directly in organisational design in order to change the behaviour of internal governance functions, influencing firm behaviour to be consistent with regulatory goals. This creates tensions in terms of the organisational loyalty of internal control functions and their regulatory mandate to pursue broader regulatory goals within the financial

---

[27] On the mis-selling of payment protection insurance to retail customers, see FSA (2010), FSA Handbook DISP 3, and Ferran (2012). On the mis-selling of interest rate swaps to small businesses, see FSA (2013a). On the manipulation of the London Inter-bank Offered Rate, see Peston (2012), BBC News (2013), discussing fifteen banks including JP Morgan in potential enforcement action against foreign exchange fixing, Aitken (2014); and Evans (2017).

[28] PRA Rulebook Risk Control, FCA Handbook, SYSC 21.

corporation (Chiu 2015). However the regulatory interventions reflect the wide-ranging measures taken in the wake of the global financial crisis to directly confront challenges of poor culture and lack of awareness of public interest in financial corporations.

Senior Persons and Individual Responsibility and Liability Regimes

The behaviour of individuals is regarded as key to the forging of bank culture, especially 'tone at the top', which refers to the behaviour of senior management (Bailey 2016). After the global financial crisis, the UK in particular pushed for greater regulatory accountability for individuals in financial corporations so as to incentivise them to take responsible decisions. The regulation of individuals is, however, not new. Already in the early 2000s, the Financial Services Authority (FSA), disbanded in 2013, introduced individual approval and conduct rules for key functions in banks and financial institutions. But in the aftermath of the global financial crisis and the subsequent conduct scandals, this regime has been considerably strengthened, especially in respect of senior executives' responsibility and personal liability (see Table 4.1 for a list of senior management functions according to the PRA Rulebook).[29]

Reforms introduced after the global financial crisis 2007–9 and in the wake of conduct crises mentioned earlier have adjusted the UK's regime in the following ways:

(a) To introduce more focused and stringent approval for senior managers;
(b) To expand the scope of other persons required for certification; and
(c) To delegate to firms to carry out certification of persons in (b).

In other words, regulatory vetting is now focused upon senior managers only, although firms have to adhere to the regulator's criteria of fitness and propriety in certifying other personnel.[30] Senior managers would be subject to stringent approval requirements as well as a framework for determining their

---

[29] Previously the FIT (Fitness and Propriety) and APER (Code of Practice for Approved Persons) modules of the Financial Services Authority Handbook. Provisions on individual responsibility and liability are now found in the FCA Handbook FIT and COCON (Code of Conduct), and the PRA Rulebook on Allocation of Responsibilities, Conduct Rules, Senior Management Function.

[30] See PRA Rulebook, *Fitness and Propriety* at http://www.prarulebook.co.uk/rulebook/Content/Part/303750/31-08-2016.

individual responsibility and liability. Although the certification process is delegated to financial corporations themselves, financial corporations are now responsible for ensuring that only appropriate people are appointed to their jobs. Further, certified persons, now a wider scope of persons than before, are subject to regulatory rules in respect of their individual conduct. Such persons are identified according to the qualitative and quantitative criteria laid out in (EU) Commission Delegated Regulation No. 604/2014, sometimes referred to as the Material Risk Takers Regulation.

Compared to the EU regulatory regime, the UK's regime in regulating senior managers is broader in scope. The Capital Requirements Directive (2013/36/EU) extends only to board appointments and does not require regulatory approval of bank executives. However, the EBA, in its non-binding but persuasive Guidelines, applies appointment criteria to 'significant function holders' (EBA and ESMA 2016), extending the scope of senior appointments beyond the board. A certain extent of convergence can be observed between the EBA's appointment criteria and the UK PRA's criteria for approval of senior appointments. The UK's regime may be regarded as the leading regime for setting standards for approval and ongoing governance of senior managers and individuals.

Table 4.1. Senior management functions, as prescribed under the PRA Rulebook

Functions	Position
Executive	Chief Executive Chief of Finance Chief of Risk Head of Internal Audit Head of key business area, where person is ultimately (and not intermediately) responsible for a business area managing more than £10 bn of assets or generating at least 20 per cent of the firm's or group's gross revenues Head of Compliance (FCA only) Significant responsibility management function (FCA only) Money-laundering oversight and reporting (FCA only)
Board	Chair Chair of Risk Committee Chair of Audit Committee Chair of Remuneration Committee Senior Independent Director Chair of Nomination Committee (FCA only) All executive and non-executive directors (FCA only)
Group level	Group entity senior manager (having significant influence upon one or more aspects of regulated activities across the group)
Other	Credit Union Senior Manager Head of overseas branch in the UK

The clear prescription of the scope of senior managers is important as the liability rules for senior managers differ from those applied to others.

The approval of senior managers is premised upon (a) a 'statement of responsibility' attached to their application for approval,[31] and (b) satisfying 'fitness and propriety' criteria.

The UK financial regulators, the PRA and the Financial Conduct Authority (FCA), have drawn up different comprehensive maps of roles of responsibilities in all financial corporations.[32] This is to ensure that firms allocate all prescribed responsibilities to individuals and it is clear to regulators who is responsible for overseeing any area of responsibility. Firms cannot omit allocating areas of responsibility, nor can they institute structures that make it difficult to ascertain 'who is ultimately responsible'.

Both senior managers and certified persons have to meet the thresholds for fitness and propriety in order to be approved, as well as on a continuing basis. The failure to adhere to these thresholds over time can result in the disqualification of the individual from working in the relevant capacity in the financial services sector.

'Fit and proper' is defined in relation to personal characteristics in relation to reputation and integrity, level of competence, knowledge and experience, and level of qualifications and ongoing training necessary for the function concerned. In terms of reputation and integrity, previous evidence of probity such as criminal convictions and professional disqualifications matters tremendously.[33] Individuals must also be vetted for 'financial soundness' including scrutinising for previous records of financial embarrassment such as bankruptcy or management of insolvent companies.

Bank misconduct is often driven by individuals and groups, but wrongdoers lack a sense of personal responsibility, as it is the firm that is made the subject of enforcement and has to pay the fine. Hence, the UK has decided to introduce rules of personal conduct to govern the behaviour of senior managers so that their behaviour and oversight of other staff can be better aligned with the needs of regulatory compliance.[34]

First, as senior managers are approved with statements of responsibility as discussed above, regulatory contraventions that occur within their areas of

---

[31] Section 60(2A), Financial Services and Markets Act 2000 as amended by the Financial Services (Banking Reform) Act 2013.

[32] PRA Rulebook, Allocation of Responsibilities; FCA Handbook, SYSC 2.

[33] For example, Financial Services and Markets Tribunal (2005a and 2005b).

[34] This was first highlighted in House of Lords and House of Commons (2013) at Vol. 1, para 110ff and Vol. II, para 1170; and brought about the Financial Services (Banking Reform) Act 2013 amending the Financial Services and Markets Act 2000 by inserting sections 64Aff.

responsibility could entail personal liability if certain conditions are satisfied.[35] A senior person who has responsibility over an area in which a regulatory contravention has occurred may be personally liable if the regulator proves that the senior person did not take such steps as a person in the senior manager's position could reasonably be expected to take to avoid the contravention.[36]

Next, senior managers are subject to a set of Rules of Conduct promulgated by the regulator (PRA or FCA).[37] In the PRA Rulebook, senior managers are subject to two sets of rules, the Individual Conduct Rules[38] and the specifically applicable Senior Manager Conduct Rules.[39] The Individual Conduct Rules apply to all certified persons and senior managers and refer to individual duties and behaviour, as set out in Table 4.2. The Senior Manager Conduct Rules, listed in Table 4.3, relate more to oversight and general organisational duties.

Finally, senior managers could be criminally liable for knowingly taking a risk that causes the failure of a bank.[40] Regulatory reforms now allow the PRA, FCA, Secretary of State, or Director of Crown Prosecutions to institute criminal proceedings against senior managers who have knowingly taken a decision for the business, being aware that a risk of failure could ensue, and in so doing has fallen below the standard of a reasonable person in that position. Such a decision must also have caused the failure of the financial institution. The section however does not extend to situations of widespread externalities.

---

[35] S66A(5) and 66B(5) of the Financial Services and Markets Act 2000 amended by the Financial Services (Banking Reform) Act 2013 and subsequently by the Bank of England and Financial Services Act 2016.

[36] Note that this is an adjustment from the position under the Financial Services (Banking Reform) Act 2013, which treated senior managers as strictly liable if a regulatory contravention occurred in their area of responsibility, subject to them being able to prove to the regulator that they had taken all reasonable steps to prevent the contravention.

[37] Sections 64A and 64B, Financial Services and Markets Act 2000 amended by the Financial Services (Banking Reform) Act 2013.

[38] Section 64A, Financial Services and Markets Act 2000 amended by the Financial Services (Banking Reform) Act 2013; PRA Rulebook, *Conduct Rules* at 2, http://www.prarulebook.co.uk/rulebook/Content/Part/302382/05-09-2016.

[39] PRA Rulebook, *Conduct Rules* at http://www.prarulebook.co.uk/rulebook/Content/Part/302382/02-09-2016.

[40] Section 36, Financial Services (Banking Reform) Act 2013. This is derived from the Parliamentary Commission's recommendation that an offence be instituted for the reckless mismanagement of a bank (House of Lords and House of Commons 2013, Vol. II: paras 1174–1186). This is intended to reflect the need for a severe and credible public interest position in bank safety and soundness, but such prosecution would likely only be undertaken rarely in the most severe of cases and not likely to be used to punish directors of small institutions. The Parliamentary Commission believed that requiring the *mens rea* of recklessness is apt, as strict criminal liability would be overly inclusive. An individual must be proved beyond a reasonable doubt to be in a mental state of 'recklessness' in managing the bank, the definition of such a mental state being well established in general criminal law jurisprudence. The offence of reckless mismanagement of a bank would only be alleged against an individual under such circumstances as bank failure with substantial costs to the taxpayer, lasting consequences for the financial system, or failures that have caused serious harm to customers.

Table 4.2. Individual conduct rules

1: You must act with integrity.
2: You must act with due skill, care, and diligence.
3: You must be open and co-operative with the FCA, the PRA, and other regulators.

Table 4.3. Senior manager conduct rules

1: You must take reasonable steps to ensure that the business of the firm for which you are responsible is controlled effectively.

2: You must take reasonable steps to ensure that the business of the firm for which you are responsible complies with the relevant requirements and standards of the regulatory system.

3: You must take reasonable steps to ensure that any delegation of your responsibilities is to an appropriate person and that you oversee the discharge of the delegated responsibility effectively.

4: You must disclose appropriately any information of which the FCA or PRA would reasonably expect notice.

Where financial consumers in many markets are adversely affected, for example, due to interest rate benchmark manipulation by banks (Wheatley 2012), the extent of externalities is severe, but this is not captured within the criminal offence.

Remuneration of Financial Corporations' Staff

A major initiative that attempts to change incentives for risk-taking behaviour has been introduced in the form of financial sector remuneration regulation.[41] The structure of financial sector remuneration has arguably given rise to a number of perverse incentives on the part of financial sector employees and management, including short-termism and excessive risk-taking (Brunnermeier et al. 2009; Financial Stability Board 2010; Sharfman 2011). This is because remuneration is structured in such a way as to include a variable remuneration component that forms a significant part of the total remuneration package. The level of variable remuneration is usually tied to performance metrics that are short-termist in nature, such as volumes of sales of product, without having due regard for the long-term performance of the product in meeting customers' needs. Hence, financial corporation employees can be incentivised

---

[41] Also see Basel Committee on Banking Supervision (2014): Principle 11.

to pursue performance strategies that would entitle them to receive high levels of variable remuneration even if such strategies may be linked to mis-selling and other forms of adverse conduct (FCA 2014: 6ff; FSA 2013b: 13ff).

The UK applies this regulatory regime to all banks, investment firms, and investment fund management companies, with exceptions for proportionate treatment of firms smaller in scale and size. The range of financial sector employees affected by the regulatory regime are categories of staff including senior management, staff engaged in control functions, and any employee receiving total remuneration that takes them into the same remuneration bracket as senior management and risk-takers, whose professional activities have a material impact on their risk profile (aka material risk-takers). Unlike in general corporate governance norms,[42] the range of individuals goes beyond board-level personnel as there are many decision-makers in various business units in banks that can generate significant risks and affect the bank's fate. As noted above with respect to 'certified persons', 'material risk-takers' are defined according to (EU) Commission Delegated Regulation No 604/2014 (amended in 2019) with reference to qualitative and quantitative criteria. The qualitative criteria refer to an individual's office or nature of responsibility, while the quantitative criteria refer to the numerical level of the individual's earnings, i.e., whether the numerical level takes the individual into the same bracket as senior management.

The regulatory regime purports to control financial sector employees' remuneration using the three-pronged approach as follows:

(a) Regulatory provisions designed to improve the governance of remu-
    neration decisions;
(b) Regulatory provisions that intervene in remuneration policies and
    principles, these being drawn from the EU Capital Requirements
    Directive 2013[43] and the Financial Stability Board's Sound Compensation
    Principles (Financial Stability Forum 2009; Financial Stability
    Board 2009); and
(c) Regulatory provisions that prescribe precise controls on the use of
    variable remuneration, as a response to the misuse of variable remu-
    neration in the years leading up to the global financial crisis.

---

[42] Mainstream corporate governance sees executive pay as problematic as levels of pay are determined by executives who have a vested interest in augmenting their package. This essential agency problem has spawned much literature relating to corporate governance best practices, e.g. Bebchuk (2012), Thomas and Hill (2016), and Cullen (2014).

[43] Art 92, Capital Requirements Directive 2013.

These are further flanked by regulatory provisions on malus and clawback, which, by providing the option to reduce or cancel unpaid remuneration or require return of compensation already paid out, are intended to incentivise long-term decision-making by material risk-takers and other individuals within the scope of the regulatory regime.

First, on regulatory provisions designed to improve the governance of remuneration decisions, each financial corporation must institute remuneration policies that are 'consistent with and promote sound and effective risk management'.[44] Next, the regulatory regime articulates optimal principles to guide the corporation's discretion in designing remuneration policies. The EBA defines remuneration as capable of being structured only as fixed or variable remuneration. Where variable remuneration is related to performance, performance criteria should incorporate multi-year business cycles, be based on the business unit as a whole, and include non-financial criteria such as sound risk management. Such principles are designed to avoid introducing overly individualistic incentives into staff behaviour.

Regulation has introduced a somewhat prescriptive regime that targets controls only on variable remuneration. Variable remuneration in theory could work as a way to manage the firm's cost in proportion to its performance. As long as variable remuneration is truly adjusted to reflect lean times/performance as well as good times/performance, it could provide the right incentives for employees to drive performance (Thannasoulis 2012). The flaw leading up to the crisis was that variable remuneration was used by banks unabashedly to inflate pay using metrics that favoured employees' short-term interests and disregarded the banks' and stakeholders' long-term interests. This is why regulatory focus has been turned in response to controlling variable remuneration. However, some of these specific prescriptions can be regarded as highly constrictive for remuneration design.

First, guaranteed variable remuneration is subject under the regulations to the express control that it has to be 'exceptional'. Guaranteed variable remuneration can only be paid out when new staff are hired and where the institution has a sound and strong capital base, and it is limited to the first year of employment.[45] Such remuneration must also adhere to the overall principles of consistency with risk management and pay for performance.[46] The control

---

[44] CRD IV Directive 2013 at Art 74(1).

[45] PRA Rulebook, *Remuneration*, at para 15.7; CRD IV Directive 2013, Art 94; Financial Stability Board (2009), Standard 11.

[46] PRA Rulebook, *Remuneration*, at para 15.7; CRD IV Directive 2013, Art 94; Financial Stability Board (2009), Standard 11.

on guaranteed variable remuneration prevents financial corporations from sidestepping remuneration rules through the power of private contracts. Next, there are a few prescriptive prohibitions in relation to the payment of variable remuneration. One is that non-executive directors cannot be paid variable remuneration.[47] The other is that financial corporations benefiting from government intervention, e.g. banks bailed out by tax-payers' money, must not pay variable remuneration to members of the management body.[48]

Third, an area of extensive prescription is remuneration composition, i.e. the structure and balance of fixed and variable components in total remuneration. It is prescribed that the fixed portion must be sufficiently high[49] to allow the operation of a fully flexible policy on variable remuneration components, including the possibility to pay no variable remuneration component. This prescription is clearly in response to the flawed use of variable remuneration design by banks prior to the global financial crisis where only ratcheting up was observed. Variable remuneration is to be capped at 100 per cent of the fixed component of remuneration,[50] and can only increase to 200 per cent of the fixed component if shareholder approval in a general meeting is obtained.[51]

Finally, the composition of variable remuneration is controlled in order to curtail short-termist incentives for financial corporation staff. Fifty per cent of variable remuneration should be paid in share instruments, and at least 40 per cent of variable remuneration should be deferred. The 40 per cent deferral rule applies to different individuals over different periods of time:

(a) A material risk-taker not falling within (b) or (c) below: a period of deferral of three years;

(b) A material risk-taker who does not perform a senior management function: a period of deferral of five years; and

(c) A material risk-taker performing a senior management function: a period of deferral of seven years.

The remuneration regulation regime is supported by mandatory malus and clawback, which allow firms not to pay out or indeed recover variable

---

[47] PRA Rulebook, *Remuneration*, para 15.3.
[48] PRA Rulebook, *Remuneration*, para 10.1, CRD IV Directive 2013, Art 93; Financial Stability Board (2009), Standard 10.
[49] PRA Rulebook, *Remuneration*, para 15.9; CRD IV Directive 2013, Art 94.
[50] PRA Rulebook, *Remuneration*, para 15.10, CRD IV Directive 2013, Art 94.
[51] PRA Rulebook, *Remuneration*, para 15.11, CRD IV Directive 2013, Art 94.

remuneration that is no longer justified.[52] It is set out clearly that up to 100 per cent of the variable remuneration in question[53] can be subject to malus or clawback. The power to do this is expressly provided in regulation as there is unlikely contractual power per se for banks to carry this out. Further, financial corporations are likely not incentivised to impair their relations with individual members of staff. However regulators see malus and clawback as providing crucial incentives to govern risk decisions on the part of individuals as they would be more likely to think of the long-term prospects of their decisions since there is 'skin in the game'.

The regulatory regime allows financial corporations to adjust their remuneration obligations in the following manner:

(a) Reduction of unvested deferred remuneration in some circumstances;
(b) Ensuring that conditions of vesting are appropriate;
(c) Recovery of vested but not yet paid out/realised remuneration through the application of malus in certain circumstances;
(d) Recovering awarded remuneration through clawback extending to a certain number of years under certain circumstances.

Where variable remuneration has vested but not yet been paid out or realised, such as in the case of shares that are awarded but subject to a retention period, financial corporations may apply malus when there is reasonable evidence of employee misbehaviour or material error; the firm or the relevant business unit suffers a material downturn in its financial performance; or the firm or the relevant business unit suffers a material failure of risk management. These can be further detailed in material adverse change clauses in employee contracts. Where variable remuneration has already been paid out, financial corporations are entitled to take action to claw back an appropriate amount of such remuneration under the same conditions as those for applying malus.[54] The potential clawback period is seven years from the date the variable remuneration is awarded. Where the remuneration awarded concerns a senior manager, clawback can potentially take place over a longer period. Financial corporations can give notice to such an employee no later than the end of the seven years, to extend the potential clawback period to ten years. The extension of the clawback period can be on the basis that the firm has commenced an investigation into facts or events which it considers could potentially lead

---

[52] Based on Financial Stability Board (2009), Standard 5.
[53] CRD IV Directive 2013, Art 94.   [54] PRA Rulebook, *Remuneration*, para 15.19.

to the application of clawback were it not for the expiry of the clawback period; or the firm has been notified by a regulatory authority (including an overseas regulatory authority) that an investigation has been commenced into facts or events which the firm considers could potentially lead to the application of clawback.

Concluding Remarks and Brief Comparative Perspectives

Regulating corporate governance in financial corporations is an attempt at providing internationally convergent standards, from the Basel Committee to the EU level, that address the public interest aspects of financial corporation governance that affect prudential safety. These do not sit easily with corporate governance traditions and soft law that have evolved in different capital markets and jurisdictions, and also do not necessarily address adverse linkages between the regulatory framework and corporate governance traditions. In the UK for example, these regulatory rules sit alongside the prevailing shareholder-centred corporate governance standards and do not challenge the importance of shareholders in corporate governance, although there is some empirical evidence regarding the potentially deleterious effects that shareholder primacy can have upon financial corporations. Indeed in the UK, shareholders continue to be asked to be engaged and active in monitoring their investee corporations, as they are assumed to have interests aligned with the public interest in ensuring that important corporations thrive and survive. These rules also do not likely affect other corporate governance traditions such as stakeholder-inclusive systems like co-determination.

At the intersection between regulatory rules and corporate governance traditions, regulatory rules now put on a mandatory footing aspects of board composition and internal control across the EU and regulate aspects of remuneration that affect the prudential safety of financial corporations. The UK has extended its regulatory reach into the regulation of individual responsibility, which distinguishes it from the EU regime and creates a distinct regime for executive personal responsibility beyond company law doctrines such as directors' duties (Chiu 2016). Regulatory rules also permeate many organisational levels that may have an impact on the risk management, conduct, and culture of the financial corporation beyond corporate governance which focuses on board-level relations.

A number of commentators (Mülbert 2009; Hopt 2013) are of the view that such regulatory intervention into corporate governance is unique to financial corporations as they clearly entail public interest concerns in relation to their viability and stability, aspects not necessarily present in other corporations. The failure of important corporations such as those with government contracts or those that entail extensive impact on the real economy due to job and contract losses[55] is beginning to capture policy-makers' attention on the need for rethinking viable models of corporate governance (Department for Business, Energy and Industrial Strategy 2017). This emerging policy attention was further sharpened after the January 2018 failure of the UK-listed corporation Carillion. Carillion, which managed many government estates and services, had extensive networks of suppliers and customers. Its failure left severe knock-on effects upon many firms, and it is queried whether the 'public interest' profile of corporations should be more widely framed in order to apply more stringent regulatory oversight, such as into corporate governance and internal organisation. It is thus timely to consider whether the shareholder-primacy basis for corporate governance rules in capital markets contradict the aims of certain public interest goals and how such tensions could be managed by regulatory policy.

References

Aitken, R. (2014). 'Big Banks Slapped With £2.6bn FX "Rate Rigging" Fines But Will They Ever Learn?', Forbes.com, 15 November. Retrieved from https://www.forbes.com/sites/rogeraitken/2014/11/15/big-banks-slapped-with-2-6bn-fx-rate-rigging-fines-but-will-they-ever-learn/ (accessed 10 January 2020).

Alchian, A. A. and Demsetz, H. (1972). 'Production, Information Costs and Economic Organisation', *The American Economic Review*, 62(5): 777–95.

Armour, J., Deakin, S., and Konzelmann, S. J. (2003). 'Shareholder Primacy and the Trajectory of UK Corporate Governance', University of Cambridge Working Paper No. 266. Cambridge: ESRC Centre for Business Research.

Armour, J., Hansmann, H., and Kraakman, R. (2017).'Agency Problems and Legal Strategies', in R. Kraakman et al. (eds.), *The Anatomy of Corporate Law*. Oxford: Oxford University Press, 35–52.

Armour, J. and Whincop, M. J. (2007). 'The Proprietary Foundations of Corporate Law', *Oxford Journal of Legal Studies*, 27(3): 429–65.

---

[55] Such as the failure of the large private company BHS, whose governance was scrutinised in the wake of public outcry over the injustice to employees and pensioners in favour of shareholders (House of Commons 2016).

Avgouleas, E. and Cullen, J. (2014). 'Corporate Governance Reform in the Banking Sector: Merits, Fallacies, and Cognitive Boundaries', *Journal of Law and Society*, 41: 28–50.

Bailey, A. (2016). 'Culture in Financial Services: A Regulator's Perspective', 9 May, London: City Week Conference. Retrieved from https://www.bankofengland.co.uk/speech/2016/culture-in-financial-services-a-regulators-perspective (accessed 10 January 2020).

Basel Committee on Banking Supervision (2015). *Guidelines: Corporate Governance Principles for Banks*. Basel: Bank for International Settlements.

Basel Committee on Banking Supervision (2014). *Guidelines: Corporate Governance Principles for Banks: Consultation Paper*. Basel: Bank for International Settlements.

Basel Committee on Banking Supervision (2010). *Principles for Enhancing Corporate Governance*. Basel: Bank for International Settlements.

BBC News (2013). 'LIBOR Scandal: RBS Fined £390m', BBC News, 6 February. Retrieved from https://www.bbc.com/news/business-21348719 (accessed 10 January 2020).

Bebchuk, L. (2012). *Pay without Performance: The Unfulfilled Promise of Executive Compensation*. Cambridge, MA: Harvard University Press.

Beltratti, A. and Stultz, R. M. (2009). 'Why Did Some Banks Perform Better during the Credit Crisis? A Cross-Country Study of the Impact of Governance and Regulation', NBER Working Paper No 15180. Cambridge, MA: National Bureau of Economic Research.

Blommestein, H. J., Hoogduin, L., and Peeters, J. J. W. (2009). 'Uncertainty and Risk Management after the Great Moderation: The Role of Risk (Mis) Management by Financial Institutions'. Retrieved from http://papers.ssrn.com/sol3/papers.cfm?abstract_id=1489826 (accessed 10 January 2020).

Boubaker, S., Nguyen, P., and Rouatbi, W. (2012). 'Large Shareholders and Firm Risk-Taking Behavior'. Retrieved from http://ssrn.com/abstract=2026038 (accessed 10 January 2020).

Brunnermeier, M. K., Crockett, A., Goodhart, C., Persaud, A. D., and Shin, H. (2009). *The Fundamental Principles of Financial Regulation, Geneva Reports on the World Economy 11*. London: Centre for Economic Policy Research.

Cheffins, B. R. (2009). 'Did Corporate Governance "Fail" During the 2008 Stock Market Meltdown? The Case of the S&P 500', ECGI Law Working Paper 124/2009. Brussels: ECGI.

Chiu, I. H-Y (2016). 'Regulatory Duties for Directors in the Financial Services Sector and Directors' Duties in Company Law: Bifurcation and Interfaces', *Journal of Business Law*, 6.

Chiu, I. H-Y (2015). *Regulating from the Inside: The Legal Framework for Internal Control at Banks and Financial Institutions*. Oxford: Hart.

Ciancanelli, P. and Reyes-Gonzalez, J. A. (2000). 'Corporate Governance in Banking: A Conceptual Framework'. Retrieved from http://papers.ssrn.com/paper.taf?abstract_id=253714 (accessed 10 January 2020).

Committee on the Global Financial System (2010). 'The Role of Margin Requirements and Haircuts in Procyclicality', CGFS Paper No 36. Basel: Bank for International Settlements.

Crouhy, M. (2010). 'Risk Management Failures During the Financial Crisis', in R. W. Kolb (ed.), *Lessons from the Financial Crisis*. New Jersey: John Wiley, 283–91.

Cullen, J. (2014). *Executive Compensation in Imperfect Financial Markets*. Cheltenham: Edward Elgar.

Davies, P. (2005). 'Enlightened Shareholder Value and the New Responsibilities of Directors', lecture delivered at the University of Melbourne Law School, 4 October. Retrieved from http://law.unimelb.edu.au/__data/assets/pdf_file/0014/1710014/94-Enlightened_Shareholder_Value_and_the_New_Responsibilities_of_Directors1.pdf (accessed 10 January 2020).

Deakin, S. (2011). 'Corporate Governance and Financial Crisis in the Long Run', in C. A. Williams and P. Zumbansen (eds.), *The Embedded Firm: Corporate Governance, Labor and Finance Capitalism*. New York: Cambridge University Press, 15–41.

Department for Business, Energy and Industrial Strategy (2017). 'Corporate Governance Reform: The Government Response to the Green Paper Consultation'. Retrieved from https://www.gov.uk/government/consultations/corporate-governance-reform (accessed 10 January 2020).

Easterbrook, F. H. and Fischel, D. R. (1991). *The Economic Structure of Corporate Law*. Cambridge, MA: Harvard University Press.

EBA (2017). *Final Report: Guidelines on Internal Governance under Directive 2013/36/EU (EBA/GL/2017/11)*. London: European Banking Authority.

EBA and ESMA (2016). *Consultation Paper: Joint ESMA and EBA Guidelines on the Assessment of the Suitability of Members of the Management Body and Key Function Holders under Directive 2013/36/EU and Directive 2014/65/EU (EBA/CP/2016/17)*. London: European Banking Authority.

Erkens, D. H., Hung, M., and Matos, P. (2012). 'Corporate Governance in the 2007–2008 Financial Crisis: Evidence from Financial Institutions Worldwide', *Journal of Corporate Finance*, 18(2): 389–411.

Evans, M. D. D. (2017). 'Forex Trading and the WMR Fix', *Journal of Banking and Finance*, 87: 233–47. doi: 10.1016/j.jbankfin.2017.09.017

FCA (2014). *Commercial Insurance Intermediaries—Conflicts of Interest And Intermediary Remuneration: Report on the Thematic Project (TR 14/9)*. London: Financial Conduct Authority.

Ferran, E. (2012). 'Regulatory Lessons from the Payment Protection Insurance Mis-Selling Scandal in the UK', *European Business Organization Law Review*, 13(2): 247–70.

Financial Services and Markets Tribunal (2005a). *Allen Philip Elliott v the Financial Services Authority*, FIN/2004/0001, Decision of 28 July 2005.

Financial Services and Markets Tribunal (2005b). *Rajiv Khungar and Khungar Home Loans Limited v the Financial Services Authority*, FIN/2004/0028, Decision of 19 October 2005.

Financial Stability Board (2015). *Transforming Shadow Banking into Resilient Market-based Finance*. Basel: Financial Stability Board. Retrieved from https://www.fsb.org/2015/11/transforming-shadow-banking-into-resilient-market-based-finance-an-overview-of-progress/ (accessed 10 January 2020).

Financial Stability Board (2010). *Thematic Review on Compensation: Peer Review Report*. Basel: Financial Stability Board.

Financial Stability Board (2009). *FSB Principles for Sound Compensation Practices: Implementation Standards*. Basel: Financial Stability Board. Retrieved from http://www.fsb.org/2009/09/principles-for-sound-compensation-practices-implementation-standards/ (accessed 10 January 2020).

Financial Stability Forum (2009). *FSF Principles for Sound Compensation Practices.* Basel: Financial Stability Board. Retrieved from http://www.fsb.org/2009/04/principles-for-sound-compensation-practices-2/ (accessed 10 January 2020).

FRC (Financial Reporting Council) (2020). *The UK Stewardship Code*. London: Financial Reporting Council.

FSA (2013a). 'FSA Confirms Full Review of Interest Rate Swap Misselling'. Retrieved from https://www.fca.org.uk/news/press-releases/fsa-confirms-start-full-review-interest-rate-swap-mis-selling (accessed 10 January 2020).

FSA (2013b). *Risks to Customers from Financial Incentives: Final Guidance.* London: Financial Services Authority.

FSA (2010). *The Assessment and Redress of Payment Protection Insurance Complaints: Feedback on the Further Consultation in CP10/6 and Final Handbook Text. Policy Statement 10/12*. London: Financial Services Authority.

Gordon, J. N. and Roe, M. J. (eds.) (2010). *Convergence and Persistence in Corporate Governance*. Cambridge: Cambridge University Press.

Govindarajan, D. (2011). 'Corporate Risk Appetite: Ensuring Board and Senior Management Accountability for Risk'. Retrieved from http://ssrn.com/abstract=1962126 (accessed 10 January 2020).

Gropp, R. and Köhler, M. (2010). *Bank Owners or Bank Managers: Who Is Keen on Risk? Evidence from the Financial Crisis*, European Business School Research Paper No 10-02. Oestrich-Winkel: European Business School.

Hall, P. A. and Soskice, D. W. (2001). *Varieties of Capitalism*. Oxford: Oxford University Press.

Hau, H. and Thum, M. P. (2009). 'Subprime Crisis and Board (In-)Competence: Private vs. Public Banks in Germany', *Economic Policy*, 24(60): 701–52.

Hopt, K. (2013). 'Better Governance of Financial Institutions', ECGI Law Working Papers No. 2017. Brussels: ECGI.

House of Commons (2016). *BHS: First Report of the Work and Pensions Committee and Fourth Report of the Business, Innovation and Skills Committee of Session 2016–17, HC 54*, published 25 July 2016. London: The Stationery Office.

House of Lords (1848). *Edward Thomas Foley v Thomas Hill and Others*, 2 HLC 28, 9 ER 1002, Judgment of 31 July, 1 August 1848.

House of Lords and House of Commons (2013). *Changing Banking for Good: Report of the Parliamentary Commission on Banking Standards (9 vols.), HL Paper 27/HC 175*. London: The Stationery Office.

Jackson, B. F. (2013). 'Danger Lurking in the Shadows: Why Regulators Lack the Authority to Effectively Fight Contagion in the Shadow Banking System', *Harvard Law Review*, 127(2): 729–50.

Jensen, M. and Meckling, W. (1976). 'Theory of the Firm: Managerial Behavior, Agency Costs and Ownership Structure', *Journal of Financial Economics*, 3(4): 305–60.

Keay, A. (2007). 'Section 172(1) of the Companies Act 2006: An Interpretation and Assessment', *Company Lawyer*, 28(4): 106–10.

Kirkpatrick, G. (2009). 'The Corporate Governance Lessons from the Financial Crisis', *OECD Financial Market Trends*, 2009/1: 61–87.

Kokkinis, A. (2018). *Corporate Law and Financial Instability*. Abingdon and New York: Routledge.

La Porta, R., Lopez-de-Silanes, F., and Shleifer, A. (2006). 'What Works in Securities Laws', *Journal of Finance* 61(1): 1–32.

Larcker, D. and Tayan, B. (2011). *Corporate Governance Matters: A Closer Look at Organisational Choices and Their Consequences*. Upper Saddle River, NJ: Pearson Education.

Lynch, E. (2012). 'Section 172: A Ground-Breaking Reform of Director's Duties, or the Emperor's New Clothes?' *Company Lawyer*, 33(7): 196–203.

Malloy, T. F. (2003). 'Regulation, Compliance and the Firm', *Temple Law Review*, 76(3): 451–531.

Mehran, H., Morrison, A., and Shapiro, J. (2012). 'Corporate Governance and Banks: What Have We Learned from the Financial Crisis?', in M. Dewatripont and X. Freixas (eds.), *The Crisis Aftermath: New Regulatory Paradigms*. London: Centre for Economic Policy Research, 11–44.

Mikes, A. (2008). 'Risk Management at Crunch Time: Are Chief Risk Officers Compliance Champions or Business Partners?'. Retrieved from http://papers. ssrn.com/sol3/papers.cfm?abstract_id=1138615 (accessed 10 January 2020).

Miller, R. T. (2010). 'Oversight Liability for Risk-Management Failures at Financial Firms', *South California Law Review*, 84(1): 47–123.

Moore, M. T. and Petrin, M. (2017). *Corporate Governance: Law, Regulation and Theory*. London: Palgrave Macmillan.

Murphy, M. E. (2011). 'Assuring Responsible Risk Management in Banking: The Corporate Governance Dimension', *Delaware Journal of Corporate Law*, 36(1). Retrieved from http://www.djcl.org/2011-%e2%80%a2-volume-36-%e2%80%a2-number-1-5 (accessed 10 January 2020).

Mülbert, P. O. (2009). 'Corporate Governance of Banks after the Financial Crisis—Theory, Evidence, Reforms', ECGI Law Working Paper No 130/2009, Brussels: ECGI.

OECD (2009). *Corporate Governance and the Financial Crisis: Key Findings and Main Messages*. Paris: OECD.

Okamoto, K. S. and Edwards, D. O. (2010). 'Risk Taking', *Cardozo Law Review*, 32: 159.

Partnoy, F. (2011). 'On Rogues, Risk-taking and Restoring Trust in Banks', *Financial Times*, 23 September. Retrieved from https://www.ft.com/content/c015e5e2-e3a0-11e0-8990-00144feabdc0 (accessed 10 January 2020).

Peston, R. (2012). 'UBS Fined £1.5bn for LIBOR Rigging', BBC News, 19 December. Retrieved from https://www.bbc.com/news/business-20767984 (accessed 10 January 2020).

Ramirez, S. A. (2009). 'Lessons From the Subprime Debacle: Stress Testing CEO Autonomy', *Saint Louis University Law Journal*, 54(1): Article 3.

Sabato, G. (2009). 'Financial Crisis: Where Did Risk Management Fail?' Retrieved from http://papers.ssrn.com/sol3/papers.cfm?abstract_id=1460762 (accessed 10 January 2020).

Schwarcz, S. L. (2008). 'Systemic Risk', *Georgetown Law Journal*, 97: 193–249.

Sharfman, B. S. (2011). 'How the Strong Negotiating Position of Wall Street Employees Impacts the Corporate Governance of Financial Firms', *Virginia Business and Law Review*, 5(3): 350–75.

Sheedy, E. (2010). 'The Future of Risk Modelling', in R. W. Kolb (ed.), *Lessons from the Financial Crisis*. New Jersey: John Wiley, 301–6.

Singh, M. (2014). *Collateral and Financial Plumbing*. London: Risk Books.

Thannasoulis, J. (2012). 'The Case for Intervening in Bankers' Pay', *The Journal of Finance*, 67(3): 849–95.

Thomas, R. S. and Hill, J. G. (eds.) (2016). *Research Handbook on Executive Pay*. Cheltenham: Edward Elgar.

Walker, D. (2009). *A Review of Corporate Governance in UK Banks and Other Financial Industry Entities: Final Recommendations*. London: The Walker Review Secretariat.

Westman, H. (2010). 'The Role of Ownership Structure and Regulatory Environment in Bank Corporate Governance'. Retrieved from http://ssrn.com/abstract=1435041 (accessed 18 March 2013).

Wheatley, M. (2012). *The Wheatley Review of LIBOR*. London: The Wheatley Review.

Williams, R. (2012). 'Enlightened Shareholder Value in UK Company Law', *UNSW Law Journal*, 35(1): 360–77.

Zingales, L. (2009). 'The Future of Securities Regulation', *Journal of Accounting Research*, 47(2): 391–425. https://doi.org/10.1111/j.1475-679X.2009.00331.x

5

Corporate Governance in Small and Medium Enterprises

Jonas Gabrielsson, Morten Huse, and Carl Åberg

Small and medium enterprises (SMEs) constitute the backbone of the world economy. They make up the vast majority of businesses, are represented in all major sectors of the economy, and provide an important source for jobs and economic growth not only in traditional manufacturing industries but also in high technology and professional services. Moreover, SMEs are typically characterised as economic change agents due to their ability to channel new combinations of knowledge and resources into new market offerings, as well as to identify and develop niches for existing products and services (Timmons 1998; Curran and Blackburn 2001; Mazzarol and Reboud 2009). As such, SMEs represent a vibrant force that drives the economy forward by converting opportunity into tangible value for their stakeholders, including customers, owners, and employees, as well as broader society.

SMEs are often classified by the number of employees and/or by the value of their assets.[1] The European Commission, for example, includes as SMEs firms with less than 250 employees while not exceeding 50 million euro in turnover or 43 million euro in balance sheet total. However, there is no universal definition of what constitutes an SME, and international institutions, national laws, and industries may define them differently (Ardic, Mylenko, and Saltane 2011). Moreover, irrespective of official definitions, SMEs are understood differently in different historical and cultural settings (Curran and Blackburn 2001; Huse 2005). When defining and understanding SMEs, we thus need to go beyond a quantitative definition and take the broader context into account, including the strong link between owners and the enterprise, the central role of the chief executive officer (CEO), the sector's

[1] For research overviews, see for example Loecher (2000); Lukács (2005); and Ayyagari, Beck, and Demirguc-Kunt (2009).

Jonas Gabrielsson, Morten Huse, and Carl Åberg, *Corporate Governance in Small and Medium Enterprises* In: *Advances in Corporate Governance: Comparative Perspectives*. Edited by: Helmut K. Anheier and Theodor Baums, Oxford University Press (2020). © Hertie School.
DOI: 10.1093/oso/9780198866367.003.0005

relatively small share of the market, as well as the typical emphasis of SMEs on value creation, including both personal and societal objectives related to entrepreneurship and innovation.

The objective of this chapter is to discuss corporate governance in relation to the heterogeneous and dynamic nature of SMEs. Corporate governance is here broadly understood as the set of principles and practices by which the enterprise is directed and controlled. In SMEs this refers to various mechanisms defining and influencing the power and decisions of the CEO, including structures and forms of ownership, the composition and functioning of management teams and boards, executive compensation, financial reporting systems, and auditing. However, it also relates to the regulatory environment of SMEs, including guidelines of best practices formalised into corporate governance codes.

We will in the chapter specifically focus on the corporate governance of unlisted SMEs whose capital stock is held, offered, and exchanged privately (Uhlaner, Wright, and Huse 2007; Voordeckers et al. 2014). These firms account for a large share of private sector employment and private sector value added in Europe. In many respects, unlisted SMEs face a greater cor- porate governance challenge than large listed companies whose governance framework may be externally imposed by various types of legal regulations and formal listing requirements. In contrast, unlisted companies have greater scope to define (or not define!) their own governance strategy. This means that unlisted companies must themselves reflect on the potential costs and benefits of various governance approaches.

A key feature that unites most privately held SMEs is that they are owned and controlled by a relatively small number of shareholders (Uhlaner, Wright, and Huse 2007). However, SMEs are also a very heterogeneous and dynamic group of firms when it comes to their goals, aspirations, and intentions (Storey 1994; Ingley, Khlif, and Karoui 2017). We acknowledge this diversity by conceptually distinguishing between three 'types' of SMEs that show marked differences when it comes to their primary ideologies and stakeholder commitments (Johannisson and Huse 2000; Gabrielsson and Huse 2005). From this stance, we develop the extended team production theory as a model of corporate governance that promotes sustained value creation in SMEs (Machold et al. 2011; Gabrielsson et al. 2016). The team production model of corporate governance rejects short-sighted distribution rules in favour of one particular stakeholder, and instead advocates mediation across all the con- stituents with a vested interest in the firm to resolve and balance competing claims on the firm and its residual earnings (Blair and Stout 1999). As such, the theory seeks to set up principles and practices that promote and sustain firm-specific investments across the full range of stakeholders that embody the firm's core capabilities (Kaufman and Englander 2005), thus creating favourable conditions for firm-specific bundles of unique expertise and know-how that generate tangible economic value for customers as well as sustained revenue streams for the firm.

We proceed as follows. In the next section, we examine the regulatory environment of SMEs by reviewing codes that have been developed to establish guidelines for good corporate governance practices for these firms. After this, we discuss literature and research on corporate governance in SMEs, where we acknowledge that theory and models of corporate governance developed in large corporations have limitations for understanding the SME context. Thereafter we develop our discussion about the specificities of SMEs, including the multiple ideologies that often co-exist in these firms and what this implies for understanding their corporate governance arrangements and needs. Then we discuss the extended team production approach as a potentially useful theoretical model for understanding corporate governance in SMEs. In the concluding part we summarise our approach and analysis and argue for its practical consequences.

Corporate Governance Codes in SMEs

Over the past two decades, corporate governance codes have become a popular means of regulating corporate behaviour. Such codes are developed to establish a set of principles or guidelines of best practices relating to issues such as relations with shareholders, board composition, remuneration, accountability, and audit. Compared to hard regulation (i.e. compulsory instructions such as laws), corporate governance codes are classified as soft regulation that follows the 'comply or explain' principle. This principle calls for standardised reporting by which for each rule in the code corporations can indicate whether they voluntarily comply or, if they do not follow the code, why not (Aguilera et al. 2008; Rapp, Schmid, and Wolff 2011). There is a wide range of collective bodies that make corporate governance codes, even within a single country, and their objectives may vary. In general, the codes that are considered to be the most important are those that include some type of sanction. The evolution of codes has been presented and discussed in several scholarly articles (e.g. Aguilera et al. 2008; Haxhi and van Ees 2010; Cuomo, Mallin, and Zattoni 2016; Clarke 2017) and throughout this volume.

The European Confederation of Directors' Associations (ecoDa) argued that the 2009 financial crisis highlighted the importance of applying good practices for SMEs since, compared to listed companies, they have been paid insufficient attention (ecoDa 2010). SMEs are often owned and controlled by single individuals or families, and shareholders have limited ability to sell their ownership stakes. In SMEs the CEO may have more entrepreneurial freedom to make decisions that have a significant influence on the long-term direction and performance of the firm, and the CEO will in most cases also be the majority shareholder and bear the main risk in the event of poor management. On the other hand, there will be a need to protect the interest of minority shareholders. Issues about related party transactions may also be important.

Corporate governance regimes are typically developed for large listed corporations, and most often these codes do not meet the needs of SMEs (Clarke 2006). However, it has been argued that, although good corporate governance may also be important for small firms, it may be unrealistic to force SMEs to comply with formal codes (Mahmood 2008). Clarke (2006) contends that a corporate governance system for SMEs should be made so that the SMEs are not overburdened and suggests a principle-based rather than rule-based approach. A principle-based approach is less influenced by law than a rule-based approach. It gives more credence to 'cultural imperatives, economic theories and political constructs that inform and shape corporate governance' (Clarke 2006: 337).

Over many years, the European Corporate Governance Institute (ecgi) has made available corporate governance codes from various countries and institutions. As of May 2018, codes from ninety-two different countries and ten cross-national institutions were published on the ecgi websites. These included corporate governance codes from forty-four European countries. In the remainder of this section we will review the codes that regulate and establish best practices for corporate governance in SMEs.

Ecgi and Corporate Governance Codes for SMEs

Most international research on and attention to governance issues are directed to listed and public corporations. Thus, among the corporate governance codes presented by ecgi in the forty-four European countries, only a few address SMEs. The Organisation for Economic Co-operation and Development also has a corporate governance code from 2005 for non-listed companies in emerging markets. While some of the codes we examined are devoted specifically to SMEs (as some codes in Belgium, Finland, France, Ireland, Italy, Switzerland, and the United Kingdom), others are combined or unified for large and small enterprises (as in Albania, Slovakia, Slovenia, and Spain), and yet others include reflections on SMEs in parts of the more general code or of that pertaining to listed companies (as in Denmark and the Netherlands). Some codes are continuously developing, and they may thus exist in several versions. There is, however, a movement in some of the above-mentioned countries to develop codes focusing on listed companies only. The corporate governance codes for SMEs available on the ecgi websites are summarised in Table 5.1.

The target audiences and objectives for the different codes vary, ranging from protecting investors, giving the company a professional image (Belgium), providing advantage in the recruitment market, ensuring continuity of the enterprise (Belgium), and in general increasing company profitability.

Albania's 2008 code specifically addresses small and large unlisted companies. This code is an adaptation of the ecoDa code. The focus is to make corporate

Table 5.1. Ecgi-listed corporate governance codes in SMEs (illustrations)

	Year	Code name	Type	Audience and objectives
Albania	2008	Corporate governance code for unlisted joint-stock companies	Unified	Unlisted joint-stock. Simplifying. Similar also for Slovenia, Slovakia, and Spain.
Belgium	2005	Code Buysse	Separate	Non-listed enterprises. Future success.
Finland	2006	Improving corporate governance for unlisted companies	Separate	Unlisted. Improving corporate governance.
France	2009	MiddleNext code	Separate	Specificities of SMEs.
Ireland	2016	Code for community, voluntary and charitable organisations	Separate	Community, voluntary, and charitable.
Italy	2017	AIdAF code	Separate	Unlisted family-controlled. Objective?
Switzerland	2006	Continuum code	Separate	Business families. Growing family businesses.
UK	2018	QCA code	Separate	Small and mid-size. Growing companies.
European Confederation of Directors' Associations	2010	ecoDa code for unlisted companies in Europe	Unified	All SMEs. Long-term continuity.

governance regulation less complex in SMEs than in large corporations. The Code Buysse, developed in 2005, targets all of Belgium's non-listed enterprises. This code is a collection of guidelines and recommendations that should help owners or managers optimise their future success (Code Buysse 2005).

In 2006, Finland's Chamber of Commerce published 'An Agenda for Improving Corporate Governance in Unlisted Companies' (Finland Central Chamber of Commerce 2006), and in 2009, the French association of small and midcap enterprises MiddleNext produced a corporate governance code (MiddleNext 2009) that focuses on the specificities of small and medium-sized companies. In Ireland there is a code for community, voluntary, and charitable organisations (2016). Such codes may be more important for SMEs than codes developed for large corporations. A corporate governance code for unlisted family-controlled companies has been proposed in Italy (AIdAF 2017), and in Switzerland a governance guide for families and their businesses lays out principles for growing the family business (Continuum and Prager Dreifuss 2008). Finally, in the UK the Quoted Companies Alliance code (QCA 2018) updates a 2013 code for small and mid-sized quoted companies.

The Swiss code distinguishes between family, corporate, and public governance, the latter of which is defined as the conduct towards external stakeholders. A main issue in the Swiss code is how to govern the family. The Belgian and French guidelines acknowledge that corporate governance challenges in various life cycle phases must be understood and that SMEs will often have more need for flexibility than large corporations will. The French guidelines in particular recognise that SMEs often face problems that are different from those in large corporations and that they frequently have a concentrated ownership and a mixture of corporate governance roles among shareholders, board members, and managers.

The Belgian Code Buysse (2005) argues that corporate governance codes in family businesses are not only good for family and its management, but also for board members and the external environment. This illustrates the significant fact that governance issues and agency perspectives in SMEs are complex and go beyond protecting shareholder values.

Variations among Codes: Audiences and Objectives

The corporate governance codes for SMEs available on the ecgi websites reflect variations in national and local challenges and business cultures.

However, corporate governance designs must also reflect that all SMEs cannot be considered under the same umbrella, as they are different and have different needs. Gabrielsson and Huse (2005) apply various theoretical perspectives and show how family businesses, venture capital-backed firms, and other SMEs use their boards and outside directors for different sets of tasks. As shown in Table 5.1, the various codes address or focus on different types of companies:

- All non-listed companies (Belgium, Finland);
- All SMEs (France, ecoDa) and listed SMEs with a focus on growing companies (UK);
- Family companies (Switzerland) and unlisted family-controlled companies (Italy);
- Community, voluntary, and charitable organisations (Ireland).

Some of the codes also make generalisations to, for example, joint ventures, subsidiaries, social companies, and state-owned enterprises (ecoDa 2010).

Good corporate governance in SMEs may contribute to establishing a framework of company processes and attitudes that add value to the business and help ensure its long-term continuity and success (ecoDa 2010). But corporate governance codes for SMEs can pursue many possible objectives. For example, the Belgian Code Buysse (2005) has the following objectives:

- Protect investors;
- Give the enterprise a professional image (legitimacy);
- Provide advantages in the recruitment market;
- Enhance the continuity of the enterprise;
- Increase profitability more generally.

Principles or Rules: The Content of Codes

Despite variations in audiences and objectives across the codes, many codes share key elements of content. Core content topics in the SME codes we examine are about ownership issues, how to contribute to long-term value creation, adapting to the context, and ethics and social responsibility.

With regards to ownership, '[m]ost unlisted enterprises are owned and controlled by single individuals or coalitions of company insiders (e.g. a family). In many cases, owners continue to play a significant direct role in management. Good governance in this context is not a question of protecting the interests of absentee shareholders' (ecoDa 2010: 12). Ownership issues are particularly important in codes with a strong focus on family businesses, but also in other SMEs. In many codes, shareholder agreements are suggested because they will improve the predictability of decision-making (ecoDa 2010). Another core topic is about change of generations and about developing successors, including self-discipline of family members (AIdAF 2017).

The SME codes are generally developed to contribute to long-term value creation in the company. Most codes make suggestions regarding boards and board composition. For example, the introduction of external board members is presented as a solution to the constraints on human resources and competencies that SMEs often experience (ecoDa 2010). Most codes also have suggestions about working structures and processes in the board (AIdAF 2017), as well as about board chairing. While the UK code remarks that (an effective) board works as a team led by the chair (QCA 2018), the Italian code requires that the board chair shall have no management power. Finally, board evaluations are frequently presented as an important development tool, for example, in the ecoDa, French, Italian, and UK codes. Boards should undertake a periodic appraisal of their own performance as well as that of individual directors.

The SME codes also generally emphasise the need to adapt rules and recommendations to the local context. A major argument for introducing a separate code for SMEs is that they need more flexibility than large corporations (Code Buysse 2005; ecoDa 2010; QCA 2018). There should thus be a dynamic approach (ecoDa 2010) and a minimum of formalism (Code Buysse 2005). SMEs should not have rule-based codes, but they should rather be principle based (QCA 2018), with the principles followed on a voluntary basis (ecoDa 2010) and the spirit more important than the form (Code Buysse 2005). The codes should be tailored to the company's individual requirements (QCA 2018). However, it is argued in the French and UK SME codes that companies that adopt the code should be expected to comply with the recommendations.

Stakeholder relations, ethics, and social responsibility are important in SME codes, as they are in codes for large companies (AidAF 2017). Likewise, transparency is just as essential in family businesses and SMEs as it is in large companies (AidAF 2017). Such codes can help contribute to ensure that the individual entrepreneur is more accountable (Code Buysse 2005) and devotes more attention to fulfilling corporate responsibility (ecoDa 2010). Furthermore, the company should not be considered a mere extension of the owner's personal property (ecoDa 2010). Finally, codes may be important for building trust with main stakeholder groups and help investors manage their risks (QCA 2018).

In sum, the regulatory environment of SMEs varies across countries when it comes to guidelines for good corporate governance practices. While specific codes have been developed in several countries, others target multiple countries. Our review shows that different corporate governance codes address different types of SMEs and that audiences and objectives vary. Nevertheless, SME codes offer similar recommendations with respect to content and are generally developed with the aim to contribute to long-term value creation. In many codes the need to adapt rules and recommendations to the local context is emphasised. In the next section, we continue this discussion via a review of research on corporate governance in SMEs.

Research on Corporate Governance in SMEs

The number of academic articles related to corporate governance in SMEs has increased significantly over the past two decades (Gabrielsson 2017). Two general observations can be made when following this stream of research. First, it is evident that SMEs face very different regulatory regimes depending on their proximate environment, most notably the country in which they operate, which then influence what formal corporate governance structure they need to adopt (Huse 2005). However, while formal structures may vary across industries and countries, it seems that SMEs have specific governance needs which make them 'decouple' formal structures from actual corporate governance practices (Voordeckers et al. 2014; Durst and Brunold 2017). In this respect, even if comparisons of SMEs display large degrees of heterogeneity in formal governance structures, they often show much more homogeneity when it comes to actual behaviour.

Second, only scarce evidence supports strong and consistent performance effects of particular corporate governance practices in SMEs. Some research has shown that an empowered board of directors could serve as a valuable resource for SMEs, especially when it comes to entrepreneurial and innovative firm behaviour (e.g., Zahra, Neubaum, and Huse 2000; Gabrielsson 2007a). However, their effectiveness and value seems to depend on a range of contingencies in and around the firm, such as owner preferences, stakeholder expectations, and the life course of the SME (Gabrielsson 2007b; Ingley et al. 2017). Thus, the available research evidence provides little guidance when it comes to the performance implications of different corporate governance arrangements across cases and contexts. Overall, this suggests that there may be a need to look closer at the specificities that characterise the principles and practices of corporate governance in SMEs.

For this analysis we have chosen four studies published in peer-reviewed academic journals to summarise existing research-based knowledge that has accumulated on corporate governance in SMEs over the years. The four studies complement each other in different ways: Two apply a systematic review methodology (Huse 2000; Li et al. 2018), while the other two present narrative reviews (Uhlaner, Wright, and Huse 2007; Bammens et al. 2011). Two focus on corporate governance (Uhlaner, Wright, and Huse 2007; Li et al. 2018), while the other two specifically focus on boards of directors (Huse 2000; Bammens et al. 2011). Table 5.2 summarises our selection of review articles.

Overall, the reviews emphasise that research is heavily dominated by agency theory and resource dependence theory (see also Gabrielsson 2017; Mair, Wolf, and Ioan, Ch. 8, and other chapters in this volume). While these theories and frameworks are heavily used and diffused, the theories are shown to be ill fitted when applied to SMEs, as they are embedded in assumptions and conceptions that have been developed for the study of large corporations. For example, agency theory emphasises how owners ensure that managers act in their interest by establishing independent governance structures (Jensen and Meckling 1976). However, the relationship between the owner and the business is much closer in SMEs than that between the shareholders and the large firm (Huse 2000), which means that this form of conflict is largely absent in most SMEs (Storey 1994). Instead, boards in SMEs are often seen as extended management teams (Zhang, Baden-Fuller, and Pool 2011) in which board members work together with the management team in pursuit of alignment and cooperation (Garg and Furr 2017). The simplified assumptions in agency theory about owners seeking to maximise shareholder wealth can also be largely questioned since owners in SMEs show much greater diversity in their objectives (Storey 1994). Furthermore, agency theory is heavily focused on the protection and distribution of value, which stands in stark contrast to the emphasis on value creation when discussing SMEs.

Resource dependence theory, on the other hand, brings issues of power to the forefront in explaining how organisations seek to manage their environments by governing relations with exchange partners (Pfeffer and Salancik 1978). In brief, resource dependence theory posits that corporate governance arrangements—most particularly its board of directors—may enable firms to minimise dependence or gain resources (Gabrielsson and

Table 5.2. Review articles on corporate governance in SMEs

	Huse (2000)	Uhlaner, Wright, and Huse (2007)	Bammens, Voordeckers, and Van Gils (2011)	Li, Terjesen, and Umans (2018)
Academic outlet	*Entrepreneurship and Regional Development*	*Small Business Economics*	*International Journal of Management Reviews*	*Small Business Economics*
Focus	Boards of directors in SMEs	Corporate governance in privately held firms	Boards of directors in family businesses	Corporate governance in entrepreneurial firms
Scope	10 selected SME journals	Entrepreneurship and small business research	Family business research	Broad search in electronic databases
Type of review	Systematic	Narrative	Narrative	Systematic
Time period	1990–99	Up to 2007	Up to 2011	Up to 2018

Huse 2010). Ample empirical evidence indicates that SMEs may benefit from recruiting external board members as a way to bring valued resources to the firm (Daily et al. 2002; Lynall, Golden, and Hillman 2003; Gabrielsson 2007a). However, the theory underplays the power of corporate governance arrangements in exercising control over the future direction of the enterprise; instead, it sees principles and practices of corporate governance as a repertoire of tactics in the hands of managers to minimise external resource dependencies. In this respect, resource dependence theory is a close ally of managerial hegemony theory (Mace 1971; Lorsch and MacIver 1989), in which board members and other corporate governance actors are reduced to 'pawns' in the service of managers.

Overall, tacit assumptions in much of the literature and research on corporate governance in SMEs contend that these firms are 'scaled down' versions of larger corporations. Nevertheless, the four reviews we examined clearly show that SMEs differ significantly from their larger counterparts that typically have distant shareholders, more hierarchical structures, and multiple layers of management. In this respect, the reviews emphasise the need to develop alternative or modified frameworks that acknowledge the specificities and diversity of the SME context when studying corporate governance practices, especially differences in ownership contexts (e.g., Huse 2000; Uhlaner, Wright, and Huse 2007). Along these lines, they also raise the topic of flexibility and argue that governance codes for SMEs should be flexible enough to take into account the different governance needs that these firms experience in different life cycle stages (Uhlaner, Wright, and Huse 2007). Furthermore, the reviews contend that more attention should be paid to stakeholder dynamics in different types of SMEs (Huse 2000; see also Huse and Zattoni 2008) and highlight how the unique corporate governance setting of SMEs influences behaviours and processes inside and outside the boardroom (Bammens et al. 2011; Uhlaner, Wright, and Huse 2007). Following these recommendations, we develop in the next section the discussion on the unique characteristics of SMEs, which in turn has implications for the application of models for corporate governance in this context.

SME Characteristics

As we noted at the outset, there is no single, uniformly acceptable definition of an SME, and their heterogeneity and dynamism often make it necessary to modify existing definitions according to the particular context in which they are examined (Storey 1994; Curran and Blackburn 2001; Ingley et al. 2017). Nevertheless, there are a few commonalities across SMEs that may serve as a basis for understanding their distinct characteristics.

First of all, SMEs are by definition smaller than large corporations, with fewer assets and fewer people employed (Mazzarol and Reboud 2009). This makes their organisational structures much simpler, or flatter, typically characterised by lower levels of formalisation. Communication channels are also more open and informal, and decision-making can be centralised at the top. Adding to this, ownership is typically located in the hands of a few people, or a single individual. Thus, as noted previously, the relationship between the business and the owner is much closer in SMEs than it is between the large firm and the shareholder. Owners and managers can also to a large extent rely on informal controls and the social capital embedded in relationships to get things going (Mustakallio 2002; Uhlaner, Floren, and Geerlings 2007). In effect, owners can have tight control over business operations, and strategic decisions that can have a major impact on the long-term direction and performance of the enterprise can be made relatively quickly (Mintzberg and Waters 1982).

Another feature common to most SMEs is that they suffer from size disadvantages, or what is often referred to as 'liabilities of smallness' (Aldrich and Auster 1986). This is reflected in challenges such as the inability to capture economies of scale (Strotmann 2007) and dependence on dominant customers (Lyons and Bailey 1993). It also relates to the difficulties SMEs experience in securing financial capital and staff (Winborg and Landström 2001) and in accessing complementary assets that are needed for developing and commercialising new products and services (Gans and Stern 2003). Overall, these disadvantages and challenges imply that SMEs need principles and practices of corporate governance that enable them to sustain their capacity to create value, while at the same time balancing the needs and priorities of major stakeholders in and around the firm (see also Mair, Wolf, and Ioan, Ch. 8 in this volume, regarding similar challenges in social enterprises).

Owners, board members, and executives are the three major forces responsible for determining the direction and performance of unlisted SMEs. Among these, owners are the most critical force as ownership assigns individuals the legal right to control the firm as well as the right to appropriate the firm's residual earnings. However, there is diversity of objectives among owners across different SMEs (Gabrielsson and Huse 2005). Some seek to pursue a particular lifestyle whilst also obtaining an acceptable level of income. Others seek to rapidly grow their firms to maximise sales or profits, and yet others aim for a slow but patient building of an empire for generations

Table 5.3. Three types of SMEs

Type of firm	Founder-centred SMEs	Investor-centred SMEs	Family-centred SMEs
Ideological base	Entrepreneurship	Management	Family institution
Dominant stakeholder	Founder/s	Financial beneficiaries	Family members
Motivation for venturing	Independence and autonomy	Monetary rewards	Tradition and family legacy
Ownership logic	Psychological	Legal/economic	Sociosymbolic
Management logic	Owner management	Professional management	Family management
Structuring principle	Networking based on trust relationships	Managerial hierarchy	Emotional hierarchy
Value creation indicator	Cash flow	Profitability	Socioemotional wealth

to come. In this respect, the varying objectives and motivations of their owners constitute a key component for understanding SMEs (Storey 1994). Table 5.3 provides a stylised overview of three main types of SMEs to analytically observe such differences.

Founder-centred SMEs can be understood as driven by entrepreneurship as the main ideology,[2] with a primary focus on creating value for the founder/s. This ideology is concerned with that which does not yet exist, but which is becoming (Gartner, Bird, and Starr 1992), and the firm is largely seen as an action-triggering device that allows the founder/s to successively engage in emerging projects. The primary motivation for venturing is independence and autonomy, which highlights the desire of the founder to control his or her life. The ownership logic is primarily psychological (Pierce, Kostova, and Dirks 2001) in the sense that it is individualistic and based on feelings of possessiveness; the founder is psychologically tied to the firm (Nelson 2003). In this vein, founding owners also see themselves as competent managers. Founder-centred SMEs are organically structured based on networks that reduce transaction costs and enhance learning (Johannisson 2000). Value creation means generating the cash flow needed to finance expansion and maintaining the venturing process by continuously identifying and exploiting entrepreneurial opportunities.

---

[2] Ideology is here defined in line with Johannisson and Huse (2000: 356) as 'a consistent and permanent way of perceiving and appreciating the world that, accompanied by emotional commitment, generates a specific mode of conduct'.

The main ideology that drives investor-centred SMEs is management, with the key goal of creating value for their financial beneficiaries. These beneficiaries can include founders but also external owners who have invested additional equity in the firm (Gabrielsson and Huse 2002). This ideology favours the implementation of professional management structures as the 'normal' way of organising economic activity, where objectives can be related to measurable units such as growth and profit (Wijbenga, Postma, and Stratling 2007). The primary motivation for venturing is monetary reward. The ownership logic is legal/economic (Monks and Minow 2012) in the sense that what is 'yours' or 'mine' is defined based on legal rights with associated economic implications. In this respect, investor-centred SMEs welcome professional management structures in which design/planning and execution/implementation are separated in time and space. Quantitative growth is the prime indicator of value creation by which owners are provided a return on their investments.

Family-centred SMEs are driven by the family institution as the principal ideology, with a focus on creating value for the family of the owners. The firm is in this respect used to create a safe domicile for the family (Miller and Rice 1967) and to maintain family traditions as well as build a future for generations to come (Gnan, Montemerlo, and Huse 2015). Family values become extremely important in this setting, where a working family life becomes a condition for the continuous survival and success of the firm (Johannisson and Huse 2000). Primary motivations for venturing are continuing an entrepreneurial tradition within the family and creating a family legacy in the local community. The ownership logic is to a large extent sociosymbolic (Etzioni 1991) in the sense that the firm is perceived as belonging to the 'whole family' based on status and identity. Family-centred SMEs are moreover organised via a clan structure (Ouchi 1979) in which hierarchies are based on seniority and kinship ties with the dominant objective of keeping the business within the family. The main indicator of value is the creation of socioemotional wealth, which according to Gómez-Mejia et al. (2007: 106) refers to 'non-financial aspects of the firm that meet the family's affective needs, such as identity, the ability to exercise family influence, and the perpetuation of the family dynasty'.

In the discussion thus far we have kept the three main types of SMEs separated on a conceptual level to enable a fine-grained theoretical analysis. At this point, however, we need to acknowledge that these types should be understood in an 'ideal-typical sense' (Doty and Glick 1994), intended to provide an abstract model that can serve as a basis for deepening our understanding of possible conflicting ideologies, values, and priorities that may persist and potentially even co-exist in SMEs. This means that a particular

SME may be more or less similar to any of these ideal types, but also that they can—and often do—host several contrasting ideologies, values, and priorities at the same time.

A dynamic life cycle approach (Ingley et al. 2017) may illustrate the development and potential clash of ideologies when SMEs continue through different growth trajectories. Such an approach acknowledges that SMEs do not follow a predictable sequence of stages characterised by increasing size and age (Wright and Stigliani 2013; Brown and Mawson 2013). Rather, they can be seen as dynamic networks of belief systems, relationships, and organising principles that enable them to navigate and adapt to changing conditions in their proximate environment (Levie and Lichtenstein 2010). Beginning with start-ups, these firms are often centred on the ideologies, values, and priorities of the founder or the founding team. The organisational structure is informal and the focus is on making and selling. However, there may be a clash of ideologies and values when start-ups survive and grow beyond the early start-up stage. At this stage, firms often implement more professional management structures and increasingly start to focus on the efficiency of operations (Scott and Bruce 1987; Storey 1994). Likewise, founder-centred SMEs that seek external equity and open up to external investors (Gabrielsson and Huse 2002) often experience increased focus on performance monitoring as well as more extensive financial reporting (Wijbenga et al. 2007; Garg 2014). Adding to this, SMEs must manage family dynamics as the venture develops and matures (Cohen and Sharma 2016), which adds to the growing complexity of the different ideologies, values, and priorities that may co-exist in the firm. In this situation, owner-managers often become board members together with other family members, starting to exert control over more junior managers by focusing on family traditions while at the same time ensuring the sustainability and growth of the firm across generations (Gnan et al. 2015; Gabrielsson et al. 2016).

Competing ideologies can be conceived as an obstacle that SMEs need to suppress or even a problem that needs to be solved, as they can result in conflicts and power games that may divert attention and resources from other seemingly more productive activities. However, Johannisson and Huse (2000) stress that the co-existence of different ideologies can be potentially functional for the viability and long-term competitiveness of SMEs as it may generate constructive tensions that continue to energise and develop the business (see also Nordqvist and Melin 2010; Ingley et al. 2017). Following this logic, a model of corporate governance in SMEs cannot rest on theoretical perspectives that favour a particular ideology, thus automatically suppressing a particular group of stakeholders over others. On the contrary, a viable theoretical model of corporate governance in SMEs should seek to balance the full range of different ideologies and stakeholder commitments that may co-exist—thus being able to equally support continued entrepreneurship *and* professional management, *as well as* continued family involvement. The next section will provide a theoretical rationale for such a model.

The Extended Team Production Model of Corporate Governance in SMEs

As argued earlier, neither agency theory nor resource dependence theory offers a balanced model of corporate governance for SMEs that acknowledges the potentially diverse set of co-existing ideologies and stakeholder commitments, while at the same time focusing attention on long-term value creation. In this section we present an extended team production approach (e.g., Machold et al. 2011; Huse and Gabrielsson 2012; Gabrielsson et al. 2016) as an alternative model of corporate governance for SMEs that may provide such a balanced perspective.

The extended team production approach is concerned with the creation of incentives to reduce the potential misalignment of interests, quite similar to agency theory. The approach is also concerned with the need to acquire or control resources critical to the survival of the firm, similar to resource dependence theory and other resource theories. However, the approach differs by specifically advocating a view of organisations as a nexus of team-specific assets, where multiple stakeholders invest firm-specific resources with the hope of benefiting from their cooperation. Team production in this setting should be understood as cooperative behaviour in which several types of resources are used, in which no single person or party holds all resources, and in which the outcome is not a sum of separable outputs of each cooperating resource (Alchian and Demsetz 1972; Kaufman and Englander 2005). This situation applies well to SMEs where resource scarcity and size disadvantages make it unlikely that any single stakeholder possesses and controls all the resources necessary to create tangible economic value for customers while at the same time generating revenue streams for the firm (Gabrielsson et al. 2016).

While SMEs must produce earnings in the current period, they must also build for the long-term to stay current with competitors and engage in innovation to meet changing customer needs. Following this logic, corporate governance in SMEs can be conceptualised as a critical coordinating mechanism for promoting and sustaining firm-specific investments to enhance its value-creating capacity. In this respect, the theory rejects short-sighted distribution rules that are made a priori for the benefit of any particular group of stakeholders (Blair 1995), for example, the sole maximisation of shareholder value. Instead, the theory emphasises that such decisions should be made for the benefit of all value-adding stakeholder groups that engage in the process of team production, in particular the stakeholders that assume risk, enhance firm value, and possess strategic information that can be used for strategy-making (Kaufman and Englander 2005; Blair and Stout 2006). The underlying argument is that it is essential to incentivise these value-adding stakeholders to sustain continued firm-specific investments as it increases firm productivity by developing firm-specific bundles of unique expertise and know-how. In this respect, the theory relates to the resource-based logic (Barney 1991) in its emphasis on heterogeneous and immobile resources as sources of competitive advantage. Unfair expropriation, on the other hand, creates a misalignment of incentives where some value-adding stakeholders may choose to withdraw from further firm-specific investments, thus harming the firm's ability to compete effectively in the marketplace (Aoki 1984).

In team production settings there is a risk that value-adding stakeholders engage in free-riding and shirking, which will reduce the competitiveness of the firm. The team production model of corporate governance rejects both ex ante division rules and ex post bargaining as effective solutions to deal with this situation (Kaufman and Englander 2005; Blair and Stout 2006). In fact, it is argued that ex ante division rules set up before team production begins encourage free-riding. Ex post bargaining, on the other hand, encourages conflict and costly fighting. The proposed solution is an empowered mediating hierarchy that will provide a long-term perspective on the value creation activities making up the firm by capturing the coalition of ideologies and interests that embody the firm's core capabilities. This kind of mediation can be elegantly performed by the board of directors (Blair and Stout 1999; Kaufman and Englander 2005), whose primary task becomes to adopt a role as independent arbiter among the various constituents with a vested interest in the firm (Huse and Gabrielsson 2012). Figure 5.1 summarises the main features of the team production model of corporate governance as applied to SMEs.

Figure 5.1 depicts that corporate governance arrangements in SMEs must seek alignment with its coalition of value-adding stakeholders that embody the core capabilities of the firm, thereby constituting its team-specific assets (Gabrielsson et al. 2016). At the same time, this coalition of stakeholders is embedded in multiple and potentially conflicting ideologies and priorities that need to be balanced in a way that promotes and sustains their firm-specific

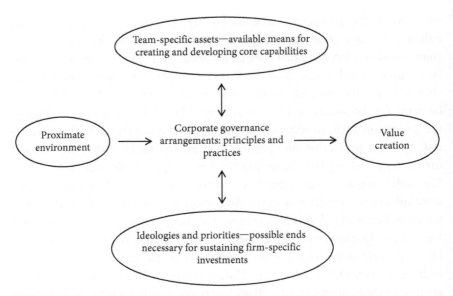

Figure 5.1. Main features of the team production model of corporate governance in SMEs

investments (Johannisson and Huse 2000). In addition to these focal interactions, Figure 5.1 acknowledges the influence from public policies, legislation, and industry norms in the proximate environment in which the firm operates (Huse 2005). In this chapter, we have presented a number of corporate governance codes that exemplify this kind of environmental influence. On the other end, the principles and processes that constitute the set of corporate governance arrangements of SMEs influence their capacity to create long-term value for the benefit of their major stakeholders, particularly their owners, but also customers, lenders, employees, and the local community where they operate. This team production logic can be summarised in three core principles that should guide corporate governance arrangements in SMEs:

- Coordinating and balancing the multiple ideologies and strategic priorities of value-adding stakeholders to sustain firm-specific investments;
- Creating and developing core capabilities to promote long-term value creation;
- Channelling the strategic information on which the firm competes into the strategic decision-making process.

Starting from these core principles, corporate governance practices in SMEs should be designed to orchestrate the productive tensions that come from the multiple ideological bases that constitute the *sine qua non* of the firm (Johannisson and Huse 2000). In this respect, the different ideologies imply different approaches to the adoption of corporate governance codes. Entrepreneurship as ideology has a flexible approach, embedded in the appreciation of the possibility to deviate if the code limits venturing opportunities. Management as ideology is generally obedient, embedded in concerns about the value of the firm and the preference to avoid potential market sanctions. The family institution as ideology is slow and hesitant, embedded in a conception of corporate governance as being an inner sanctum for the family.

In a similar vein, the different ideologies entail different approaches to the control of internal management actions and performance. Entrepreneurship prioritises making and selling, which call for control systems that emphasise market results. In addition to salary, executives are thus preferably remunerated with individual and team bonuses based on market performance. The management ideology prioritises profitability and is in this respect concerned with the gains or losses generated on investments relative to invested resources. Executives are hence preferably compensated with profit-sharing and stock options, thereby bonding their behaviour via a claim on the residual. The family institution seeks stability and survival and emphasises operational efficiency and cost control. Executives are preferably remunerated with fixed salaries combined with merit increases.

There is also a need to acknowledge that the different ideologies have different approaches to the board of directors. Entrepreneurship as ideology regards the board of directors much as an extended executive team, in which the chairperson acts as a figurehead that represents the SME in relation to external groups and actors. The primary task of the board then is to develop linkages with the proximate environment to enable access to scarce resources via networking and lobbying (George, Wood, and Khan 2001). As such, social capital and relational competence become critical board member qualifications. Management as ideology considers the board of directors as an independent decision-making body, in which the chairperson is a liaison representing the constituents with a vested interest in the firm. The board's primary task is to engage in external oversight by monitoring managerial and firm performance (Garg 2014). Here, questioning skills and analytical competence constitute key board member qualifications. The family institution as ideology regards the board of directors much as an integrated family council, where the chairperson acts as a mentor or supporter for the CEO and other board members. The board's main task is to provide advice and counsel, meaning that board member's functional and firm-specific competence are

Table 5.4. Preferred corporate governance practices across different types of ideologies

	Entrepreneurship as ideology	Management as ideology	Family institution as ideology
Compliance with corporate governance codes	Flexible	Obedient	Slow and hesitant
Control system emphasis	Market results	Profitability	Efficiency of operations
Executive remuneration	Individual and team bonuses	Profit-sharing and stock options	Salary and merit increases
Role of board in firm	Extended executive team	Independent decision-making body	Integrated family council
Board tasks	Networking	Monitoring	Advice and counsel
Chairperson profile	Figurehead	Liaison	Mentor
Board qualifications	Social capital and relational competence	Questioning skills and analytical competence	Functional and firm-specific competence

important board member qualifications (Gabrielsson et al. 2016). The preferred corporate governance practices across the different ideologies are depicted in Table 5.4.

The different preferences in Table 5.4 need to be balanced and integrated into the corporate governance practices of the focal firm. The tension that may be created when different ideologies clash should be seen as constructive conflicts that energise and strengthen the competitiveness and long-term viability of SMEs (Johannisson and Huse 2000). Depending on the specific situation of SMEs, the importance and emphasis on different ideological bases may vary, and, as noted earlier, the emphasis may also change over a firm's life course. The team production logic developed in this chapter thus calls for a flexible and dynamic approach, where corporate governance practices and control systems are carefully implemented based on their potential to contribute to sustainable value creation.

Conclusion

Unlisted SMEs make a major contribution to economic job creation and growth, however, their specific corporate governance arrangements have so far been relatively neglected. In this chapter we have examined and challenged existing knowledge and practice about corporate governance in SMEs. Scholars often uncritically adopt theories and frameworks developed for large listed corporations that are ill fitted to the specifics of SMEs. In contrast, we have discussed some of the core features that characterise SMEs and how multiple ideologies that often co-exist in these firms need to be integrated in their corporate governance arrangements. In the chapter we have also presented core assumptions and consequences of the extended team production approach and argued for its application for developing corporate governance practices that contribute to long-term value creation in SMEs.

The extended team production approach supplements and goes beyond traditional theoretical perspectives on corporate governance that favour one particular stakeholder group. It does so by emphasising the need to have a balancing perspective that acknowledges the full range of value-adding stakeholders in SMEs. At the same time, the approach provides a theoretical logic embedded in both economic and behavioural approaches that generate a set of guiding principles for the specific governance needs and challenges of SMEs. The theoretical logic shows the importance of aligning corporate governance practices in SMEs with the coalition of value-adding stakeholders that embody the core capabilities of the firm. The board of directors is a critical coordinating body in this process assigned with the overall responsibility of balancing the potentially diverse range of co-existing ideologies and strategic priorities of different stakeholder coalitions. In addition, successful mediation by the board of directors builds a trustful corporate governance climate that enables board members to channel the expertise and know-how by which the firm competes into the strategic decision-making process, thereby enhancing the firm's value creation potential.

The approach and analysis presented in this chapter may provide SMEs with principles and practices to improve the value-creating potential of their corporate governance arrangements. The board of directors is often the target for corporate governance reforms advocating the recruitment of external board members and an emphasis on independent oversight and control. The team production model presented and developed in this chapter opens up for a more dynamic and flexible approach that calls attention to how corporate governance arrangements may contribute to sustainable value creation. In this respect, boards in SMEs can be seen as tools that create legitimacy, balance different ideologies and strategic priorities, and distribute power and influence among the full range of value-adding stakeholders that make up the firm. Our approach and analysis can thus be used to illuminate the principles on which corporate governance arrangements in SMEs should build to promote sustainable, long-term value creation.

An implication of our theory and framework for policy-makers is its highlighting of the systemic interaction between the often-competing ideologies underlying SMEs and their role in concurrently energising and sustaining the long-term value creation capacity of the firm. Mainstream models of corporate governance, most notably agency theory, are in many ways ill fitted to the specificities and diversity of SMEs. Our review and theoretical discussion show that SMEs need corporate governance principles and practices that acknowledge the potentially diverse set of ideologies and stakeholder commitments that often co-exist, especially differences in ownership contexts. If not properly addressed, there is otherwise a risk that policy initiatives aimed at strengthening the competitiveness of SMEs either via hard law or soft regulations might impede their path to financial viability and long-term, sustainable growth. Thus, when policy-makers focus on supporting corporate governance principles and practices in SMEs, we recommend that a tailored approach be taken that acknowledges the multiple ideologies at play in this setting as well as the specific governance needs and challenges involved.

References

Aguilera, R. V., Filatotchev, I., Gospel, H. and Jackson, G. (2008). 'An Organizational Approach to Comparative Corporate Governance: Costs, Contingencies, and Complementarities', *Organization Science*, 19(3): 475–92.

AIdAF (Associazione Italiana delle Aziende Familiari) (2017). *Corporate Governance Principles for Unlisted Family-controlled Companies: Code of Corporate Governance*. Milan: AIdAF.

Alchian, A. A. and Demsetz, H. (1972). 'Production, Information Costs, and Economic Organization', *American Economic Review*, 62: 777–95.

Aldrich, H., and Auster, E. R. (1986). 'Even Dwarfs Started Small: Liabilities of Age and Size and Their Strategic Implications', in L. L. Cummings and B. M. Staw (eds.), *Research in Organizational Behavior* Vol. VIII. Greenwich, CT: JAI Press, 165–98.

Aoki, M. (1984). *The Cooperative Game Theory of the Firm*. Oxford, UK: Clarendon Press.

Ardic, O. P., Mylenko, N., and Saltane, V. (2011). 'Small and Medium Enterprises: A Cross-country Analysis with a New Data Set', Policy Research Working Paper 5538. Washington, DC: World Bank.

Ayyagari, M., Beck, T., and Demirguc-Kunt, A. (2009). 'Small and Medium Enterprises Across the Globe', *Small Business Economics*, 29(4): 415–34.

Bammens, Y., Voordeckers, W., and Van Gils, A. (2011). 'Boards of Directors in Family Businesses: A Literature Review and Research Agenda', *International Journal of Management Reviews*, 13(2): 134–52.

Barney, J. (1991). 'Firm Resources and Sustained Competitive Advantage', *Journal of Management*, 17(1): 99–120.

Blair, M. (1995). *Ownership and Control: Rethinking Corporate Governance for the Twenty-first Century*. Washington, DC: Brookings Institution.

Blair, M. and Stout, L. A. (1999). 'A Team Production Theory of Corporate Law', *Virginia Law Review*, 85: 247–328.

Blair, M. and Stout, L. A. (2006). 'Specific Investment: Explaining Anomalies in Corporate Law', *Journal of Corporation Law*, 31(3): 719–44.

Brown, R. and Mawson, S. (2013). 'Trigger Points and High-growth Firms: A Conceptualisation and Review of Public Policy Implications', *Journal of Small Business and Enterprise Development*, 20(2): 279–95.

Clarke, A. (2006). 'Small and Medium-sized Enterprises (SMEs) and Corporate Governance: Politics, Resources and Trickle-down Effects', *Keeping Good Companies*, 58(6): 332–37.

Clarke, T. (2017). *International Corporate Governance: A Comparative Approach*. Abingdon, UK: Routledge.

Code Buysse (2005). *Corporate Governance—Aanbevelingen voor niet-beursgenoteerde ondernemingen*. Brussels: UNIZO. Retrieved from http://www. ecgi.org/codes/documents/code_buysse_nl.pdf (accessed 10 January 2020).

Cohen, A. R. and Sharma, P. (2016). *Entrepreneurs in Every Generation: How Successful Family Businesses Develop Their Next Leaders*. Oakland: Berrett-Koehler Publishers.

Continuum and Prager Dreifuss (2008). *Code G: Governance Guide for Families and Their Businesses*. Zürich: Continuum, Prager Dreifuss. [Original German edition published in 2006.]

Cuomo, F., Mallin, C. and Zattoni, A. (2016). 'Corporate Governance Codes: A Review and Research Agenda, *Corporate Governance: An International Review*, 24(3): 222–41.

Curran, J. and Blackburn, R. A. (2001). *Researching the Small Enterprise*. London: SAGE Publications.

Daily, C. M., McDougall, P. P., Covin, J. G., and Dalton, D.R. (2002). 'Governance and Strategic Leadership in Entrepreneurial Firms', *Journal of Management*, 28(3): 387–412.

Doty, D. H. and Glick, W. H. (1994). 'Typologies as a Unique Form of Theory Building: Toward Improved Understanding and Modelling', *Academy of Management Review*, 19(2): 230–51.

Durst, S. and Brunold, J. (2017). 'Corporate Governance Practices in Smaller Privately Held Businesses—Insights from the Rhine Valley Region', in J. Gabrielsson (ed.), *Handbook of Research on Corporate Governance and Entrepreneurship*. Cheltenham, UK: Edward Elgar Publishing, 201–23.

ecoDa (European Confederation of Directors' Associations) (2010). *Corporate Governance Guidance and Principles for Unlisted Companies in Europe.* Brussels: ecoDa.

Etzioni, A. (1991). 'The Socio-economics of Property', *Journal of Social Behavior and Personality*, 6(6): 465–68.

Finland Central Chamber of Commerce (2006). *Improving Corporate Governance of Unlisted Companies*. Helsinki: Finland Central Chamber of Commerce.

Gabrielsson, J. (2017). 'Corporate Governance and Entrepreneurship: Current States and Future Directions', in J. Gabrielsson (ed.), *Handbook of Research on Corporate Governance and Entrepreneurship*. Cheltenham, UK: Edward Elgar, 3–26.

Gabrielsson, J. (2007a). 'Boards of Directors and Entrepreneurial Posture in Medium-size Companies: Putting the Board Demography Approach to a Test', *International Small Business Journal*, 25(5): 511–37.

Gabrielsson, J. (2007b). 'Correlates of Board Empowerment in Small Companies', *Entrepreneurship: Theory and Practice*, 31(5): 687–711.

Gabrielsson, J., Calabrò, A., and Huse, M. (2016). 'Boards and Value Creation in Family Firms', in R. Leblanc (ed.), *The Handbook of Board Governance: A Comprehensive Guide for Public, Private, and Not-for-Profit Board Members*. Hoboken, New Jersey: John Wiley and Sons.

Gabrielsson, J. and Huse, M. (2010). 'Governance Theory: Origins and Implications for Researching Boards and Governance in Entrepreneurial Firms', in H. Landström and F. Lohrke (eds.), *The Historical Foundations of Entrepreneurship Research*. Cheltenham, UK: Edward Elgar, 27–62.

Gabrielsson, J. and Huse, M. (2005). '"Outside" Directors in SME Boards: A Call for Theoretical Reflections', *Corporate Board: Roles, Duties and Composition*, 1(1): 28–37.

Gabrielsson, J. and Huse, M. (2002). 'The Venture Capitalist and the Board of Directors in SMEs: Roles and Processes', *Venture Capital*, 4(2): 125–46.

Gans, J. S. and Stern, S. (2003). 'The Product Market and the Market for "Ideas": Commercialization Strategies for Technology Entrepreneurs', *Research Policy*, 32: 333–50.

Garg, S. (2014). 'Microfoundations of Board Monitoring: The Case of Entrepreneurial Firms', *Academy of Management Review*, 39(1): 114–17.

Garg, S. and Furr, N. (2017). 'Venture Boards: Past Insights and Future Directions', *Strategic Entrepreneurship Journal*, 11: 326–43.

Gartner, W. B., Bird, B. J., and Starr, J. A. (1992). 'Acting "As if": Differentiating Entrepreneurial from Organizational Behavior', *Entrepreneurship Theory and Practice*, 17: 13–31.

George, G., Wood, D. R. Jr., and Khan, R. (2001). 'Networking Strategy of Boards: Implications for Small and Medium-sized Enterprises', *Entrepreneurship and Regional Development*, 13(3): 269–85.

Gnan, L., Montemerlo, D., and Huse, M. (2015). 'Governance Systems in Family SMEs: The Substitution Effects Between Family Councils and Corporate Governance Mechanisms', *Journal of Small Business Management*, 53(2): 355–81.

Gómez-Mejia, L. R., Haynes, K. T., Nunez-Nickel, M., Jacobson, K. J. L., and Moyano-Fuentes, J. (2007). 'Socioemotional Wealth and Business Risks in Family-controlled Firms, Evidence from Spanish Olive Oil Mills', *Administrative Science Quarterly*, 52(1): 106–37.

Haxhi, I. and van Ees, H. (2010). 'Explaining Diversity in the Worldwide Diffusion of Codes of Good Governance', *Journal of International Business Studies*, 41(4): 710–26.

Huse, M. (2005). 'Corporate Governance: Understanding Important Contingencies', *Corporate Ownership and Control*, 2: 41–50.

Huse, M. (2000). 'Boards in SMEs: A Review and Research Agenda', *Entrepreneurship and Regional Development*, 12(4): 271–90.

Huse, M. and Gabrielsson, J. (2012). 'Board Leadership and Value Creation: An Extended Team Production Approach', in T. Clarke and D. Branson (eds.), *The SAGE Handbook of Corporate Governance*. London: Sage Publications, 233–51.

Huse, M. and Zattoni, A. (2008). 'Trust, Firm Life Cycle, and Actual Board Behavior: Evidence from "One of the Lads" in the Board of Three Small Firms', *International Studies of Management and Organization*, 38(3): 71–97.

Ingley, C., Khlif, W., and Karoui, L. (2017). 'SME Growth Trajectories, Transitions and Board Role Portfolios: A Critical Review and Integrative Model', *International Small Business Journal*, 35(6): 729–50.

Jensen, M. C. and Meckling, W. H. (1976). 'Theory of the Firm: Managerial Behavior, Agency Costs and Ownership Structure', *Journal of Financial Economics*, 3: 305–60.

Johannisson, B. (2000). 'Networking and Entrepreneurial Growth', in D. L. Sexton and H. Landström (eds.), *The Blackwell Handbook of Entrepreneurship*. Malden, MA: Blackwell, 368–86.

Johannisson, B. and Huse, M. (2000). 'Recruiting Outside Board Members in the Small Family Business: An Ideological Challenge', *Entrepreneurship and Regional Development*, 12(4): 353–78.

Kaufman, A. and Englander, E. (2005). 'A Team Production Model of Corporate Governance', *Academy of Management Executive*, 19(3): 9–22.

Levie, J. D. and Lichtenstein, B. B. (2010). 'A Terminal Assessment of Stages Theory: Introducing a Dynamic States Approach to Entrepreneurship', *Entrepreneurship Theory and Practice*, 34(2): 317–50.

Li, H., Terjesen, S., and Umans, T. (2018). 'Corporate Governance in Entrepreneurial Firms: A Systematic Review and Research Agenda', *Small Business Economics*, published ahead of print. https://doi.org/10.1007/s11187-018-0118-1

Loecher, U. (2000). 'Small snd Medium-Sized Enterprises—Delimitation and the European Definition in the Area of Industrial Business', *European Business Review*, 12(5): 261–64.

Lorsch, J. W. and MacIver, E. (1989). *Pawns or Potentates: Reality of America's Corporate Boards*. Brighton, Massachusetts: Harvard Business Review Press.

Lukács, E. (2005). 'The Economic Role of SMEs in the World Economy, especially in Europe', *European Integration Studies*, 4(1): 3–12.

Lynall, M. D., Golden, B. R., and Hillman, A. (2003). 'Board Composition from Adolescence to Maturity: A Multitheoretic View', *Academy of Management Review*, 28(3): 416–31.

Lyons, B. R. and Bailey, A. (1993). 'Small Subcontractors in UK Engineering: Competitiveness, Dependence and Problems', *Small Business Economics* 5(2): 101–9.

Mace, M. (1971). *Directors: Myth and Reality*. Cambridge: Harvard University.

Machold, S., Huse, M., Minichilli, A., and Nordqvist, M. (2011). 'Board Leadership and Strategy Involvement in Small Firms: A Team Production Approach', *Corporate Governance: An International Review*, 19(4): 368–83.

Mahmood, S. (2008). 'Corporate Governance and Business Ethics for SMEs in Developing Countries: Challenges and Way Forward', International Society of Business, Economics, and Ethics World Congress, Cape Town, South Africa, 15–18 July 2008.

Mazzarol, T. and Reboud, S. (2009). *The Strategy of Small Firms: Strategic Management and Innovation in the Small Firm*. Cheltenham: Edward Elgar.

MiddleNext (2009). *Code de gouvernement d'entreprise pour les valeurs moyennes et petites. Cahier No. 4*. Paris: MiddleNext.

Miller, E. J. and Rice, A. K. (1967). *Systems of Organization*. London: Tavistock.

Mintzberg, H. and Waters, J. A. (1982). 'Tracking Strategy in an Entrepreneurial Firm', *Academy of Management Journal*, 25(3): 465–99.

Monks, R. A. G. and Minow, N. (2012). *Corporate Governance*. Hoboken, NJ: Wiley.

Mustakallio, M. (2002) *Contractual and Relational Governance in Family Firms: Effects on Strategic Decision-Making Quality and Firm Performance.* Helsinki University of Technology, Doctoral Dissertation 2002/2.

Nelson, T. (2003). 'The Persistence of Founder Influence: Management, Ownership, and Performance Effects at Initial Public Offering', *Strategic Management Journal*, 24(8): 707–24.

Nordqvist, M. and Melin, L. (2010). 'Entrepreneurial Families and Family Firms', *Entrepreneurship and Regional Development*, 22(3–4): 211–39.

Ouchi, W. G. (1979). 'A Conceptual Framework for the Design of Organizational Control Mechanisms', *Management Science*, 25(9): 833–48.

Pfeffer, J. and Salancik, G. R. (1978). *The External Control of Organizations: A Resource Dependence Perspective.* New York: Harper and Row.

Pierce, J. L., Kostova, T., and Dirks, K. T. (2001). 'Toward a Theory of Psychological Ownership in Organizations', *Academy of Management Review*, 26(2): 298–310.

QCA (Quoted Companies Alliance) (2018). *The QCA Corporate Governance Code.* London: Quoted Companies Alliance.

Rapp, M. S., Schmid, T., and Wolff, M. (2011). 'Hard or Soft Regulation of Corporate Governance?' HHL Research Paper Series in Corporate Governance, electronic copy available at: http://ssrn.com/abstract=1930847

Republic of Albania, Ministry of Economy, Trade and Energy, Competitiveness Policy Department (2008). *Corporate Governance Code for Unlisted Joint-Stock Companies in Albania.* Tirana: Republic of Albania.

Scott, M. and Bruce, R. (1987). 'Five Stages of Growth in Small Businesses', *Long Range Planning*, 20(3): 45–52.

Storey, D. (1994). *Understanding the Small Business Sector.* London: Routledge.

Strotmann, H. (2007). 'Entrepreneurial Survival', *Small Business Economics*, 28: 87–104.

Timmons, J. (1998). *America's Entrepreneurial Revolution: The Demise of Brontosaurus Capitalism.* Babson Park, Massachusetts: Olin Graduate School of Business, Babson College.

Uhlaner, L., Floren, R., and Geerlings, J. (2007). 'Owner Commitment and Relational Governance in the Privately-held Firm: An Empirical Study', *Small Business Economics*, 29(3): 275–93.

Uhlaner, L., Wright, M., and Huse, M. (2007). 'Private Firms and Corporate Governance: An Integrated Economic and Management Perspective', *Small Business Economics*, 29(3): 225–41.

Voordeckers, W., Van Gils, A., Gabrielsson, J., Politis, D., and Huse, M. (2014). 'Board Structures and Board Behaviour: A Cross-country Comparison of

Privately Held SMEs in Belgium, the Netherlands and Norway', *International Journal of Business Governance and Ethics*, 9: 197–219.

Wijbenga, F. H., Postma, T. J. B. M., and Stratling, R. (2007). 'The Influence of the Venture Capitalist's Governance Activities on the Entrepreneurial Firm's Control Systems and Performance', *Entrepreneurship Theory and Practice*, 31(2): 257–77.

Winborg, J. and Landström, H. (2001). 'Financial Bootstrapping in Small Businesses: Examining Small Business Managers' Resource Acquisition Behaviors', *Journal of Business Venturing*, 16: 235–54.

Wright, M. and Stigliani, I. (2013). 'Entrepreneurship and Growth', *International Small Business Journal*, 31(1): 3–22.

Zahra, S., Neubaum, D. C., and Huse, M. (2000). 'Entrepreneurship in Medium-size Companies: Exploring the Effects of Ownership and Governance Systems', *Journal of Management*, 26(5): 947–76.

Zhang, J., Baden-Fuller, C., and Pool, J. K. (2011). 'Resolving the Tensions Between Monitoring, Resourcing and Strategizing: Structures and Processes in High Technology Venture Boards', *Long Range Planning*, 44: 95–117.

6

Corporate Governance Regulation for Public Benefit Foundations in Europe

Hanna Surmatz

Do corporate governance principles apply to public benefit foundations, taking into account the specific structure of philanthropic foundations as asset-based and purpose-driven organisations without owners and shareholders, and, if so, in which ways? This chapter suggests that the corporate governance discourse needs adaptation for public benefit foundations since they have to take into account both internal and external governance mechanisms such as reporting regulations, external audits, and state oversight. Unlike companies and associations, public benefit foundations generally have no members or shareholders who control board members and executive staff and who safeguard that the statutory purposes are pursued. In some academic disciplines this is reflected in wording that foundations 'own' themselves. Hence foundations' internal governance control mechanisms may appear less strong, and there could be a (real or perceived) risk that the board or the executive could bend the foundation in a way that is not aligned with the statutory purposes.

This chapter reviews internal and external governance rules of public benefit foundations as tools to safeguard the will of the founder and pursuance of the statutory public benefit purpose in a comparative perspective and places them in the context of recent policy. It takes stock of the current state of play in terms of existing internal and external governance regulation (hard law and soft law) and points to potential trends and ways forward. The underlying legal analysis covers European countries—hence the geographical focus of the chapter is Europe—but the discourse has a wider geographical application.

Public benefit foundations are among the oldest forms of social institutions and, since the 1990s, have experienced a significant growth period (Anheier and Leat 2013; Anheier 2018) in Europe with an estimated 110,000

Hanna Surmatz, *Corporate Governance Regulation for Public Benefit Foundations in Europe* In: *Advances in Corporate Governance: Comparative Perspectives.* Edited by: Helmut K. Anheier and Theodor Baums, Oxford University Press (2020). © Hertie School.
DOI: 10.1093/oso/9780198866367.003.0006

foundations in 2009 (Hopt et al. 2009) and 147,000 in 2016 (Breen 2018: 8). Foundations play a vital role in our societies, yet data on the actual size of the sector produce at best a very rough estimation, and research on corporate governance questions and approaches from a comparative perspective is still scarce.

Quite some research has emerged on the roles of philanthropic foundations in society more generally (e.g. Anheier and Leat 2013; Prewitt et al. 2006; Fleishman 2007; Hammack and Anheier 2013), to some extent taking into account transparency, accountability, and governance questions related to the specific structure of public benefit foundations. While newer international and European comparative research on foundations and their operating frameworks exists, only little of it focuses specifically on foundation governance. That which does (e.g. Bethmann et al. 2014; Boesso et al. 2015; De Andrés-Alonso et al. 2010; Hopt and von Hippel 2010; Van der Ploeg et al. 2017) is certainly challenged by the great diversity of the sector and related problems of classification (Boesso et al. 2015). Comparative research on governance regulation is hindered also because of the different legal traditions and concepts and the complex interplay between hard law/soft law and state supervision (but see Van Veen 2007, 2010, the latter analysing self-regulation and government regulation of fund-raising).

In addition, some research on non-profit organisation (NPO) governance has focused on governance in a narrower sense (governing boards) and has rather not taken into account the influence of the wider external governance system, including regulators and audit and inspection bodies (see Cornforth 2012). Furthermore, this research on the NPO sector tends to cover a very diverse group of entities and has focused more on the largest category among NPOs, namely those that are organised as limited liability companies or associations, which have a membership or shareholder/ownership structure (see Chapters 7 and 8 in this volume for analyses of governance in NPOs and social enterprises, respectively). Foundation governance is however distinct, since a foundation as a legal form (where it exists as a specific legal form) generally has no members and shareholders.[1]

---

[1] Though no common legal definition of a foundation exists in Europe, a few civil law countries allow an associative structure for foundations.

Definitions, Specific Structure of Public Benefit Foundations, and Perceived Risks

Definitions and Framing Questions

As noted in the introduction to this volume, corporate governance refers to rules and procedures for decision-making, accountability and transparency, and distributional rights. Academic literature has long focused on a narrower concept of corporate governance, namely on rules and procedures for decision-making in publicly traded or listed companies, where control over capital by management is separated from ownership of capital by shareholders in the context of solving conflicts between principals (owners/shareholders) and agents (managers). By the 1990s, research began to address specificities of NPOs, including to some extent foundations in the United States and Europe (Rey-Garcia et al. 2012; Ch. 7 in this volume). Corporate governance research has however mostly focused on the composition, role, and effectiveness of governing boards and more recently also the role of executive staff and its interplay with the board (Bethmann et al. 2014) and has not sufficiently taken account of the wider governance system including regulators and audit and inspection or supervisory bodies (with a few notable examples, e.g. Van Veen 2008), which is the approach taken here.

Accountability is understood as an obligation or willingness of a public benefit foundation to account for its actions towards its multiple stakeholders (including downwards to beneficiaries and the public at large as well as upwards to donors or governments and internal accountability). The often conflated term transparency is understood as an obligation or willingness to publish and make available (also via supervisory body, tax authority, or other) information about the organisation (e.g. basic data regarding establishment: name, address, purpose, founder, decision-making body), its finances (e.g. publishing financial reports, undergoing audits), and its programmes and operations (e.g. publishing annual activity reports). Transparency is considered an indispensable mechanism for enacting accountability of a public benefit foundation to different stakeholders throughout its lifetime (EFC and DAFNE 2011; Ebrahim 2010).

The concept and definition of a public benefit foundation differs from country to country, and there is no common international or European legal definition for it. Furthermore, different criteria may apply for civil law and for tax law (Van Veen 2004; Anheier and Then 2004). While in civil law countries the foundation is a distinct legal form with a specific legal definition, in common law countries different legal forms exist, such as trusts or limited liability companies, but the foundation as a legal form does not exist.

The European Foundation Centre (EFC) uses the term 'institutional philanthropy' to be able to recognise and embrace the full variety and structures that exist for such philanthropic organisations. Taking a functional rather than a legalistic approach, there is a common thread of characteristics which European public benefit foundations share and which form the proposed working definition for this chapter: an independent organisation serving a public benefit purpose for which a founder (or founders) has provided assets and determined the foundation's purpose and statutes.[2] This definition does not cover private interest foundations such as family foundations, which benefit private interests and which exist in around half of the European Union (EU) countries (EFC 2015: 16). In many countries the framework legislation does not distinguish between private interest and public benefit foundations. Rather, the distinction is made only by tax law or specific public benefit status. Trusts (where they exist), similar legal institutions, and other arrangements such as non-autonomous foundations without legal personality (which exist in many civil law countries) have a specific governance structure and, even though in some cases functionally comparable to foundations, are generally not included in the scope of the chapter (though some parts of the chapter speak to them as well).[3]

There is also no common legal definition of what a corporate foundation is. Companies create foundations and often provide the capital either through continued financial contributions or the creation of an endowment—often in the form of a major shareholding in the company itself. In many cases there are even governance links when board seats are filled by staff from the related companies (Rey-Garcia et al. 2012: 79).

Implications of the Specific Features of Foundations for Corporate Governance

The specific structure of foundations as (in many cases tax-exempt) asset-based and purpose-driven organisations without owners or shareholders

---

[2] This definition corresponds to a large extent with the one used for the feasibility study of a European Foundation Statute (Hopt et al. 2009: 13).

[3] While civil law foundations have separate legal personality and 'own themselves', in the case of trusts it is the trustees who are the legal owners of the property of the trust and they are answerable to the charitable purpose (in charitable trusts) or the beneficiaries (in the case of private trusts).

shapes corporate governance questions also in the context of the rationale for internal and external governance, transparency, and accountability regulation. The governance discourse and regulation have been influenced by many different factors as described in the following.

Principal–agent Theory and Potential Adaptations for Public Benefit Foundations

First, there has been a growing argument that the foundation sector should adopt its own version of a 'principal–agent' approach (Jensen and Meckling 1976), which was developed for the corporate sector in order to address how an organisation should be governed and controlled to prevent abuse by governing bodies (Hopt et al. 2005: 246f; von Hippel 2007; EFC and DAFNE 2011: 9). Applying the principal–agent theory to companies, different principal–agent relationships can be identified within a for-profit company. The governing board and management of a for-profit company are the 'agent' which acts on behalf of and in the interest of the owners or shareholders as the 'principal'. The danger is that the agents may in some cases act more in their own interest, for instance though self-dealing. Therefore, it is mandatory that decisions made by the governing board and management are transparent so that owners and shareholders are informed and can react when decisions appear risky and/or when the behaviour of the governing board or management is deemed negligent. The principal–agent approach has been criticised as being based on the assumption that individuals are driven by the promotion of their own interest, even though most managers and governing boards act to the best of their abilities, whereas others argue that the approach does not take into account interests other than just shareholder and member interests (Van Veen 2008).

Many researchers are of the opinion that the essence of the principal–agent theory could also apply to NPOs (Caers et al. 2006; von Schönfeld 2017: 28; see also Chapter 7 in this volume) and public benefit foundations (Hopt et al. 2005: 246f; von Hippel 2007; Jakob 2006: 530; EFC and DAFNE 2011: 9). However, in this context it is important to stress that foundations potentially lack 'built-in' cross-check mechanisms to avoid abuse since they do not have owners/shareholders or members. It has already been stated that the good governance of a foundation depends to a large extent on the ethical standing of its board (EFC and DAFNE 2011). If one would want to apply the principal–agent theory to foundations, the question arises who the stakeholder or 'principal' would be in whose interest the governing board/management acts as agent? In the case of public benefit foundations beneficiaries claim no proprietary rights on the assets. Founders or donors dedicate their money to the purpose of the foundation and do not have any own economic interest in the foundation; their interest is therefore not comparable to that of shareholders in a for-profit company. In addition, foundations are often set up for a very long period beyond their founders' lifetimes. Therefore, even if one could argue that the founder does retain a vested interest in checking board activities (Thymm 2007: 221f.), this would hardly be maintained beyond their lifetime (von Schönfeld 2018: 137). Hence the board rather acts on behalf of the foundation itself and not on behalf of the founder or beneficiaries.

In the context of the principal–agent theory it is argued that while donors/ founders delegate the control functions to a governing board, the board members delegate management and decisions to 'internal agents', but the board retains ultimate control over the internal agents (De Andrés-Alonso et al. 2010). The founders have not simply delegated the management to the board, but the founders as 'principals' have been superseded by the foundation itself. The board is accountable to the foundation (and not to the founder or the beneficiaries since neither of them can claim proprietary rights). The civil law foundation owns itself and has no external owners or shareholders (EFC and DAFNE 2011: 16). This specific structure leads to a control issue (von Schönfeld 2017: 28f.) which is addressed by transparency and accountability rules and external supervisory structures (Van Veen 2008). In particular in civil law countries, the argument is used that transparency and accountability are important tools to ensure that the will of the founder (i.e. the public benefit purpose) and the foundation as an independent entity are protected against misconduct by the foundation board or other organs and misuse of the foundation funds. As mentioned earlier, this is different for those organisations that do not have separate legal personality such as trusts or non-autonomous foundations, which are only to some extent referred to in this chapter. While civil law foundations own itself/own the assets, it is the trustees who are the legal owners of the trust property and they have onerous fiduciary obligations to carry out the trust.

Some researchers argue that traditional theories of corporate governance such as the agency theory should be expanded for application to public benefit foundations to incorporate a cognitive dimension (De Andrés-Alonso et al. 2010). Instead of board size and independence, knowledge diversity inside the boardroom and the active character of board members are argued to have a positive influence on effectiveness and resource allocation. While the research focused on a sample of Spanish foundations, it can be argued that the cognitive dimension of an expanded model of governance could also apply beyond Spain. Charreaux (2005) already advocated for a model of governance that is built on the agency framework but adds a more cognitive approach, which corresponds to the findings of legal analysis that the ethical standing of the board is a crucial element in foundation corporate governance. Further research in the context of Italian foundations of banking origin supports these findings but argues also that governance systems in which a powerful and longer term chairperson coexists with strong board processes are associated with more sophisticated strategic approaches (Boesso et al. 2015). How much such a cognitive dimension can be incorporated into the agency theory for foundations needs further analysis. In particular more research is needed on whether and to what extent the suggested cognitive dimension goes beyond a mere call for a board with diverse backgrounds.

So-called 'participatory grantmaking' and stakeholder involvement in foundation governance could also be seen as ways to further develop the principal–agent approach for public benefit foundations. Community foundations often have more participatory governance elements in their set-up and are considered by some as tools to strengthen local control (Walkenhorst 2008). Also other parts of institutional philanthropy (going beyond community and local contexts) have been discussing and developing models to strengthen participation of third actors in governance and decision-making structures (Van Veen 2008). This could either be limited to decisions about grantmaking or it could go beyond that. There has been some analysis done as to how an enhanced stakeholder approach to philanthropy could change decision-making and governance in (local) philanthropy, and what the potential rewards and risks are (Harrow 2011: 2). In the context of local philanthropy, the demands on governance are subject to the lens of public scrutiny and community involvement. It is also considered that the legitimacy of foundations may be enhanced by their stakeholder responsiveness through explicit governance change (Harrow 2011: 11).

Arguing that social change is a negotiated, contested political process, and not simply a question of better management (Anheier and Leat 2013, 2006), different philanthropy set-ups are discussed. Foundations (in local contexts and beyond) may consider an engagement strategy via their governance. It is argued that especially in uncertain times, foundations can benefit from interacting more openly with their stakeholders in order to identify needs and develop best strategies to address them. Such an approach would however imply a major shift in governance thinking for the foundation world (Harrow 2011: 12). Another more pragmatic rationale for considering more stakeholder interaction is the need to act in cases of falling foundation income. Some researchers also argue that in addition to regulatory control and governance mechanisms, market forces (in particular the fundraising market) could indeed provide for external corporate governance elements and for solving the principal–agent conflict in the case of NPOs (von Schönfeld 2018: 145; von Hippel 2007: 104f.).

A desirable effort to clarify some of these issues would be an analysis of how engaging other stakeholders in the governance of public benefit foundations could potentially be seen as creating a proxy for members of associations or shareholders in companies in the agency theory context and beyond.

Further analysis is also needed as to how other theoretical approaches discussed in the literature on corporate governance such as stewardship theory have influenced governance discussions and governance regulation for the public benefit foundation sector. The stewardship theory suggests that managers, left on their own, will act as responsible stewards of the assets they control (Donaldson and Davis 1991). Stewardship theorists argue that given a choice between self-serving behaviour and pro-organisational behaviour, a steward will place higher value on cooperation than defection. One may argue that the stewardship idea has already influenced the internal governance approach within the foundation sector, since the good governance of a foundation under current regulation to a large extent depends on the ethical standing and good stewardship of its managers and governing board. However, this would need further research.

Creditor Protection and Legal Security Arguments
In addition to the adaptation of the principal–agent approach, legal security and creditor protection arguments shape the context of governance regulation of foundations. Regulation related to governance, accountability, and transparency ensures overall legal security and creditor protection as a consequence of creating a legal entity. The granting of legal personality normally protects the capital of a civil law foundation from the founders' or donors' creditors. Regardless of a foundation's specificities, any legal person may be required to present its basic data (including information about its legal representative or beneficial ownership according to new EU rules) and annual accounts in a public register, as a means to ensure that credible information is provided to all parties with whom the foundation enters into contracts.

Exchange for Tax Exemptions
Another element influencing governance questions of public benefit foundations is related to a specific tax status that foundations may wish to acquire. In

exchange for tax benefits, the state (and tax-payers) expects a public benefit foundation to have good governance in place and to be subjected to more detailed transparency and accountability requirements to show that it supports the general public interest. Governments give up part of their tax income via tax incentives because public benefit foundations are supposed to benefit the whole community. Tax exemption is often seen as an instrument for division of labour between the state and private actors when it comes to benefiting the general public. Private initiatives may therefore only receive tax privileges if they have checks and balances in place and can show in a transparent and accountable manner (towards the tax authorities and the general public) that they benefit the public at large and how they do it (EFC and DAFNE 2011).

The Interest of the General Public

Since many foundations aim to tackle problems in society and wish to bring about social change, it is also argued that the public at large has a legitimate interest in obtaining information about foundations and their governance and management. Where foundations take the role to determine public priorities in a modern democracy, they need to be transparent and accountable. For foundations as organisations without shareholders, members, or customers and with 'clients' unlikely to criticise them (Anheier and Leat 2013: 466), demands on internal and external governance are seen in this context.

Some researchers even put forward that increased demands for transparency and accountability can be made since they consider 'foundations as largely undemocratic institutions promoting their version of the public good often via tax protected resources, creating a state protected power asymmetry between those who control resources and those who seek them' (Prewitt et al. 2006). Alongside the suspicion of individual selfishness and misuse of foundations, irritation about inefficiency and inflexibility sometimes associated with foundations or disagreement with use of foundations as instruments of power or corporate control are also mentioned (Wijkström 2001). Matters of power and legitimacy are also considered problematic in developed democracies when it comes to philanthropy (Bernholz et al. 2016). However, on the other side, the case is also made that foundations enjoy fundamental rights, such as the freedom of property and the freedom of speech, which are crucial to their role in civil society (Van der Ploeg et al. 2017: Chapter 2, 268ff.).

Sector Interest and Sector Efforts Around Internal and External Good Governance

It should be stressed in this context that many public benefit foundations are working in the spirit of an internally driven, ethical commitment to good corporate governance, transparency, and accountability stemming from their mission as public benefit foundations (EFC and DAFNE 2011: 10). Good governance, sound management, transparency, and accountability are considered essential parts of good foundation practice. Often there are also strategic considerations for foundations to adopt these principles and practices and thus to maintain public trust in the sector. Foundations need to undertake efforts to prevent and anticipate scandal in a climate of increased suspicion. In addition, they consider that being open to innovations and to change in society will help them to improve their philanthropic activity and respond to new ideas and trends in society. There are a set of sector infrastructure organisations working on sector-driven guidance and recommendations covering also good governance questions (see for example the EFC Principles of Good Practice covering independent governance, sound management, transparency, and accountability).

Specific Case of Company-linked Foundations

Corporate governance questions have special relevance in the case of corporate foundations, especially in those cases where company managers (and not the shareholders) decide whether the company will endow or fund the foundation and for which purposes (Rey-Garcia et al. 2012: 79). Research on corporate foundations concludes that since corporate foundations (and one may analyse this question also for endowed foundations, more generally) do not tend to raise funds from external donors, they potentially lack an intrinsic incentive for transparency towards external stakeholders and the general public that characterises fundraising foundations (Rey-Garcia et al. 2012: 86). Governance questions specifically related to company-linked foundations may deserve more research; within the scope of this chapter only some basic issues could be mentioned.

Perceived Risks and Perceived Lack of Effectiveness Related to Public Benefit Foundations Impacting Governance, Transparency, and Accountability Questions

Public benefit foundations have their public benefit mission and non-distribution constraint in common with the wider non-profit sector. While

NPOs may not be more vulnerable to scandal and abuse compared to the for-profit sector, their public benefit mission may render them more susceptible to public disappointment (Rey-Garcia et al. 2012: 78).

Their public benefit mission and status (often leading to tax exemptions) implies a certain level of legitimate interest of policy-makers, legislators, and the general public. The tax-exempt status (where applicable) of NPOs implies certain legal requirements on transparency and accountability introduced also for maintaining society's trust, which makes the tax-exempt non-profit sector resemble public bodies when it comes to transparency and accountability duties (Leat 1994).

Public benefit foundations as well as organisations in the wider non-profit sector have over the past decade come under increased scrutiny and criticism for different reasons, including for instance the perceived risk of abuse for money laundering purposes, terrorism financing, and tax evasion; as well as individual cases in the media of wrongdoing related to excessive executive compensation, conflict of interest, corruption, and abuse of power structures in other ways.

Additionally, questions around effectiveness have increased public distrust and led to more regulation, including self-regulation. The effectiveness of the NPO and the public benefit foundation sector has been criticised by the media and the general public; a study undertaken within the German foundation sector concluded that there are deficiencies with regard to strategic management, asset administration, control, and overall management (Sandberg 2007). Some experts claim that this perceived lack of effectiveness arises from a deficit in management and controlling structures (von Schönfeld 2018: 127).

In recent years, in particular the security agenda (prevention of terrorism financing and money laundering) has been a key driver for more transparency regulation (in some cases over-regulation) impacting on the foundation and wider non-profit sectors. The European Commission's Supra-National Risk Assessment report (European Commission 2017: 186–9) stated that the money laundering and terrorism financing threat (likelihood) and vulnerability (weakness) are significant for NPOs (level 3), and for those NPOs receiving institutional funding they are moderately significant (level 2). The report highlighted that parts of the non-profit sector are exposed to a higher level of money laundering and terrorism financing risks, in particular for cross-border philanthropic flows. The lack of traceability of sources and destinations of transfers of philanthropic capital flows when sent abroad was seen as a specific issue of concern.

This European risk perception of the philanthropy and NPO sector by policy-makers corresponds with the global context. The European framework is to a large extent based on recommendations adopted by the global policy-setter on money laundering and terrorism financing prevention policy, namely the Financial Action Task Force (FATF), which had until 2016 used a policy recommendation that described the NPO sector in its entirety as particularly vulnerable to abuse for terrorism financing. In 2016, however, FATF moved to an approach that explicitly acknowledges that now only parts of the non-profit sector are likely to be at risk, and governments should apply a risk-based approach with targeted and proportionate measures to address potential terrorism financing risks. This policy change also reflects the success of the Global NPO coalition on FATF, which is led by the US Charity and Security Network, the European Center for Not-for-Profit Law, the EFC, and the Human Security Collective, and supported by others (Romaniuk and Keatinge 2018; Breen 2018).

The FATF and EU security agenda and policy to address terrorism financing, money laundering, and tax evasion have changed the discourse around public benefit foundation and NPO internal and external governance regulation as tools to address certain perceived risks. In the context of assessing potential risks for abuse, existing measures such as hard law and self-regulation must be taken into account by governments worldwide, according to FATF policy. The security agenda has hence created a certain momentum for policy-makers and the sector to review the effectiveness of internal and external governance questions with a view to avoid over-regulation in cases where existing mechanisms already address potential risks.

In terms of reviewing their own governance and risk management, many larger public benefit foundations have adopted more sophisticated and professionalised risk management approaches, which cover not only areas of security and safety but also fiduciary, legal, reputational, operational, and information risks.

Key Empirical Points on Regulatory and Self-Regulatory Approaches within Foundation Governance

This section aims to present an empirical analysis as to how existing mechanisms, be they regulatory or self-regulatory foundation practices, shape the governance of public benefit foundations, taking into account the specific structure of public benefit foundations as organisations with no owners, shareholders, or members. These governance mechanisms can be internal procedures or practices of the foundation and governance rules as well as 'external' governance via reporting rules and other regulations, external audits, and supervisory structures.

Working with national legal experts, the EFC has conducted comparative analysis on national rules and self-regulatory approaches around foundation governance in thirty countries (EFC 2015), which provides the key source for the following section, which focuses on Europe.

Internal Governance Regulation

Founders generally have the freedom to design the internal governance structure of the foundation created, but the law prescribes some basic issues that need to be addressed and how it should be done (the level of detail varies across countries). Foundations are legally required to have a governing board as the key governing organ. The board is the key mechanism of governance in the non-profit world (De Andrés-Alonso et al. 2010). Private foundation supervisory mechanisms, e.g. supervisory boards and monitoring by auditors or other third parties, are mandatory only in some countries. Rights of third parties are generally not included in the laws (see Van Veen 2008 arguing that a right of participation of third parties could be included by legislators). Generally foundation laws do not describe detailed regulations on governance and internal checks and balances (Van Veen 2008), but there has been room for self-regulation in order to cover some of these issues.

Role of Founders in Governance According to the Law

Founders typically have no decision-making power in the running of the foundation. Their engagement generally ends with the creation process. Some founders continue to engage during their lifetime generally by staying involved in the governance structure, e.g. by being a board member or by preserving some control functions, but this does not go beyond the lifetime of the founder or in some cases the first generation thereafter (von Schönfeld 2018: 137). The founders of public benefit foundations give away the assets to the foundation and hence do not own the assets once the transfer of funds has happened. The founder has no proprietary rights on the assets of a public benefit foundation and cannot benefit financially from it.

Governing Board

All European foundation laws recognise that there must be someone who is responsible for the management of the foundation (Hopt et al. 2006: 133).

In most countries, the only mandatory governing organ is a governing board, but foundations are free to set up other organs if they deem it necessary (Surmatz and Ibbotson 2015). In some countries, the board may delegate some duties to other persons (Hopt et al. 2006: 134).

Approximately half of the EFC surveyed countries require a foundation to have a collective governing body, with more than one board member (Surmatz and Ibbotson 2015: 11). Most countries in which this is regulated prescribe at least three members for the board of directors. In most countries, the board can be composed of individuals as well as legal entities, with the exception of some cases (Austria for public benefit foundations; Czech Republic, Denmark, Finland, Hungary, and Latvia allow only 'natural persons'; Surmatz and Ibbotson 2015). Generally, founders are allowed to be members of the board; however in Hungary, they along with their relatives must be in the minority, while in Sweden a founder must not be the sole board member.

Some countries prescribe that the members of the board must not be related or closely connected, while others expressly stipulate that persons with a financial interest such as employees cannot become board members (Hopt et al. 2006: 161).

In most of the countries surveyed, founders are free to define in the statutes how board members are appointed, and they usually make the initial appointments. The power to appoint new board members can rest with the founder(s), with another natural or legal person, with the supervisory board of the foundation, or with the members of the board of directors (co-option system, also called a self-perpetuating board). Only a small number of countries have mandatory rules regarding board appointments. Only a few countries provide legislation detailing rules on quorum, voting, and minutes, whereas in other countries such rules are part of internal regulation (Hopt et al. 2006: 135).

The European laws do not generally provide for a system of inside and outside directors (as exists in the US), which may provide for more checks and balances within a board. Hence the tasks, interests, and approaches of European board members may be too homogeneous (Hopt 2009).

Remuneration of board members of public benefit foundations is allowed in half of the EFC surveyed countries. In most cases this is however subject to a notional restriction that the amount must be reasonable since the assets have to be used to pursue the public benefit purpose (Surmatz and Ibbotson 2015). In a small number of countries board remuneration is prohibited altogether (e.g. France and Spain; see also Hopt et al. 2006: 148; Van der Ploeg et al. 2017: 113ff, 333). Common law countries regard the role of charity trustees as a voluntary one since no direct or indirect benefit may derive from their position.

Supervisory Board

Some countries foresee a supervisory board to strengthen the internal control of the foundation and its governing board with the aim of guaranteeing that foundations fulfil their duties to pursue the public benefit purposes. Ten of the surveyed countries (Austria, Bulgaria, Czech Republic, Estonia, Italy, Poland, Portugal, Romania, Slovakia, and Ukraine) legally require some form of a supervisory body, the tasks of which usually include control over the governing board, as well as the appointment of an auditor and board members. Estonia and Portugal require all foundations to have a supervisory board in addition to a governing board. Four countries (Bulgaria, Italy, Poland, and Ukraine) oblige foundations with a public benefit status to have a supervisory board, while Czech Republic, Slovakia, and Hungary stipulate a supervisory body for larger foundations. In Hungary, the obligation to have a supervisory board applies only to organisations which both hold public benefit status and have budgets of a certain size. In Austria meanwhile, supervisory boards are only required for private foundations.

The role of such a supervisory body has not yet been analysed in a comparative or more systematic way. Although some countries require an additional supervisory board in order to control the governing board, no general consensus has been reached as to whether such an extra supervisory board should be regulated or recommended from a general European perspective, and whether the requirement of such a supervisory board could address some of the above-mentioned credibility and control issues.

Duty of Care/Duty of Loyalty of Board Members

Generally, the governing board has the task of properly managing the foundation and ensuring that the public benefit purpose is pursued and regulations are complied with. The board represents the foundation towards third parties. In most countries, this representation function may be delegated to a director or officers of the foundation. The duty of care and the duty of loyalty of board members are recognised in all surveyed countries and are part of the respective legal provisions even though not always explicitly mentioned.

The duty of loyalty relates to a perceived stewardship principle and arises out of the principal–agent theory and its application to the philanthropic foundation sector. The founders have not simply delegated the management to the board, but they have been superseded by the foundation itself. The board therefore is accountable to the foundation (and not to the founder or to the beneficiary, since in public benefit foundations neither of these can claim proprietary rights). Because the foundation owns itself and has no external owners/shareholders, controlling mechanisms become a crucial aspect of a foundation's functioning (EFC and DAFNE 2011; Van Veen 2008).

Experts describe the duty of loyalty as a normative attempt to counterbalance the natural self-interest of board members. The duty of loyalty is provided for within legislation, with rules inter alia on conflict of interest and non-distribution constraint. Legislation also regulates the remuneration of board members. As mentioned above, most countries set limitations on the extent to which board members may be remunerated, while remuneration is entirely prohibited in some countries.

The duty of care implies that board members must use their own skills to diligently manage the foundation. This duty is implemented by national legislation in different ways: board members must, according to the respective laws, ensure that the public benefit purpose is pursued, taking into account the deed, statutes, or law and the will of the founders. While board members have the right to amend foundations' statutes in the majority of countries, when doing so the foundation laws usually require that board members take into account the original will or intention of the founder. Members of the board are in most countries personally liable in cases of losses caused by (at least) grossly negligent acts or wilful defaults on their part (breach of duty). The liability of board members aims to ensure board members' duties of care and loyalty are enforceable, in particular the duty of proper management of foundations' activities and assets, and pursuance of their public benefit purposes (EFC and DAFNE 2011).

Role of the Executive Director and Staff

The laws generally only require public benefit foundations to have a governing board. The actual activity of running and governing an organisation is often executed by more people than the members of the governing board (Bethmann et al. 2014). In particular, executive staff play a key role in the governance of public benefit foundations, but they are mentioned only marginally in the laws. While board members often constitute the key governing bodies of an organisation, the senior management does the actual running of the organisation and often gets representation rights.

In practice, when it comes to corporate governance questions, actual responsibility does not always correspond to the legal allocation of duties and powers, which in fact lawyers consider 'disorderly situations' (Van Veen 2008). Bethmann et al. (2014) elaborate and apply a model of four governance patterns: the board-dominant model, the shared model, the staff-dominant model, and the bystander model.

Rights of Beneficiaries and Other Third Parties

There is no provision for the rights of beneficiaries and other third parties in most countries. Beneficiaries may receive information rights in a few countries (e.g. in Austria, Germany, Greece, Italy, and Switzerland), and third parties may receive these rights in a few countries as well (Netherlands, England, Wales, and the US) (Hopt et al. 2009: 70; Van Veen 2007: 267ff.).

External Governance Regulation

Governance of public benefit foundations as understood in a wider context also includes transparency, accountability, and external audit and supervision regulation. All EFC surveyed European countries have a minimum level of external supervision over foundations, however, the form and extent of supervision vary greatly (Van Veen 2007; Van der Ploeg et al. 2017: 145ff, 281ff). Tax-exempt foundations are usually subject to supervision by the tax authority, and most countries have non-tax related supervisory agencies with powers to inspect and intervene in management decisions, for instance in the case of mismanagement, and to dissolve a foundation in specific cases. Already in the creation phase of the legal entity some involvement of an external supervisory structure or a court is generally needed. In eighteen of the thirty EFC 2015 surveyed countries, state approval or court registration is required to set up a public benefit foundation. State approval or court registration guarantees that the legal requirements for the establishment of a foundation are checked and reviewed by a state authority or a court.

All thirty countries surveyed by the EFC require foundations to prepare annual reports and annual financial records, and most countries require them to be filed with the relevant authorities. However, there are great differences between the content and form of these reports and how these are submitted and checked (or not), and whether they are made available to the public, as well as the extent of reporting (e.g. whether an audited report is needed or not). So, while there is a general effort to introduce control mechanisms, there is heterogeneity in the approach and execution of those mechanisms.

The Public Benefit Status or Tax-exempt Status

The regulatory framework for the public benefit or tax status has implications for the external governance and supervision of foundations. To become tax-exempt, a foundation must share its information with either its country's tax authorities or (in cases of automatic exemption) the foundation authority. As both authorities act on behalf of the wider public, they have a vested interest in seeing to it that a foundation that receives tax exemptions actually pursues its public benefit purpose. In case a foundation does not pursue its public benefit purpose, it runs the risk of losing its public benefit status and tax exemptions. In the majority of European countries, foundations must request special recognition from the tax authority, and only in few cases is this automatic (i.e. granted in relation to the legal form of a foundation). Several countries have established a distinct 'public benefit' or 'charitable' status through separate acts that may confer obligations and benefits on the organisations with this status beyond tax exemptions (Van der Ploeg et al. 2017: 191ff, 298ff).

Generally, tax-exempt foundations have to provide evidence to the tax authorities through their financial or annual reports that the income is spent on public benefit purposes.

The tax law definition of a public benefit purpose will often include conditions related to the target group (e.g. the general public or a part of it, the needy or marginalised, etc.) and even conditions related to the dominance or exclusivity of pursuing these purposes (e.g. in the Netherlands, Germany, and the UK). In the vast majority of countries, foundations are required by law (in most cases by tax law) to follow a non-distribution constraint. This means that benefits cannot be distributed either directly or indirectly to any founder, donor, board member, or employee of the foundation. In almost all countries, it is regulated by law that the assets of a public benefit foundation cannot revert to private ownership upon its dissolution. In case of dissolution, the assets must be used for public benefit purposes. Most commonly, this is to take place through the transfer of the assets to another organisation with the same or similar purpose to that of the dissolved foundation. In seven of the countries surveyed by the EFC, the legislation also refers to a maximum that can be spent on administration costs. In an additional seven countries, administration costs must be 'reasonable' or 'bona fide'. In Germany, many of the local (state-level) foundation laws demand that administration costs should be as low as possible. In general, the tax exempt status defines a strict approach in terms of external governance of those organisations that seek it.

Increased Transparency: Registers and Beneficial Ownership Registers

Registration in some type of foundation or company register or a court is generally required. In most countries, public benefit foundations are logged in a register that is publicly available, giving access to key data on foundations, including details about the founder; the purpose, name, and registered office of the foundation; and in many cases the starting assets and the names of board members. Information about a dissolution is also frequently kept in the foundation register, or the foundation is removed from the register in case of dissolution. However, in some countries these registries, while they are public by law, are not easily accessible, especially where registration lies with the local courts (EFC and DAFNE 2011; Surmatz and Ibbotson 2015). So public accessibility is a relative category depending on the national rules.

With the 4th EU Anti Money Laundering Directive (Directive 2015/849 of 20 May 2015) and its implementation at the national level, publicly available registers of so-called 'beneficial owners' (BOs) of legal entities have been introduced throughout the EU. Policy-makers decided to make the BO concept applicable to legal entities and trusts whether for private or public interest. The BOs of different types of organisations are defined in Article 3 (6) of the Directive as any natural person(s) who ultimately owns or controls the customer and/or the natural person(s) on whose behalf a transaction or activity is being conducted. Since public benefit foundations have no external owners (they own themselves), the individuals who control foundations should be identified and listed. Hence, in the future, information about legal representatives are to be accessible in such BO registers.

Reporting and Access to Reports

Public benefit foundations are also required to prepare financial information and reports in all surveyed countries and in general must file this with one or more authorities (EFC and DAFNE 2011; Surmatz and Ibbotson 2015). More than half of the EFC surveyed countries also require the submission of a report on the activities of the foundation. In countries where a public benefit status exists, activity reporting is usually part of the annual report, in which there can be additional requirements relating to the use of budgetary resources or a demonstration of compliance with the public benefit status requirements. In a few countries such as Latvia and Spain, foundations are even required to submit an annual action plan to the administrative authority, in addition to their annual report. The majority of countries stipulate that foundations' financial or activity reports should be publicly available, with ten countries stipulating that all information disclosed to the authorities should also be in the public arena. However, in some countries (e.g. Austria, Germany, Latvia, Slovenia, and Turkey) reporting does not have to be made public, while in others only certain types of foundations are required to publish their reports. In summary, the requirements on which reports should be made available and shared with the general public greatly vary across countries.

Audit

External audit is mandatory for all foundations in seven of the EFC surveyed countries, and for practically all foundations in a further three countries. In twelve countries, a foundation's size determines whether it is subject to an audit. Size is most often determined by annual income and/or assets, and in some countries also by the number of people employed by the foundation. In a few countries, the type of foundation is the factor determining whether an audit would be required. There are only seven countries where there is no audit requirement at all (EFC and DAFNE 2011; Surmatz and Ibbotson 2015). This suggests that auditing is seen as a valid instrument of control in most of the EFC surveyed countries, especially for foundations of a certain size.

External Supervisory Authorities

External supervision of foundations established for public benefit purposes is generally more extensive than for private-purpose foundations. In some countries only foundations with a public benefit status are supervised, while tax-exempt foundations are generally supervised by the tax authorities. Most countries have a competent ministry entrusted with the supervision of foundations. Furthermore, courts play a supervisory role in many countries, but the supervisory powers of courts are usually limited to actions upon initiation of an interested third party or the public prosecutor (Surmatz and Ibbotson 2015). Only three countries are without specific legal or regulatory provisions to supervise foundations other than what is prescribed for any legal person.

The legal and procedural powers granted to state supervisory bodies vary greatly across the thirty EFC countries surveyed. For the most part, state supervisory bodies have the right to obtain information or to initiate inquiries. The board of a foundation must send annual reports and annual accounts to the relevant state supervisory authority as a means of preventive supervision (EFC 2015: 34–5). In some cases certain acts, governance decisions, or documents must be approved by the relevant authority. In nine of the countries, only limited powers are given to the supervisory authorities, such as courts acting upon requests from other stakeholders or public authorities with powers for receiving and reviewing annual reports. However, in other countries, the authorities have much greater powers to, among other things, undertake inspections on site; intervene in case of management failure; order the board to take a specific action; dismiss the board or its members; or appoint a 'commissioner' or new director (EFC 2015). It has been argued that such supervisory structures alone are not able to compensate for the lack of 'principal' with own self-interest (Hopt and Von Hippel 2010: 49).

The general public or third parties have no enforcement rights but may for example inform the supervisory authority about certain circumstances, and may also inform the police or state attorney in case of potential criminal acts. Thus though some level of control by external supervisory authorities is considered, the level of intervention rights and actions differ in the countries considered here.

Self-regulation and Own Practice

In addition to hard law, internal and external governance issues are shaped by self-regulatory efforts (Van Veen 2008; Van der Ploeg et al. 2017: 124ff). For the purposes of this chapter, self-regulation includes sector-designed regimes including the use of principles of good practice and initiatives promoting ethical codes of conduct instead of, or as a complement to, hard law. Research on the interaction between non-profit self-regulation and hard law has sought to unpack the relationship between the two modes of regulation and to better understand the factors prompting the adoption of one mode over the other and the basis for switching from soft to hard law (Breen et al. 2017; Breen 2018).

Since the early 1990s there has been a growing sector interest in self-regulatory frameworks. While the threat of government action and under-regulation were identified as drivers for self-regulation efforts, the impetus from public benefit foundations' side stems from the will of foundations to improve their governance, forge a professional and efficient sector, and even support learning and sharing of good practice and strengthen trust in the sector (EFC and DAFNE 2011). A regulatory gap and the wish to rebuild trust may be seen as a driver in some cases (Breen et al. 2017).

Advantages associated with self-regulation that come from the foundation sector itself have been described as:

(a) The direct relevance of the principles developed by and on behalf of the sector;
(b) More flexibility compared to hard law;
(c) An opportunity to raise governance standards more effectively than externally imposed compliance-based regulation that is based on a command and control model (EFC and DAFNE 2011);
(d) A tool to pre-empt the state introducing statutory regulation or inform the later statutory regulation adopted.

Disadvantages associated with self-regulatory codes are the lack of active monitoring of compliance levels and effective sanctions. Without the pressure of legal enforcement, low participant take-up rates can also lead to a lack of critical mass for the code's acceptance. Research has shown that state support is often crucial to the initial establishment of self-regulatory codes, as is the state's willingness to step in with regulation in the event that the self-regulatory code is unsuccessful. An interesting statutory power in this regard is the power of the Irish Charity Regulator under the Charities Act 2009 to approve existing self-regulatory codes, thereby 'promoting' a voluntary code developed by the sector (Breen 2018).

The 2011 study conducted by the EFC and the Donors and Foundations Networks of Europe (DAFNE) of self-regulatory regimes in twenty-four countries found some common features of the reviewed codes: they were mainly self-certifying, there was no active monitoring of compliance, and there was generally no certification procedure as such. The list of those who signed up to adhere to the codes of practice was generally published on a website. While many of the codes indicated that non-compliance with the code principles could incur sanction, only one DAFNE member reported having excluded a member for non-compliance with the self-regulatory mechanism (EFC and DAFNE 2011: 25). Anecdotal evidence suggests that self-regulatory codes have helped to clarify conditions for membership of national associations, have helped to raise professional standards, and are primarily perceived as motivating instruments encouraging self-reflection and performance improvement, rather than as compliance instruments (Breen 2018).

The codes analysed in the 2011 EFC and DAFNE report focused on issues relating to governance and management, reporting requirements, and ensuring proper use of funds. A number of codes also covered administration and overhead costs, board remuneration, 'know your beneficiary rules', and fiduciary principles relating to the control and use of funds. Guidance on governance and management was included in the majority of codes reviewed by the EFC/DAFNE report, and a number of them clearly even go beyond the hard law provisions. In terms of 'knowing your beneficiary' and 'knowing your donor', one could, however, argue that self-regulation has in part been overruled by the recent wave of hard law involving money laundering and terrorism financing legislation, which has put tighter controls on philanthropic and other money flows. Specific rules on human resource policies, diversity in board composition, and conflict of interest are also included in the majority of reviewed codes, in particular in countries where the hard law lacks conflict of interest rules.

Since hard law leaves quite some flexibility in terms of board composition, soft law approaches play an important role in giving some voluntary guidance to the foundation sector (Van Veen 2008). Board composition, beyond its size and independence, is a crucial element of good governance. Researchers and codes of conduct emphasise the benefits of including outsiders in the board as a means to assure objectivity when monitoring the management of the organisations (De Andrés-Alonso et al. 2010), though also arguing that given the voluntary role and lack of remuneration, it might be difficult to find engaged outsiders to fulfil such a role. Recent research argues that the cumulative nature and heterogeneity of the knowledge of the board have a positive effect on the foundation's efficiency (De Andrés-Alonso et al. 2010; Boesso et al. 2015). The philanthropy sector certainly has enlarged its toolkit of actions and evolved from grant-giving to more complex grant making and operational strategies. The board composition and diverse experience of board members hence becomes an even more crucial element in order for a board to be able to perform its more demanding strategic role. While foundation practice seems to be taking this on as a natural development, this has only to a limited extent found its way into self-regulation approaches. Referring to the idea of different governance models for public benefit foundations with more participatory or external elements in decision-making, it is also interesting to note that in 2011 only very few codes recommended that foundations should involve (potential) grantees or beneficiaries in programme design or evaluation, but this may have moved in the meantime. It appears that given the great variety of philanthropic actors and approaches, no one-size-fits-all approach would ever work, and regulatory and self-regulatory approaches are advised to continue to leave enough flexibility and openness.

From the foundations' perspective, self-regulatory mechanisms already seem to have increased transparency, accountability, and good governance standards, and have also enhanced the level of trust in and credibility of the sector among stakeholders and society (EFC and DAFNE 2011).

EU-level Attempts to Design Soft Law Approaches with Relevance for Corporate Governance

The European Commission has made some attempts to enter the 'soft law' framework for the entire non-profit sector operating in the EU. In 2005 the Commission issued a Communication (The Prevention of and Fight Against Terrorist Financing through Enhanced National Level Coordination and Greater Transparency of the Non-Profit Sector, COM (2005) 620 final), recommending a Framework for a Code of Conduct to enhance transparency and accountability of NPOs and to reduce the risk of abuse of the non-profit sector. The actual provisions related to the need for registration of NPOs and the proper keeping of accounts. Despite subsequent European Council endorsement of the Code and Commission attempts to encourage widespread application, implementation has been sporadic (Breen 2018).

Building on its 2005 Framework for a Code of Conduct, the Commission issued a 4-page discussion paper to a select group of invited NGOs and Member State representatives at a conference in 2010. The discussion paper identified six specific areas for guidance, namely: a) basic principles for good NPO practice; b) good governance; c) accountability and transparency; d) relations to the donor; e) relations to the beneficiary; and f) suspicious activity reporting. The principles were aimed at entities that use their assets 'exclusively for charitable or other legitimate purposes' and whose activities are 'directed towards the attainment of the organisation's stated public benefit goals' (Breen 2018). To date, these guidelines have not been published in the form of a Commission Communication and have hence not played any directional role.

Hard Law versus Soft Law and Internal versus External—No One-Size-Fits-All

The design elements of internal and external governance of public benefit foundations found in various hard law and soft law frameworks are based on legal cultures and traditions that vary across the different countries. It is hence hardly possible to do an overall assessment of whether the systems work, or if there is a need for more hard law regulation or governance codes. Some issues may nonetheless be highlighted.

Internal corporate governance questions are less regulated by hard law, and apart from establishing a governing board, there is flexibility in the design of the internal governance structure. There are however limitations to this flexibility to avoid the dominant influence of the founder(s), and conflict of interest rules for board members exist in many countries. One additional quite common requirement is collective governance (i.e. boards composed of more than one person) in order to ensure appropriate checks and balances in the decision-making process. Currently, just over half of European countries require more than one person on the board of the public benefit foundation, and in a number of countries a collective board structure is suggested by the self-regulatory mechanisms used by foundations. Only a few countries require a supervisory board structure, a control organ that some researchers argue could provide additional checks and balances in public benefit foundations (von Schönfeld 2018: 147). Generally, the laws and soft laws focus on governing board elements and do not pay attention to the executive staff, which actually runs and governs the organisation in most cases. Governance and management requirements if included in self-regulatory mechanisms are generally not enforced and continue also to depend, within the remit of the law, on the ethical behaviour of the board and executive staff.

From an external governance perspective, during the creation process, the hard law generally requires a (non-discretionary) act involving a public authority or court to obtain legal personality, which includes a cross-check that legal requirements (including the creation of the appropriate governance structure) are met. In this process, foundations are accountable to the involved authority (legal and/or tax) and the general public. During its lifetime a foundation is in most countries regularly monitored to ensure that the requirements for its specific status are met (by tax authorities, supervisory authorities, or in some cases even the general public if they have access to certain types of information). Supervisory authorities generally monitor compliance with the law and whether the public benefit purpose is pursued. They also monitor whether governance requirements are lawfully implemented and whether reporting and auditing are undertaken (EFC and DAFNE 2011). How comprehensively these supervisory structures are able to work given budget cuts in the public sector goes beyond the scope of this chapter.

The hard law generally appears to provide sufficient protection for creditors (EFC and DAFNE 2011), but are mechanisms to prevent mismanagement and abuse sufficient? As mentioned above, foundations often do not have a 'built-in' mechanism to control against abuse within their internal governance structure since they have no owners or shareholders who would have a vested interest—i.e. direct incentives—to protect the organisation. It is especially after the foundation is formed that the will of the founder needs further support or protection, and mechanisms to prevent mismanagement and abuse must function. Initial analysis (EFC and DAFNE 2011) suggests that existing regulation (a combination of transparency and accountability regulation and external supervisory structures) provides for a system of control over foundations and their governing bodies that takes the specific governance structure into account. The duty of loyalty of board members is expressed in a number of ways, including by conflict of interest rules, non-distribution constraint, and limitation of remuneration of board members. The duty of care of board members is also implemented by national legislation: when changing the statutes, the will of the founder generally needs to be taken into account, and members of the boards are in most countries personally liable in cases of losses caused by (at least) grossly negligent acts or wilful defaults on their part (breach of duty). It therefore appears that national foundation laws provide for a regulatory framework with regard to governance and duties of board members, which play a significant role in ensuring accountability and control of foundations.

In addition, external supervisory structures are important mechanisms for control of the governing board and for the prevention of mismanagement and abuse. The authority acts on behalf of various stakeholders (founder, beneficiaries, donors, the public at large), which all have a legitimate interest in the proper management of the foundation. In many countries with stricter transparency requirements, where annual activity reports and annual financial statements are publicly available, the public at large also ensures that a foundation pursues its public benefit purpose in line with the will of the founder.

Where the foundation receives tax exemption, the tax authorities, when checking requirements of tax exemption, also play a role in preventing abuse and mismanagement.

Some national legislation foresees that internal control mechanisms be developed through supervisory boards. Several researchers and practitioners argue in favour of requiring such an additional supervisory organ (von Schönfeld 2018: 149). An international study in the context of developing a European supranational legal form for foundations suggested a supervisory board for larger foundations (Hopt et al. 2006). Since the effectiveness of such supervisory boards has been questioned and there are additional costs and administration involved, it may appear advisable not to include this as a hard law requirement but rather promote it as an optional soft law measure for larger organisations (the latter currently already being suggested in several countries' soft law approaches). The hard law could be accompanied by governance codes, and potentially supervision could be reduced if the governance codes work well (Van Veen 2008).

Finally, many foundations have integrated transparency and accountability into their management practices, usually beyond legislative requirements (EFC and DAFNE 2011). The general public cannot however rely on this since it is simply an autonomous decision of the foundation to conduct itself in this way.

To sum up, it appears that given the great variety of philanthropic actors and approaches, no one-size-fits-all approach would ever work, and regulatory and self-regulatory approaches are advised to continue to leave enough flexibility and openness. Some researchers also argue that strict governance regulation may hinder foundations' flexibility in reacting quickly to changing environments (Bethmann et al. 2014).

Conclusion

From a theoretical point of view, the classical principal–agent theory is not suitable for public benefit foundations. Hence a more comprehensive principal–agent theory of public benefit foundations, which combines agency theory elements with aspects of a cognitive dimension, stewardship theory, and empirical data on the governance and management of public benefit foundations, should be further developed and tested. Governance codes appear to follow a stewardship point of view, where the starting point is not the premises of intrinsic self-interest of directors, but rather promoting the functioning of boards and enhancing public trust, based on the conviction that public benefit foundations can fulfil their mission if they are transparent and trusted. Such theoretical approaches should also take into account and analyse the effectiveness of external governance mechanisms such as reporting regulations, external audits, state oversight, and the role of executive staff in foundation governance as suggested above.

The design elements of internal and external governance of public benefit foundations found in various hard law and soft law frameworks are based on legal cultures and traditions that vary across the different countries. Given the great variety of different types of organisations, a tight one-size-fits-all approach does not seem feasible either for hard law or for soft law approaches. This chapter concludes that in a European context generally the interplay of hard law and soft law as well as internal and external governance elements seems to provide appropriate governance approaches for different cultural contexts.

Given the specific structure of public benefit foundations, as entities without owners, members, or shareholders, external governance mechanisms such as reporting requirements, audits, and state or court supervision play a role in protecting the will of the founder, the pursuance of the public benefit purpose, and conformity with statutes and the law and prevention of abuse.

Internal corporate governance questions are less regulated by hard law, and, apart from establishing a governing board, there is a level of flexibility to design the internal governance structure. Soft law approaches, which further outline good practice for independent governance and sound management as well as transparency and accountability approaches, could be further developed and strengthened. Consideration could be given to optional elements of participatory grantmaking and two-tier structures with additional supervisory boards for larger foundations. If self-regulation becomes stronger on governance questions, potentially external governance elements may play a lesser role in the future.

References

Anheier, H. K. (2018). 'Philanthropic Foundations in Cross-national Perspectives: A Comparative Approach', *American Behavioral Scientist*, 62(12): 1591–1602.

Anheier, H. K. and Leat, D. (2013). 'Philanthropic Foundations: What Rationales', *Social Research*, 80(2): 449–72.

Anheier, H. K. and Leat, D. (2006). *Creative Philanthropy: Toward a New Philanthropy for the Twenty-First Century*. Abingdon and New York: Routledge.

Anheier, H. K. and Then, V. (eds.) (2004). *Zwischen Eigennutz und Gemeinwohl, neue Formen und Wege der Gemeinnützigkeit*. Gütersloh: Verlag Bertelsmann Stiftung.

Bernholz, L., Cordelli, C., and Reich, R. (eds.) (2016). *Philanthropy in Democratic Societies: History, Institutions, Values*. Chicago: University of Chicago Press.

Bethmann, S., von Schnurbein, G., and Studer, S. (2014). 'Governance Systems of Grantmaking Foundations', *Voluntary Sector Review*, 5: 75–95.

Boesso, G., Cerbioni, F., Menini, A., and Parbonetti, A. (2015). 'Philanthropy by Decree: Exploring the Governance and Philanthropic Strategies of Foundations of Banking Origin', *Nonprofit Management & Leadership*, 25(3): 197–213.

Breen, O. B. (2018). *Enlarging the Space for European Philanthropy*. Brussels: European Foundation Centre and Donors and Foundations Networks in Europe.

Breen, O. B., Dunn, A., and Sidel, M. (eds.) (2017). *Regulatory Waves: Comparative Perspectives on State Regulation and Self-Regulation Policies in the Nonprofit Sector*. Cambridge: Cambridge University Press.

Caers, R., Du Bois, C., Jegers, M., De Gieter, S., Schepers, C., and Pepermans, R. (2006). 'Principal-Agent Relationships on the Steward-Agency Axis', *Nonprofit Management & Leadership*, 17(1): 25–47.

Charreaux, G. (2005). 'Pour une gouvernance d'entreprise "comportementale"', *Revue Française de gestion*, 31: 215–38.

Cornforth, C. (2012). 'Non-profit Governance Research: Limitations of the Focus on Boards and Suggestions for New Directions', *Non-profit and Voluntary Sector Quarterly*, 41(6): 1116–35.

De Andrés-Alonso, P., Azofra-Palenzuela, V., and Romero-Merino, M. E. (2010). 'Beyond the Disciplinary Role of Governance: How Boards Assess Value to Spanish Foundations', *British Journal of Management*, 21(1): 100–14.

Donaldson, L. and Davis, J. H. (1991). 'Stewardship Theory or Agency Theory: CEO Governance and Shareholder Returns', *Australian Journal of Management*, 16(1): 49–64.

Ebrahim, A. (2010). *Handbook of Non-profit Leadership and Management* (3rd edition). San Francisco: Jossey-Bass.

European Commission (2017). 'Report from the Commission to the European Parliament and the Council on the assessment of the risks of money laundering and terrorist financing affecting the internal market and relating to cross-border activities'. COM(2017) 340 final. Brussels.

European Foundation Centre (EFC) (2015). *Comparative Highlights of Foundation Laws*. Brussels: European Foundation Centre.

European Foundation Centre (EFC) and Donors and Foundations Networks in Europe (DAFNE) (2011). *Exploring Transparency and Accountability: Regulation of Public-benefit Foundations in Europe*. Brussels: European Foundation Centre.

Fleishman, J. L. (2007). *The Foundation. A Great American Secret: How Private Wealth Is Changing the World*. New York: Public Affairs.

Hammack, D. C. and Anheier, H. K. (2013). *A Versatile American Institution: The Changing Ideals and Realities of Philanthropic Foundations*. Washington, D.C.: Brookings Institution Press.

Harrow, J. (2011). 'Governance and Isophormism in Local Philanthropy', *Public Management Review*, 13(1): 1–20.

Hopt, K. J. (2009). 'The Board of Non-profit Organizations: Some Corporate Governance Thoughts from Europe', European Corporate Governance Institute—Law Working Paper No. 125/2009.

Hopt, K. J. and von Hippel, T. (eds.) (2010). *Comparative Corporate Governance of Non-Profit Organisations*. Cambridge, UK: Cambridge University Press.

Hopt, K. J., von Hippel, T., Anheier, H. K., Then, V., Ebke, W., Reimer, E., and Vahlpahl, T. (2009). *Feasibility Study on a European Foundation Statute. Final Report*. Heidelberg; Max Planck Institute for Comparative and International Private Law and University of Heidelberg, Centre of Social Investment and Investigation.

Hopt, K. J., Walz, W. R., von Hippel, T., and Then, V. (eds.) (2006). *The European Foundation—A New Legal Approach*. Cambridge: Cambridge University Press.

Hopt K. J., von Hippel, T., and Walz, W. R. (eds.) (2005). *Non-Profit Organisationen in Recht, Wirtschaft und Gesellschaft*. Tübingen: Mohr-Siebeck.

Jakob, D. (2006). *Schutz der Stiftung*. Tübingen: Mohr-Siebeck.

Jensen, M. C. and Meckling, W. H. (1976). 'Theory of the Firm: Managerial Behavior, Agency Costs and Ownership Structure', *Journal of Financial Economics*, 3(4): 305–60.

Leat, D. (1994). *Challenging Management: An Exploratory Study of Perceptions of Managers Who Have Moved from For-profit to Voluntary Organisations*. London: Centre for Voluntary Sector and Non-profit Management, City University School of Business.

Prewitt, K., Dogan, M., Heydemann, S., and Toepler, S. (eds.) (2006). *The Legitimacy of Philanthropic Foundations: United States and European Perspectives*. New York: Russell Sage Foundation.

Rey-Garcia, M., Martin-Cavanna, J., and Alvarez-Gonzalez, L. I. (2012). 'Assessing and Advancing Foundation Transparency: Corporate Foundations as a Case Study', *Foundation Review*, 4(3): 77–89.

Romaniuk, P. and Keatinge, T. (2018). 'Protecting Charities from Terrorists…and Counterterrorists: FATF and the Global Effort to Prevent Terrorist Financing Through the Non-profit Sector', *Crime, Law and Social Change*, 69(2): 265–82.

Sandberg, B. (2007). *Stand und Perspektiven des Stiftungsmanagements in Deutschland: eine empirische Studie zur betriebswirtschaftlichen Orientierung von Stiftungen*. Berlin: Berliner Wissenschafts-Verlag.

Surmatz, H. and Ibbotson N. (2015). 'Summary Analysis', in European Foundation Centre, *Comparative Highlights of Foundation Laws: The Operating Environment for Foundations in Europe*. Brussels: European Foundation Centre, 8–14.

Thymm, N. (2007). *Kontrollproblem der Stiftung und die Rechtsstellung der Destinatäre*. Erlangen: Carl Heymanns Verlag.

Van der Ploeg, T. J., Van Veen, W. J. M., and Versteegh, C. R. M. (eds.) (2017). *Civil Society in Europe, Minumum Norms and Optimum Conditions of its Regulation*. Cambridge: Cambridge University Press.

Van Veen, W. J. M. (2010). 'Comparing Regulation of Fundraising: Self-regulation or Government Regulation?', in K. J. Hopt and T. von Hippel (eds.), *Comparative Corporate Governance of Non-Profit Organisations*. Cambridge, UK: Cambridge University Press, 662–98.

Van Veen, W. J. M. (2008). 'Corporate Governance for Non-Profit Organisations—A Legal Approach', in H. Kohl, F. Kübler, C. Ott, and K. Schmidt (eds.), *Zwischen Markt und Staat, Gedächtnisschrift für Rainer Walz*. Köln: Carl Heymanns Verlag, 757–68.

Van Veen, W. J. M. (2007). 'Stiftungsaufsicht in Europa', in A. Richter and T. Wachter (eds.), *Handbuch des Internationalen Stiftungsrechts*. Bonn: Nomos and Zerb Verlag, 257–99.

Van Veen, W. J. M. (2004). 'Public Benefit Law from a Comparative Perspective', in P. Bater, F. W. Hondius, and P. K. Lieber (eds.), *The Tax Treatment of NGOs*. Alphen aan den Rijn: Kluwer Law International, 239–52.

Von Hippel, T. (2007). 'Grundprobleme von Nonprofit-Organisationen/Key problems of non-profit organisations', Tübingen. Presented as Habilitation (professor thesis) to the Hamburg University Law faculty in 2005/2006.

Von Schönfeld, F. (2018). 'Zur Notwendigkeit eines Aufsichtsorgans in großen gemeinnützigen Organisationen [The Need for a Supervisory Body in Large Charitable Organisations]', in Bucerius Law School, *Non Profit Law Yearbook 2017*. München: C.H. Beck, 127–60.

Von Schönfeld, F. (2017). *Leitungs- und Kontrollstrukturen in gemeinnützigen Organisationen*. Hamburg: Bucerius Law School Press.

Walkenhorst, P. (ed.) (2008). *Building Philanthropic and Social Capital: The Work of Community Foundations*. Gütersloh: Verlag Bertelsmann Stiftung.

Wijkström, F. (2001). 'Om svenska stiftelser', in H. Westlund (ed.), *Social ekonomi i Sverige*. Stockholm: Nordsteds, 257–77.

7

Non-profit Governance

Gemma Donnelly-Cox, Michael Meyer, and Filip Wijkström

Non-profit organisations (NPOs) are actors at the local, national, and transnational level. Now more than ever, they play important roles in our societies.[1] For the past several decades, issues of legitimacy and representativeness as well as matters of accountability and responsibility have come to the forefront, raising crucial questions about non-profits' internal governance as well as their external relations with government, for-profit corporations, and affected groups of stakeholders and constituencies. Members, donors, volunteers, employees, and clients have always had claims on how the organisations are run. With the rolling back of the state and government solutions in many countries during the 1980s and 1990s, the non-profit sector has experienced a period of continuous economic growth in most western societies. At the same time, non-profit and voluntary organisations have also become exposed to new types and new levels of critique and scrutiny from internal as well as external sources and actors.

For non-profit actors, governance has emerged as a multi-level phenomenon. It stretches from polycentric governance of highly complex economic systems (Ostrom 2010), multi-level governance running well beyond the nation-state (e.g. Bache and Chapman 2008; Ruzza 2004), and the role of non-profits within multi-level systems (see e.g. section 5 in Cornforth and Brown 2014), to co-governance (e.g. Bode 2006; Cheng 2018), governance exercised in networks (Provan and Kenis 2008; Sørensen and Torfing 2005), and organisational governance. While in this chapter we will focus on organisational governance for non-profit and voluntary organisations

---

[1] To define a non-profit organisation, we use the widely accepted Johns Hopkins Comparative Nonprofit Sector Project definition (Salamon and Anheier 1997: 33f) which incorporates five elements: organised, private, self-governing, the non-distribution constraint, and voluntary. Non-profits are formal organisations (statutes, structure, membership regulations) in a position of control of their own decisions; they are separate from government as well as from individual for-profit corporations; they can keep their profits and reinvest them to serve their mission; and they involve a meaningful degree of voluntary participation to govern and run the organisation.

Gemma Donnelly-Cox, Michael Meyer, and Filip Wijkström, *Non-profit Governance* In: *Advances in Corporate Governance: Comparative Perspectives.* Edited by: Helmut K. Anheier and Theodor Baums, Oxford University Press (2020).
© Hertie School.
DOI: 10.1093/oso/9780198866367.003.0007

(i.e. non-profit governance), it is important to keep the wider picture in mind (cf. Reuter, Wijkström, and Meyer 2014), as many elements of non-profit governance are both empirically and theoretically influenced by what is happening at these other levels and inspired by developments in these other domains.

The chapter is structured as follows. First, we provide an overview of the development of the governance concept and its application to non-profits. Second, we examine the role of constituencies or stakeholders, i.e. different groups of actors whose interests in a NPO should be balanced and integrated in organisational decision-making, as discussed in academic literature. Third, we sketch out some of the most distinctive theoretical positions identified in non-profit governance. Fourth, we provide a brief outline of the various models of good organisational governance that have emerged in the field of non-profits. We end with a brief discussion and outlook of upcoming issues in non-profit governance.

History and Perspectives of Non-profit Governance

We begin with an outline of some of the recent history of non-profit governance in studies on non-profit management discourse and in non-profit research. All the questions that governance is expected to answer existed in non-profits long before the notion of governance appeared: it is about power dynamics, how to steer the organisation, and how to integrate different interests into decision-making. Until the 1990s, however, these questions were discussed under different headings in the literature. One interesting and early alternative way to conceptualise this dimension of the NPO would be to understand its governance as 'the government of associations' (Glaser and Sills 1966). The first applications of the term governance as a way to steer non-profits and to balance tensions between board, management, and external actors, however, dates back to the early 1990s (Abzug et al. 1993; Drucker 1990).

Besides organisational internal needs and demands for governance, isomorphic patterns (DiMaggio and Powell 1983) have accelerated the spread of organisational practices. Governance in non-profits appeared as a topic of increased interest on the agenda almost simultaneously with the peak in interest in corporate, i.e. for-profit, governance (see, for example, the seminal publications of Alexander and Weiner 1998; Saidel and Harlan 1998; Zingales 1998). At the same time, the discussion of accountability of non-profits gained momentum (Bogart 1995; Fama and Jensen 1983b; Young, Bania, and Bailey 1996). In addition to isomorphic processes, the importance of the idea of 'residual claimants' and key themes such as the separation of ownership and control (Fama and Jensen 1983b), substitution of trust by control (Ortmann and Schlesinger 1997), and the transformation from choice to contract (Williamson 2002) have all contributed strongly to the growing discussion of non-profit governance that took off at the beginning of the new millennium.

In most countries, NPOs have been positioned in the space or opening between the state, the household sector, and the market. They organise people on the basis of relations other than that of citizens, family members, or customers. They contribute to the production and delivery of goods and services that are neither provided by actors on the market nor in family settings nor by the government. They are found in arrangements supporting the state or government as agents in many fields, e.g. in health care, social services, arts and culture, and sports, or contributing through advocacy and community-building for the common good (Neumayr and Meyer 2010). They are political actors pushing and lobbying both national governments and for-profit corporations around the world to change the agenda and to further their missions (Boli and Thomas 1999; Walker 1983). Traditionally, economists have been able to explain the existence of a third or non-profit sector by failure performance models (Hammack and Young 1993; Badelt 1990), where NPOs are understood to respond to market and state failures and fill these gaps. A close proximity to the governmental sector has become reality in many countries, and public funding in different forms is now an essential resource for many NPOs (Pennerstorfer and Neumayr 2017; Saglie and Sivesind 2018).

Consequently, the NPO world is touched by both strands of broader governance theory: (1) political science-oriented governance and (2) organisational, i.e. corporate, governance (Renz and Andersson 2014; Steen-Johnsen, Eynaud, and Wijkström 2011; Wijkström and Reuter 2015). In political science and policy-making, the concept of governance emerged as an answer to the increasing complexity of political actors and networks (Anheier 2013). Governance has become an issue of increasing relevance at different levels of political policy-making, as the concept integrates non-state actors that participate in generating regulations (e.g. Ansell and Gash 2008; Pierre and Peters 2000; Rhodes 2007; Risse 2013; Sahlin et al. 2015; Stoker 1998). In this very general sense, governance refers to all modes of coordinating social action in society, e.g. by markets, hierarchies, or networks (Williamson 1975).

In a more narrow sense, concentrating on the political system, governance has come to mean the 'various institutionalized modes of social coordination to produce and implement collectively binding rules, or to provide public goods' (Risse 2013: 9). Hereby, the focus shifts from actors and structures to networks and processes. In Europe, the recent experience of European integration and the increasingly complex interplay of governmental and non-governmental actors at supranational, national, regional, municipal, and local level have contributed to the fostering and development of the concept of multi-level governance (e.g. Bache and Chapman 2008; Eising 2004). European policy-makers learned from the critique of a democratic deficit and actively encouraged both research on multi-level governance and non-profits building umbrella organisations that could participate in the European Commission's efforts in various policy fields.

At the level of organisations, corporate governance has a longer tradition and is closely related to the development of shareholder capitalism. Morck and Steier (2005) conclude—based on an international comparison of financial history in Canada, China, France, Germany, India, Italy, Japan, the Netherlands, Sweden, the United Kingdom, and the United States—that the history of corporate governance is path dependent. In some countries, financial collapses resulted in a distaste for financial markets, as is reported for France. Others, such as Britain, underwent financial crises and responded by regulating but sustaining financial markets. The US pioneered the transition from family capitalism to shareholder capitalism, and consequently was in the vanguard of introducing corporate governance regulations. More recently, the scandal surrounding Enron, an American energy company that systematically defrauded its shareholders (Healy and Palepu 2003; McLean and Elkind 2013), accelerated the global spread of corporate governance regulations. In the US, Enron's bankruptcy led to the passage of the Sarbanes-Oxley Act (SOX) in 2002. SOX is nearly 'a mirror image of Enron: the company's perceived corporate governance failings are matched virtually point for point in the principal provisions of the Act' (Deakin and Konzelmann 2004: 134). According to Google©-Trends, corporate governance peaked as a search term in the early years of the new millennium.[2]

These developments spilled over to the non-profit sector, meeting strong internal demands there and building an intense flow of discourse. SOX has also had consequences for non-profits (Mulligan 2007; Saxton and Neely 2019; Yallapragada, Roe, and Tomas 2010), and it has been argued that it has

---

[2] https://trends.google.com/trends/explore?date=all&q=Corporate%20Governance; 12 August 2019.

functioned as a blueprint also for the non-profit sector, but the fact that the sector's 'growing significance and reliance on public funds has also attracted increased scrutiny' (Cornforth 2014: 1) also played a central role. In research as well as practice, the composition of boards, board roles, responsibilities, and effectiveness as well as the relationship between boards and managers have emerged as the major topics. Thus, the discussion of non-profit governance in the early 2000s closely mirrored the mainstream of corporate governance issues and was initially coined and conceptualised primarily by US scholarship. It was within the European perspective that the distinction between organisational governance and governance at a societal level was identified and introduced (e.g. Hodges 2005; Osborne 2010; Steen-Johnsen, Eynaud, and Wijkström 2011; Wijkström and Reuter 2015), due to the strong intertwining of the public and the non-profit sector found in many European countries.

Meanwhile, relevant research has continued to broaden the field of non-profit governance studies significantly (Renz and Andersson 2014). The field now also comprises individual roles and actors in boards; board composition, roles, practices, and effectiveness; the embeddedness of governance within organisations and hybrid forms of organisations; network governance; and the role of non-profits and voluntary associations in societal governance.

Understandings of non-profit governance vary widely. Unsurprisingly, the academic fault lines run along disciplines and theories. In non-profit practice, conceptions of governance vary across countries, which tends to increase the complexity. At least three academic disciplines offer a particular set of perspectives on governance and civil society: economics, sociology, and political science. With a few notable exceptions (e.g. Stone and Ostrower 2007), these perspectives have been used in splendid isolation (Maier and Meyer 2011).

From an economics perspective, non-profit governance is understood as a particular form of corporate governance (e.g. Jegers 2009; Speckbacher 2008; Young 2011). The core question addressed is which stakeholders make valuable and specific investments in NPOs that are not sufficiently protected by contracts. It is argued that their residual rights of control should be protected by governance mechanisms such as boards, legal protection, or the standardisation of outputs.

The sociological perspective, mainly developed in organisation studies, points to governance structure, embracing formal goals, ownership, distribution of residual claims, decision-making procedures, control and accountability mechanisms, and embedded incentives (Enjolras 2009; Rhodes 2007). It is argued that governance systems should foster collective action and emphasise collective ownership, democratic checks and balances, a broad range of incentives, and participatory procedures (Enjolras 2009; LeRoux 2009).

The political science (public policy) perspective introduces the macro concept of 'new' and 'soft' governance to emphasise the reduced influence of traditional government and the shift of responsibilities in many cases for public policy implementation to non-governmental actors. Governance thus comprises the formal authority as well as the informal exercise of judgement by numerous actors involved in both advocating and implementing public policies and programmes (Lynn, Heinrich, and Hill 2000: 4; Blomgren Bingham, Nabatchi, and O'Leary 2005; Heinrich and Lynn 2000; Liou 2001).

As a common denominator of these different approaches, we understand governance as 'the system and processes concerned with ensuring the overall direction, control, and accountability of an organization' (Renz and Andersson 2014: 18). Non-profit governance practice shows considerable differences according to national contexts. If the focus of research serves as an indicator, US/Anglo-Saxon notions of governance tend to concentrate on board governance of NPOs and their relations with executive staff (Bradshaw 2002, 2009; Ostrower and Stone 2006, 2010; Saidel and Harlan 1998; Zimmermann and Stevens 2008). This stands in stark contrast to governance practice in many European countries, especially in northern Europe, where many organisations in civil society are democratically governed membership organisations (Enjolras 2009: 769).

Beyond this, there are vibrant discussions within the legal studies in many countries. In Germany, for instance, the Institute for Foundation Law and the Law of Non-Profit-Organisations, initiated at Bucerius Law School in Hamburg, contributes remarkably to legal aspects of non-profit governance (e.g. Leuschner 2016; Hasenpflug 2011), especially to foundation governance (Voigt de Oliveira and Wendt 2012). Hereby many suggestions have been made regarding how to shape governance systems and codes (Gräwe 2013; Kalss 2014). As legal forms and tools differ so much between countries and their legal systems, we will not go into detail on this discussion here.

Context and Constituencies

In this chapter so far, we have teased out the influence of both political science-derived and corporate governance theory contexts on the concept of non-profit governance. We now turn our focus to constituencies, the different groups of actors whose interests in an NPO are to be balanced and integrated in organisational decision-making. Amongst scholars who have invested considerable effort to carve out and conceptualise the particularities of non-profit governance, a common point of departure has been to consider the influence of various stakeholders and the ways in which they contribute to the distinctiveness of non-profit governance. Multiple constituencies or stakeholders, it is argued, contribute to the complexity and distinctiveness of the non-profit governance task (Stone 1996), and they are also central to the conduct of 'good governance' (Anheier 2013).

A useful starting point for addressing stakeholders is to consider what these approaches bring to our understanding of non-profit governance. The stakeholder approach taken by Speckbacher (2008) focuses not on the mechanisms of governance at the outset, but rather on the particular problems—in his analysis, economic—that are solved by a stakeholder approach to non-profit governance. He then identifies the rules or institutional arrangements that equate with good governance (Speckbacher 2008: 298).

Themes of effectiveness, efficiency, and accountability arise repeatedly throughout the stakeholder literature. Herman and Renz (1997) have emphasised that multiple constituencies beyond organisational decision-makers make judgements of organisational effectiveness, such that the effectiveness of the organisation cannot be assessed independent of multiple stakeholder judgements (Herman and Renz 1997: 202). This has implications for how the organisation communicates with its various stakeholders, as well as for the approaches boards take to evaluating organisational effectiveness (Herman and Renz 1997: 203). One dimension of effectiveness is stakeholder management, and one way of managing multiple and diverse stakeholder perceptions and perspectives is to attempt to align them (Wellens and Jegers 2014).

Addressees of accountability in NPOs differ significantly from public and business organisations, as do the ways that accountability is established and achieved (Dicke and Ott 1999; Young, Bania, and Bailey 1996). Non-profits are accountable not only to those constituencies that provide them with resources (governments, donors, members, volunteers, etc.), but also towards beneficiaries and towards their overall mission. Usually, research differentiates between upward and downward accountability (e.g., Hug and Jäger 2014). Most obviously, balancing these directions of accountability in governance is a tough challenge for NPOs (Ebrahim 2005, 2009).

Themes beyond accountability and effectiveness addressed through stakeholder approaches include collaborative and network arrangements. For example, stakeholder approaches may be applied in understanding how key actors in non-profit–public sector collaboration respond to important internal tensions (Cornforth, Hayes, and Vangen 2015).

A factor that further increases the complexity of conceptualising stakeholders in non-profit governance research is the large variety of non-profit forms, including charities, foundations, membership associations, social businesses, and the like. With different organisational types come different stakeholder groupings and implications and varying stakeholder demands (Leroux, 2009), for example, the central but ambiguous role assigned to members in many large, federative organisations (S. Einarsson 2012; T. Einarsson 2012; Skocpol 2003).

Different NPOs and their governance systems have to fulfil not only upward and downward accountabilities to funders and beneficiaries, but also various kinds of horizontal accountabilities towards different member groups, membership types, employees, volunteers, donors, etc. at the same time as actually fulfilling their mission. It is therefore not surprising to see that different scholars have been arguing for different focus and weight to different groups of beneficiaries or stakeholders, pointing to the fact that a variety of governing combinations may be required in different types of NPOs (Young 2011). The matter of who has a legitimate claim on the non-profit is actually one of the most important distinguishing factors separating different governance theories or approaches from each other, as we will see in the next section.

An important point of departure for us is therefore that non-profit governance cannot be easily pressed into the Procrustean bed of corporate governance without the risk of hurting the organisations and even running the risk of neglecting specific constituencies.

Theoretical Approaches and Discourses

The study of non-profit and voluntary organisations and their ways to organise and go about their activities has often been conducted in the domestic, often legally defined context where the particular organisations of interest reside. This is of course important in order to understand the organisations and their behaviour in the local setting, but it has so far been difficult to draw more generalised organisation theory lessons from this line of research, especially when addressing the matter of governance. In this section we briefly outline three major and popular theoretical approaches of a more general character which have been applied in the growing literature aimed at addressing non-profit governance. Although less contextually biased than other types of study, these approaches however still widely mirror theories of corporate, for-profit governance in the way they have been dealt with in many earlier non-profit governance studies.

The theoretical godfather of corporate governance is agency theory, an approach which has recently been used also for understanding and developing NPOs. Most visibly, this theory has been propelled into non-profit studies through the application of the very influential classical principal–agent version (Jegers 2009; Steinberg 2008), but also through the modified stewardship approach (Caers et al. 2006; Donaldson and Davis 1991). Stakeholder theory has also been suggested as a useful frame for understanding non-profit governance (Wellens and Jegers 2014; Speckbacher 2008; Young 2011). Often, these clearly normative approaches have provided recommendations for the design of governance structures and new procedures in non-profits: 'Principal agency theory has been extremely influential, particularly in proposing changes to governance processes; and it can be seen informing a range of measures such as codes of practice and share option schemes for senior managers' (Spear 2004: 34). Interesting and valuable progress has been made in the field through comparative or integrative approaches, in which these different approaches have been combined or compared in various ways (Bernstein, Buse, and Bilimoria 2016; Kreutzer and Jacobs 2011; Van Puyvelde et al. 2012).

Beyond this, we can also see contingency approaches being applied (Bradshaw 2009), different forms of hybrid governance arrangements being studied, for example in social enterprises as well as in other forms (Anheier and Krlev 2015; Defourny and Nyssens 2017; Donnelly-Cox 2015), and new institutionalism being brought in to explain how the new governance wave has entered the non-profit sector as a topic. These are all developments which we interpret as both a steadily increasing interest in and a growth of knowledge about non-profit governance. In this chapter, we will however briefly focus on outlining some of the major similarities and differences between the three main approaches we identified.

An important starting point is Fama and Jensen's (1983b: 321) argument that one reason that non-profit governance is distinctive is the absence of normal 'residual claims'. In their terms: 'Again, however, the decision control structures of complex non-profits have special features attributable to the absence of alienable residual claims.' On a more general level, Anheier (2000: 13) has further argued that 'because of their complicated governance structure and minimal influences from markets and the electorate to check on performance, non-profits can easily be manoeuvred into a state of hidden failure', further stressing one major difference of non-profit organisations in comparison to either government or for-profit corporations.

Despite this existing understanding of non-profits as different, the study of non-profit governance still leans heavily on approaches and theories developed in or for the for-profit sector. Young (2011: 573) for example seeks the answer to a rhetorical question which we argue on a more general level still guides a substantial amount of the non-profit governance research: 'However, one may ask, could non-profit governance be redesigned to resemble the ownership model so that non-profit boards would behave more forcefully to fulfil their duties?' (see also Viader and Espina 2014). It could thus be argued that a substantial amount of further adaption and transformation of earlier models and theories developed primarily for for-profit governance would still be needed when applying them to the world of non-profit and voluntary organisations.

The Principal–agent Approach

In its simplest form, the principal–agent model assumes a kind of contractual relationship between, on the one hand, a principal, i.e. the owner or shareholder as the 'residual claimant', in the language of Fama and Jensen (1983b), and, on the other, an agent internal to the organisation, often the chief executive officer (CEO) or a person in a corresponding executive function. As a result of an analytical separation of ownership and control, the governance approach pioneered in Fama and Jensen's seminal work, the principal hires the agent to conduct some kind of activity in the interest of the principal, and in the process, authority and power are delegated to the agent.

In a slightly more complex version within a large and complex non-profit organisation, applying the principal–agent approach can be likened to seeing the organisation as a vertical chain of command running along a number of intertwined principal–agent links downwards in the organisation where authority and command flow from the principal to the agent in each of the links.

Apart from the assumption of a vertical chain of command in the form of contracts between principals and agents, there are two other important assumptions that make the principal–agent model especially powerful. The first assumption is that there exists, for different reasons, an information asymmetry between the principal and the agent. Since the agent is closer to the operations than the principal is and because of the greater amount of time spent, the agent has an information advantage. This is an asymmetry that the agent might use to further their own interests. This possibility brings us to the other important assumption: that the interests of the principal and those held by the agent are different (Waterman and Meier 1998).

The problem (also known as the agency dilemma) arises when the agent and the principal have different interests, at the same time as there is an asymmetry of information between the principal and the agent, who has more and better information (cf. Jegers 2009). 'This theory is concerned with economistic, rational-choice theories of how the principal (usually determined by property rights, i.e. the owner/member) can control the agent (the manager of the enterprise) so that the agent manages effectively in the principal's interests' (Spear 2004: 34).

Fama and Jensen, in their two highly influential articles, further argue that 'the decision control structures of complex non-profits have special features attributable to the absence of alienable residual claims' (Fama and Jensen 1983b: 321) and that this absence of residual claims 'does not mean that non-profits make no profits. It means that alienable claims to profits do not exist' (Fama and Jensen 1983a: 342). They thus maintain that non-profits have no residual claimants. However, this position held by Fama and Jensen is not uncontested, which indicates the fuzziness and complexity of the basic assumptions that come with the territory of non-profit governance. To the contrary, Williamson (1983: 358) for example argues that 'because the beneficiaries, real or pretended, are among those who stand to lose most if non-profits are badly run, beneficiaries can be said to have residual claimant status in the non-profit organization' (see also Reuter and Wijkström 2018).

The Stewardship Approach

A key criticism particularly relevant to NPOs relates to the image of the relationship between the principal and the agent as an eternal struggle over different interests within the organisation. The principal–agent model's focus on distrust and control has been criticised as a simplification of human and organisational behaviour (Jensen and Meckling 1994; Steinberg 2008), and stewardship theory has been suggested as an alternative. 'While agency theory privileges controlling behaviour, stewardship theory emphasizes the coaching behaviour of boards' (Kreutzer and Jacobs 2011: 613). As an example of one of the few attempts to study which of the two models best fit with practice, researchers asked both CEOs and board chairs in the same 474 NPOs a set of questions about board performance and claim to have found 'more support for [...] agency theory than [...] stewardship theory' (Bernstein, Buse, and Bilimoria 2016: 494).

Stewardship theory, which traces its roots to sociology and psychology, emphasises governance mechanisms that facilitate and empower rather than those that monitor and control (Davis, Schoorman, and Donaldson 1997). One such mechanism of potential stewardship identified by Donaldson and Davis (1991) is the situation in which the CEO is also the chairperson of the governing board. In the classical principal–agent approach and based on an assumption of a manager behaving as an 'economic man', the board is a key structural mechanism intended to curtail managerial opportunism. According to this approach: 'Where the chief executive officer is chair of the board of directors, the impartiality of the board is compromised' (Donaldson and Davis 1991: 50–51).

However, from another theoretical angle, the CEO could be understood as a 'steward'. This is an approach where 'organisational role-holders are conceived as being motivated by a need to achieve, to gain intrinsic satisfaction through successfully performing inherently challenging work, to exercise responsibility and authority and thereby to gain recognition from peers and bosses' (Donaldson and Davis 1991: 51). Thus, it is instead assumed that the intentions and interests of the 'steward' (as opposed to those of the classical 'agent' in the principal–agent model proper) can be compatible or even aligned with those of the board and the principals. Based on an alignment of interest between the steward and the principal, the steward will be motivated to act in line with the intentions and interests of the principal (Sundaramurthy and Lewis 2003). This scenario has been said to fit better with the reality of many voluntary or non-profit organisations (e.g. Caers et al. 2006; Kreutzer and Jacobs 2011). Here, the literature suggests that when the representatives of an organisation are provided with adequate challenges and responsibility, self-control will develop automatically (Davis, Schoorman, and Donaldson 1997: 33).

To conclude, with a stewardship approach to non-profit governance, the principal–agent model's basic idea of an internal vertical chain of command is retained as the core of the governance system, but instead it offers a different— less negative—conceptualisation of the relationship between the principal and the agent. Organisational governance is better conceived of, it is argued, as being based on collaboration, participation, and an understanding shared by the principal and the agent (the steward) regarding both the goal of the organisation and how to best realise it. In formal terms, it is the principal–agent model's base assumption of different or even conflicting interests between principal and agent that is made void, or at least less relevant. Concerning who has a legitimate claim on the organisation, its activities, or its outcomes, however, the stewardship approach brings nothing new to the table to solve this analytical challenge.

The Stakeholder Approach

The second serious challenger to the principal–agent model as a proper basis for non-profit corporate governance is one step further removed. While the stewardship model relaxes the assumption of conflict of interest between the agent and the principal, it still regards actors within the organisation as the primary and most legitimate holders of claims on or interests in the organisation. The stewardship approach also maintains the basic vertical 'chain of command' character, as discussed above. With the stakeholder approach, however, the step is taken to fully include in the analysis also those stakeholders ('claimants') that reside outside of the organisation and even outside of its mission statement. Further, it does so while recognising as relevant not only vertical relationships, but also horizontal ones, for example in a network approach. Nevertheless, even with this increased clarity, classical non-profit or voluntary sector constituents such as donors (Jegers 2009; Young 2011), volunteers (McClusky 2002; Rehli and Jäger 2011), or organisational members (Balduck, Van Rossem, and Buelens 2010; S. Einarsson 2012) are notoriously difficult to place clearly on either side of the boundary between what is to be understood as inside of the organisation and what is instead constructed as its environment. In reality, this often differs from case to case, from one organisation to the other.

In different stakeholder approaches, the definition of a stakeholder can range from the wide to the narrow. For example, according to Freeman's (1984: 46) broad definition, 'a stakeholder in an organization is [...] any group or individual who can affect or is affected by the achievement of the organization's objectives'. By contrast, Speckbacher (2008) defines a non-profit governance stakeholder rather narrowly as a party (i) that contributes specific resources, (ii) that creates value for the organisation, and (iii) whose claims on the return from the investment are (at least partly) unprotected.

Thus, claimants who are traditionally understood as being 'outsiders' to the organisation and its more immediate group of beneficiaries and clients can have legitimate claims on the results or effects of the operations of a voluntary or non-profit organisation. Such claimants can be understood to have a stake in the output or effects of the particular organisation, and therefore—from a certain normative perspective—they also are (or should be) included among the organisation's claimants in its governance.

We consider the basic and primary idea propelled into the non-profit governance debate by the stakeholder approach as highly relevant. It is a welcome contribution to the debate, but it is equally important to note that this type of approach would depart from the classical organisational (corporate) governance approach as it might allow, for example, the local municipality or actors that are formally outside of the organisation proper but close in other ways to be viewed as legitimate claimants. From an organisational governance perspective, it might be possible to further develop the stakeholder approach for NPOs along the 'network' or 'collaborative' governance approach, a recent trend in public administration (Ansell and Gash 2008; Provan and Kenis 2008; Sørensen and Torfing 2015).

The Role of the 'Residual Claimant'

One important difference in how scholars have used and conceptualised the three models concerns how they deal with the questions 'for whom?' or 'for what purpose?' the non-profit or voluntary organisation exists or operates. It would take us too far astray to go into substantial detail, but it suffices to bring back the different approaches developed, on the one hand, by Fama and Jensen (1983a), who asserted that non-profits do not really have any 'residual claimants', and, on the other hand, by Williamson (1983), who argued instead that the beneficiaries of the organisation should be seen as having a claim on the organisation. With this 'claim' lens applied to different accounts of governance, a number of interesting positions can be identified.

Closely related to this question about claimants is the idea of efficiency, which is central in most economic literature and even in the study of NPOs (Speckbacher 2003, 2008; Wellens and Jegers 2014). But for efficiency goals to play their powerful role in the organisation—and to provide its governance system with direction—we need to be able to define both to whom or what and under which constraints the organisation is supposed to deliver its particular version of the greater or common good. Until these basic decisions are taken, it is almost impossible to analyse the efficiency of the governance system of a non-profit or voluntary organisation. Perhaps the fuzziness regarding the complex goal functions of many NPOs and the conceptual unclarity about who the legitimate claimants would be are the reasons why much of the literature instead focuses on what we know with certainty is inefficient, such as embezzlement, corruption, and fraud, and on the measures and aspects that studies on for-profit corporate governance have handed us. Or maybe it is the central position of the owner and the often unproblematised profit motive defining traditional for-profit governance that lead us astray. There is, however, an obvious risk that such approaches might actually divert us from the search for better models and sharper theories for non-profit governance.

In the best of all worlds, a clear and readily distinguishable goal function for all non-profits would simplify the task. But, unlike for for-profits, this would be impossible in the non-profit world, since the voluntary and non-profit actors populating it have nothing in common other than the requirement not to make (or rather, not to distribute) a profit. This is not really the goal of the organisation but a condition under which the organisation should operate, and which can also be met in different ways. Further, unlike in for-profits, there is no simple way within most NPOs to compare different options or types of investments with each other. In the for-profit sector, the very efficient and comparative tool 'return on investment' offers a powerful mechanism to increase the efficiency of the organisation by shifting resources from one part of the organisation (region, type of products or services, etc.) to another with a better promise to deliver higher yield per invested unit.

In one noteworthy contribution to the stakeholder approach discussed earlier, Speckbacher (2008: 297) argues: 'From an economic point of view, the objective of a corporate governance system is to facilitate cooperation among stakeholders, that is, to make it more efficient.' This is an interesting approach, but, unfortunately, it does not solve the core riddle of non-profit governance as we have defined it here: the lack of coherent mission or goal function. To paraphrase an old saying by Peter Drucker, by going down the efficiency lane we run the obvious risk of focusing on 'doing things right' instead of 'doing the right things', which is a crucial dimension central to any kind of governance arrangement.

Instead of despair, however, we would like to offer what we believe is a useful analytical tool when moving forward theoretically in non-profit

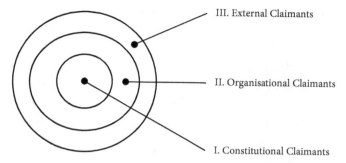

Figure 7.1. Schematic model of different types of claimant for non-profit organisations

governance studies and when seeking to better understand how NPOs are dealing with this matter. Instead of trying to find the one and only replacement for 'owners' or 'investors' in non-profits—which seems to be a direction in which the non-profit governance field is currently going—we suggest that we should retain the original idea of 'claimants' offered by Fama and Jensen (1983a). But instead of focusing on the 'residual claimants'—which implies financial returns or at least economic benefits and risks taking the discussion in the wrong direction—we suggest replacing the idea of a 'residual' with that of a 'result'. By addressing the result instead of the residual of the organisation's activities or operations, we allow for a wider and more relevant picture of the kind of organisational output upon which someone or something could have a claim. One benefit of this approach is that it would also be a step closer towards the important contribution of the stakeholder approach according to which not only economic interests are supposed to be factored into the governance equation. Legal particularities also help to define that 'result': there will be differences in how important specific stakeholders (and the 'results' relevant for them) are, depending on whether they are membership-based non-profits (e.g. associations), asset-based non-profits (e.g. foundations; see Surmatz, Chapter 6 in this volume), or shareholder-based non-profit forms (e.g. limited liability companies, B corporations, social enterprises; see Mair, Wolf, and Ioan, Chapter 8 in this volume, on governance of social enterprises).

However, to maintain our clear focus on and interest in organisational governance, we propose that we place in the centre any category or item with a (I) constitutional claim on the results of the organisation (see Figure 7.1). By constitutional claim, we mean that this entity is mentioned or pointed to in the organisation's statutes or mission statement in terms that would signify that a claim could be formulated. This could of course be a category of people, such as children, soccer players, talented youth, single mothers, metal work-ers, or refugees. But it could also refer to indigenous or endemic animals or old houses (as in mission phrase 'the preservation of historic buildings'). The first category of claimants could be specified as people or animals 'in need', but also to less easily individualised entities such as those at the centre of 'save-the-rainforest' types of mission or the restoration of 'God's kingdom on earth' (cf. Wijkström and Reuter 2015), i.e. the claimants being the rainforest and God (or possibly 'God's kingdom'), respectively. Admittedly, this solution is still complex and difficult, and it also leaves a great deal for the different parties in the governance of the organisations to define, interpret, or negoti-ate, but what else can be done when the organisations themselves constantly decide to place such endeavours at the centre of their reason for existence?

In the second ring of legitimate claimants, for enhanced analytical clarity we suggest placing the more traditional civil society 'citizens' that are (II) internal to the non-profit or the voluntary association (Lundström and Wijkström 2015) such as volunteers, donors, members, employees, or other staff and function-aries. This category of claimants we choose to define as organisational claim-ants. This distinction would help us not only to better distinguish between different approaches to non-profit governance, but it would also—we argue—lend more analytical structure to the future study of how non-profit gover-nance actually is conceptualised and practiced in the many different forms of organisations operating in this sector (Young et al. 2016).

Finally, within the third ring of this analytical frame we embrace the important contribution of the stakeholder approach and also include (III) the category consisting of the many different but relevant claimants found in the external environment of the organisation (as it is meanwhile also done in many for-profits). Examples would include the local community in which the organisation resides or operates, the municipality as an official partner or granter of subsidies, different foundations supporting the organisations, corporate sector philanthropic partners, or other actors like legislators, trade unions, and industry umbrella associations.

The increased clarity regarding different claimant categories that follows will aid us in distinguishing between different governance models, theories, or analytical approaches suggested by scholars or others, as well as provide us with a useful tool in future governance studies. The idea of some form of claimant—we would dare to argue—is a feature central to any type of gover-nance theory, and with the schematic model suggested in this section, we contribute to creating a tool for a better and more elaborated conceptualisa-tion of the non-profit claimant.

Developing Governance Practice in Non-profits

Recommendations based on normative theories notwithstanding, various models of good organisational governance have emerged in the field of NPOs. They are partly aligned with institutional logics (Thornton and Ocasio 1999, 2008), partly with the fields that non-profits work in (S. Einarsson 2012; T. Einarsson 2012), partly with different discourses that promote ideal types of non-profits. Accordingly, particular non-profit logics are based on particular assumptions about how 'good' non-profit governance should work (Maier and Meyer 2011).

The blueprint of the managerialist governance mode resembles corporate governance in business organisations. Core topics within this discourse are effectiveness, efficiency, resources, and strategy. Non-profits should choose methods that will lead to efficient and effective mission achievement. Donors and funding institutions are the main addressees of accountability activities that report effective and impactful performance.

Professional non-profits concentrate on the quality of their substantive work. The organisation is most accountable to those who represent professional standards, i.e. peers and external professional associations. Performance means meeting professional standards and succeeding in evaluation by peers.

In civic non-profits, the organisation is constructed as a kind of *res publica*. Positions, units, and practices within the organisation resemble governments and public administrations, thus mirroring representative democracies. Governance is grounded in the support of a majority of members. Formal procedures translate this support into decisions. Much effort is given to talking about proper, formal, written procedures. Active members are the final addressees in a formal ladder of accountability (management, board, general assembly), and the mobilisation of the majority's support per se is an indicator of successful performance.

Domestic non-profits organise themselves like families. Founders play a core role and personalise the non-profit's mission. They prefer uncomplicated direct activity. Personal issues are central to the organisation. For example, when talking about the organisation, references are made to people, not to positions. The organisation is seen as a unique family, and its members are expected to be devoted idealists. The non-profit is primarily accountable to its beneficiaries, because they lack representation at the family table, where employees are core participants. Mission achievement is the focus of accountability, though dependent on intuitive judgement and not measurable.

Finally, grassroots NPOs present the ideal image of a domination-free space. These organisations revolve around principles and fundamental positions. Since the organisation's goals are typically abstract and difficult to realise, being true to one's principles is considered an indicator of success. In governance, these organisations prioritise accountability to activists, who contribute their work to the organisation.

Only three of these five discourses offer normative models of governance that resonate in a wide range of non-profits, i.e. the managerial, the professional, and the civic models with their particular notions of constituencies, accountability, and steering. Domestic and grassroots non-profits, however, serve as the negative counter models of 'irrational' governance that we must overcome. To tackle the accountability challenge, many suggestions have been made on how to shape structures and processes in non-profit governance. We present here four practices, drawing from contemporary scholarship: board composition and function (Ostrower and Stone 2015), transparency regulations (Hale 2013), governance codes (von Schnurbein and Stöckli 2010), and, most recently, accountability clubs (Tremblay-Boire, Prakash, and Gugerty 2016).

Giving boards a central role in governance implies two characteristics of non-profits, both typical for Anglo-Saxon voluntary sectors. First, the board is the main governance organ of a non-profit, and it is juxtaposed with the executive management team. Second, non-profits coming out of a charity tradition often adopt a managerial logic that mimics the structure of for-profit business companies. Neither of these characteristics are as prevalent in Continental or northern Europe as they are in the UK and the US. In Scandinavia, for example, typical non-profit and voluntary organisations have developed from popular movements and follow a civic logic, characterised by a strong influence of membership and annual general membership gatherings building three-stage governance systems and democratic elections for executive and governance boards (Hvenmark 2008). In countries characterised by a corporatist non-profit regime such as Germany, France, Switzerland, and Austria, we also find three-stage governance systems in large non-profits, but a prevalence of two-stage systems in the majority of non-profits with a general assembly and an executive board, but no separate governance body (Djukic et al. 2015).

Board composition comprises mainly three questions: Who should serve on the board? Which factors determine the composition of boards? What are the consequences of board composition? Literature suggests that a specific kind of stakeholder must be represented on boards, i.e. those providing valuable specific resources without the protection of a comprehensive contract that details exactly how the organisation is to use these resources (Speckbacher 2008). Such stakeholders seek decision and control rights in order to direct the use of the resources they have provided. In many cases, these stakeholders encompass beneficiaries, individual donors donating rather small sums, and volunteers. Given the fundamental problem of defining the residual claimant that we discussed in the prior section, even this far-reaching recommendation might be too myopic.

Though board composition has been a popular issue in research and we already know much about the ethnic composition of boards and the correlation between CEOs' and board members' characteristics (Ostrower and Stone 2015; Stone and Ostrower 2007), we still lack research on the degree to which valuable but unprotected stakeholders have access to boards.

The roles and activities of governance boards are influenced by diverse factors. Tensions emerge from three partly conflicting functions that boards have to fulfil: controlling and monitoring, coaching and enabling, and fundraising and resource development (Ostrower and Stone 2006, 2010). Board work is contingent on environmental conditions, so that monitoring roles are preferred under stable conditions and boundary-spanning roles under unstable conditions (Brown and Guo 2010). Very often boards react in response to changes of external funding sources, e.g. by reducing community representation on the board when government funding increases (Guo 2007).

Research reveals a number of factors that positively influence board effectiveness: board member commitment (Preston and Brown 2004), planned recruitment, member orientation, and member performance evaluation (Brown 2005, 2007). A more recent study has shown that a decision-oriented but still critical culture in boards, board cohesiveness, diversity in terms of members' industry background, and human and social capital are strongly related to non-profits' capacity for innovation (Jaskyte 2018).

The second bundle of practices concerns transparency, which is a symbol for accountability. Calls for increased accountability and greater degrees of transparency among non-profits are common, not least in relation to public sector cooperation. In a recent study of Norwegian voluntary associations and public regulation, the researchers for example conclude 'that one aspect of state–civil society relations has changed in a more general way: there is a greater emphasis on accountability and transparency, in particular in welfare service provision, disaster preparedness and foreign aid' (Saglie and Sivesind 2018: 305). In the US, federal policy aimed at non-profit transparency relies on formal regulation, which is not as extensive as that applying to the public sector. Non-profits turn to trust and collaboration in order to be considered transparent in the current environment (Hale 2013). In the US, non-profits are more likely to provide access to their financial statements if they are larger organisations or have more debt, a larger contribution ratio, or a higher compensation expense ratio (Behn, DeVries, and Lin 2007, 2010). Another study (Atan, Zainon, and Wah 2012) shows that the sum of donations received is related to the extent of disclosure of information in NPOs' reports. The study's authors suggest that if non-profits improve their disclosure of information in their reporting, they will convince stakeholders that the resources are used efficiently in the provision of charity services.

In Continental Europe, non-profit transparency is more controversial. Transparency correlates with legal form and national regulatory frameworks. For some legal forms (e.g. corporations), there are mandatory laws (commercial code, tax laws) that enforce transparency. For others, only tax laws demand specific forms of accounting (but no public transparency). In some countries, non-profit governance codices have been published (e.g. Kalss 2014), but 'comply or explain' rules have not been enforced. For foundations, transparency regulations differ significantly between countries (see Surmatz, Chapter 6 in this volume, for more on variations in foundation governance). Many large non-profits are reluctant to publish their financial statements, as they fear that knowledge of their total assets might deter individual donors. However, non-profits account for a sizeable share of social service delivery in countries like Germany, Austria, and Switzerland. Some of the world's largest non-profit conglomerates are, for example, found in Germany (e.g. Caritas and Diakonie), together employing almost one million full-time equivalent employees. Both accountability and transparency requirements there are rather low and largely part of formalistic reporting to tax authorities. What is more, there is a general paucity of available information on non-profit organisations, combined with low levels of awareness among stakeholders as to potential accountability and transparency problems, and a lack of political will among non-profit representatives and policy-makers to change the status quo (Anheier, Hass, and Beller 2013).

Non-profits are still rather hesitant to increase transparency, even though this might enhance public confidence and trust and increase donations and memberships. Even in the US, many non-profit organisations have not adopted the recommended disclosure practices, though a recent study (Blouin, Lee, and Erickson 2018) shows that disclosure is strongly correlated to donations. Fundraising success is related to the performance indicators shown in the disclosures, particularly the ratio of programme expenditures to total expenditures.

In governance codes, both transparency and board regulations are standard content. As traditional law-making has become less effective in meeting the needs of various agents, reliance on soft law has increased, especially on corporate governance codes, which has fostered global governance standards for for-profit corporations (Harnay 2018). Also for non-profits, the adoption of a code of governance is a way to create external legitimacy. It might also strengthen internal legitimacy and reinforce board members' perceptions that the board is well governed. At the same time, codes constrain board autonomy (Walters and Tacon 2018). In business, regulations apply the 'comply or explain' approach (e.g. in the UK, Germany, the Netherlands). Rather than setting out binding laws, government regulators set out a code, which listed companies may either comply with or, if they do not comply, explain their reasons publicly. Manifestations in the non-profit sphere are the manifold certification marks and quality regulations for charities that compete for donations. In some countries such as Scotland, government regulatory agencies issue certification marks that indicate charity compliance with the code (e.g. McDonnell and Rutherford 2018) in order to safeguard the interests of donors (Cordery and Baskerville 2007).

Regulations and governance codes for NPOs are issued not only by public regulatory agencies (e.g. in the UK), but also by private accountability clubs (Gugerty and Prakash 2010; Tremblay-Boire, Prakash, and Gugerty 2016), i.e. voluntary associations of non-profits with the goal of providing them with monitoring and reputation enhancement. 'Accountability clubs can be viewed as voluntary mechanisms for regulation by reputation. Reputations are judgements that one set of actors make about others regarding an issue....Non-profits can seek to enhance their reputation for responsible management by joining an accountability club' (Tremblay-Boire, Prakash, and Gugerty 2016: 713). More generally, we find three modes of self-regulative governance practices: (1) compliance self-regulation (e.g. in Germany), where non-profits must conform to a set of behaviours imposed on them by external actors, such as third-party evaluation or accreditation entities; (2) adaptive self-regulation (e.g. in the UK) that is oriented toward market mechanisms to moderate accountability behaviour and resource exchanges; and (3) professional self-regulation models (e.g. in Poland) designed to enact practice-based norms, values, and rules and to improve perceptions of non-profit legitimacy (Bies 2010).

Board composition and practices, transparency regulations, governance codes, and more recently accountability clubs provide different mechanisms for improving organisational governance in non-profits. Meanwhile, as non-profits increasingly work in collaboration with other non-profits, businesses, or public authorities, governance has to go beyond organisational borders (e.g. Vangen, Hayes, and Cornforth 2015; Cornforth, Hayes, and Vangen 2015). Governance must deal with continuing give-and-take between network partners, it has been argued, caused by the need to exchange resources and negotiate shared purposes, with game-like interactions that are rooted in trust and are regulated by rules of the game that have to be negotiated (Rhodes 2007: 1246). The need to deal with continuous negotiation of the rules of the game places severe tensions on initial sets of governance rules and structures (task forces, meetings, and the like) within individual non-profits, e.g. between efficiency and participation, conflicting priorities, and changing leadership. Organisational inertia, lack of resources, lack of skills, and unwillingness to cooperate all may interfere with efforts to improve collaborative governance structures (Cornforth, Hayes, and Vangen 2015: 792). While research has produced some findings that provide hints for advancing non-profit organisational governance by improving both the composition and practices of the boards and by adopting transparency rules and governance codes, comparatively few findings have yet emerged in the field of network governance.

Discussion and Outlook

We have addressed the heterogeneity of different types of non-profits and their plurality of constituencies with theoretical approaches that have been mainly applied to and originally developed for the template of for-profit business corporate governance. Some of them are more helpful for addressing the various problems of non-profit accountability, some of them less so. Further work, beyond the scope of this chapter, could enhance their analytical and explanatory power if they were more explicitly complemented by theories of democracy, professionalism, participation, social movements, and the like.

In this assessment we would like to repeat what Hough, McGregor-Lowndes, and Ryan (2005: 3) wrote more than a decade ago when they concluded that 'a multi-theory and multi-disciplinary perspective is needed if research on governance of non-profit organisations is to be complete in scope, rich in content, and relevant'. We have already suggested a first step concerning a more synthesised approach to the role of claimants and beneficiaries that we believe would bring more clarity if applied to non-profit governance studies as well as to the more normative work by some scholars. In this final part, however, we would like to point to three other areas in which further exploration would contribute significantly to non-profit governance research.

In particular three lacunae in much of the previous non-profit governance research can be identified which we see as promising avenues for future studies. First of all, many empirical studies and attempts at theory development in non-profit governance scholarship seem to borrow from its predecessor, i.e. corporate for-profit governance, a focus on the part of the organisation's governance architecture that more or less begins and ends with the governing board, occasionally flows downward in the study of or normative prescriptions regarding the design of the board–executive relationship, and more rarely continues in a vertical cascade of successive principal–agent links. In this, much of what goes on in governance terms above, before, or parallel to the board has been neglected.

While the aim of many for-profit firms is often quite straightforward, i.e. some form of economic profit, the goal function of non-profit institutions and voluntary associations is more complex and often consists of multiple conflicting goals (Brickley and Van Horn 2002; Eldenburg et al. 2001). While the profit motive is central to the for-profit firm (if this type of organisation in the long run did not deliver any economic profits to be distributed or shared, it would normally go out of business and disappear), the only thing we know for sure about NPOs—and this is one of the few conditions that, analytically speaking, brings them together in a common sector or sphere—is that they are not intended for distributing profit. Otherwise, these organisations differ substantially from each other in how they formulate their purpose or mission, and this has clear implications for their governance, as also noted by Willems et al. (2016: 1425): 'Non-profit organizations are incredibly heterogeneous with regard to mission and purpose, which has important governance consequences. Several goals might be at the origin of existence for a single organization.' The organisations might differ with respect to for whom they exist, what role they are tasked to play in society, or why people should join together in them. This wide range of missions replaces the simple profit motive that lies at the core of corporate for-profit governance.

To be able to deal with the complexity of goal functions, many of the organisations populating civil society have been equipped with complex governance superstructures consisting of both formal bodies and processes overarching or preceding the board. For example, in the US 'most charitable non-profits have self-perpetuating boards. New members of a self-perpetuating board are selected by the existing members of the board who identify and enlist individuals according to criteria established by the board itself' (Worth 2016: 77). Apart from this very special form, different types of nominating committees, electorates, annual or general assemblies, principals, or voting systems exist in many organisations (Chatelain-Ponroy, Eynaud and Sponem 2015; Young 2011: 575f.) both within and beyond the still dominant Anglo-Saxon civil society regimes, but they are not yet really dealt with in the existing research literature.

While in comparison with for-profit firms or government agencies, NPOs often remain weak in the bottom part of the governance architecture (from the board downwards), the principles, processes, and structures developed in the upper part of the governance architecture are sometimes substantial. For example it is in this upper part where the governance conflicts or overlaps between the intentions and ambitions of the different factions or orientations found among member categories, donor groups, or other stakeholders become more visible and are pitched against each other, and later percolated down into the board. Since this upper section of the governance architecture can be expected to be particularly relevant in a type of organisation that is often value-driven, more and deeper studies to remedy this lacuna in the non-profit governance literature would be highly valuable.

Our second concern is the current apparent obsession with vertical governance mechanisms, such as the principal–agent chain of command, that are assumed or prescribed in much of the literature. What we miss are studies to help us better understand the horizontal governance mechanisms actually operating in many non-profit or voluntary organisations. Particularly interesting and relevant would be an effort to conceptualise the many voluntary or non-profit organisations that are part of, or that have historically been related to, the larger organisational complex very often associated with many of the traditional social or popular movements.

In particular at the upper level of the governance architecture, i.e. higher up constitutionally than the governing board, neither information asymmetries nor conflicts of interest would really be expected to play out in a vertical manner. We would instead expect these elements or components of the governance architecture to be horizontally organised with people and representatives of different groups, factions, orders, or schools of thought being in close and more lateral dialogue and contention with each other.

Even at the lower levels in the vertical chain of command, we would expect both interesting and important governance mechanisms, configurations, and processes to exist, for example, between different parallel lines of operations in larger non-profits, which Anheier (2000: 10) describes as 'conglomerates of multiple organizations or component parts' with multiple bottom lines. In a for-profit entity, the most efficient and profitable line or unit typically should receive more of the collective resources in the future. But, in a non-profit organisation or voluntary association, according to what goal function are resources being prioritised between different operations or branches?

Qualitative and comparative case studies would contribute to a better understanding of how conflict or cooperation between different groups, coalitions, or categories of top-level claimants or stakeholders play out in the governance of non-profit or voluntary organisations (see, for example, S. Einarsson 2012). Also in-depth case studies with a focus on the inner governance life of non-profit organisations below the board level—where the statutes or mission statements are translated (or not) into management decisions, procedures, and organisational priorities between different parts of the organisation—would be a welcome contribution to the continued study of non-profit governance.

Third, although a bourgeoning literature on the many different forms of membership-based voluntary associations and their governance exists (T. Einarsson 2012; Hvenmark 2008; von Schnurbein 2009; Spear 2004; Young et al. 1999), our assessment is that there is still more to be said and done on this topic. Several authors from the social movement tradition have pointed to the relative lack of attention in the current non-profit governance literature to matters like representation, citizenship, and democracy. For example, Enjolras and Steen-Johnsen (2015: 191), when they discuss the term 'democratic governance', highlight the role of civil society organisations to contribute to an active citizenship 'through creating possibilities for participation and empowerment; and through allowing for representation in a public sphere'. In doing so they point to both the external and the internal dimensions of non-profit governance (see also Wijkström and Reuter 2015).

The multi-faceted plethora of membership associations around the world and the challenges in many of these organisations as a result of increased professionalisation (Skocpol 2003) and new relations with government (Smith and Lipsky 1993) offer a fascinating and promising laboratory of governance study with high-yield potential. In his article on 'the rest of the non-profit sector', Smith (1997) early on identified this sub-population as a 'dark matter' ignored in much non-profit research, which also holds true for the study of non-profit governance. In his reflection, Spear (2004: 33) for example observed that 'in those voluntary organisations which are charities the historical development of charity law has tended to marginalise members in relation to trustees and management' (cf. Lansley 1996). As a result of recent decades of empirical research responding to earlier critique (cf. Cornforth and Simpson 2002), we now know more about how the boards of non-profit charitable institutions (particularly in the US) are composed and what is going on inside the non-profit boardroom.

At the current formative stage in the study of non-profit governance—leaving aside for the moment the more normative and practical dimension of the topic— we believe that both more rigour and structure are needed, as well as more theoretical openness when addressing a number of conceptual challenges inherent to the field. The economics approach has contributed substantially to getting us this far, and there are still a number of important tasks for this discipline in the continued development of governance scholarship in non-profit and voluntary organisations. We contend, however, that additional efforts along the lines proposed above from other academic disciplines as wide and disparate as sociology, organisational behaviour, psychology, public administration, ethnology, management, political science, and history would very much enhance our understanding—and thus also our capacity to generate relevant analytical models—of the rich and complex field of non-profit governance.

References

Abzug, R., DiMaggio, P., Gray, B. H., Useem, M., and Kang, C. H. (1993). 'Variations in Trusteeship: Cases from Boston and Cleveland, 1925–1985', *Voluntas: International Journal of Voluntary and Nonprofit Organizations*, 4(3): 271–300.

Alexander, J. A. and Weiner, B. J. (1998). 'The Adoption of the Corporate Governance Model by Non-profit Organizations', *Nonprofit Management and Leadership*, 8(3): 223–42.

Anheier, H. K. (2013). 'Governance: What Are the Issues?', in Hertie School of Governance (ed.), *The Governance Report*. Oxford: Oxford University Press, 11–31.

Anheier, H. K. (2000). *Managing Non-Profit Organisations: Towards a New Approach* (Vol. 1). London: Center for Civil Society at the London School of Economics.

Anheier, H. K., Hass, R., and Beller, A. (2013). 'Accountability and Transparency in the German Nonprofit Sector: A Paradox?', *International Review of Public Administration*, 18(3): 69–84. doi: 10.1080/12294659.2013.10805264

Anheier, H. K. and Krlev, G. (2015). 'Governance and Management of Hybrid Organizations', *International Studies of Management & Organization*, 45(3): 193–206.

Ansell, C. and Gash, A. (2008). 'Collaborative Governance in Theory and Practice', *Journal of Public Administration Research & Theory*, 18(4): 543–71.

Atan, R., Zainon, S., and Wah, Y. B. (2012). 'Quality Information by Charity Organizations and Its Relationship with Donations', in M. K. Jha, M. Lazard, A. Zaharin, and K. Sopian (eds.), *Recent Advances in Business Administration: Proceedings of the 6th WSEAS International Conference on Business Administration*. Athens: WSEAS Press, 118–23.

Bache, I. A. N. and Chapman, R. (2008). 'Democracy through Multilevel Governance? The Implementation of the Structural Funds in South Yorkshire', *Governance*, 21(3): 397–418. doi: http://dx.doi.org/10.1111/j.1468-0491.2008.00405.x

Badelt, C. (1990). 'Institutional Choice and the Nonprofit Sector', in H. K. Anheier and W. Seibel (eds.), *The Third Sector. Comparative Studies of Non-Profit Organizations*. Berlin/New York: Springer, 53–64.

Balduck, A.-L., Van Rossem, A., and Buelens, M. (2010). 'Identifying Competencies of Volunteer Board Members of Community Sports Clubs', *Nonprofit and Voluntary Sector Quarterly*, 39(2): 213–35.

Behn, B. K., DeVries, D. D., and Lin, J. (2010). 'The Determinants of Transparency in Nonprofit Organizations: An Exploratory Study', *Advances in Accounting*, 26(1): 6–12.

Behn, B., DeVries, D., and Lin, J. (2007). 'Voluntary Disclosure in Nonprofit Organizations: An Exploratory Study'. Retrieved from https://ssrn.com/abstract=727363 (accessed 10 January 2020).

Bernstein, R., Buse, K., and Bilimoria, D. (2016). 'Revisiting Agency and Stewardship Theories', *Nonprofit Management and Leadership*, 26(4): 489–98.

Bies, A. L. (2010). 'Evolution of Nonprofit Self-Regulation in Europe', *Non-profit and Voluntary Sector Quarterly*, 39(6): 1057–86.

Blomgren Bingham, L., Nabatchi, T., and O'Leary, R. (2005). 'The New Governance: Practices and Processes for Stakeholder and Citizen Participation', *Public Administration Review*, 65(5): 547–58.

Blouin, M. C., Lee, R. L., and Erickson, G. S. (2018). 'The Impact of Online Financial Disclosure and Donations in Non-profits', *Journal of Non-profit & Public Sector Marketing*, 30(3): 251–66. doi: 10.1080/10495142.2018.1452819

Bode, I. (2006). 'Co-governance Within Networks and the Non-profit–For-profit Divide. A Cross-cultural Perspective on the Evolution of Domiciliary Elderly Care', *Public Management Review*, 8(4): 551–66.

Bogart, W. T. (1995). 'Accountability and Nonprofit Organizations: An Economic Perspective', *Non-profit Management and Leadership*, 6(2): 157–70.

Boli, J. and Thomas, G. M. (eds.) (1999). *Constructing World Culture: International Nongovernmental Organizations since 1875*. Stanford: Stanford University Press.

Bradshaw, P. (2009). 'A Contingency Approach to Nonprofit Governance', *Nonprofit Management & Leadership*, 20(1): 61–81.

Bradshaw, P. (2002). 'Reframing Board-Staff Relations', *Nonprofit Management & Leadership*, 12(4): 471–84.

Brickley, J. A. and Van Horn, R. L. (2002). 'Managerial Incentives in Nonprofit Organizations: Evidence from Hospitals', *The Journal of Law and Economics*, 45(1): 227–49.

Brown, W. A. (2007). 'Board Development Practices and Competent Board Members: Implications for Performance', *Nonprofit Management and Leadership*, 17(3): 301–17.

Brown, W. A. (2005). 'Exploring the Association between Board and Organizational Performance in Non-profit Organizations', *Nonprofit Management and Leadership*, 15(3): 317–39.

Brown, W. A. and Guo, C. (2010). 'Exploring the Key Roles for Nonprofit Boards', *Nonprofit and Voluntary Sector Quarterly*, 39(3): 536–46.

Caers, R., Du Bois, C., Jegers, M., DeGieter, S., Schepers, C., and Pepermans, R. (2006). 'Principal-Agent Relationships on the Stewardship-Agency Axis', *Nonprofit Management & Leadership*, 17(1): 25–46.

Chatelain-Ponroy, S., Eynaud, P., and Sponem, S. (2015). 'Civil Society Organization Governance: More than just a Matter for the Board', in J.-L. Laville, D. R. Young, and P. Eynaud (eds.), *Civil Society, the Third Sector and Social Enterprise. Governance and Democracy*. Oxon and New York: Routledge, 58–74.

Cheng, Y. (2018). 'Exploring the Role of Nonprofits in Public Service Provision: Moving from Coproduction to Cogovernance', *Public Administration Review*, 79(2): 203–14.

Cordery, C. J. and Baskerville, R. F. (2007). 'Charity Financial Reporting Regulation: A Comparative Study of the UK and New Zealand', *Accounting History*, 12(1): 7–27. doi: 10.1177/1032373207072806.

Cornforth, C. (2014). 'Nonprofit Governance Research', in C. Cornforth and W. A. Brown (eds.), *Nonprofit Governance: Innovative Perspectives and Approaches*. London and New York: Routledge, 1–14.

Cornforth, C. and Brown, W. A. (eds.). (2014). *Nonprofit Governance: Innovative Perspectives and Approaches*. London and New York: Routledge.

Cornforth, C., Hayes, J. P., and Vangen, S. (2015). 'Nonprofit–Public Collaborations: Understanding Governance Dynamics', *Nonprofit and Voluntary Sector Quarterly*, 44(4): 775–95.

Cornforth, C. and Simpson, C. (2002). 'Change and Continuity in the Governance of Nonprofit Organizations in the United Kingdom: The Impact of Organizational Size', *Nonprofit Management and Leadership*, 12(4): 451–70.

Davis, J. H., Schoorman, F. D., and Donaldson, L. (1997). 'Toward a Stewardship Theory of Management', *Academy of Management Review*, 22(1): 20–47.

Deakin, S. and Konzelmann, S. J. (2004). 'Learning from Enron', *Corporate Governance: An International Review*, 12(2): 134–42.

Defourny, J. and Nyssens, M. (2017). 'Fundamentals for an International Typology of Social Enterprise Models', *VOLUNTAS: International Journal of Voluntary and Nonprofit Organizations*, 28(6): 2469–97.

Dicke, L. A. and Ott, J. S. (1999). 'Public Agency Accountability in Human Service Contracting', *Public Productivity & Management Review*, 22(4): 502–16.

DiMaggio, P. J. and Powell, W. W. (1983). 'The Iron Cage Revisited: Institutional Isomorphism and Collective Rationality in Organizational Fields', *American Sociological Review*, 48: 147–60.

Djukic, B., Schober, C., Horak, C., and Meyer, M. (2015). 'Stakeholderbasierte NPO-Governance als Möglichkeit zur Ressourcenmobilisierung am Beispiel des Österreichischen NPO-Governance Kodex', in R. Andessner, D. Greiling, M. Gmür, and L. Theuvsen (eds.), *Ressourcenmobilisierung Durch Nonprofit-Organisationen*. Linz: Trauner, 356–68.

Donaldson, L. and Davis, J. H. (1991). 'Stewardship Theory or Agency Theory: CEO Governance and Shareholder Returns', *Australian Journal of Management*, 16(1): 49–64.

Donnelly-Cox, G. (2015). 'Civil Society Governance: Hybridization within Third-Sector and Social Enterprise Domains', in J.-L. Laville, D. R. Young, and P. Eynaud (eds.), *Civil Society, the Third Sector and Social Enterprise. Governance and Democracy*. Oxon and New York: Routledge, 52–66.

Drucker, P. F. (1990). 'Lessons for Successful Nonprofit Governance', *Nonprofit Management and Leadership*, 1(1): 7–14. doi:10.1002/nml.4130010103

Ebrahim, A. (2009). 'Placing the Normative Logics of Accountability in "Thick" Perspective', *American Behavioral Scientist*, 52(6): 885–904. doi: 10.1177/0002764208327664

Ebrahim, A. (2005). 'Accountability Myopia: Losing Sight of Organizational Learning', *Nonprofit and Voluntary Sector Quarterly*, 34(1): 56–87.

Einarsson, S. (2012). 'Ideology Being Governed: Strategy Formation in Civil Society', PhD thesis (Stockholm School of Economics, Stockholm).

Einarsson, T. (2012). 'Membership and Organizational Governance', PhD thesis (Stockholm School of Economics, Stockholm).

Eising, R. (2004). 'Multilevel Governance and Business Interests in the European Union', *Governance*, 17(2): 211–45.

Eldenburg, L., Hermalin, B. E, Weisbach, M. S., and Wosinska, M. (2001). 'Hospital Governance, Performance Objectives, and Organizational Form',

NBER Working Paper No. 8201. Cambridge, MA: National Bureau of Economic Research.

Enjolras, B. (2009). 'A Governance-Structure Approach to Voluntary Organizations', *Nonprofit and Voluntary Sector Quarterly*, 38(5): 761–83. doi: 10.1177/0899764008320030

Enjolras, B. and Steen-Johnsen, K. (2015). 'Democratic Governance and Citizenship', in J.-L. Laville, D. R. Young, and P. Eynaud (Eds.), *Civil Society, the Third Sector and Social Enterprise. Governance and Democracy*. Oxon and New York: Routledge, 191–204.

Fama, E. F. and Jensen, M. C. (1983a). 'Agency Problems and Residual Claims', *Journal of Law and Economics*, 26(2): 327–49.

Fama, E. F. and Jensen, M. C. (1983b). 'Separation of Ownership and Control', *The Journal of Law and Economics*, 26(2): 301–25.

Freeman, R. E. (1984). *Strategic Management: A Stakeholder Approach*. Boston: Pitman/Ballinger.

Glaser, W. A. and Sills, D. L. (eds.) (1966). *The Government of Associations. Selections from the Behavioral Sciences*. Totowa (NJ): Bedminister Press.

Gräwe, D. (2013). 'Zur Notwendigkeit der Ausgestaltung von Nonprofit Governance-Systemen', *Zeitschrift für Stiftungs- und Vereinwesen*, 11(3): 81–120.

Gugerty, M. K. and Prakash, A. (2010). *Voluntary Regulation of NGOs and Nonprofits: An Accountability Club Framework*. Cambridge, UK: Cambridge University Press.

Guo, C. (2007). 'When Government Becomes the Principal Philanthropist: The Effects of Public Funding on Patterns of Nonprofit Governance', *Public Administration Review*, 67(3): 458–73.

Hale, K. (2013). 'Understanding Nonprofit Transparency: The Limits of Formal Regulation in the American Nonprofit Sector', *International Review of Public Administration*, 18(3): 31–49. doi: 10.1080/12294659.2013.10805262

Hammack, D. C. and Young, D. R. (1993). *Nonprofit Organizations in a Market Economy. Understanding New Roles, Issues, and Trends*. San Francisco: Jossey Bass.

Harnay, S. (2018). 'Explaining the Production and Dissemination of Global Corporate Governance Standards: A Law and Economics Approach to Corporate Governance Codes as a Global Law-Making Technology', in J.-S. Bergé, S. Harnay, U. Mayrhofer, and L. Obadia (eds.), *Global Phenomena and Social Sciences: An Interdisciplinary and Comparative Approach*. Cham: Springer International Publishing, 63–78.

Hasenpflug, T. (2011). 'Stand der Einführung neuer Corporate Governance Strukturen in deutschen NonProfit-Organisationen nach Vorbild des US

Sarbanes-Oxley Acts', *npoR Zeitschrift für das Recht der Nonprofit-Organisationen*, 1: 11–15.

Healy, P. M. and Palepu, K. G. (2003). 'The Fall of Enron', *Journal of Economic Perspectives*, 17(2): 3–26.

Heinrich, C. J. and Lynn, L. E. (eds.). (2000). *Governance and Performance: New Perspectives*. Washington, DC: Georgetown University Press.

Herman, D. R. and Renz, D. O. (1997). 'Multiple Constituencies and the Social Construction of Nonprofit Organization Effectiveness', *Nonprofit and Voluntary Sector Quarterly*, 26(2): 185–206.

Hodges, R. (2005). *Governance and the Public Sector*. Cheltenham: Edward Elgar Publishing.

Hough, A., McGregor-Lowndes, M., and Ryan, C. M. (2005). 'Theorizing About Board Governance of Nonprofit Organizations: Surveying the Landscape'. Paper for the 34th Annual Conference of the Association for Research on Nonprofit Organizations and Voluntary Action, Washington, DC, 17–19 November.

Hug, N. and Jäger, U. P. (2014). 'Resource-Based Accountability: A Case Study on Multiple Accountability Relations in an Economic Development Nonprofit', *Voluntas*, 25(3): 772–96. doi: http://dx.doi.org/10.1007/s11266-013-9362-9

Hvenmark, J. (2008). 'Reconsidering Membership: A Study of Individual Members' Formal Affiliation with Democratically Governed Federations', PhD thesis (Stockholm School of Economics, Stockholm).

Jaskyte, K. (2018). 'Board Attributes and Processes, Board Effectiveness, and Organizational Innovation: Evidence from Nonprofit Organizations', *VOLUNTAS: International Journal of Voluntary and Nonprofit Organizations*, 29(5): 1098–11. doi: 10.1007/s11266-017-9945-y

Jegers, M. (2009). '"Corporate" Governance in Nonprofit Organizations', *Nonprofit Management & Leadership*, 20(2): 143–64.

Jensen, M. C. and Meckling, W. H. (1994). 'The Nature of Man', *Journal of Applied Corporate Finance*, 2: 4–19.

Kalss, S. (2014). 'Der österreichische Corporate Governance-Kodex für Non-Profit-Organisationen', in: R. Hüttemann, P. Rawert, K. Schmidt, and B. Weitemeyer (eds.), *Non Profit Law Yearbook 2013/2014*. Hamburg: Bucerius Law School Press, 125–61.

Kreutzer, K. and Jacobs, C. (2011). 'Balancing Control and Coaching in CSO Governance. A Paradox Perspective on Board Behavior', *Voluntas: International Journal of Voluntary and Nonprofit Organizations*, 22(4): 613–38.

Lansley, J. (1996). 'Membership Participation and Ideology in Large Voluntary Organisations: the Case of the National Trust', *Voluntas: International Journal of Voluntary and Nonprofit Organizations*, 7(3): 221–40.

LeRoux, K. (2009). 'Paternalistic or Participatory Governance? Examining Opportunities for Client Participation in Nonprofit Service Organizations', *Public Administration Review*, 69(3): 504–17.

Leuschner, L. (2016). 'Zwischen Gläubigerschutz und Corporate Governance: Reformperspektiven des Vereinsrechts', *npoR Zeitschrift für das Recht der Nonprofit-Organisationen*, 3: 99–104.

Liou, K. T. (2001). 'Governance and Economic Development: Changes and Challenges', *International Journal of Public Administration*, 24(10): 1005–22.

Lundström, T. and Wijkström, F. (2015). 'Rekonstruktionen av det frivilliga: De nya civilsamhällesmedborgarna', in J. von Essen, M. Karlsson, L. Blomquist, E. Forssell, and L. Trägårdh (eds.), *Med kärlek till det oordnade*. Stockholm: Ersta Sköndal Bräcke Högskola, 179–215.

Lynn, L. E., Heinrich, C. J., and Hill, C. J. (2000). 'Studying Governance and Public Management: Why? How?', in C. J. Heinrich and L. E. Lynn (eds.), *Governance and Performance: New Perspectives*. Washington, D.C.: Georgetown Unversity Press, 1–33.

Maier, F. and Meyer, M. (2011). 'Managerialism and Beyond: Discourses of Civil Society Organization and Their Governance Implications', *Voluntas: International Journal of Voluntary and Nonprofit Organizations*, 22(4): 731–56. doi: 10.1007/s11266-011-9202-8

McClusky, J. E. (2002). 'Re-Thinking Nonprofit Organization Governance: Implications for Management and Leadership', *International Journal of Public Administration*, 25(4): 539–59.

McDonnell, D. and Rutherford, A. C. (2018). 'The Determinants of Charity Misconduct', *Nonprofit and Voluntary Sector Quarterly*, 47(1): 107–25. doi: 10.1177/0899764017728367

McLean, B. and Elkind, P. (2013). *The Smartest Guys in the Room: The Amazing Rise and Scandalous Fall of Enron*. New York: Penguin.

Morck, R. and Steier, L. (2005). 'The Global History of Corporate Governance: An Introduction', in R. K. Morck (ed.), *A History of Corporate Governance around the World: Family Business Groups to Professional Managers*. Chicago: University of Chicago Press, 1–64.

Mulligan, L. N. (2007). 'What's Good for the Goose Is Not Good for the Gander: Sarbanes-Oxley-Style Nonprofit Reforms', *Michigan Law Review*, 105(8): 1981–2009.

Neumayr, M. and Meyer, M. (2010). 'In Search of Civicness: An Empirical Investigation of Service Delivery, Public Advocacy, and Community Building by Civil Society Organizations', in T. Brandsen, P. Dekker, and A. Evers (eds.), *Civicness in the Governance and Delivery of Social Services*. Baden-Baden: Nomos, 201–26.

Ortmann, A. and Schlesinger, M. (1997). 'Trust, Repute and the Role of Non-Profit Enterprise', *Voluntas*, 8(2): 97–119.

Osborne, S. P. (ed.) (2010). *The New Public Governance: Emerging Perspectives on the Theory and Practice of Public Governance*. London: Routledge.

Ostrom, E. (2010). 'Beyond Markets and States: Polycentric Governance of Complex Economic Systems', *Transnational Corporations Review*, 2(2): 1–12. doi: 10.1080/19186444.2010.11658229

Ostrower, F. and Stone, M. M. (2015). 'Governing Boards and Organizational Environments: Growing Complexities, Shifting Boundaries', in J.-L. Laville, D. R. Young, and P. Eynaud (Eds.), *Civil Society, the Third Sector and Social Enterprise. Governance and Democracy*. Oxon and New York: Routledge, 75–90.

Ostrower, F. and Stone, M. M. (2010). 'Moving Governance Research Forward: A Contingency-Based Framework and Data Application', *Nonprofit and Voluntary Sector Quarterly*, 39(5): 901–24. doi: 10.1177/0899764009338962

Ostrower, F. and Stone, M. M. (2006). 'Governance: Research Trends, Gaps, and Future Prospects', in W. W. Powell and R. Steinberg (eds.), *The Nonprofit Sector: A Research Handbook* (2nd ed.). New Haven, Conn.: Yale University Press, 612–28.

Pennerstorfer, A. and Neumayr, M. (2017). 'Examining the Association of Welfare State Expenditure, Non-Profit Regimes and Charitable Giving', *Voluntas: International Journal of Voluntary and Nonprofit Organizations*, 28: 532–55. https://doi.org/10.1007/s11266-016-9739-7

Pierre, J. and Peters, G. B. (2000). *Governance, Politics and the State*. Basingstoke: Macmillan.

Preston, J. B. and Brown, W. A. (2004). 'Commitment and Performance of Nonprofit Board Members', *Nonprofit Management and Leadership*, 15(2): 221–38.

Provan, K. G. and Kenis, P. (2008). 'Modes of Network Governance: Structure, Management, and Effectiveness', *Journal of Public Administration Research and Theory*, 18(2): 229–52. doi: 10.1093/jopart/mum015

Rehli, F. and Jäger, U. P. (2011). 'The Governance of International Nongovernmental Organizations: How Funding and Volunteer Involvement Affect Board Nomination Modes and Stakeholder Representation in International Nongovernmental Organizations', *Voluntas: International Journal of Voluntary and Nonprofit Organizations*, 22(4): 587–611.

Renz, D. O. and Andersson, F. O. (2014). 'Nonprofit Governance: A Review of the Field', in C. Cornforth and W. A. Brown (eds.), *Nonprofit Governance: Innovative Perspective and Approaches*. London and New York: Routledge, 17–39.

Reuter, M. and Wijkström, F. (2018). 'Three Parallel Modes of Governance in Civil Society. The Steering and Control of Welfare Provision in the Church of Sweden', paper prepared for the 34th EGOS Colloquium in Tallinn, July 5–7.

Reuter, M., Wijkström, F., and Meyer, M. (2014). 'Who Calls the Shots? The *Real* Normative Power of Civil Society', in M. Freise and T. Hallmann (eds.), *Modernizing Democracy*. New York: Springer, 71–82.

Rhodes, R. A. W. (2007). 'Understanding Governance: Ten Years On', *Organization Studies*, 28(8): 1243–64.

Risse, T. (2013). *Governance without a State? Policies and Politics in Areas of Limited Statehood*. New York: Columbia University Press.

Ruzza, C. (2004). *Europe and Civil Society: Movement Coalitions and European Governance*. Manchester: Manchester University Press.

Saglie, J. and Sivesind, K.-H. (2018). 'Civil Society Institutions or Semi-Public Agencies? State Regulation of Parties and Voluntary Organizations in Norway', *Journal of Civil Society*, 14(4): 292–310.

Sahlin, K., Wijkström, F., Dellmuth, L., Einarsson, T., and Oberg, A. (2015). 'The "Milky Way" of Intermediary Organisations: A Transnational Field of University Governance', *Policy & Politics*, 43(3): 407–24.

Saidel, J. R. and Harlan, S. L. (1998). 'Contracting and Patterns of Nonprofit Governance', *Nonprofit Management and Leadership*, 8(3): 243–259.

Salamon, L. M. and Anheier, H. K. (1997). *Defining the Nonprofit Sector: A Cross-National Analysis*. Manchester: Manchester University Press.

Saxton, G. D. and Neely, D. G. (2019). 'The Relationship between Sarbanes–Oxley Policies and Donor Advisories in Nonprofit Organizations', *Journal of Business Ethics*, 158(2): 1–19.

Skocpol, T. (2003). *Diminished Democracy: From Membership to Management in American Civic Life*. Norman: University of Oklahoma Press.

Smith, D. H. (1997). 'The Rest of the Nonprofit Sector: Grassroots Associations as the Dark Matter Ignored in Prevailing "Flat Earth" Maps of the Sector', *Nonprofit and Voluntary Sector Quarterly*, 26(2): 114–31.

Smith, S. R. and Lipsky, M. (1993). *Nonprofits for Hire, the Welfare State in the Age of Contracting*. Cambridge: Harvard University Press.

Spear, R. (2004). 'Governance in Democratic Member-Based Organisations', *Annals of Public and Cooperative Economics*, 75(1): 33–60.

Speckbacher, G. (2008). 'Nonprofit Versus Corporate Governance: An Economic Approach', *Nonprofit Management & Leadership*, 18(3): 295–320.

Speckbacher, G. (2003). 'The Economics of Performance Management in Nonprofit Organizations', *Nonprofit Management and Leadership*, 13(3): 267–81.

Steen-Johnsen, K., Eynaud, P., and Wijkström, F. (2011). 'On Civil Society Governance: An Emergent Research Field', *Voluntas: International Journal of Voluntary and Nonprofit Organizations*, 22(4): 555. Doi: 10.1007/s11266-011-9211-7

Steinberg, R. (2008). *Principal-Agent Theory and Nonprofit Accountability*. St Louis: Federal Reserve Bank of St Louis.

Stoker, G. (1998). 'Governance as Theory: Five Propositions', *International Social Science Journal*, 50(155): 17–28.

Stone, M. M. (1996). 'Competing Contexts: The Evolution of a Nonprofit Organization's Governance System in Multiple Environments', *Administration & Society*, 28(1): 61–89.

Stone, M. M. and Ostrower, F. (2007). 'Acting in the Public Interest? Another Look at Research on Nonprofit Governance', *Nonprofit and Voluntary Sector Quarterly*, 36(3): 416–38. doi: 10.1177/0899764006296049

Sundaramurthy, C. and Lewis, M. (2003). 'Control and Collaboration: Paradoxes of Governance', *Academy of Management Review*, 28(3): 397–415.

Sørensen, E. and Torfing, J. (2005). 'Network Governance and Post-Liberal Democracy', *Administrative Theory & Praxis*, 27(2): 197–237.

Thornton, P. H. and Ocasio, W. (2008). 'Institutional Logics,' in R. Greenwood, C. Oliver, K. Sahlin. and R. Suddaby (eds.), *The Sage Handbook of Organizational Institutionalism*. London: Sage, 99–128.

Thornton, P. H. and Ocasio, W. (1999). 'Institutional Logics and the Historical Contingency of Power in Organizations: Executive Succession in the Higher Education Publishing Industry, 1958–1990', *American Journal of Sociology*, 105(3): 801–43.

Tremblay-Boire, J., Prakash, A., and Gugerty, M. K. (2016). 'Regulation by Reputation: Monitoring and Sanctioning in Nonprofit Accountability Clubs', *Public Administration Review*, 76(5): 712–22. doi: 10.1111/puar.12539

Vangen, S., Hayes, J. P., and Cornforth, C. (2015). 'Governing Cross-Sector, Inter-Organizational Collaborations', *Public Management Review*, 17(9): 1237–60.

Van Puyvelde, S., Caers, R., Du Bois, C., and Jegers, M. (2012). 'The Governance of Nonprofit Organizations: Integrating Agency Theory With Stakeholder and Stewardship Theories', *Nonprofit and Voluntary Sector Quarterly Nonprofit and Voluntary Sector Quarterly*, 41(3): 431–51. doi: 10.1177/0899764011409757

Viader, A. M. and Espina, M. I. (2014). 'Are Not-for-profits Learning from For-profit-organizations? A Look into Governance', *Corporate Governance*, 14(1): 1–14. doi: 10.1108/CG-11-2012-0083

Voigt de Oliveira, S. and Wendt, M. (2012). 'Corporate Governance und Compliance Management in Stiftungen', *npoR Zeitschrift für das Recht der Nonprofit-Organisationen*, 1/: 19–22.

von Schnurbein, G. (2009). 'Patterns of Governance Structures in Trade Associations and Unions', *Nonprofit Management and Leadership*, 20(1): 97–115.

von Schnurbein, G. and Stöckli, S. (2010). 'Die Gestaltung von Nonprofit Governance Kodizes in Deutschland und der Schweiz—Eine Komparative Inhaltsanalyse', *Die Betriebswirtschaft*, 70(6): 493–509.

Walker, J. L. (1983). 'The Origins and Maintenance of Interest Groups in America', *The American Political Science Review*, 77(2): 390–406.

Walters, G. and Tacon, R. (2018). 'The "Codification" of Governance in the Non-Profit Sport Sector in the UK', *European Sport Management Quarterly*, 8(4): 1–19. doi: 10.1080/16184742.2017.1418405

Waterman, R. W. and Meier, K. J. (1998). 'Principal-Agent Models: An Expansion?', *Journal of Public Administration Research and Theory*, 8(2): 173–202.

Wellens, L. and Jegers, M. (2014). 'Effective Governance in Nonprofit Organizations: A Literature Based Multiple Stakeholder Approach', *European Management Journal*, 32(2): 223–43.

Wijkström, F. and Reuter, M. (2015). 'Two Sides of the Governance Coin: The Missing Civil Society Link', in J.-L. Laville, D. R. Young, and P. Eynaud (eds.), *Civil Society, the Third Sector and Social Enterprise. Governance and Democracy*. Oxon and New York: Routledge, 122–38.

Willems, J., Andersson, F. O., Jegers, M., and Renz, D. O. (2016). 'A Coalition Perspective on Nonprofit Governance Quality: Analyzing Dimensions of Influence in an Exploratory Comparative Case Analysis', *Voluntas: International Journal of Voluntary and Nonprofit Organizations*, 28(4): 1422–47. doi: 10.1007/s11266-016-9683-6

Williamson, O. E. (2002). 'The Theory of the Firm as Governance Structure: From Choice to Contract', *The Journal of Economic Perspectives*, 16(3): 171–95.

Williamson, O. E. (1983). 'Organization Form, Residual Claimants, and Corporate Control', *The Journal of Law and Economics*, 26(2): 351–66.

Williamson, O. E. (1975). *Markets and Hierarchies*. New York: Free Press.

Worth, M. J. (2016). *Nonprofit Management: Principles and Practice* (4th ed.). Los Angeles: Sage.

Yallapragada, R. R., Roe, C. W., and Toma, A. G. (2010). 'Sarbanes-Oxley Act of 2002 and Non-Profit Organizations', *Journal of Business & Economics Research*, 8(2): 89–93.

Young, D. R. (2011). 'The Prospective Role of Economic Stakeholders in the Governance of Nonprofit Organizations', *Voluntas: International Journal of Voluntary and Nonprofit Organizations*, 22(4): 566–86.

Young, D.R., Bania, N., and Bailey, D. (1996). 'Structure and Accountability a Study of National Nonprofit Associations', *Nonprofit Management and Leadership*, 6(4): 347–65.

Young, D. R., Searing, E. A. M., and Brewer, C. V. (eds.) (2016). *The Social Enterprise Zoo. A Guide for Perplexed Scholars, Entrepeneurs, Philanthropists, Leaders, Investors, and Policymakers.* Cheltenham (UK): Edward Elgar Publishing.

Young, D. R, Koenig, B. L, Najam, A., and Fisher, J. (1999). 'Strategy and Structure in Managing Global Associations', *Voluntas: International Journal of Voluntary and Nonprofit Organizations*, 10(4): 323–43.

Zimmermann, J. A. M. and Stevens, B. W. (2008). 'Best Practices in Board Governance: Evidence from South Carolina', *Nonprofit Management & Leadership*, 19(2): 189–202.

Zingales, L. (1998). 'Corporate Governance', in P. Newman (ed.), *Palgrave Dictionary of Economics and the Law*. London: Macmillan, 497–503.

8

Governance in Social Enterprises

Johanna Mair, Miriam Wolf, and Alexandra Ioan

Social Enterprises and Their Governance Challenges

Social enterprises are organisations that pursue a social mission using market mechanisms (Mair and Marti 2006; Huysentruyt et al. 2016). From a policy perspective, they are promising vehicles to create both social and economic value for society in times when public funds are shrinking and the financial viability of charities and non-profit organisations (NPOs) is increasingly at stake (European Commission 2017). From a civil society perspective, they are an important organisational form to ensure longevity, financial viability, and sustainability of mission-driven organisations. Social enterprises are neither typical charities nor typical businesses but combine aspects of both, using commercial activities as means toward social ends. They are often small or medium-sized[1] and do not draw on highly elaborated governance arrangements as do larger for- or non-profit organisations. Governance often resembles a grey zone for these organisations, and the approach social enterprises adopt ranges from formal, legally binding arrangements to more flexible and context-based ones. Well-known examples of social enterprises are work integration organisations like Specialsterne or auticon, both of which draw on the strengths of people on the autism spectrum in the information technology field by enabling them to participate in the regular labour market as opposed to sheltered workshops that have been known for decades and have mainly followed a deficit-oriented approach.

As such, social enterprises stand for a larger population of organisations that are not easy to categorise: a population that has no legally defined form, scope, and mandate and no clearly defined roles for stakeholders. What characterises them is a commitment to address a social problem and/or achieve

---

[1] For an overview of the average size of social enterprises across countries (full-time employees and volunteers) see SEFORÏS cross-country report (SEFORÏS 2017: 29).

Johanna Mair, Miriam Wolf, and Alexandra Ioan, *Governance in Social Enterprises* In: *Advances in Corporate Governance: Comparative Perspectives*. Edited by: Helmut K. Anheier and Theodor Baums, Oxford University Press (2020).
© Hertie School.
DOI: 10.1093/oso/9780198866367.003.0008

social change, while pursuing organisational goals such as reaching break-even, running a profit, attracting funding and financial capital, hiring and retaining talented people, growing and scaling targets that reflect the magnitude of the social problem they address, and so on.

The multiplicity of goals poses challenges for both theory and practice. Over the last years, scholars have turned to the label of hybrid organisations (Battilana and Dorado 2010; Besharov and Smith 2014; Mair et al. 2015) to highlight tensions and contradictions arising from pursuing multiple goals (economic, social, and/or environmental). What makes the pursuit of multiple goals challenging for social enterprises and interesting for scholars of organisational governance is the relationship between goals, stakeholders, and accountability. Stakeholders such as funders, beneficiaries, employees, or governments act as 'principals' of social enterprises that can lead the organisation to prioritise some goals over others. At the same time, multiplicity of goals may also lead to more leeway for managers of organisations, as judgement and measurement of performance become more complex. The different stakeholders of social enterprises also differ in the way they hold and can execute Hirschman options—exit, voice, and loyalty (Anheier and Krlev 2015)—which reflects on the very distinct power sources and negotiation and bargaining power these stakeholders have. Being accountable to such a diverse set of stakeholders requires social enterprises to pay particular attention to different dimensions of accountability—accountability for what and to whom.

Navigating and/or aligning multiple goals and interests of stakeholders is critical for social enterprises to avoid mission drift, i.e. losing sight of their social mission, while navigating market and political pressures (Cornforth 2014; Ebrahim et al. 2014). Governance has been identified as a key mechanism that helps social enterprises to avoid mission drift—to 'stay hybrid', fulfilling multiple goals and attending to demands of multiple stakeholders (Mair et al. 2015). Governance, scholars suggest, enables social enterprises to thrive amidst multiple institutional pressures, preventing them from drifting too far towards either social or commercial goals, and allowing them to account for and respond to multiple stakeholder demands. However, empirical evidence regarding how governance in social enterprises addresses these challenges is scarce, and we still know little about governance and the specific mechanisms that enable social enterprises to avoid drifting away from their social mission and be co-opted by internal or external pressures (Mair et al. 2015).

The objective in this chapter is to review canonical theoretical approaches on corporate governance and assess their usefulness to understand governance of social enterprises. We will highlight productive angles to examine social enterprise governance and provide first empirical insights on how social enterprises govern in order to inform future research in this domain.

Probing the Usefulness of Corporate Governance Research to Understand Social Enterprises

Governance from an organisational perspective has been defined as 'the structures, systems and processes concerned with ensuring the overall direction, control and accountability of an organisation' (Cornforth and Chambers 2010). Throughout the last decades, a number of different approaches to governance have been developed by scholars coming from different disciplines, shaping theory and practice alike. Common to all of them is the view that governance refers to an established set of structures and practices that maintain stability within but also beyond the organisation. We will refer here to three of these approaches considered as canonical to the study of corporate governance.

The Agency Approach

The agency approach to governance emphasises the need for control within the organisation. Developed from economic theory, it starts from the assumption that an agent taking decisions on behalf of another actor, i.e. the principal, will take those decisions in her own best interests rather than in the interest of the principal (which are usually the owners or the shareholders of the organisation) (Eisenhardt 1989). According to the literature, the agency problem is likely to arise in any context where the interests of the principal and agent are not aligned and/or access to information is asymmetric. Control thus allows diminishing the risk associated with the agent deviating from the principal's interests. While a variety of control mechanisms have been discussed in the literature, the most established mechanism to tackle the agency problem remains the board with formal decision-making power representing the shareholders in the organisation (Dalton et al. 2007). The primary function of boards is to monitor actions to ensure that the management operates in the interests of shareholders by carrying out functions such as controlling the chief executive officer (CEO), monitoring strategy, and financial oversight (Rindova 1999). The agency approach to governance is particularly dominant in Anglo-Saxon literature and the literature regarding for-profit governance, supporting the one-tier model of shareholder orientation and composition of boards.

While the agency approach has dominated both literature and the practice of organisational governance for decades, scholars suggest that this approach may not be apt to study and develop governance mechanisms in social enterprises. The agency problem becomes more accentuated in social enterprises where it is difficult to settle on 1) who the principal is and 2) what the mandate of the organisation is. In social enterprises multiple stakeholders—funders, beneficiaries, donors, and clients—typically all act as principals. However, they are more or less powerful in influencing the organisation, and they differ in their expectations and the pressures they put on the organisation (Mair et al. 2015; Anheier and Krlev 2015; Ostrower and Stone 2006). Social enterprises therefore are likely to face multiple accountability disorder (Koppell 2005, 2011). They may at times emphasise the directives of funders, while at other times they may focus on customers' or beneficiaries' interests. In the long run, this may lead to stakeholders being displeased and the organisation struggling between multiple goals and accountabilities, ultimately facilitating mission drift.

Agency theory assumes that human behaviour is individualistic and self-serving, motivated primarily by external drivers such as status or financial incentives; it emphasises the extrinsic motivations of agents. Empirical studies have shown however that managers in social enterprises have a high level of intrinsic motivation too, wanting to contribute to achieve the goals of the organisation, sometimes even at the expense of their own interests. This view conflicts with the narrow economic self-interest suggested by agency theory and does not allow for the complexity of social enterprises aiming to deliver on multiple goals while being embedded in a complex web of stakeholders with different interests, expectations, and power.

The Stewardship Approach

The stewardship approach to governance starts from the assumption of a more intrinsic motivation of agents. Emerging from sociological and psychological theory, it starts from the assumption that managers will in fact act as responsible stewards of their organisation and its goals. It posits that actors aspire to higher purposes, that they are not self-serving individuals as suggested by agency theory, but that they act with altruism and intrinsic motivation for the benefit of the organisation, its stakeholders, and the public good (Davis et al. 1997; Donaldson and Davis 1991). The key question in stewardship theory is thus not how to control narrow self-interest and principal–agent problems but how to build organisational structures that support and empower actors in working towards organisational goals. Failure to do so, scholars suggest, arises from structural problems rather than principal–agent problems (Van Puyvelde et al. 2012). The stewardship approach has been particularly present in European literature and the literature regarding non-profit governance (see Chapter 6), supporting a two-tier model of governing boards where employees and other stakeholders are represented.

However, while emphasising intrinsic motivation, stewardship theory struggles to explain variations of this intrinsic motivation within the organisation. For instance, in work integration organisations, some members may prefer scaling the social performance of the organisation in terms of providing more support for their employees with special needs, while others may prefer scaling in terms of providing more jobs for more people belonging to a disadvantaged group. This may be the case in co-determined boards.

While such internal conflicts may occur and may trigger mission drift, in social enterprises also external relationships tend to become challenging for the organisation. Although the organisation and actors within the organisation may be motivated to act in the interest of their principals—donors, target groups, customers, or the public—those interests may not always be aligned, thus facilitating mission drift. This may be aggravated by informational asymmetries. For instance, if the beneficiaries of the social enterprise differ from its customers, market feedback may come more explicitly from customers that guarantee the economic sustainability of the organisation than from the target group the organisation aims to support through its social mission (Ebrahim et al. 2014). In this vein, work integration social enterprises for example may struggle to balance special needs and performance variations of their consultants and expectations of their customers that demand quick, high-quality services and products. These informational asymmetries can have an influence on the way in which managers interpret their stewardship role in the organisation. Thus, also stewardship theory has only partial potential to account for multiple goals and different interests and expectations that internal and external stakeholders place upon social enterprises.

The Resource Dependence Approach

The third approach to organisational governance is based on resource dependence theory (Pfeffer and Salancik 1978). In contrast to agency and stewardship theory that focus mostly on internal aspects of the organisation, the resource dependence approach accounts for the multiple external pressures placed upon organisations. The resource dependence approach to governance starts from the assumption that organisations are dependent on their environment and that they have to manage these dependencies in order to survive.

Similar to the agency approach, the resource dependence approach gives high relevance to the board as a key governance body which, in this view, assumes a service function rather than a control function and allows the organisation to benefit from and align with its external environment: 'When an organization appoints an individual to a board, it expects the individual will come to support the organization, will concern himself with its problems, will variably present it to others, and will try to aid it' (Pfeffer and Salancik 1978: 163). Board members engage in facilitating the acquisition of resources that are critical to the firm's success, building relationships with key stakeholders (Boyd 1990; Hillman et al. 2001), facilitating access to capital (Mizruchi and Stearns 1988), enhancing company reputation and image (Selznick 1949), and establishing contacts with the external environment (Zahra and Pearce 1989). In this regard, boards provide a co-optation mechanism by 'absorbing new elements into the leadership or policy-determining structure of an organization as a means of averting threats to its stability or existence' (Selznick 1949: 34). Co-optation, as Selznick proposes, is related to the process by which an institutional environment impinges itself upon an organisation and effects changes in its leadership and policies. It also involves commitment, in the sense that the groups to which adaptation has been made constrain the field of choice available to the organisation or leadership in question.

Since the 1980s, resource dependence approaches to governance have come to dominate the literature on non-profit and charity organisations. Boards assuming a service function are often associated with NPOs that depend on external financial support to sustain their activities (Guo 2007). However, they have been criticised for limiting community access to governance (such as for beneficiaries or the public they aim to serve) and prioritising co-optation of financial resource providers. In the context of social enterprises, fault lines, i.e. hypothetical dividing lines splitting a group into relatively homogeneous subgroups, and power imbalances in boards have emerged as problematic in diverse boards that aim to manage and co-opt diverse external pressures (Crucke and Knockaert 2016; Mair et al. 2015). For instance, while beneficiary involvement in boards has been considered a promising avenue to ensure downwards accountability and adherence to the social mission, target groups may not possess enough confidence, skills, and power to actively voice their needs, while other members such as donors and funders may more strongly voice their interests. Ultimately, absorbing resource providers into the organisation may thus exacerbate rather than help control the risk of mission drift, as some groups may gain more power over the organisation's decisions and management.

Dominant Governance Approaches

Table 8.1 summarises the different approaches to governance and the limitations they have in helping social enterprises to manage the risk of mission drift and diverse internal and external pressures. As shown previously, while each of the governance approaches brings important insights to governance issues, none of them provides a solution to the particular governance challenges of social enterprises, specifically, balancing multiple goals and stakeholder pressures.

In particular, we find that the multiplicity of both internal and external goals and interests of principals is a challenge that is not or only partly addressed by the three approaches.

Productive Lenses to Examine Social Enterprise Governance

In order to meet the limitations of existing theoretical approaches on corporate governance, particularly in regard to avoiding mission drift and co-optation by powerful groups of stakeholders, scholars have discussed how mechanisms such as board governance (Ebrahim et al. 2014; Mair et al. 2015), new legal forms (Brakman Reiser 2010; Cooney 2013), and mechanisms to ensure accountability (Ebrahim and Rangan 2010) could contribute to successful governance of social enterprises.

Table 8.1. Approaches to governance and their limitations for governance of social enterprises

	Agency	Stewardship	Resource dependence
Theoretical basis	Economics	Sociology/Psychology	Economics/Sociology
Basis of literature	Anglo-Saxon literature, for-profit literature	European literature, non-profit literature	Anglo-Saxon and European non-profit literature
Dominant view of board	One tier-model: shareholder orientation and composition	Two-tier model: co-determination of employees and representatives of the public interest on the boards	Governance not principally driven by boards but affected by diverse external forces and power relationships
Approach	Control	Collaboration	Co-optation
Principal–agent relationship	Goal conflict	Aligned goals	Multiple goals
Agent's motivation	Intrinsic	Intrinsic	Extrinsic
Human behaviour	Individualist	Collectivist	Dependent
Governance mechanisms	Monitoring, incentives	Empowering structures	Absorbing external elements
Limitations for governance of social enterprises	- Focuses on a single principal or principals with homogenous interests - Does not account for intrinsic motivation - Focuses on internal agency problems - Assumes goal conflict between principal and agent	- Focuses on a single principal or principals with homogenous interests - Does not account for differences in motivations - Focuses on internal structures - Assumes goal congruence	- Does not provide solutions for power imbalances and fault lines - May exacerbate risk of mission drift - May create principal–agent problems

Source: Adapted from Van Puyvelde et al. 2012.

Governing Boards

As mentioned in the previous section, governing boards have long been considered both by agency and resource dependence theorists an effective means to either control agents in organisations in order to make them contribute to organisational goals rather than maximise self-interest (Dalton et al. 2007) or to act as intermediaries between the organisation and its external environment (Ostrower and Stone 2006). As social enterprises are often small organisations with less than fifty employees (SEFORÏS 2017), they rarely draw on large, formalised board arrangements. This also reduces bargaining and power struggles within the board and between board and management, processes that can be more visible and relevant in larger organisations.

In social enterprises boards have been depicted as playing a major role in avoiding mission drift, as they could internalise, manage, and arbitrate external pressures and conflicting interests (Mair et al. 2015; Jones 2007; Weisbrod 2004). When representing different types of stakeholders, boards are expected to play a role in balancing divergent expectations and interests from key actors such as investors and beneficiaries (Huybrechts 2010; Pache and Santos 2010). In this vein, governing boards become an interface between organisations and their external environment, acting as carriers of pressures from the environment, while simultaneously being a buffer for the organisation in regard to these pressures. More recently, however, scholars have pointed towards the potential conflicts arising from diverse boards. Subgroups defending different and sometimes competing interests and goals may lead to the emergence of fault lines within the board. Tensions and power imbalances between different subgroups can make it difficult to achieve a clear purpose and may block decision-making processes (Crucke and Knockaert 2016; Spear et al. 2009) thus ultimately not solving governance challenges but exacerbating them.

The key role of boards in governing organisations more broadly is increasingly challenged by scholars who propose that they are a 'useless, if mostly harmless, institution carried on out of inertia' (Gillespie and Zweig 2010) and that they do not in fact make much of a difference in most cases (Boivie et al. 2016). Those scholars also suggest that it is time to move beyond the 'one-size-fits-all' approaches that have been advocated for a long time regarding board composition and role. They argue in favour of building specific solutions for specific needs, so that boards can actually make a difference. Social enterprises provide an opportunity to go down this avenue. Until today however, we have little empirical evidence about the actual importance of board governance in social enterprises, about the functions the boards fulfil, about the composition of the boards, and how board governance enables social enterprises to thrive.

Scholars also suggest it is time to move on from the assumption that boards are the solution to all governance challenges organisations face. They invite us to examine governance mechanisms beyond the board, such as new legal forms and stakeholder groups that can put pressure on organisations to stay true to the multiple goals they set out to pursue (Aguilera et al. 2015; Boivie et al. 2016).

Legal Forms

Legal forms 'define relations of competition, cooperation, and market-specific definitions of how firms should be organized' (Fligstein 1996). Both organisational and legal scholars have pointed out the constraints that traditional non-profit and for-profit legal forms place on social enterprises. While boundaries between sectors are increasingly blurring (Bromley and Meyer 2017), legal forms are still tied to neat divisions (Cooney 2013). The assumption is that a for-profit legal form will force social enterprises to single-mindedly focus on profit, with little opportunity to legally protect the social mission of the entity or its founders.[2] Under a non-profit legal form, on the other hand, the social vision can be protected, but business strategies, particularly equity capital, are foreclosed (Brakman Reiser 2010; Mair et al. 2015). This often forces social enterprises to limit their revenue-generating activities and rely on donations or grants.

Establishing hybrid legal forms has been discussed as one major aspect to help social enterprises to thrive. Allowing for the combination of characteristics from both for-profit and non-profit legal forms would make it easier for organisations to pursue both a revenue-generating activity and a social mission at the same time (Ebrahim et al. 2014). In some countries, like in the United States and the United Kingdom, hybrid legal forms such as benefit corporations or community interest companies (CICs) that allow generating profits and assets for the public good have been established since the 2000s to offer more flexible legal arrangements. Brakman Reiser and Dean (2017) suggest that what they call mission-protected hybrids can allow protecting adherence to a social mission and controlling the risk of selling out the social mission for profit, while at the same time opening opportunities to raise capital. In their view legislation can become an ally that does not frustrate

---

[2] Legal forms and legislative frameworks, however, differ greatly across different countries. For an overview of legal forms adopted by social enterprises in different countries see SEFORÏS cross-country report (SEFORÏS 2017). Additional resources on legal frameworks of social enterprises also available in Galera and Borzaga (2009).

but rather empowers social enterprises in their efforts to simultaneously pursue multiple goals.

This, they propose, will be ensured when the social enterprise prioritises social good in the aggregate. For instance, they suggest that a mission-protected hybrid that manufactures and distributes low-cost lanterns in the developing world to combat poverty would not violate the prioritisation mandate by choosing a supplier that produces the metal sheeting it needs at the lowest price point, even if choosing a more expensive supplier could imply higher pay for some low-income workers. As long as the entity in its broader constellation of actions prioritises its anti-poverty mission, such individual business decisions will not conflict with the relevant purpose requirements (Brakman Reiser and Dean 2017).

While the examples they study show that potential legal forms have to empower social enterprises to thrive and stay true to multiple goals, in the majority of countries social enterprises are still forced to pursue their dual mission under a non-hybrid for-profit or non-profit legal form. Despite this, we know little about what legal forms social enterprises actually assume and how they deal with restrictions associated with different legal forms.

Accountability Relationships

As discussed previously, one major challenge that social enterprises face is how to manage competing pressures from multiple principals. A major question in this regard is whether and how social enterprises are being held accountable for their activities and decisions and whether and how stakeholder groups have the opportunity to monitor activities and decisions (Ebrahim 2003).

Upward accountability to donors, foundations, governments, and clients (if they are not also beneficiaries) is often focused on providing evidence that designated funding is being spent for designated purposes, while downward accountability to stakeholders such as beneficiaries and target groups hinges on mechanisms that ensure the organisation is providing the services and products the target groups considers valuable (Edwards and Hulme 1996; Ebrahim et al. 2014).

Scholars consider reporting to be the basis of any accountability relationship as it facilitates judgements about behaviour and performance of the organisation. This, in turn, allows stakeholders to monitor and consequently to question or sanction activities of the organisation, i.e. to hold it accountable

(Bovens 2006; Koppell 2011). However, while stakeholders such as capital providers have an exit option when unsatisfied, beneficiaries often have limited or no alternatives in case they are not satisfied with the services and products provided to them. They mostly lack an exit option and therefore can only mediate the accountability relationship through voicing their concerns (Ebrahim et al. 2014). This, in turn, relates back to the issue of inclusion of beneficiaries and target groups on boards in order to ensure that social performance is reported and that the feedback of the target group is taken into consideration in decision-making.

For social enterprises, however, dependence on powerful principals bears the risk of emphasising upward accountability mechanisms, while losing connection to the target group and their needs and requirements. Until now, we know little about the reporting practices by which social enterprises ensure upwards and downwards accountability and how those enable or hinder social enterprises to stay true to multiple goals and stakeholder demands.

Empirical Insights: Governance at Play in Social Enterprises

To advance our understanding of social enterprise governance and to sharpen theoretical approaches we propose to look at how social enterprises govern. Especially the analysis of practice and structures relating to boards, legal forms, and reporting practices of social enterprises in different countries might be helpful to systematically build a knowledge base and at the same time to inform theorising efforts. We do so by drawing on both qualitative and quantitative data. Combining findings from survey and case data across different countries and sectors allows us to identify prevailing established governance practices and structures across social enterprises, while also accounting for emerging, not yet formalised structures, practices, and developments over time.

Our data stem from a unique and large-scale study about social enterprises supported and funded by the European Commission and carried out by an international research team (www.seforis.eu). The Social Enterprises as a Force for more Inclusive and Innovative Societies (SEFORÏS) research project was conducted over a period of three years in nine countries (China, Germany, Hungary, Portugal, Romania, Russia, Spain, Sweden, and UK). The study was based on in-depth qualitative and quantitative interviews with managers of social enterprises. We use the resulting twenty-five in-depth case studies and the large dataset including 1,030 social enterprises to shed light on concrete governance structures and practices that social enterprises make use of across the world (SEFORÏS 2018; Huysentruyt et al. 2016).

In the following sections we report on insights and patterns we found on governing boards, legal forms, and reporting practices. In each section we first report on our quantitative results and then share qualitative findings.

Boards: From Symbolic to Substantive?

In our sample, 90 per cent of the surveyed social enterprises indicated that they have a board with formal decision-making power. However, we find that the majority of boards are set up for symbolic reasons, i.e. to comply with legal pressures or interests of powerful stakeholders: 65.8 per cent of the entrepreneurs indicate that they had established a board because it was a legal requirement or a requirement from funders. On the other hand, our survey findings show that fewer social enterprises (21.9 per cent) establish a board for substantive reasons and to face the particular challenges of social enterprises, including as a mechanism to balance interests of different stakeholders or receive external feedback.

Regarding the functions that the boards fulfil, we find that most organisations imitate board governance from for-profit organisations based on the agency approach. The boards have control functions (including tasks such as financial oversight, monitoring programmes and services, evaluating the CEO, contributing to internal policy, and serving as a sounding board for management) and strategic functions (planning for the future of the organisation). Fewer organisations indicate having boards assuming service functions as suggested by resource dependence theory (including tasks such as fundraising, building community relations, influencing policy, and educating the public). Of the respondents, 36.9 per cent also stated that boards fulfil tasks corresponding to different functions of control, of ensuring hybridity, or others depending on the particular needs of the organisations.

In terms of board diversity, the majority of the surveyed social enterprises had boards with only one (39.4 per cent of organisations) or two (36.5 per cent of organisations) different types of representatives, with most boards consisting of representatives from business and/or the social sector. Only 24.0 per cent of the organisations surveyed indicated having three or more different types of stakeholders on the board. Board inclusiveness—including beneficiary representatives on the boards—is also not a dominant practice: only a third of all surveyed organisations have beneficiary representatives on the board.

While our survey findings indicate that boards of social enterprises do not always include a wide range of stakeholders and that beneficiary representatives are rather the exception than the rule, our case studies show that organisations establish structures or positions beyond the board that allow them to account for multiple stakeholder groups and their particular interests. For instance, in the UK an organisation has created a beneficiary committee in order to ensure input from beneficiaries. As the social enterprise's representative described it, 'This would be a small board of about 4–6 people, former beneficiaries of [the organisation]. They would be consulted every now and then on matters that directly influence the service users of [the organisation].'

In Germany, we found that organisations establish positions within the organisation but outside the board with the main purpose to mediate between different stakeholder groups and goals of the organisation. Thus, even if employees are not formally included in the board, they are engaged in organisational governance from a different position. As an employee of a German social enterprise explained, 'My role [...] is defined by representing the interests of our (beneficiaries). And that you have to align with the economic needs that exist in the organisation.'

Our findings suggest that the establishment of governance mechanisms beyond the board may enable the organisations to maintain and manage multiple goals and relationships with multiple stakeholders with diverse interests and needs.

Legal Forms: From Constraining to Enabling?

Our survey findings show that social enterprises across countries assume a broad variety of legal forms: non-profit, for-profit, and hybrid. In some countries (for example China and the UK) the majority of social enterprises assumes a for-profit legal form, whereas in other countries (for example, Romania, Hungary, and Germany) social enterprises have mostly non-profit legal forms. Our survey findings also indicate that social enterprises combine legal forms flexibly in order to conduct their activities and respond to external pressures: 16.1 per cent of the organisations combine traditional legal forms, a for-profit and a non-profit organisation. As shown in Table 8.2,

Table 8.2. Selective overview of the variety of legal forms assumed by social enterprises across countries

Germany (N=107)	Sweden (N=106)	UK (N=135)	Spain (N=125)
Eingetragener Verein (e.V.) 'Registered Association' (45%)	Ideell förening 'Non-profit organisation' (40%)	Private company limited by guarantee (Ltd) (41%)	Fundación (sin ánimo de lucro) 'Foundation' (25%)
Gemeinnützige GmbH (gGmbH) 'Limited Liability Company with public benefit status' (17%)	Aktiebolag (AB) 'Ltd' Minimum capital SEK50,000 (20%)	Charity (36%) Community interest company (CIC) (10.5%)	Asociación 'Association' (20%) Cooperativa de Trabajo Asociado 'Worker's cooperative' (19%)
Gesellschaft mit beschränkter Haftung (GmbH) 'Limited Liability Company' (15%) Other (6%)	Ekonomisk förening (Ek. för.) 'Economic association' (20%) Stiftelse 'Foundation' (11%)	Private company limited by shares (8%) Industrial and Provident Society (1.5%)	Sociedad Limitada Nueva Empresa 'New Enterprise Limited Company' (17%) Other (5.5%)
Gesellschaft bürgerlichen Rechts (GbR) 'Private Partnership' (5.5%)	Aktiebolag med särskild vinstutdelnings-begränsning (SVB) 'Limited liability company with dividend restrictions' (3%)		

Note: For a full overview see the SEFORÏS cross-country report (2017).

which provides an overview of legal forms in a selection of the countries in our sample, 10.5 per cent of the organisations in the UK assume a new hybrid legal form (CIC). It is the only country represented in our sample where such a legal form is available.

While we find that social enterprises assume and combine diverse legal forms, our qualitative findings indicate that social enterprises do not necessarily stick with one legal form over time. While social entrepreneurs give much thought to the implications of choosing legal forms initially, particularly related to how they generate revenues and the type of stakeholders they engage with, we find that organisations change legal forms as the organisations develop and external and internal demands change.

Legal forms are used by some organisations to manage external pressures. For instance, the founder of a German social enterprise successfully operating under a for-profit legal form told us that they decided to add a non-profit legal form not necessarily because it was needed for functional reasons but more in order to manage expectations from external stakeholders. As the founder explained, 'We did this [combining legal forms] so that people take us seriously. We do not really need this [non-profit] legal form for our work. But people think only a non-profit is appropriate for this. If we say we are a for-profit they think we want to make money out of it.' Thus, while the for-profit legal form allows the organisation to operate successfully on the market, the non-profit legal form allows them to gain external legitimacy and emphasise commitment to the social mission.

Another example is changing the legal form as a reaction to shifts in the way organisations generate revenues. While younger organisations often assume a non-profit legal form to absorb public funding and minimise tax burden, organisations that increase self-generation of revenues and reduce dependence on public funding or donations over time decide to change to a for-profit legal form. However, as indicated previously, they may also maintain a non-profit legal form for legitimacy reasons and for taxation benefits.

Thus, our findings suggest that legal forms not only constrain social enterprises but are also used strategically as a tool. They contribute to relating to and gaining legitimacy from particular stakeholder groups, such as funders and the general public, and they also serve to manage changing internal needs of the organisation such as tax exemptions or access to particular sources of funding.

Reporting Practices

Our survey findings show that most social enterprises report and measure their social performance. Social performance measurement and reporting is still in its infancy in the non-profit and philanthropic sector. In 2010 only 13 per cent of German philanthropic organisations had a printed annual report (Albrecht et al. 2013). In our sample, however, 65 per cent of the social enterprises surveyed systematically assess their social performance and report on it. The largest share of organisations (40 per cent) focuses on reporting their social performance to capital providers. However, a much smaller proportion of organisations (20 per cent) indicated that they feel most accountable to their capital providers. A much higher percentage (40 per cent), in turn, feels most accountable to the beneficiaries, but only 10 per cent of the organisations report to them. This depicts a decoupling between reporting practices and the actual commitment of the organisations towards particular stakeholder groups. Nevertheless, 93.8 per cent of all organisations indicated that they measure at least once a year how satisfied the beneficiaries are with their organisation and its activities. Moreover, even if figures are not necessarily reported, they are used internally: almost all (99.6 per cent) of the organisations surveyed indicated that they use beneficiary feedback to improve their services and products.

Our case study findings confirm that social performance measurement and reporting serve primarily as means to ensure funding and maintain partnerships with powerful stakeholders. The majority of social enterprises use quantitative measures to assess their social performance, focusing on the number of beneficiaries or clients served. As a social entrepreneur in Portugal put it, 'The monitoring is tuned to the needs of the main funding body's report [...] We are adjusting the tools to fit the needs of the stakeholders or for whoever it is essential that we would produce the report to maintain the partnership.'

Our case study findings indicate that while funders often push particular measurement and reporting requirements on the organisations, those are often decoupled from the organisation's actual activities. Formal reporting is primarily used as a tool to ensure upwards accountability, while playing a minor role for downwards accountability.

However, as noted earlier, social enterprises do in fact establish additional internal mechanisms to qualitatively measure beneficiary satisfaction, collect feedback, and use the findings to improve the services and products they provide to the beneficiaries. As a German social entrepreneur explains, 'We speak with the families and with the volunteers and discuss how things went. You ask for feedback, also negative feedback, how did it go, what could have been done better, what are your suggestions to improve?'

Thus, while reporting to stakeholders such as capital providers is focused on communicating success and quantitative indicators, internal performance measurement focuses on qualitative measures that allow the organisation to learn and constantly improve services and products to better fit the needs of the beneficiaries. While focusing on only one of these types of performance measurements may compromise either the financial viability of the organisation or the quality of the services provided, combining both orientations may enable organisations to perform well both financially and in terms of the quality of their social service provision.

Looking Ahead

Our assessment of current literature and first insights from how social enterprises govern suggests that a more thorough theoretical and empirical understanding of social enterprise governance is imminent. Moreover, advancing the knowledge base in a theoretically meaningful and empirically accurate way will be critical to inform this vibrant field of practice currently in search of the appropriate policies.

Our findings show that a more nuanced and in-depth empirical study of governance structures, practices, and mechanisms in social enterprises can lead the way to identify emerging governance arrangements such as adapting dual or hybrid legal forms, changing legal forms over time, or establishing particular bodies, positions, or mechanisms to ensure involvement of beneficiaries. Those may be important governance mechanisms that allow social enterprises to remain hybrid and balance multiple goals and the needs and interests of multiple stakeholders with different recourse to power.

In this chapter, we have not discussed drivers and consequences of these governance arrangements. Preliminary analysis indicates that organisations combining two legal forms outperform for-profit organisations in terms of social performance and that organisations that report their social performance to diverse stakeholders achieve better social performance. Therefore, organisations developing new governance mechanisms such as those ensuring engagement of beneficiaries or dealing flexibly with established legal forms seem to be more successful than others that draw on established governance structures and mechanisms for primarily symbolic and less for substantive reasons. However, more research is needed to understand the particular governance solutions social enterprises develop to meet their specific needs and challenges.

As the aim of this chapter was to gain a general understanding of governance in social enterprises across countries, we were not able to account for variations among countries and cases. However, our findings do indicate differences in the flexibility of social enterprises in dealing with legal forms and in their reasons for establishing a board. We also found variations in how social performance is measured. Further research is needed to unpack the role of context in the development of all these governance arrangements.

Our findings also raise questions about institutionalisation processes and isomorphic pressures (DiMaggio and Powell 1983; Mizruchi and Fein 1999).

While the informal structures and practices we identified are implemented by some organisations and not by others, the establishment of internal performance measures or multi-level structures may spread and become more formalised as more and more organisations adopt such structures and practices. This may in the long run trigger changes in prevailing conceptions of control (Fligstein 1990).

The findings reported on in this chapter also have implications for policy-makers, raising questions regarding the way in which emerging practices and structures can and should be formalised. Some of these questions for instance can be related to establishing an umbrella mechanism coupling for-profit and non-profit legal forms to better regulate the use of legal forms for legitimacy reasons. Other questions refer to formalising governance structures that ensure the involvement of beneficiaries in organisational governance.

This is a first step towards advancing a more empirically anchored research agenda that looks into governance starting from the concrete experiences and practices of organisations. This view can further our understanding at a theoretical level of how the changing organisational landscape influences governance, and this in turn can better serve the advancement of good practices in organisations. Our research also responds to the increasingly diverse needs of people inhabiting organisations that demand variety within capitalism in order to build effective and well-governed organisations.

Acknowledgements

The present research has been developed with the support of the SEFORÏS Project 'Social Entrepreneurship as a Force for more Inclusive and Innovative Societies'. This project has received funding from the European Union's Seventh Framework Programme for research, technological development, and demonstration under grant agreement no 613500. We thank Nikolas Rathert, Ute Stephan, and Marieke Huysentruyt for their support.

References

Aguilera, R. V., Desender, K., Bednar, M. K., and Lee, J. H. (2015). 'Connecting the Dots. Bringing External Corporate Governance into the Corporate Governance Puzzle', *The Academy of Management Annals*, 9(1): 483–573.

Albrecht, K., Beck, S., Hoelscher, P., Plazek, M., and von der Ahe, B. (2013). *Wirkungsorientierte Steuerung in Non-Profit-Organisationen*. Berlin: Phineo.

Anheier, H. K. and Krlev, G. (2015). 'Governance and Management of Hybridity. Special Issue', *International Studies of Management & Organization*, 45(3): 193–281.

Battilana, J. and Dorado, S. (2010). 'Building Sustainable Hybrid Organizations: The Case of Commercial Microfinance Organizations', *Academy of Management Journal*, 53(6): 1419–40.

Besharov, M. L. and Smith, W. K. (2014). 'Multiple Institutional Logics in Organizations: Explaining Their Varied Nature and Implications', *Academy of Management Review*, 39(3): 364–81.

Boivie, S., Bednar, M. K., Aguilera, R. V., and Andrus, J. L. (2016). 'Are Boards Designed to Fail? The Implausibility of Effective Board Monitoring', *Academy of Management Annals*, 10(1): 1–93.

Bovens, M. (2006). 'Analysing and Assessing Public Accountability. A Conceptual Framework', *European Law Journal*, 13(4): 447–68.

Boyd, B. (1990). 'Corporate Linkages and Organizational Environment: A Test of the Resource Dependence Model', *Strategic Management Journal*, 11:6: 419–30.

Brakman Reiser, D. (2010). 'Governing and Financing Blended Enterprise', *Chicago-Kent Law Review*, 85(2): 619–54.

Brakman Reiser, D. and Dean, S. A. (2017). *Social Enterprise Law. Trust, Public Benefit and Capital Markets*. Oxford: Oxford University Press.

Bromley, P. and Meyer, J. W. (2017). ' "They Are All Organizations": The Cultural Roots of Blurring Between Nonprofit, Business and Government Sectors', *Administration and Society*, 49(7): 939–66.

Cooney, K. (2013). 'Mission Control: Examining the Institutionalization of New Legal Forms of Social Enterprise in Different Strategic Action Fields', in B. Gidron and Y. Hasenfeld (eds.), *Social Enterprise: An Organizational Perspective*. Basingstoke, Hampshire: Palgrave Macmillan, 198–221.

Cornforth, C. (2014). 'Understanding and Combating Mission Drift in Social Enterprises', *Social Enterprise Journal*, 10(1): 3–20.

Cornforth, C. and Chambers, N. (2010). 'The Role of Corporate Governance and Boards in Organisational Performance', in K. Walsh, G. Harvey, and P. Jas (eds.), *Connecting Knowledge and Performance in Public Services: From Knowing to Doing*. Cambridge, UK: Cambridge University Press, 99–127.

Crucke, S. and Knockaert, M. (2016). 'When Stakeholder Representation Leads to Faultlines. A Study of Board Service Performance in Social Enterprises', *Journal of Management Studies*, 53(5): 768–93.

Dalton, D. R., Hitt, M. A., Certo, S. T., and Dalton, C. M. (2007). 'The Fundamental Agency Problem and Its Mitigation. Independence, Equity, and the Market for Corporate Control', *The Academy of Management Annals*, 1(1): 1–64.

Davis, J. H., Schoorman, F. D., and Donaldson, L. (1997). 'Toward a Stewardship Theory of Management', *The Academy of Management Review*, 22(1): 20–47.

DiMaggio, P. J. and Powell, W. W. (1983). 'The Iron Cage Revisited: Institutional Isomorphism and Collective Rationality in Organizational Fields', *American Sociological Review*, 48(2): 147–60.

Donaldson, L. and Davis, J.H. (1991). 'Stewardship Theory or Agency Theory: CEO Governance and Shareholder Returns', *Australian Journal of Management*, 16(1): 49–64.

Ebrahim, A. (2003). 'Accountability in Practice: Mechanisms for NGOs', *World Development*, 31(5): 813–29.

Ebrahim A. and Rangan, V. K. (2010). 'Putting the Brakes on Impact: A Contingency Framework for Measuring Social Performance', *Academy of Management Annual Meeting Proceedings*, 2010(1). doi: 10.5465/ambpp.2010.54500944

Ebrahim, A., Battilana, J., and Mair, J. (2014). 'The Governance of Social Enterprises: Mission Drift and Accountability Challenges in Hybrid Organizations', *Research in Organizational Behavior*, 34: 81–100.

Edwards, M. and Hulme, D. (1996). 'Too Close for Comfort? The Impact of Official Aid on Nongovernmental Organizations', *World Development*, 24(6): 961–73.

Eisenhardt, K. M. (1989). 'Agency Theory: An Assessment and Review', *Academy of Management Review*, 14(1): 57–74.

European Commission (2017). *Social enterprises*. (Online) Retrieved from http://ec.europa.eu/growth/sectors/social-economy/enterprises_en (accessed 20 August 2017).

Fligstein, N. (1990). *The Transformation of Corporate Control*. Cambridge, MA: Harvard University Press.

Fligstein, N. (1996). 'Markets as Politics: A Political-Cultural Approach to Market Institutions', *American Sociological Review*, 61(4): 656–73.

Galera, G. and Borzaga, C. (2009). Social Enterprise: An International Overview of its Conceptual Evolution and Legal Implementation', *Social Enterprise Journal*, 5(3): 210–28.

Gillespie, J. and Zweig, D. (2010). *Money for Nothing: How CEOs and Boards Are Bankrupting America*. New York: Free Press.

Guo, C. (2007). 'When Government Becomes the Principal Philanthropist: The Effects of Public Funding on Patterns of Nonprofit Governance', *Public Administration Review*, 67(3): 458–73.

Hillman, A.J., Keim, G. D., and Luce, R. A. (2001). 'Board Composition and Stakeholder Performance: Do Stakeholder Directors Make a Difference?', *Business & Society*, 40(3): 295–314.

Huybrechts, B. (2010). 'The Governance of Fair Trade Social Enterprises in Belgium', *Social Enterprise Journal*, 6(2): 110–24.

Huysentruyt, M., Mair, J., and Stephan, U. (2016). 'Market-Oriented and Mission-Focused: Social Enterprises around the Globe', *Stanford Social Innovation Review*. (Online) Retrieved from https://ssir.org/articles/entry/market_oriented_and_mission_focused_social_enterprises_around_the_globe (accessed 19 October 2019).

Jones, M. B. (2007). 'The Multiple Sources of Mission Drift', *Nonprofit and Voluntary Sector Quarterly*, 36 (2): 299–307.

Koppell, J. G. S. (2005). 'Pathologies of Accountability: ICANN and the Challenge of "Multiple Accountabilities Disorder"', *Public Administration Review*, 65(1): 94–108.

Koppell, J. G. S. (2011). 'Accountability for Global Governance Organizations', in M. J. Dubnick and H. G. Frederickson (eds.), *Accountable Governance: Problems and Promises*. New York: Routledge, 55–79.

Mair, J. and Martí, I. (2006). 'Social Entrepreneurship Research: A Source of Explanation, Prediction, and Delight', *Journal of World Business*, 41(1): 36–44.

Mair, J., Mayer, J., and Lutz, E. (2015). 'Navigating Institutional Plurality: Organizational Governance in Hybrid Organizations', *Organisation Studies*, 36(6): 713–39.

Mizruchi, M. S. and Fein, L. C. (1999). 'The Social Construction of Organizational Knowledge: A Study of the Uses of Coercive, Mimetic, and Normative Isomorphism', *Administrative Science Quarterly*, 44(4): 653–83.

Mizruchi, M. S. and Stearns, L. B. (1988). 'A Longitudinal Study of the Formation of Interlocking Directorates', *Administrative Science Quarterly*, 33(2): 194–210.

Ostrower, F. and Stone, M. M. (2006). 'Governance: Research Trends, Gaps, and Future Prospects', in W. W. Powell and R. Steinberg (eds.) *The Nonprofit Sector: A Research Handbook*. New Haven: Yale University Press, 612–28.

Pache, A. C. and Santos, F. (2010). 'When Worlds Collide: The Internal Dynamics of Organizational Responses to Conflicting Institutional Demands', *Academy of Management Review*, 35(3): 455–76.

Pfeffer, J. and Salancik, G. R. (1978). *The External Control of Organizations: A Resource Dependence Perspective*. New York: Harper & Row.

Rindova, V. (1999). 'What Corporate Boards Have to Do with Strategy: A Cognitive Perspective', *Journal of Management Studies*, 36(7): 953–75.

SEFORÏS (2018). www.seforis.eu (accessed 22 February 2019).

SEFORÏS (2017). Cross Country Report. (Online) Retrieved from www.seforis.eu/cross-country-report (accessed 22 February 2019).

Selznick, P. (1949). *TVA and the Grass Roots*. New York: Harper & Row.

Spear, R., Cornforth, C., and Aiken, M. (2009). 'The Governance Challenges of Social Enterprises: Evidence from a UK Empirical Study'. *Annals of Public and Cooperative Economics*, 80(2): 247–73.

Van Puyvelde, S., Caers, R., Du Bois, C., and Jegers, M. (2012). 'The Governance of Nonprofit Organizations: Integrating Agency Theory with Stakeholder and Stewardship Theories', *Nonprofit and Voluntary Sector Quarterly*, 41(3): 431–51.

Weisbrod, B. A. (2004). 'The Pitfalls of Profits', *Stanford Social Innovation Review*, 2(3): 40–54.

Zahra, S. A. and Pearce, J. A. (1989). 'Boards of Directors and Corporate Financial Performance: A Review and Integrative Model', *Journal of Management*, 15(2): 291–334.

9

The Governance of International Organisations

Structural Components, Internal Mechanisms, and Contemporary Challenges

Cecilia Cannon and Thomas Biersteker

International organisations (IOs), especially the United Nations (UN) and the Bretton Woods institutions, are key players in the architecture of global governance—from international peace and security to global economic governance, humanitarian assistance, and achieving the world's sustainable development goals. While IOs cannot and should not be equated with global governance, they play critically important, and often leading, roles in global governance. They draw on their store of expertise and the legitimacy they derive from representativeness to facilitate international cooperation to address shared global challenges, and in recent years, they have worked alongside, and at times in partnership with, other institutional actors, such as civil society organisations and global business.

In this chapter, we examine the means and mechanisms through which IOs are governed. We begin with a general introduction to IOs, focusing on the three foundational bodies that generally constitute the governance of IOs: member states (the legislative branch of IOs), IO secretariats (the executive branch of IOs), and IO executive boards (that advise member states and oversee the secretariat's work). We also examine the oversight and accountability mechanisms put in place in IOs to address the challenges of mismanagement, corruption, and failed programmes. We then consider four design features of IOs that vary across different IOs and affect their governance, including an IO's mandate, financing, rule-making and processes of decision-making, and engagement with non-state actors. In this section, we additionally demonstrate how certain design features adapt and reform over time. Finally, we reflect on some of the contemporary

Cecilia Cannon and Thomas Biersteker, *The Governance of International Organisations: Structural Components, Internal Mechanisms, and Contemporary Challenges* In: *Advances in Corporate Governance: Comparative Perspectives.*
Edited by: Helmut K. Anheier and Theodor Baums, Oxford University Press (2020). © Hertie School.
DOI: 10.1093/oso/9780198866367.003.0009

challenges IOs are facing with respect to their governance and describe different ways IOs are adapting and reforming to address some of these challenges.

For a definition of our subject, we take as our starting point Pevehouse, Nordstrom, and Warnke's (2004: 103) definition of an IO as '1) A formal entity; [that] 2) has states as members; and 3) possesses a permanent secretariat or other indication of institutionalization such as headquarters and/or permanent staff.'

Foundations of the Governance of International Organisations

The governance foundations of IOs are fundamentally different from those of other organisations explored in this volume. To begin, IOs are composed principally of individual sovereign *member states*, who delegate authority and operations to a *secretariat*, and who often establish an *executive board* to advise member states and to oversee the secretariat's operations (Saz Carranza et al. 2016). This tripartite governance relationship, frequently referred to as the 'operational structure' in the literature on institutional and organisational design, forms the foundation on which most intergovernmental organisations are governed. States delegate authority to IOs for a variety of different purposes—to solve collective action problems, to address public goods concerns, and/or to pursue national interests within and through IOs.

IOs are founded upon internationally recognised treaties, conventions, or constitutions that are adopted by the member states of an IO at the time the organisation is created, and which can be amended with the approval of the IO's member states. The World Health Organization (WHO), for example, was established through the founding Constitution of the World Health Organization, which was signed by sixty-one states at the International Health Conference in 1946 and entered into force in April 1948.[1] These founding agreements contain the baseline procedures and rules of behaviour for IO member states, secretariats, and executive boards. They also stipulate the procedures for settling disputes concerning the interpretation or application of the founding agreements. Article 75 of WHO's founding constitution, for example, stipulates that disputes not settled by negotiation or by the Health Assembly shall be referred to the International Court of Justice, unless concerned parties agree to an alternative mode of settlement.

---

[1] Amendments to the Constitution were adopted by WHO member states at the 26th, 29th, 39th, and 51st World Health Assemblies, and entered into force in 1977, 1984, 1994, and 2005, respectively.

While member states, secretariats, and executive boards constitute the core, foundational units of governance of most IOs, there is tremendous variation in their form and type. Most theories of IOs rely on some variant of a principal–agent model to describe the mechanisms of governance used by states to delegate authority, and to control, regulate, and thus govern IOs (Hawkins et al. 2006). That is, states are the principals, and IOs are the agents mandated to carry out their collective actions and goals. The roles of the IO secretariats and the IO executive boards in such models are frequently conflated in IO research. Only a small number of scholars have shown the important monitoring function IO boards are expected to play in aligning secretariat decisions with the demands of IO member states, and as deliberative forums for addressing divergent stakeholder expectations and interests (Martinez-Diaz 2009; Hinna and Scarozza 2015; Federo and Saz Carranza 2018b).

The foundational elements that constitute the operational structure of IOs can vary in significant ways, as illustrated below, namely through membership composition, the degree of secretariat autonomy from member states, the degree and nature of involvement of executive boards, and the oversight and accountability mechanisms put in place to govern their activities.

Membership Composition

Membership is among the most contested issues in the creation of new IOs (Koremenos, Lipson, and Snidal 2001: 770). If explicit criteria are articulated for membership, such as in the World Trade Organization (WTO) or the European Union (EU), there is a guarantee (at least at the outset) that members will share certain beliefs, institutional forms, or procedures that may facilitate their reaching agreement. If, on the other hand, the IO pursues universal membership, it may find reaching agreement on controversial or politically polarising issues more difficult. As Mancur Olson argued in *The Logic of Collective Action* (Olson 1965), the more members of an institution, the more difficult it can be for the institution to make decisions. This is particularly true if the organisation is governed by consensus decision-making (discussed in more detail later in the chapter).

Koremenos et al. (2001: 794) argued that institutional flexibility tends to decrease with the number of members of an international organisation: 'All else equal, states will introduce less flexibility into institutions with larger numbers because larger numbers increase the costs associated with flexibility more than they increase its benefits.' Since their primary examples include very large member institutions (like the WTO) designed to reinforce member state commitments, their proposition is less directly applicable to smaller organisations like the UN Peacebuilding Commission with its mandate for institutional coordination. The range and scope of the issues taken up by an IO also tend to increase with the number of its members, potentially increasing the likelihood of policy gridlock (Hale, Held, and Young 2013). While organisations with large numbers of members have more difficulty reaching agreement, there are conditions under which issue linkage among actors with heterogeneous interests 'may generate new opportunities for resolving conflicts and reaching mutually beneficial arrangements' (Koremenos et al. 2001: 785–6).

The membership composition of IOs can change over time, in terms of both numbers and types of members. The International Labour Organization (ILO), for example, expanded from a small club of Western European states at its founding in 1919, to include members with very different labour governance approaches, such as the United States, socialist states, and developing countries. Given that the ILO's member state delegations are composed of two government delegates, an employer organisation delegate and a worker organisation delegate, the type of polity joining the organisation has had consequences for coalition formation and patterns of voting within the organisation over time.

Membership composition of the World Intellectual Property Organization (WIPO) also changed substantially from the time the organisation was founded in 1970,[2] having profound implications for the organisation's mandate and scope of work, not to mention limiting the extent of control of the founding member states over the organisation's activities. Prior to WIPO formally joining the UN system in 1974, very few developing countries were members. When the organisation became a specialised UN agency, membership suddenly opened to all UN member states, and many developing countries joined WIPO (Bogsch 1992). This change in membership composition had ramifications for the organisation's mandate, with the UN–WIPO agreement tasking WIPO with the additional role of facilitating the transfer of technology related to industrial property to the developing countries to accelerate economic, social, and cultural development (Ladas 1975). This gave rise to tensions that endure to this day between WIPO members who want

---

[2] In 1970, WIPO was created to replace the United International Bureaux for the Protection of Intellectual Property (BIRPI), which had previously, in 1893, united the Paris Convention for the Protection of Industrial Property and the Berne Convention for the Protection of Literary and Artistic Works.

the organisation to prioritise a development agenda versus members who prioritise intellectual property (IP) protection.

Autonomy of the Secretariat

The degree of autonomy member states grant to an IO's secretariat illustrates the shifting balance of power between the legislative and executive branches of IOs (Koppell 2010: 118). Most secretariats are constrained in their ability to take on new initiatives and, as a result, look to authorisation from their member state-dominated governing bodies prior to embarking on new initiatives. This depends very much on the leadership of the secretariat, however. While Dag Hammarskjold, second Secretary General of the UN, famously described the office of the UN Secretary-General as 'more secretary than general', he demonstrated that some heads of IOs are more charismatic and innovative than others and can embark on initiatives, commonly in association with key member states of the organisation that share similar goals. The amount of autonomy granted to secretariats can also increase over time, as secretariats build on their considerable stores of expertise in different issue domains to propose new initiatives and internal IO reforms. One of the comparative advantages of IOs is their accumulated expertise on technical issues related to global standard-setting and regulation that enable them to play a disproportionate role in global governance far beyond their numbers, constitutional mandate, or resource base (Barnett and Finnemore 1999).

As Johnson (2014) has noted in her research on organisational progeny, many IOs are founded not only by states operating exclusively amongst themselves, but in conjunction with other IOs. She finds that when IOs participate in the creation of other IOs, they design the new organisations with features that give their secretariats greater autonomy. She also draws on principal–agent theory to argue that when member states become concerned about the increasing autonomy of IO secretariats, they have a number of institutional vehicles for reasserting their control, ranging from budgetary constraints and changes of leadership to the commissioning of periodic reviews of the organisation. Member states can reduce the level of their annual financial contribution, restrict or limit the purposes for which their contributions can be used, or provide supplemental financial resources to fund specific objectives. Periodic changes of leadership are the norm in all IOs, but some member states may try to replace an incumbent whose leadership they do not like with one they prefer. The commissioning of periodic reviews of performance and thematic content of an IO is another way of reasserting control.

Degree and Nature of Involvement of Executive Boards

Although they are often core to the operational structure of IOs, there is great variation in the design of executive boards and the degree to which they become actively involved in an IO's day-to-day governance. As suggested earlier, IO boards are expected to play an important role monitoring the activities of an IO in order to align the secretariat's decisions and operations with member states' demands and to establish deliberative forums for addressing divergent stakeholder expectations and interests (Martinez-Diaz 2009; Hinna and Scarozza 2015; Federo and Saz Carranza 2018b). Through an examination of the boards of sixteen intergovernmental organisations, Ryan Federo and Angel Saz Carranza (2018a) show that in addition to advising IO secretariats about the formulation of strategy, some IO executive boards also actively initiate, design, and evaluate IO strategies. By contrast, the boards of corporations and public and non-profit organisations are usually only consulted when the chief executive officer (CEO) designs the organisation's strategy, and they generally do not themselves formulate or implement strategies (Federo and Saz Carranza 2018a).

The UN Educational, Scientific and Cultural Organization (UNESCO), for example, consists of three governing bodies: the General Conference, the Executive Board, and the Secretariat. The General Conference, made up of representatives of UNESCO's member states, assigns tasks to UNESCO's Executive Board every two years. The Executive Board is made up of fifty-eight members elected by the General Conference that represent the General Conference's diverse cultures and geographic origins. It meets twice per year and is responsible for UNESCO's management, for preparing the General Conference's programme of work, and for overseeing implementation of the General Conference's decisions by UNESCO's Secretariat. The Board additionally undertakes work based on agreements concluded between UNESCO and the UN, the specialised UN agencies, and other intergovernmental organisations (UNESCO 2018). The Secretariat, meanwhile, carries out UNESCO's day-to-day work and is composed of the Director-General and his or her staff.

The International Monetary Fund (IMF), by contrast, has two advisory Ministerial Committees—the International Monetary and Financial Committee (IMFC) and the Joint Ministerial Committee of the Boards of Governors of the Bank and Fund on the Transfer of Real Resources to Developing Countries (the Development Committee).[3] These Committees report to IMF's Board of Governors, IMF's legislative branch made up of IMF member state representatives, who have weighted voting rights based on their financial contributions to the IMF. The Board of Governors delegates authority to the IMF Executive Board, chaired by IMF's Managing Director, and composed of twenty-four members that are selected via the Board of Governor's weighted voting procedure. The Executive Board meets several times weekly and is responsible for carrying out IMF's day-to-day activities (IMF 2018a; 2018b).

A 2008 evaluation of IMF's executive board (Martinez-Diaz 2008) identified four key roles of IO executive boards: political counterweight, performance police, democratic forum, and strategic thinker. The study found that the IMF faced a crisis of relevance and legitimacy due to the organisation's major donor member states exerting tight control over the use of their financial contributions through their selected Executive Board members. This was found to inhibit the ability of the Board to act as a democratic forum, performance police, and strategic thinker (Martinez-Diaz 2008).

Federo and Saz Carranza (2018a) find that the optimal level of board involvement in the strategy formulation of IOs depends on an organisation's level of complexity. Using organisation theory, they define complex organisations as those that provide multiple products or services that require carefully integrated processes and resources (Robson, Katsikeas, and Bello 2008). For IOs, level of complexity thus refers to breadth of mandate (Hooghe and Marks 2015). Federo and Saz Carranza (2018a) find that greater IO board involvement can yield positive effects on strategy formulation in complex IOs. Three development banks in their sample—the Asian Development Bank, the Inter-American Development Bank, and the World Bank—represent highly complex organisations with enhanced information-processing needs. All three organisations demonstrated active board involvement, with the presence of full-time directors, high frequency of board meetings, participation on many board committees, and involvement in CEO selection. The

---

[3] IMF's advisory committees meet twice every year. The IMFC is made up of twenty-four of the organisation's 189 governors. It discusses management of the international monetary and financial system, including current events, and reviews the Executive Board's proposals to amend IMF's Articles of Agreement. Operating by consensus, it guides the IMF's work programme and provides strategic direction to the work and policies of the IMF. The joint Development Committee is made up of twenty-five finance and development ministers. It advises the Boards of Governors of the IMF and the World Bank on economic development in emerging market and developing countries and the financial resources needed to foster economic development in developing countries (IMF Factsheet 2018a; 2018b).

World Bank board, for example, was found to be actively engaged in strategy formulation. Directors on the board possess the required expertise to serve on the board, they frequently meet with the World Bank's President, and the board committees often work with senior management of the World Bank, share and process information, and contribute to strategy development (Federo and Saz Carranza 2018a: 9).

By contrast, board involvement in the less complex IOs in Federo and Saz Carranza's sample demonstrate far less board involvement in strategy formulation. The UN Environment Programme, the United Nations Children's Fund (UNICEF), and the International Fund for Agricultural Development all have relatively narrow mandates, and all recorded lower frequency of board meetings, the absence of an executive committee, and the absence of involvement in CEO selection (Federo and Saz Carranza 2018a: 9). Federo and Saz Carranza argue that while greater board involvement enables acquisition, processing, and sharing of information to facilitate better strategy formulation, less complex organisations require less information sharing and lower information-processing, reducing the need for input from board directors during strategy formulation. While board involvement improves information-processing, it also incurs bureaucratic and coordination costs, costs that can be absorbed by complex IOs, but less so by less complex ones (Federo and Saz Carranza 2018a: 12).

Oversight and Accountability Mechanisms

Following the association of a number of IOs with corruption, mismanagement, and controversial, failed programmes in the late 1990s and early 2000s, member states introduced oversight offices and mechanisms to many IOs, such as the UN, the African Development Bank, and the Organization of American States. This came following increased debate about the 'democratic deficit' and lack of accountability of European and global intergovernmental organisations more generally (Majone 1998; Dahl 1999; Nye 2001; Grigorescu 2010: 871). The UN's Iraq Oil-for-Food Programme scandal that came to light in the early 2000s involved charges of corruption that even reached the Office of then Secretary-General Kofi Annan (Volcker et al. 2005).

Anderson (2010) laments the lack of legal accountability of IOs. He says,

International organizations such as the UN have massive failure problems...the problems range from rent-seeking to major criminal corruption and fraud. They arise from a treaty structure deliberately designed to shield the organization and its agents from judicial accountability...the result is to put the UN and international organizations and their agents in fundamental ways outside of the rule of law in the most ordinary sense.

As IO bureaucracies came to be seen as powerful rogue international actors operating beyond the control of their member states, member states introduced oversight mechanisms in order to reassert control over IO bureaucracies and to reduce unwanted independent IO actions (Grigorescu 2010). The newly created oversight offices were tasked with conducting internal audits, inspections, investigations, and evaluations, and many IOs additionally crafted policies that sought to identify conflicts of interest, increase transparency around financial transactions of officials working in the organisations, and protect whistle-blowers. While a few IOs were already undertaking some of these tasks, the newly established oversight offices formalised and expanded them (Grigorescu 2010).

As Grigorescu (2010) notes, IOs were initially more likely to adopt oversight mechanisms if decision-making processes were based on weighted voting, rather than unanimity, if they had greater financing from member states that actively participated in the IO's work, and if they had large budgets. Membership composition made up primarily of democratic states also gave rise to creation of oversight offices. As more and more organisations established such mechanisms, oversight mechanisms spread more broadly across IOs through policy and norm diffusion, as part of the spread of the norm of democratic governance in the 1990s and 2000s (Grigorescu 2010).

The Integrity and Anti-Corruption Department (IACD) of the African Development Bank Group, for example, was established in November 2005. According to the IACD's web page, it was mandated to carry out 'independent investigations into allegations of corruption, fraud and other sanctionable practices in Bank Group Financed Operations—internal corporate procurement issues and operations financed by the Bank Group'. The department also conducts risk assessments and surveillance and works to prevent and reduce the potential for corruption, fraud, misconduct, and other sanctionable practices within the Bank Group Financed Operations (African Development Bank Group 2018).

In 2007, member states of the African Development Bank Group adopted the Whistle Blowing and Complaints Handling Policy. The Policy was developed, it states, 'in furtherance of the Bank Group's desire to strengthen the Bank's system of integrity and the fight against corruption and related offences'. It lays out the conditions and procedures for investigations of allegations of corruption, fraud, and other forms of misconduct. It continues, 'In order to enhance good governance and transparency, the main aims of the Policy are to provide an avenue for raising concerns related to Fraud, Corruption or any other Misconduct and to assure that persons who disclose information related to fraud, corruption or any other misconduct will be protected from Retaliation' (African Development Bank Group 2007).

Notwithstanding the introduction of oversight offices, legal scholars such as Parish (2010) have argued for heightened legal scrutiny of IO actions, since many IOs have frequently acted in violation of fundamental international standards of the rule of law. Parish argues that the internal legal mechanisms of IOs lack sufficient means to hold IOs accountable and that structural reasons inhibit international courts and tribunals from conducting adequate review of day-to-day IO decisions and actions. He finds insufficient reasoning to justify the legal immunities of many IOs. He proposes that IO accountability be improved through increased international judicial oversight and abrogation of certain IO immunities, making them subject to domestic courts where they operate (Parish 2010).

Design Features Affecting the Governance of IOs

In addition to the three foundational bodies that constitute the basis of governance of IOs—member states, the secretariat, and executive boards—and the oversight and accountability mechanisms just described, there are a number of other IO design features that have profound effects on their governance. A great deal of attention is given to the design of IOs when they are first created. In an introduction to a special issue of the journal *International Organization* devoted to the analysis of the rational design of institutions, Koremenos, Lipson, and Snidal argued that 'states use international institutions to further their own goals, and they design institutions accordingly' (Koremenos et al. 2001: 762). They contended that the design of different international institutions is 'the result of rational, purposive interactions among states and other international actors to solve specific problems' (Koremenos et al. 2001: 762).

States tend to be risk averse and design institutions to maintain their sovereign prerogatives. Design features are key to maintaining control of IOs once they are created as separate bodies with delegated authority. Institutional design scholars have identified a number of core elements subject to variation in IOs that affect how IOs are governed. Koppell's empirical analysis of the organisational design of twenty-five global governance organisations highlights variation that can be found in the areas of representation and administration, the rule-making process, adherence and enforcement, and interest group participation (Koppell 2010). Koremenos et al. (2001) identify five variations in IO design, including membership rules, scope of issues covered, centralisation of tasks, rules for controlling the institution, and flexibility of arrangements.

Building on the work of Koppell (2010), Koremenos et al. (2001), and Tallberg et al. (2013), we identified four key IO design features subject to variation that affect the governance and performance of IOs in significant ways, not only at their founding, but also as they develop and change over time. These include (1) the scope and substance of an IO's *mandate*; (2) how an IO is *financed*; (3) the *rule-making and decision-making processes* within an IO; and (4) an IO's *engagement with different types of non-state actors*. As will be discussed below, some of these design features can be used to claw back member state control, should the IO as agent become too independent of states or appear to become independently 'powerful' in international relations.

Mandate

The scope and substance of an IO's mandate is often contested among member states and can vary from the broad to the very narrow. IO mandates are frequently subject to reinterpretation and redefinition during processes of institutional adaptation over time, as well as to reform initiatives. Member states can control the scope and type of work an IO undertakes by granting it the authority to carry out four potential functions: production, service, mobilisation, and governance (Koppell 2010). Koppell argues that those organisations endowed with the authority to carry out wide-ranging responsibilities (a broader mandate) are more likely to be engaged in what he calls positive governance production, as compared with those endowed with narrower mandates (Koppell 2010: 74–9).

Broad mandates can be enabling for secretariats and can be used to justify actions taken within an IO that may not have been anticipated when the organisation was first created. Excessively narrow mandates, by contrast, can prevent an organisation from adapting to a changing environment or anticipating and dealing adequately with emerging phenomena. Discussing the challenges of measuring IO performance and effectiveness, Gutner and

Thompson (2010) have emphasised that member states frequently endow IOs with 'lofty' mandates that provide insufficient specific criteria for judging IO performance.

Countering the prevalent claim that IOs seek to increase their mandate, i.e. engage in mission creep, in order to increase their influence (Lawrence 2008; Littoz-Monnet 2017), Helfer (2006) illustrates, through the case of the ILO, that some IOs have narrowed their mandates over time. The ILO first broadened its mandate during the post-World War II period to include new areas of labour to correspond to changes in its law-making, monitoring functions, and decision-making procedures, and in response to demands from a larger and more diverse membership. During the 1990s and early 2000s, however, the ILO experienced an increasing gap between treaty adoption and treaty ratification by ILO member states. In response, the organisation, led by its then-Director General, strategically narrowed its mandate to emphasise promoting universal compliance with a core group of fundamental labour rights (Helfer 2006).

Financing

The financing of IOs is a critical design feature affecting the extent of control member states have over an IO's activities (Koppell 2010). At their founding, most IOs are financed by assessed contributions from member states, i.e. the fees member states pay to enjoy the privileges and benefits of membership in an IO. The amount is generally calculated using a formula agreed to by member states that often reflects their level of development, or the country's GDP. Member states are often categorised into different tiers, which determine the amount of their assessed financial contribution to the IO. As such, states with greater financial wherewithal may contribute more or subsidise the participation of others, without necessarily asking for greater voting rights.

Over time, as IOs take on new responsibilities, member states with a particular interest in or normative support for certain activities carried out by an IO may supplement their assessed contributions with voluntary contributions. Sometimes, these voluntary contributions are non-specified, that is, they are for general activities of the IO. In June 2018, for example, Sweden entered into multi-year core funding agreements with the UN Development Programme, UNICEF, UN Women, and the UN Population Fund (UNFPA). Sweden voluntarily committed SEK 6.8 billion to the core funding of these agencies, which the UN agencies argue allows them to carry out their mandates with increased flexibility and predictability (UNDP, UNICEF, UNFPA and UN Women 2018). More often, however, voluntary contributions are earmarked for specific policy initiatives, to be used in specific countries and on specific projects (also known as 'specified' or 'attributed' voluntary contributions).

Today, in an environment characterised by decreasing proportions of mandatory, assessed government contributions to IOs (discussed in more detail below), some IOs supplement their government financing with voluntary, typically earmarked, contributions from private donors. The contributions of the Bill and Melinda Gates Foundation to the activities of the WHO are a prominent example of private financing, just as contributions from private pharmaceutical companies are among the most controversial sources of income for the organisation. In 2016, only 19 per cent of WHO's USD 2,364 million income came from member states' assessed contributions, while 42 per cent came from member states' voluntary contributions, 13 per cent from philanthropic foundations (primarily the Bill and Melinda Gates Foundation), 9 per cent from the UN and other IOs and development banks, 7 per cent from non-governmental organisations (NGOs) (with the Rotary Foundation contributing the majority), 5 per cent from partnerships administered at WHO, and 2 per cent from the private sector, including pharmaceutical companies (World Health Organization 2017). Table 9.1 illustrates WHO's changing composition of assessed vis-à-vis voluntary sources of financing over time.

Some IOs have supplemented their financing by charging fees for the provision of services and goods, or from income derived from public–private partnerships hosted at an IO. The WIPO is the most prominent example of an IO financing its activities through fees charged for the provision of services and goods. In 2016, 95 per cent of WIPO's revenue was generated through fees for the various international protection systems administered by the organisation. In recent years, member states, such as the US, have raised questions about the extent to which this type of IO financing leads to excessive control by the WIPO secretariat over WIPO activities, decreasing member state control (Cannon and Biersteker 2018). The WHO, as mentioned above, supplements some of its revenue with fees from partnerships it administers.

When examining the motives behind member state–driven reforms of IO funding rules, some scholars have argued that the shift of powerful member states towards voluntary contributions enables them to control (and limit) the budget available to IOs, and thus limit the activities in which an IO could engage (Sridhar and Woods 2013). Challenging this view, Graham (2017) has argued that the funding rules design and changes at UN economic

Table 9.1. WHO's changing composition of financing over time (in US dollars)

Year	Mandatory assessed contributions (% of total income)	Voluntary contributions (% of total income)	Other revenue (% of total income)	Total income
1949*	4,270,145 (90%)	460,878** (10%)		4,731,023***
1958	13,305,047 (91%)	754,506 (5%)	530,474 (4%)	14,590,027
1968	54,571,931 (87%)	2,595,242 (4%)	5,455,275 (9%)	62,622,448
1978	170,035,937 (64%)	93,606,272** (36%)		263,642,209
1988	294,857,127 (37%)	292,504,464 (37%)	205,017,829 (26%)	792,379,420
1998	418,751,000 (41%)	520,909,519 (50%)	93,589,420 (9%)	1,033,250,939
2008	470,062,155 (27%)	1,111,325,223 (64%)	162,788,729 (9%)	1,744,176,107
2016	470,036,000 (19%)	1,751,810,509 (72%)	195,461,821 (9%)	2,426,758,000

Notes: * WHO was created in 1948, however 1949 was the first full year of WHO's operations.
** It was not possible to distinguish between 'voluntary contributions' and 'other income' for this year.
*** Total income for 1949 does not include WHO's Working Capital Fund (total assets at close of 1949 USD 2,588,648.33) because it was not possible to distinguish income in 1948 from income in 1949.
Source: Data compiled and calculated from WHO annual and biennial financial reports.

development institutions had other roots. She contends that funding rule reforms permitting voluntary contributions from member states were driven by states that supported the UN, who were seeking to expand the organisation's activities beyond the tightly controlled mandate and programmes approved by the collective membership. Voluntary contributions offered these individual countries more flexibility and control.

At the same time, Mathiason (2007) has shown that member states can constrain IO secretariat activities by creating an environment of instability of funding. Other scholars, like Johnson (2014), emphasise the strategic efforts IO bureaucrats can make to alter an IO's design, including its funding mechanisms, in order to create more autonomy from member states. Johnson explains, 'States can design an [IO] to be financed only by themselves, but over time the international bureaucrats within the [IO] can decrease this vulnerability by diversifying their funding sources beyond states' (Johnson 2014: 53).

Questioning the extent to which such efforts are entirely strategic, we argue elsewhere that increased earmarked voluntary contributions to WHO, from both member states and private donors, appear to have led to decreased control of the organisation by both the collective member states and WHO's secretariat, with enhanced control going to the individual private and member state donors, which attach strict requirements for how the WHO can spend their funds in specific countries and on specific projects (Cannon and Biersteker 2018). By contrast, in the case of WIPO, generation of income through charging fees for the various international copyright protection systems administered by WIPO appears to have led to increased control of the secretariat over its activities and decreased member state control. As noted above, as the US begins to lose predominance in the technology innovation and intellectual property fields to China, and to a lesser extent to the EU, the US has started questioning WIPO's autonomy with respect to the use and allocation of the organisation's funds generated through fee-paying clients.

Among the effects produced by such changes in IO financing is decreased member state control over IO activities (Cannon and Biersteker 2018). This leads us to challenge conventional principal–agent models of governance, with the IOs now servicing multiple principals. At what point does an IO stop being a traditional 'intergovernmental' organisation and start being a multi-stakeholder organisation or a public–private partnership in and of itself, no longer solely receiving financing and mandates from the collective member states, but also receiving financing and mandates from other actors, including business, philanthropic foundations, NGOs, research institutes, or fee-paying clients? This could have substantive implications for priority-setting and future directions of the organisation.

Rule-making and Decision-making Processes

The rule-making and decision-making processes built into an IO's design can have profound effects on the governance of IOs. For example, reliance on consensus decision-making, the requirement of a super-majority, and the provision of a veto to a few member states are all ways to maintain control of an organisation. Koppell illustrates variation in the rule-making process, distinguishing between formal processes, in which requirements are specific and inflexible, and informal processes, in which the requirements are less rigid (Koppell 2010: 146–51). With reference to the decision-making process, he distinguishes between majoritarian, super-majoritarian, majoritarian with veto, and consensus procedures (Koppell 2010: 154–7). Many IOs exhibit combinations of several of these types of decision-making processes within their complex structures depending on the issue under consideration.

How an organisation's bureaucracy is structured also matters. Egeberg (2003) argues that the structure of a bureaucracy can affect its capacity to intervene in decision-making processes and influence outcomes. More functionally oriented bureaucracies engage member states more regularly in decision-making processes, while those that play a supporting role participate in rule-crafting (Koppell 2010). In short, IO bureaucracies can play a role in agenda-setting by controlling important information and/or resources. These varying features of IO design are also subject to change over time.

How decisions are made within the organisation also varies widely across different IOs. In most instances, the governing body of member state representatives tends to possess final authority, but an organisation may also operate with informal governance mechanisms that effectively give the direction of the organisation to its leadership and secretariat. There is also wide variation in the ways decisions are taken. In some institutions, like the UN General Assembly, majority rule is the norm (though there are instances like Charter reform that require a two-thirds majority). Many IOs operate on the principle of consensus, which implies a unit veto by any individual member state. The meaning of consensus, and how it operates in practice, varies considerably, however, from one institution to another. While the UN Disarmament Conference has been deadlocked for years over the opposition of a single member state to the adoption of its agenda, the International Telecommunications Union (with hundreds of participants from both the public and private sector) operates with an informal understanding of consensus that avoids divisive votes at all costs (Mraz 2018).

Other IOs provide vetoes to key member states, primarily to ensure that they remain within the organisation. The UN Security Council is the most notable example, with its provision of the veto to the major powers at its founding (essentially, the victorious alliance at the end of World War II). It also operates with a majority plus one (assuming no vetoes) in order to pass a resolution. Finally, there are some IOs that operate on a weighted voting basis, such as the international financial institutions. In the cases of the IMF and the World Bank, a member state's share of the vote is determined by the size of its financial contribution to the organisation.

In the rule-making and decision-making process, states can further limit the potential powers of an IO with reference to types of rules organisations can produce. IOs that administer binding international treaties and regulations, for example, are endowed with more power to hold states accountable for violations of those agreements than IOs that administer non legally binding international agreements, such as principles, standards, and recommendations (Koppell 2010: 86–9).

Engagement with Non-state Actors

How IOs engage non-state actors in their work is a final characteristic that varies significantly across different institutional settings, one with important implications for how IOs are governed. Tallberg et al.'s (2013) research on the opening up of international organisations shows that IOs can grant formal access to non-state actors in four policy functions: 1) policy formulation; 2) decision-making; 3) implementation; and 4) monitoring and enforcement. Most IOs have granted non-state actors increased formal access to their international policy processes over the past fifty years. There is significant variation in the degree and nature of this access, with the greatest in the domain of human rights and the least in the areas of finance and security. Whether the motivation for this is to fill a functional demand or provide a means of legitimation, IOs tend to view this development in normative terms as 'good' governance (Tallberg et al. 2013). International organisations are increasingly pressured to engage with non-state actors in their work, by their member states and financial contributors (whether government or private donors) who, for the most part, increasingly favour a 'whole of society' approach to addressing global challenges today.[4]

As of 2018, the WHO, for example, engaged with 729 non-state actors in its work, including 298 NGOs, forty-four private sector entities, twenty-four philanthropic foundations, and 363 academic institutions (WHO 2018). Non-state actors engage with WHO for technical collaboration, advocacy, the provision of knowledge and evidence on technical issues, and participation in WHO meetings (WHO 2016). They enter into official relations with WHO by submitting an application to the Executive Board, which reviews the applications to ensure that the established criteria and other requirements set out in the Framework for Engagement with Non-state Actors, including due diligence, are fulfilled.

As the WHO began to engage more frequently with non-state actors to fulfil its work, member states articulated procedures and rules of behaviour for how and when the WHO secretariat and member states should engage with non-state actors. WHO's Framework, adopted by WHO member states at the 69th World Health Assembly in 2016, consists of an overarching framework and four specific policies for engagement with NGOs, private sector entities, philanthropic foundations, and academic institutions. It contains

---

[4] As observed during the Agenda 2030 and the Sustainable Development Goals High Level Political Forum sessions in 2017, and during the preparatory and negotiation sessions for the Global Compact for Migration in 2017 and 2018.

standards of procedure for the management of potential conflicts of interest and other risks of engagement, stipulates how the framework relates to other WHO policies, designates responsibility for oversight of engagement to WHO's Executive Board, outlines how non-compliance with the framework should be addressed, specifies how the framework should be implemented, and details procedures for monitoring and evaluation of the framework (WHO 2016).

Contemporary Challenges Facing IOs and How IOs Are Addressing Them

There is a widespread perception that existing IOs are either underperforming or deficient in some important respects. According to many international relations scholars, formal IOs and the global cooperation they were designed to facilitate are failing (Weiss 2009; Hale et al. 2013). This 'policy gridlock' can be seen in issue domains as diverse as security, trade, the global economy, and the environment. Just as states are turning to alternative governance arrangements to address shared concerns when the institutional status quo does not offer an appropriate venue for prevailing cooperation problems, scholars are also turning to examine these new institutional forms, such as informal intergovernmental organisations (IIGOs) (Vabulas and Snidal 2013; Hale et al. 2013), public–private partnerships (Andonova 2010; 2017), and multi-stakeholder initiatives (Jerbi 2012).

Most IOs were originally designed by their founding member states to respond collectively to and to address optimally the challenges they faced at the time the IOs were first created. As such, there is an ongoing need for IOs to adapt and reform to meet constantly evolving contexts, changing member state compositions, new issue demands, and new global challenges. As the work and design of an IO evolve, additional procedures and rules of behaviour are introduced and adopted by an IO's member states. For example, as the WHO began to engage more frequently with non-state actors to fulfil its work, member states articulated procedures and rules of behaviour for how and when the WHO secretariat and member states should engage with non-state actors, already described above. The rational-legal authority granted to IOs endows them with the potential to behave independently from the states that created them, and the rules that define an IO's bureaucracy can at times either inhibit their ability or overshadow their willingness to carry out the mandate member states have bestowed on them (Snidal 1996; Barnett and Finnemore 1999).

While a great deal of the theoretical focus of international relations scholars has been on the initial design of international organisations, all organisations, once created, invariably become engaged in processes of change, reform, adaptation, and institutional development. This can lead either to advances in corporate governance, or to the so-called 'Frankenstein problem' where the IO transforms itself in ways not anticipated by its creators (Guzman 2013). Sometimes the motivation for reform is to maintain an IO's relevance and salience to an issue domain by broadening its original mandate. Public choice theorists remind us that one of the principal goals of any organisation is to ensure its survival and perpetuate itself, and this can be one of the central motivations for mandate expansion (Vaubel 2006). There are other motivations for reform and change, both exogenous and endogenous, including changes of leadership, reductions in financing, or the emergence of new global challenges. While the reasons for reform are important, this is not our central focus in this chapter. Rather, we are interested in identifying different types of reform, the challenges they address, and how to assess their consequences, rather than their origins.

Most of the predominant IOs of today were created nearly seventy-five years ago between 1944 and 1949. Their ability to adapt to changing demographic and global power distributions is key to the maintenance of their legitimacy. Yet beyond reforms to specific design features, core institutional reforms of the operational structure of major post-World War II IOs have proven difficult. Everyone acknowledges the increasingly non-representative nature of the UN Security Council, and there have been a great many innovative ideas about how to reform the Council ranging from proposals to increase the number of members (without the veto) to ideas about reforming the use of the veto itself. Significant progress on UN Security Council reform was made during the High-Level Review of the UN prior to the adoption of the 2005 World Summit Outcome document, but opposition to the proposals for membership enlargement from key member states was widespread within the organisation. While the UN Security Council has expanded its membership from the time of its founding to fifteen members today, the permanent membership of the Council (and the veto powers associated with it) remains as it was when founded in 1945. The international financial institutions created at Bretton Woods are also demonstrating difficulties in reform and adjustment, and the inability to achieve US Congressional support for reforms of the institutions prompted the creation of new development banks in Asia and among the BRICS (Brazil, Russia, India, China, and South Africa).

Cutbacks in member state funding of IOs have forced many of them increasingly to look beyond member state contributions for financial resources. As already discussed in the preceding section, the WHO was almost fully funded by member state assessed contributions at its founding. As of 2016, assessed contributions account for only 19 per cent of the WHO's operating revenue (refer to Table 9.1). As a result of declining assessed contribution revenue, it has turned to voluntary contributions from member states and contributions from private foundations, corporations, and other non-state actors to make up for the shortfall. This pattern of reductions in assessed contributions and increased reliance on other sources of revenue is common across most IOs today. This calls into question some of the basic premises of conventional principal–agent models of governance of intergovernmental IOs described at the beginning of this chapter. It also raises the prospect that non-state actors, by virtue of their ability to issue mandates directly to IOs through their provision of financing for them, are beginning to play the role of principals directing IO agents to carry out their projects (Cannon and Biersteker 2018).

Beyond their growing financial role, private sector institutions like advocacy groups, corporate firms, and philanthropic foundations are beginning to offer solutions to collective action problems and address public goods problems with their own ideas and approaches. As a result, formal international (intergovernmental) organisations (FIGOs) are increasingly competing with IIGOs (Vabulas and Snidal 2013) and a variety of different transgovernmental initiatives (or TGIs). IIGOs like the G-groups (Group of Seven, Group of Twenty) are easier to establish, offer more institutional flexibility, and are less costly to maintain (since they do not have permanent secretariats). They are also easier to control and offer opportunities for forum-shopping for individual states unhappy with the restraints of formal intergovernmental treaty-based organisations. As a result, FIGOs, i.e. traditional IOs, can no longer assume that they are the sole recipients of delegated authority from member states or other key actors. While they can refer to the authority of their original mandates or the authority of their accumulated expertise, they are increasingly forced to compete with other actors in a 'global market for authority' (Sending 2018). This may be one of the reasons we see the increased reliance on public–private partnerships, TGIs, multi-stakeholder initiatives, transnational policy networks, and other innovative institutional forms of governance at the global level.

As a result of these institutional developments, there appears to be an increasing reliance on informal governance mechanisms. As Westerwinter, Abbott, and Biersteker (2017) have argued, there are three different types of informal governance at the global level: informality in institutional form, informality within formal IOs, and informality among the networks of expertise operating around formal IOs. The rate of creation of new FIGOs has stalled in recent years, while there has been a steady growth in IIGOs and a nearly exponential growth of TGIs (Westerwinter, Abbott, and Biersteker 2017). Informal procedures *within* formal IOs—maintained by institutional cultures that determine which nationalities traditionally occupy certain key positions or how the institution of consensus operates within the organisation—are also increasingly apparent. Informal networks of expertise operating *around* formal IGOs, as indicated by the so-called 'Third UN' (Weiss et al. 2009) or transnational policy networks of expertise, have emerged in most areas and are particularly apparent in new or emerging issue domains.

Finally, in recent years, some of the core norms that have defined the post-World War II period have experienced significant erosion and even degradation, not only in the realm of global security, but also in the governance of the global political economy. Global security norms against territorial annexation by force, the use of siege warfare, the deliberate targeting of schools and hospitals, the targeting of humanitarian personnel, and the use of chemical weapons have all been violated, sometimes by major powers themselves. A similar degradation is also taking place with regard to global political economy norms, with the unilateral application of tariffs without recourse to the WTO by the US, giving rise to recent concerns about the future of the WTO itself.

Conclusion

International organisations are historically governed by principal–agent relationships, with authority delegated by individual member states to a secretariat, and with an executive board that both states and secretariats can appeal to in adjudicating their relationship. Despite these core governance attributes, however, neither the foundational operational structure of IOs nor central elements of their internal design are fixed in time or place.

Although they share some fundamental governance characteristics, IOs vary both in their initial design and in their subsequent development, change, and reform. In the first section of this chapter, we illustrated variation over time in their membership, the autonomy of their secretariats, the degree of involvement of their governing bodies, and their oversight and accountability mechanisms. The historical context of their founding has profound effects on all four elements, and all four also change over the life of the institution, with globally shared events like twentieth-century decolonisation having had profound effects on all of them (particularly with regard to membership and expanded issue mandates).

Beyond their core operational structure, however, other design features also vary significantly, as our brief survey of the literature indicates. The mandates, financing, decision-making processes, and relationships with non-state actors have all shown significant variation both across different IOs and over time within them. These design features can lead to variation in the degree of member state control over an IO as well as to reform efforts within them. These design features adapt and are subject to reform over time for a variety of reasons, both exogenous and endogenous, that have motivated scholars of IOs for decades.

All of this change in the governance of IOs is taking place at a time when the demand for the services that the UN and IOs in general provide continues to be high and has arguably even increased in recent years, as new global and transnational problems have been placed on the global agenda. IOs remain first among equals in many issue domains by virtue of some of their broad governance or institutional characteristics (inclusivity, representativeness, and the extensiveness and depth of their expertise). Despite this, however, it is perhaps time that we begin to change the way we traditionally think about IOs and their internal governance. The intergovernmental nature of the organisations and their core governance by principal–agent relationships among member states, secretariats, and executive boards need to be rethought and reconceptualised as increasingly hybrid governance arrangements emerge in a competitive marketplace for global governance authority.

While much existing research on IOs has focused on the conditions under which institutions change, more attention should be given to the relationship between reforms in IO design and the organisation's levels of effectiveness. The UN and other IOs today face complex, new global challenges. Their ability to adapt and reform to address these challenges will determine not only their own fate as institutions, but also that of the peoples they represent. We need to improve our understanding of the nature and consequences of IOs' varying abilities to reform in order to contribute to enhancing their effectiveness going forward. Scholars should scrutinise the origins and initial purposes of IOs and assess whether the underlying rationale for their existence has substantially changed. They should interrogate whether intergovernmental organisations can be sufficiently supplemented by other forms of governance and/or whether they play a unique normative role that other hybrid forms of governance cannot. Finally, we need to explore whether there is merit in safeguarding the political nature of intergovernmental organisations, even if the going is slow and gridlock often emerges.

Acknowledgement

The research on which this chapter is partially based is funded by the Swiss National Science Foundation project 'Can an international organisation's propensity to reform help its member states break through policy gridlock?'.

References

African Development Bank Group (2007). 'Whistle Blowing and Complaints Handling Policy', Tunis, January. Retrieved from https://www.afdb.org/en/documents/document/whistle-blowing-and-complaints-handling-policy-10527 (accessed 10 January 2020).

African Development Bank Group (2018). 'Integrity and Anti-Corruption'. Retrieved from https://www.afdb.org/en/about-us/organisational-structure/integrity-and-anti-corruption/ (accessed 8 July 2018).

Anderson, K. (2010). 'Legal Accountability of International Organizations and Their Agents'. Blog post in *Opinio Juris*, 16 September 2010. Retrieved from http://opiniojuris.org/2010/09/16/legal-accountability-of-international-organizations-and-their-agents/ (accessed 8 July 2018).

Andonova, L. (2010). 'Public-Private Partnerships for the Earth: Politics and Patterns of Hybrid Authority in the Multilateral System', *Global Environmental Politics*, 10(2): 25–53.

Andonova, L. (2017). *Governance Entrepreneurs: International Organizations and the Rise of Global Public-Private Partnerships*. Cambridge, UK: Cambridge University Press.

Barnett, M. and Finnemore, M. (1999). 'The Politics, Power, and Pathologies of International Organizations', *International Organization*, 53(4): 699–732.

Bogsch, A. (1992). *Brief History of the First Twenty-five Years of the World Intellectual Property Organization*. Geneva: WIPO Publications.

Cannon, C. and Biersteker, T. (2018). 'Tracing the Effects of IO Financing Reforms', paper for the 2018 International Studies Association Conference, San Francisco, CA, USA, April 2018.

Dahl, R. (1999). 'Can International Organizations Be Democratic? A Skeptic's View', in I. Shapiro and C. Hacker-Cordon (eds.), *Democracy's Edges*. Cambridge, UK: Cambridge University Press, 19–36.

Egeberg, M. (2003). 'How Bureaucratic Structure Matters: An Organizational Perspective', in B. G. Peters and J. Pierre (eds.) *Handbook of Public Administration*. Thousand Oaks, CA. Sage Publications, 116–26.

Federo, R. and Saz Carranza, A. (2018a). 'A Configurational Analysis of Board Involvement in Intergovernmental Organizations', *Corporate Governance: An International Review*, 26(6): 414–28.

Federo, R. and Saz Carranza, A. (2018b). 'A Typology of Board Designs for Highly Effective Monitoring in Intergovernmental Organizations under the United Nations System', *Regulation and Governance*. doi: 10.1111/rego.12216

Graham, E. (2017). 'The Institutional Design of Funding Rules at International Organizations: Explaining the Transformation in Financing the United Nations', *European Journal of International Relations*, 23(2): 365–90.

Grigorescu, A. (2010). 'The Spread of Bureaucratic Oversight Mechanisms across Intergovernmental Organizations', *International Studies Quarterly*, 54, 871–86.

Gutner, T. and Thompson, A. (2010). 'The Politics of IO Performance', *The Review of International Organizations*, 5(3): 227–48.

Guzman, A. (2013). 'International Organizations and the Frankenstein Problem', *European Journal of International Law*, 24(4): 999–1025.

Hale, T., Held, D., and Young, K. (2013). *Gridlock: Why Global Cooperation Is Failing When We Need It Most*. London: Polity Press.

Hawkins, D. G., Lake, D. A., Nielson, D. L., and Tierney, M. J. (2006). *Delegation and Agency in International Organizations*. Cambridge, UK: Cambridge University Press.

Helfer, L. R. (2006). 'Understanding Change in International Organisations: Globalisation and Innovation in the ILO', *Vanderbilt Law Review*, 59(3): 649–726.

Hinna, A. and Scarozza, D. (2015). 'A Behavioral Perspective for Governing Bodies: Processes and Conflicts in Public Organizations', *International Studies of Management & Organization*, 45(1): 43–59.

Hooghe, L. and Marks, G. (2015). 'Delegation and Pooling in International Organizations', *The Review of International Organizations*, 10(3): 305–28.

IMF (2018a). Factsheet 'How the IMF Makes Decisions', 8 March 2018. Retrieved from https://www.imf.org/en/About/Factsheets/Sheets/2016/07/27/15/24/How-the-IMF-Makes-Decisions (accessed 22 October 2018).

IMF (2018b). Factsheet 'A Guide to Committees, Groups and Clubs', 8 March 2018. Retrieved from https://www.imf.org/en/About/Factsheets/A-Guide-to-Committees-Groups-and-Clubs (accessed 22 October 2018).

Jerbi, S. (2012). 'Assessing the Roles of Multi-Stakeholder Initiatives in Advancing the Business and Human Rights Agenda', *International Review of the Red Cross*, 94(887): 1027–46.

Johnson, T. (2014). *Organizational Progeny: Why Governments Are Losing Control Over the Proliferating Structures of Global Governance*. Oxford: Oxford University Press.

Koppell, J. G. S. (2010). *World Rule: Accountability, Legitimacy, and the Design of Global Governance*. Chicago: The University of Chicago Press.

Koremenos, B., Lipson, C., and Snidal, D. (2001). 'The Rational Design of International Institutions', *International Organization*, 55(4): 761–99.

Ladas, S. P. (1975). *Patents, Trademarks, and Related Rights: National and International Protection*. Cambridge, MA: Harvard University Press.

Lawrence, R. Z. (2008). 'International Organisations: The Challenge of Aligning Mission, Means and Legitimacy', *The World Economy*, 31(11): 1455–70.

Littoz-Monnet, A. (2017). 'Expert Knowledge as a Strategic Resource: International Bureaucrats and the Shaping of Bioethical Standards', *International Studies Quarterly*, 61: 584–95.

Majone, G. (1998). 'Europe's Democratic Deficit', *European Law Journal*, 4(1): 5–28.

Martinez-Diaz, L. (2008). 'Executive Boards in International Organizations: Lessons for Strengthening IMF Governance', IEO Background Paper BP/08/08. Washington, DC: Independent Evaluation Office of the International Monetary Fund.

Martinez-Diaz, L. (2009). 'Boards of Directors in International Organizations: A Framework for Understanding the Dilemmas of Institutional Design', *The Review of International Organizations*, 4: 383–406.

Mathiason, J. (2007). *Invisible Governance: International Secretariats in Global Politics*. Bloomfield: Kumarian Press.

Mraz, P. (2018). 'Beyond the Charter Reform: Breaking UN Deadlocks through Greater Use of Expertise', paper presented at the annual meeting of the Academic Council on the UN System, Rome, July.

Nye, J. (2001). 'Globalization's Democratic Deficit: How to Make International Institutions More Accountable', *Foreign Affairs*, 80: 2–6.

Olson, M. (1965). *The Logic of Collective Action: Public Goods and the Theory of Groups*. Cambridge, MA: Harvard University Press.

Parish, M. (2010). 'Essay on the Accountability of International Organizations', *International Organizations Law Review*, 7(2): 277–342.

Pevehouse, J., Nordstrom, T., and Warnke, K. (2004). 'The Correlates of War 2 International Governmental Organizations Version 2.0', *Conflict Management and Peace Science*, 21(2): 101–19.

Robson, M. J., Katsikeas, C. S., and Bello, D. C. (2008). 'Drivers and Performance Outcomes of Trust in International Strategic Alliances: The Role of Organizational Complexity', *Organization Science*, 19(4): 647–65.

Saz Carranza, A., Federo, R., Fernández Marín, X., and Losada Marrodán, C. (2016). 'The Boards of International Governmental Organizations: Resource Providers or Delegated Controllers?', paper presented at the 9th Annual Conference on the Political Economy of International Organizations, University of Utah, Salt Lake City (USA).

Sending, O. J. (2018). 'How Rule Generates Authority', paper presented at the Global Governance Centre, Graduate Institute, Geneva, 23 April.

Snidal, D. (1996). 'Political Economy and International Institutions', *International Review of Law and Economics*, 16: 121–37.

Sridhar, D. and Woods, N. (2013). 'Trojan Multilateralism: Global Cooperation in Health', *Global Policy*, 4: 325–35.

Tallberg, J., Sommerer, T., Squatrito, T., and Jönsson, C. (2013). *The Opening Up of International Organizations*. Cambridge, UK: Cambridge University Press.

UNESCO (2018) [website]. 'UNESCO Executive Board'. Retrieved from https://en.unesco.org/executiveboard (accessed 22 August 2018).

UNDP, UNICEF, UNFPA and UN Women (2018). 'Joint Statement: Contribution Will Help Us Deliver Better Results for the Communities We Serve', 12 June. Retrieved from https://www.unwomen.org/en/news/stories/2018/6/joint-statement-swedens-multi-year-commitment-to-core-funding (accessed 10 January 2020).

Vabulas, F. and Snidal, D. (2013). 'Organization without Delegation: Informal Intergovernmental Organizations (IIGOs) and the Spectrum of Intergovernmental Arrangements', *The Review of International Organizations*, 8(2): 193–220.

Vaubel, R. (2006). 'Principal-agent Problems in International Organizations', *The Review of International Organizations*, 1(2): 125–38.

Volcker, P. A., Goldstone, R. J., and Pieth, M. (2005). 'Independent Inquiry Committee into the United Nations Oil-For-Food Programme: Manipulation of the Oil-for-food Programme by the Iraqi Regime'. 27 October 2005. Retrieved from https://www.files.ethz.ch/isn/13894/ManipulationReport.pdf (accessed 23 March 2020).

Weiss, T. (2009). *What's Wrong with the UN and How to Fix It*. Cambridge, UK: Polity Press.

Weiss, T. G., Carayannis, T., and Jolly, R. (2009). 'The "Third" United Nations', *Global Governance: A Review of Multilateralism and International Organizations*, 15(1): 123–42.

Westerwinter, O., Abbott, K., and Biersteker, T. (2017). 'Informal Governance in World Politics', paper presented at the Swiss Network of International Studies conference on Informal Governance, University of St Gallen, May 2017.

World Health Organization (2016). 'Framework for Engagement with Non-State Actors'. Retrieved from http://www.who.int/about/collaborations/non-state-actors/A69_R10-FENSA-en.pdf?ua=1 (accessed 22 October 2018).

World Health Organization (2017). *World Health Organization 2016 Financial and Budget Report*. Geneva: The World Health Organization.

World Health Organization (2018). 'English/French List of 214 Non-State Actors in Official Relations with WHO Reflecting Decisions of the 142th Session of the Executive Board, January 2018'. Retrieved from www.who.int/about/collaborations/non-state-actors/non-state-actors-list.pdf?ua=1 (accessed 22 October 2018).

10

Public Corporate Governance

Ulf Papenfuß

The provision of public services with new institutional arrangements has made state-owned enterprises (SOEs) increasingly relevant in many countries over the last decades. Studies from different countries demonstrate the significant role of SOEs in terms of their economic relevance and in providing public services (Bruton et al. 2015; Millward 2011). SOEs often provide critical infrastructure and services in areas where high reliability is required, for example, public hospitals, electricity, water, public transport, and the like.

For major societal issues such as the implementation of the sustainable development goals of the United Nations, digital transformation, coping with demographic change, debt crises, and citizen engagement, public corporate governance (PCG) and integrated management of administration and SOEs are crucial issues for society and research (OECD 2015). To describe corporate governance for SOEs in an increasing number of countries, scholars and practitioners use the term 'public corporate governance' (see, for example, German Federation 2009; Bundeskanzleramt Österreich 2012; Steiner, Raess Brenner, and Saxenhofer 2014). PCG can be defined as the legal and actual regulatory framework for control, supervision, and management of public sector organisations with independent economic management. In comparison to other terms used, the term public corporate governance is more precise, and it could help researchers to conceptualise and describe the field more accurately and in a differentiated manner.

Governance deficits and a lack of accountability have led to discussions in the context of PCG about which models, mechanisms, instruments, and processes public authorities can use to ensure effective, efficient, and sustainable provision of public services (OECD 2015; Florio and Fecher 2011; Bruton et al. 2015; Grossi, Papenfuß, and Tremblay 2015; Verhoest et al. 2012). The design and effects of governance reforms and governance issues are of special importance.

The outlined challenges call for integrated governance approaches by public authorities for administration as well as for SOEs and agencies. Policy-makers

Ulf Papenfuß, *Public Corporate Governance* In: *Advances in Corporate Governance: Comparative Perspectives.*
Edited by: Helmut K. Anheier and Theodor Baums, Oxford University Press (2020). © Hertie School.
DOI: 10.1093/oso/9780198866367.003.0010

such as the European Union (EU) and the International Monetary Fund (IMF) increasingly focus on SOEs, e.g. in terms of accountability and efficiency (European Commission 2016), and on ownership policy, oversight, and governance frameworks (IMF 2017).

PCG is an important topic for the future for both practitioners and scholarly debate. Reasons for this increasing relevance are the large number of SOEs, the scope and heterogeneity of their tasks in the context of public service provision, the large number of SOEs' employees, the high amount of investments undertaken by SOEs, and the debts held by SOEs. Public service provision and budget consolidation cannot be realised effectively and efficiently without powerful SOE governance and management. From a public policy perspective SOEs are important policy instruments, and the aim of PCG is to integrate them in all phases of the policy cycle in an adequate manner (Thynne 1994, 2011).

This chapter proceeds with an overview on PCG, presenting the theoretical and conceptual basics. The next section outlines major PCG challenges addressed in empirical studies in the international literature, followed by a reflection on the research situation. Looking then at the Organisation for Economic Co-operation and Development (OECD) Guidelines on Corporate Governance of State-Owned Enterprises, the next section provides an overview of the diffusion of public corporate governance codes in Germany and reflects on crucial differences between the varying codes in order to highlight opportunities for further international PCG research developments.

Definition and Theoretical Conceptualisation

Definition and Relevance of SOEs

SOEs are defined as enterprises that are under the control of public authorities at all government levels, either by majority ownership by one or more public authorities or otherwise by exercising an equivalent degree of control (European Commission 2016; Grossi et al. 2015; OECD 2015). They are characterised by their dual goal system with public service and financial goals. In the international debate several terms are used for these types of enterprises and organisations: SOEs, municipally-owned enterprises, public enterprises, government-owned companies, local corporations, government business enterprises, government-sponsored enterprises, government corporations, mixed enterprises, indirect or direct holdings of the government, type 2 and type 3 agencies (Van Thiel 2012), and other combinations of these elements (Papenfuß and Keppeler 2020). However, the term most often used by scholars and practitioners is SOEs (e.g. OECD 2015; OECD 2005; European Commission 2016; Bruton et al. 2015; Papenfuß and Keppeler 2020; Aharoni 1981).

The rationale for state ownership of enterprises varies among countries, public authorities within a country, and industries. It can typically be said to comprise a mix of social, economic, and strategic interests. Examples include public service provision, industrial policy, regional development, the supply of public goods, as well as the existence of 'natural' monopolies. However, over the last few decades, globalisation of markets, technological changes, and deregulation of previously monopolistic markets have led to readjustment and restructuring of the public sector in many countries on all government levels and therefore made SOEs crucial for sustainable public service provision and social policy goals (OECD 2015).

Moreover, SOE participation in international trade and investment has grown significantly. While SOEs once were solely engaged in providing basic infrastructure or other public services within their domestic markets, they are increasingly becoming important actors outside their territories. In tandem with this development is the proliferation of state-owned investment vehicles, which adds complexity to the relationship between governments and the enterprises they own (OECD 2015).

Worldwide, SOEs represent approximately 10 per cent of global gross domestic product (GDP) (Bruton et al. 2015). An OECD study covering thirty-four countries shows that in 2012, SOE portfolios combined a value of USD 2 trillion and 6 million employees; in some countries such as Norway representing up to 10 per cent of national employment (OECD 2014). In Germany, there are more than 16,500 SOEs with total proceeds of above EUR 550 billion (German Federal Statistical Office 2018). These companies employ 6.4 million workers, which represent approximately 20 per cent of all employees in German enterprises. Nearly 15,000 of those SOEs exist on the local level. Here, empirical studies show that 50 per cent of the employees in the public sector work not in the administration, but in SOEs and comparable public organisations (German Federal Statistical Office 2019). SOEs undertake more than half of the public sector's investments, and the debt ratio of SOEs is often even higher than that of the administration (Hesse, Lenk, and Starke 2017). Empirical studies for other countries show similar institutional arrangements of public service provision (Aharoni 1981; OECD 2017; Voorn, van Genugten, and van Thiel 2017).

Definition and Theoretical Conceptualisation of Public Corporate Governance

Since the 1990s the term corporate governance has been frequently used in the private management debate. A uniform definition of corporate governance has not yet evolved. In a generally accepted short definition, corporate governance refers to the legal and factual (practical, concerned with what is actually the case) regulatory framework for management and monitoring of a company (Hodges, Wright, and Keasey 1996; European Commission 2011; Clarke and Branson 2012).

In the international academic debate, different terms and concepts are discussed, such as corporate governance, public governance, public sector governance, and public service governance. However, all these terms and concepts do not specifically focus on corporate governance and management of organisations of public authorities with independent economic management. The term 'public corporate governance' is more precise because the specifications 'corporate' and 'public' make it possible to address this type of public organisations in a specific and differentiated manner. Moreover, PCG more effectively conveys the fact that the administration is involved in this area and that researchers' investigations cover more than just the boards of SOEs. Until now, the term has seldom been used in international journals. PCG could be understood as a synonym for 'corporate governance of SOEs'. However, as outlined, the term 'public corporate governance' yields a clearer understanding of the subject.

Regarding the specific conditions of SOEs, PCG can be defined as the legal and factual regulatory framework for control, supervision, and management of organisations of public authorities with independent economic management. Furthermore, PCG includes the implemented steering, management, and supervision as well as the behaviour of the people working within the regulatory framework.

PCG relates both to (external) control and supervision *of* the organisations with independent economic management by political bodies and the administration and to the (internal) management *in* independent organisational entities. PCG deals with the design of all components of the public authority control system and therefore also with the administration (e.g. corporation management unit) and the respective political body (city council, mayor, parliament, and the like). This combination of internal and external perspective is a key characteristic of PCG and underlines the interdisciplinary character of the research field.

According to the definition, PCG is not limited to a certain legal form. The term 'corporate' merely specifies the focus on public organisations with independent economic management. Criteria for independent economic management are an own annual financial statement or a separate appendix in the budget of the public authority. The respective entities may be profitable or loss-making and may operate in a competing or non-competing market environment.

The aim of and motivation for regulation of PCG is to enhance the effectiveness and efficiency of public organisations with independent economic management providing public services. The public authority should act as an effective and informed shareholder. PCG should improve the control quality and administrative capacity of public authorities.

In Germany, the corporate governance system is organised based on a two-tier board system. The management board with the executive directors is responsible for the day-to-day management of the enterprise. The supervisory board with the non-executive directors supervises and advises the members of the management board and is involved in decisions of fundamental importance. Because of greater competencies and more operational influence in the German two-tier system, the management board is of special importance (Papenfuß and Schmidt 2015). In SOEs, the supervisory board is appointed by the public authority. Its members are politicians, members of the administration, external business experts, and representatives of trade unions (German Federation 2009).

As evident from the literature on public management (Lane 2005) and corporate governance (Clarke and Branson 2012; Wright et al. 2013), agency theory is the dominant theoretical perspective for analysing PCG (Shaoul, Stafford, and Stapleton 2012; Van Slyke 2006; Whincop 2005). Political decisions regarding the outsourcing of public services to SOEs have led to greater information asymmetries such as hidden characteristics, hidden information, and hidden actions between numerous principals and agents including the general public, politicians, administration, and supervisory and management boards (Papenfuß, Steinhauer, and Friedländer 2017; Hodges, Wright, and Keasey 1996). Hence, there is a complex constellation of actors with multiple principal–agent relationships and overlapping responsibilities in public corporate governance.

Information asymmetries enable agents to pursue their own interests, allowing for the possibility of opportunistic behaviour. Institutions have to ensure that the agents act according to the first principal's interests and that their performance is observable and can be evaluated.

Stewardship theory places higher values on mutual alignment with overall objectives and assumes collective, cooperative, and pro-organisational behaviour of actors. Intrinsic motivation, trustworthiness, and information exchange are underlying motives for action (Van Slyke 2006; see also Anheier and Abels, Chapter 2 in this volume). In the intense debate on agency theory and stewardship theory, it would be helpful to gain a better understanding of the circumstances, if any, under which responsible actors should follow the recommendations of agency theory or, alternatively, those of stewardship theory or how the lessons of the theories could be integrated in the specific context of PCG.

According to property rights theory, the responsibilities, rights, and obligations of the relevant actors of SOEs must be clearly established and demonstrated. From this perspective, corporate governance reporting must clearly show which actors have which property rights. This includes information on clear responsibility structures for controlling and reporting on SOEs but also the responsibilities of individual persons and committees within the management board and supervisory body.

From the perspective of stakeholder theory, all stakeholders need to be adequately informed about SOEs.

Key Challenges of Public Corporate Governance

PCG is a major challenge for governments and public authorities on all government levels. SOEs face unique governance challenges (World Bank 2014; OECD 2015). On the one hand, public owners interpreting their role in a very passive way may result in insufficient oversight. In this case, SOEs' and their staff's incentives to act in the best interest of the public is limited, increasing the risk of self-serving behaviour. On the other hand, SOEs may suffer from undue hands-on and politically motivated ownership interference, leading to unclear lines of responsibility, a lack of accountability, and efficiency losses in corporate operations and supervision. The risk of self-serving or inefficient behaviour is amplified due to the complex chain of agents (management, board, ownership entities, ministries, the government, and the legislature) the general public representing the principal has to rely on. Additional governance issues arise because SOEs operate in a dual goal system. They should implement a given public policy while simultaneously carrying out economic activities successfully (Aharoni 1981; Bernier 2015).

At the state-government level conflicts may arise when state regulators are responsible for taking action against state-controlled entities or when the entities have to fulfil both economic and public policy obligations. Therefore transparency, evaluation, and policy coherence are of paramount importance for efficient decision-making and good corporate governance (OECD 2015).

Compared to private companies, SOEs encounter additional governance challenges arising from the following (OECD 2015):

- Multiple and often competing goals and objectives;
- Specific ownership structures with multiple principals;
- Protection from competition;
- Politicisation or patronage in boards and management;
- Low levels of accountability and transparency.

Implementing external and internal corporate governance control elements is based on two options: 'exit' and 'voice'. 'Voice' aims at influencing the transaction partner's behaviour by actively advocating one's own interests at shareholders' meetings or similar events. 'Exit' refers to termination of the transactional relationship. For designing PCG, it is of substantial importance that, due to the public service obligations of SOEs, governments' exit options are limited in many cases. Furthermore, financial success is not always necessary for SOEs. Hence, in the context of PCG, exercising 'voice' rights is relatively more important. Therefore, PCG is highly dependent on internal corporate governance mechanisms. Whereas private companies are pressured and controlled by capital markets, SOEs require effective elements of corporate governance to replace those pressures and controls. Empirical studies still show significant deficits in PCG. In general, criticism related to PCG scandals primarily focuses on failures in implementation, although some cases show relevant conceptual deficits (OECD 2015; Daiser, Ysa, and Schmitt 2017).

Both scholars and international organisations such as the OECD, the EU, and the World Bank stress the need and opportunities for PCG development (Verhoest et al. 2012; World Bank 2014; OECD 2015; Grossi, Papenfuß, and Tremblay 2015). Sometimes the expression 'darkroom of democracy' is used to describe PCG and to show how important decisions in this context are taken outside of democratic political control.

Research on SOEs and PCG

Given the relevance of SOEs and PCG, one might expect research on SOEs to make up a large proportion of corporate governance research output. However, the vast majority of empirical research on corporate governance focuses on private sector companies. The scholarly debate in journals on this field is active and elaborate. Significant contributions even seem to have led to a state of maturity in terms of methodology and content for specific subtopics. In contrast to the high number of contributions regarding private companies, corporate governance in SOEs has received little attention (Bruton et al. 2015; Daiser, Ysa, and Schmitt 2017). In their examination of journals of the *Financial Times'* top 45 list (FT 45) from 2000 to 2014, Bruton et al. (2015: 94) found that 'only 39 articles out of thousands published by the FT 45 top journals during the most recent 15-year period actually focused on the management of SOEs. Although inquiry into SOEs is on the rise…there is still a dearth of research on the topic.' Similarly, in the public management literature, there are also disproportionately more empirical studies on public administration in comparison to SOEs (Papenfuß and Keppeler 2020).

The lack of empirical research on SOEs and PCG also holds for leading scientific journals in other disciplines. Changes in institutional arrangements for public service provision have given rise to new challenges that should be ample fodder for several disciplines. Nevertheless, those challenges have not yet been addressed to the extent that other phenomena have been. These research gaps gain additional relevance as both scholars and practitioners increasingly call for improvement in the way PCG is designed and implemented.

Although there is an observable move towards more empirical studies of SOEs (Andrews et al. 2019; Jia, Huang, and Man Zhang 2019), empirical PCG research is far from achieving a level of output consistent with SOEs' sociopolitical and economic relevance. The comparatively limited literature on corporate governance of SOEs has triggered recurring calls to enhance the empirical state of knowledge about the factual, practised governance structures and the effects of changed governance rules (Bruton et al. 2015; Daiser, Ysa, and Schmitt 2017).

From a conceptual and theoretical point of view the research imbalance is important because the organisational differences between SOEs, public administration, private companies, and other entities have implications. SOEs need to be dealt with separately from administrative units or private firms for three main reasons: the dual goal system of SOEs, their complex ownership structure, and their different legal framework.

First, SOEs are characterised by their dual goal system with public service provision goals and financial goals. Under the laws of many countries, the provision of public services is a constitutive feature of SOEs. However, regardless of whether a focus on financial ratios is desirable and/or legally necessary, it cannot be denied that financial results play a very important role in daily life for the management and control of SOEs. Existing research confirms differences between public and private entities at the organisational level. SOEs lie somewhere in between—as an intermediate organisational form between public and private entities. On the one hand, SOEs provide public services, and it could be the case that empirical theory-testing would lead to comparable results as for the administration. On the other hand, corporatisation and agencification have led to significant intra-organisational changes related to organisational culture, goals, and rationalities, which might have a strong influence on empirical findings investigating theories and concepts (Papenfuß and Keppeler 2020).

Second, SOEs cannot be treated in the same way as conventional private sector enterprises because state ownership influences the goals and performance of SOEs. SOEs are characterised by public service provision goals, distinguishing them from the single focus on profit in the private business sector. According to the well-established theory of goal-setting, this difference in organisational goals can significantly influence individual motivation, effort, and performance.

Third, SOEs act within a different legal framework which, for example, allows them to increase pay-for-performance components more strongly than in the administration, which is determined by rigid civil service law. Whereas public personnel law often limits administrations, SOEs may have more freedom in human resource management practices. On the other hand, following the argument that, as a public employer, they have a model role, they cannot act as freely as private firms.

According to a recent systematic literature review PCG 'is a dynamic, diversified field of research that does not have a clear mainstream' (Daiser, Ysa, and Schmitt 2017: 455). Often investigated topics identified in their literature review are 'firm performance, ownership, governance framework, M&A and restructuring, and control mechanisms', but there are important topics with little research coverage, e.g. 'financial and portfolio management as well as alliance and interfirm governance' (Daiser, Ysa, and Schmitt 2017). In addition, the review highlights a 'methodical imbalance' with an over-reliance on secondary data, regression analyses, and data on China in neglect of other countries. Many studies measure company performance against purely financial criteria, and as a result there are calls for researchers to focus more on the non-economic goals of SOEs.

Regarding control mechanisms, the review comes to the conclusion that 'future investigations should concentrate on owners, their behaviour, context, and abilities to control...effects of contract management, trust, and accountability in hybrid organisations as well as how governments can engage in the private sector and still maintain a sound regulatory and policy framework' (Daiser, Ysa, and Schmitt 2017). Moreover, there is a need for studies on the effects of privatisation on firm value as well as on the consequences of insufficient risk disclosure. The academic community draws mainly on private sector governance research—a fact that amply justifies investing in a reflection on specific concepts in this field.

A systematic literature review on the performance of municipal-owned enterprises (MOCs) found that while such enterprises were often more efficient than local bureaucracies in providing some services, they also had high initial failure rates. The high initial failure risk resulted in part from goal conflict and principal–agent problems, i.e. PCG problems, which could be mitigated by building capacity to manage complex contracts (Voorn, van Genugten, and van Thiel 2017). The authors' research also uncovered 'tentative evidence that MOCs used for inter-municipal cooperation can gain efficiency when scale economies are present only if problems of dispersed ownership can be overcome' (Voorn, van Genugten, and van Thiel 2017: 836).

Chances and Diffusion of Public Corporate Governance Codes

In the international public management debate on the improvement of corporate governance, public corporate governance codes (PCGCs) play a crucial role (OECD 2015; Aguilera and Cuervo-Cazurra 2004; Grossi, Papenfuß, and Tremblay 2015; Haxhi and van Ees 2015). As propagators of such codes, the World Bank, the OECD, and the European Commission have promoted their development and use also in SOEs (Aguilera and Cuervo-Cazurra 2004; Grossi, Papenfuß, and Tremblay 2015; OECD 2015). A PCGC prescribes regulations for the management and supervision of companies and contains internationally and nationally recognised standards for good and responsible governance. Companies can diverge from the code, but then are obliged to disclose and justify the deviations ('comply or explain' principle). This enables companies to reflect on sector- and enterprise-specific requirements.

There are several classifications of self-regulation differentiating a continuum between 'voluntary self-regulation' and 'mandated self-regulation'. In the case of mandated self-regulation, the rules are mandated by the government; in the case of voluntary self-regulation, there is no direct or indirect government involvement. German PCGCs are classified as mandated self-regulation, since the rules have been developed by governmental and social groups and thereafter are passed by the responsible political or governmental body of a public authority (e.g. city council, state parliament, or cabinet).

PCGCs define goals, responsibilities, duties, rights, instruments, und processes for various areas. They often cover the following:

- Public authority as shareholder;
- Directors (supervisory board);
- Executive directors (management board);
- Interaction between directors (supervisory board) and executive directors (management board);
- Accounting;
- Auditing;
- Transparency.

According to most PCGCs, the management and supervisory boards must issue annual reports on the corporate governance of the company (corporate governance report). In particular, the report must state whether the SOE has complied with the recommendations of the PCGC and whether it continues to do so. In the countries which implement the 'comply or explain' principle, any instances of deviations from the recommendations must be explained and justified in a short declaration.

Owing to flexibility in compliance, PCGCs can give more precise and more far-reaching requirements for governance and controlling than inflexible laws can (see Baums, Chapter 3 in this volume, for more on corporate governance codes more generally). Typically, laws can only regulate standard cases not occurring frequently in practice. Therefore, laws necessarily leave regulatory gaps and loopholes, for which a PCGC can compensate. PCGCs regulate enterprises less strictly than laws and leave room for situational decision-making. Therefore, PCGCs do not restrict enterprises' freedom to make decisions, which for good reasons has been strengthened.

PCGCs are supposed to summarise and explain central aspects of the corporate governance system in place. Therefore, for all stakeholders, PCGCs provide an exploratory summary of the relevant rules, standards, and laws, for example, by referring to the relevant paragraphs in the PCGC. PCGCs also supplement this basic information by addressing frequently occurring issues of corporate governance, regulatory gaps, and uncertainties about recommendations that go beyond what is legally required.

From an agency theory point of view, self-regulation can help to mitigate agency problems in the specific public sector context. Here, self-regulation is to be understood as a flexible and transparent contract between all the actors involved in the PCG system in order to concretise incomplete contracts between the various principals and agents. With explicit recommendations and suggestions on corporate accountability, management, and responsibility, diverging interests can be harmonised and information asymmetries can be reduced sustainably. From a theoretical point of view, especially declarations of compliance and the 'comply or explain' mechanism contribute significantly to the monitoring and reporting system and foster the work of agents with different governance rules.

In the international context, the OECD's *Guidelines on Corporate Governance of State-owned Enterprises*, which are designed to support international exchange and promotion of policies, warrant special attention. In 2005 the OECD working group on corporate governance of SOEs established a public corporate governance code and in 2015 published a revised version after an intensive consultation process (OECD 2015).

PCGCs have spread around the world, for instance to Austria at the federation level and the federal state of Salzburg and to the Swiss Canton Aargau. In the Netherlands, PCGCs exist for several sub-sectors within the public sector. These PCGCs differ, but are all derived from the commercial code for listed companies (Papenfuß et al. 2018).

In Germany, since 2001 there has been a corporate governance code for listed enterprises of the government commission German Corporate Governance Code (see Baums, Chapter 3 in this volume, for more on the German corporate governance code). According to §161 of the German Stock Corporation Act, publicly listed enterprises are required to disclose online a declaration of compliance to the government's Commission on the German Corporate Governance Codex published by the Federal Ministry of Justice and Consumer Protection.

In the context of PCG it is important in the federal German system that each local authority at the different government levels (federation, federal states, municipalities) has self-governing and legislative authority according to Article 28 of the German Constitution. Against this background, since 2005 German public authorities on all levels have been developing various PCGCs. First, Berlin and Brandenburg published their PCGC in 2005; Stuttgart and Bremen followed in 2006 and 2007. The German Federal Ministry of Finance presented its PCGC for SOEs of the German Federation in 2009. In the meantime, some fifty German public authorities have adopted a code; several more are in the running to establish a PCGC.

The basic concept and the structure of the German PCGCs are the same, but there are crucial differences in their formulation and implementation. For PCGCs there is no legal requirement for declaration of compliance as outlined above for the German Corporate Governance Code for listed companies, although it would be possible to implement it in the different municipal laws and the state budget laws. For this reason it is crucial and necessary to incorporate the compulsory disclosure of a declaration of compliance to a PCGC in the company statutes of the respective SOE in order to make the declaration of compliance legally obligatory for SOEs. Each public authority with a PCGC should have a clear rule that the obligation to prepare and publish the declaration of compliance should be written into the statutes of the company.

German PCGCs provide flexibility in terms of choosing which recommendations to follow. It is permissible to deviate from the PCGC and can be justified as a sign for good public corporate governance. However, the declaration of compliance covering a detailed and reasonable explanation of the decision to deviate from recommendations is compulsory because it is anchored in the company's statutes and more than just a declaration of intent. The big advantage in terms of regulation is the possibility to adapt to specific company situations by deviating from recommendations, if those deviations can be justified well. Given the special responsibility of SOEs it is appropriate to require supervisory board members and executives to systematically reflect on the state of the enterprise in terms of the recommendations and give a short but well-argued declaration of compliance on a yearly basis. This is not additional or unnecessary bureaucracy but can be done in a short and precise manner and can help in day-to-day operations to improve governance and management of and in the enterprise.

However, analyses of the various German PCGCs show striking deviations from recommendations and major differences in their implementation. Many fail on transparency criteria, and often the number and type of recommendations differ. In addition, many categorise recommendations, which should be reported on, as mere suggestions, which do not have to be reported on. Major areas of governance on which these PCGCs differ include: responsibility and procedures for strategy and goal development, inclusion of political bodies in PCG, evaluation of the supervisory board's efficiency, content of reports of the executive board to the supervisory board, prevention and disclosure of conflicts of interest, test of appropriateness of executive compensation, internal audit, and provision of relevant information on corporate governance on the corporate website.

For the most part, PCGCs—given proper design and implementation—are considered to deliver valuable improvements to PCG, and studies show effects (Steiner, Raess Brenner, and Saxenhofer 2014; Perego and Verbeeten 2015). However, a PCGC is not the 'one and only' tool for PCG and is not a replacement for central corporate governance tools. Instead, a PCGC can serve as a conceptual framework delivering helpful contributions for various areas. A PCGC that meets the requirements derived from theories and recommendations, especially including a statement of compliance in the articles of association of the company, provides helpful contributions for public authorities but also support for individual actors for everyday working life.

A current and important evolution is the development of the German Public Corporate Governance Model-Code, published in January 2020. Various authors have criticised the significant differences among German PCGCs and principles of responsible PCG and have demanded the development of a model PCGC. To that end, this author initiated and coordinated the development of an expert commission and the German Public Corporate Governance Model-Code.[1] The Model-Code could be used to ease the establishment and evaluation of PCGCs in individual public authorities, which today requires the investment of significant labour and other resources in detailed analyses of what other authorities are doing and what developments might necessitate changes. With regard to sociopolitical discussions, the use of the German Public Corporate Governance Model-Code provides comprehensive additional value and individual benefits for everyday work and can offer relevant contributions to maintain and regain trust in public organisations and for democratically legitimised action options and political control.

Conclusion and Research Perspectives

The empirical data on the relevance of SOEs prove that, in many areas, sustainable public service provision and budget consolidation cannot be realised effectively and efficiently without powerful management and control of SOEs and responsible PCG.

---

[1] German Public Corporate Governance-Modelcode (G-PCGM), Eds. Ulf Papenfuß, Klaus-Michael Ahrend, and Kristin Wagner-Krechlok, version as of 7 January 2020, available at: www.pcg-musterkodex.de.

Multitudinous studies focus on corporate governance of private—especially listed—enterprises. In comparison, the scholarly community has conducted little empirical research on SOEs, despite their obvious relevance. Moreover, in some important fields there are disproportionately more empirical studies on the public administration than on SOEs.

Empirical research on many PCG questions and on the effects of models and instruments which public authorities could use to steer and control SOEs is clearly needed. From a theoretical point of view, researchers of different disciplines could test the explanatory power of existing theories, concepts, and constructs in the specific context of SOEs. With regard to future research this chapter can highlight several aspects which deserve special attention from a PCG point of view.

First, when researching the effects of different variables in the context of SOEs, researchers must be aware that financial performance measurements are not sufficient to capture the sum of SOE performance. As described above, SOEs are characterised by their dual goal system with public service provision goals and financial goals. Although analysis of financial indicators is relevant and provides meaningful insights, non-financial performance indicators for public service provision are particularly important. An exclusive control and research focus on financial results can lead to dysfunctional effects on public service provision. However, very often SOEs and public authorities do not report on performance indicators for the public service provision goals. Gathering data to monitor achievement of the public service goal is a big challenge for all current large-scale research studies covering various sectors in this field. Nevertheless, for upcoming research it would be beneficial to identify meaningful performance data for the public service goal and integrate them into databases for use by forthcoming studies.

A second aspect that requires greater attention by researchers is the discourse on the explanatory power of agency theory and stewardship theory in the specific context of SOEs. In contrast to research on private companies, there are hardly any empirical tests on the explanatory power of these theories in relation to SOEs.

Third, the question as to whether SOE managers should be paid like bureaucrats without performance-based pay is particularly relevant. According to several studies (Papenfuß and Keppeler 2020), organisational goals and ownership structure can influence the performance effects of pay for performance and public service motivation. In the context of SOEs, it is necessary to understand whether the special SOE characteristics have the same (in)direct effect and, if so, how.

Fourth, it seems worthwhile to assess, by means of quantitative and qualitative approaches, the behaviour control effects of PCGCs in the context of SOEs and administrations for different governance areas and rules. Moreover, comparative studies could be especially interesting in the fields of politicisation of executive directors, compensation transparency, and representation of women in the boards, for example.

Overall, with regard to empirical data for outsourced public sector entities concerning services, employees, investments, or debts, PCG deserves more empirical research as well as discussions with practitioners regarding the implications of the research findings. Strengthening comparative approaches and efforts in this field seems especially valuable as a means of gathering new ideas and of benefiting from the insights of other countries for improving the effectiveness and efficiency of public service provision. PCG is relevant for society and science and merits more empirical research and a broad discussion of the results.

References

Aguilera, R. V. and Cuervo-Cazurra, A. (2004). 'Codes of Good Governance Worldwide: What Is the Trigger?', *Organization Studies*, 25(3): 415–43.

Aharoni, Y. (1981). 'Performance Evaluation of State-Owned Enterprises: A Process Perspective', *Management Science*, 27(11): 1340–7.

Andrews, R., Ferry, L., Skelcher, C., and Wegorowski, P. (2019). 'Corporatization in the Public Sector: Explaining the Growth of Local Government Companies', *Public Administration Review*. doi: https://doi.org/10.1111/puar.13052

Bernier, L. (2015). *Public Enterprises Today: Missions, Performance and Governance.* Brussels: Peter Lang.

Bruton, G. D., Peng, M. W., Ahlstrom, D., Stan, C., and Xu, K. (2015). 'State-Owned Enterprises Around the World as Hybrid Organizations', *Academy of Management Perspectives*, 29(1): 92–114.

Bundeskanzleramt Österreich (2012). *Public Corporate Governance Kodex. Grundsätze der Unternehmens- und Beteiligungsführung im Bereich des Bundes.* Vienna: Bundeskanzleramt.

Clarke, T. and Branson, D. (2012). *The SAGE Handbook of Corporate Governance.* Los Angeles: Sage.

Daiser, P., Ysa, T., and Schmitt, D. (2017). 'Corporate Governance of State-Owned Enterprises: A Systematic Analysis of Empirical Literature', *International Journal of Public Sector Management*, 30(5): 447–66.

European Commission (2016). *State-Owned Enterprises in the EU: Lessons Learnt and Ways Forward in a Post-Crisis Context.* Luxembourg: Publications Office of the European Union.

European Commission (2011). *Green Paper: The EU Corporate Governance Framework COM(2011) 164 final.* Brussels: European Commission.

Florio, M. and Fecher, F. (2011). 'The Future of Public Enterprises: Contributions to a New Discourse', *Annals of Public and Cooperative Economics,* 82(4)361–73.

German Federal Statistical Office (2018). Public funds, institutions and enterprises. Retrieved from https://www.destatis.de/EN/Themes/Government/Public-Finance/Public-Funds-Institutions-And-Enterprises/_node.html;jsessionid=260 BD27547806ECDB151E3445745CF4E.internet721 (accessed 15 November 2018).

German Federal Statistical Office (2019). Personnel of public employers [Personal des öffentlichen Diensts]. Retrieved from https://www.destatis.de/DE/Themen/Staat/Oeffentlicher-Dienst/Publikationen/Downloads-Oeffentlicher-Dienst/personal-oeffentlicher-dienst-2140600187004.pdf?__blob=publicationFile (accessed 4 December 2019).

German Federation (2009). *Public Corporate Governance Code of the Federation.* Berlin: Federal Ministry of Finance.

Grossi, G., Papenfuß, U., and Tremblay, M. (2015). 'Corporate Governance and Accountability of State-Owned Enterprises: Relevance for Science and Society and Interdisciplinary Research Perspectives', *International Journal of Public Sector Management,* 28(4): 274–85.

Haxhi, I., and van Ees, H. (2015). 'Explaining Diversity in the Worldwide Diffusion of Codes of Good Governance', *Journal of International Business Studies,* 41(4): 710–26.

Hesse, M., Lenk, T., and Starke, T. (2017). *Investitionen der Öffentlichen Hand. Die Rolle der Öffentlichen Fonds, Einrichtungen und Unternehmen* [Public Investments. The Role of Public Funds, Entities and Enterprises]. Gütersloh: Bertelsmann Foundation.

Hodges, R., Wright, M., and Keasey, K. (1996). 'Corporate Governance in the Public Services: Concepts and Issues', *Public Money & Management,* 16(2): 7–13.

IMF (2017). *State-Owned Enterprises in Emerging Europe: The Good, the Bad, and the Ugly.* Washington, DC: International Monetary Fund.

Jia, N., Huang, K., and Man Zhang, C. (2019). 'Public Governance, Corporate Governance, and Firm Innovation: An Examination of State-Owned Enterprises', *Academy of Management Journal,* 62(1): 220–47.

Lane, E. (2005). *Public Administration and Public Management: The Principal-Agent Perspective.* London: Routledge.

Millward, R. (2011). 'Public Enterprise in the Modern Western World: An Historical Analysis', *Annals of Public and Cooperative Economics,* 82(4): 375–98.

OECD (2017). *The Size and Sectoral Distribution of State-Owned Enterprises.* Paris: OECD Publishing.

OECD (2015). *Guidelines on Corporate Governance of State-Owned Enterprises.* Paris: OECD Publishing.

OECD (2014). *The Size and Sectoral Distribution of SOEs in OECD and Partner Countries.* Paris: OECD Publishing.

OECD (2005). *OECD Guidelines on Corporate Governance of State-Owned Enterprises.* Paris: OECD Publishing.

Papenfuß, U., and Keppeler, F. (2020). 'Does Performance-related Pay and Public Service Motivation Research Treat State-owned Enterprises like a neglected Cinderella? A Systematic Literature Review and Framework for Future Research on Performance Effects', *Public Management Review*, 22 (7): 1119–45.

Papenfuß, U., van Genugten, M., de Kruijf, J., and van Thiel, S. (2018). 'Implementation of EU Initiatives on Gender Diversity and Executive Directors' Pay in Municipally-Owned Enterprises in Germany and the Netherlands', *Public Money & Management*, 38(2): 87–96.

Papenfuß, U., and Schmidt, C. (2015). 'Pay for Performance in German State-Owned Enterprises: Evidence and Reflection for Organizational Success Research with Undistorted and "Right" Data', *Corporate Ownership & Control*, 13(2): 336–50.

Papenfuß, U., Steinhauer, L., and Friedländer, B. (2017). 'Clearing the Fog for an Overall View on State-Owned-Enterprises: Quality of Aggregate Holdings Reporting by Public Administrations in 12 Countries', *International Review of Administrative Sciences*, 85(3): 1–21.

Perego, P., and Verbeeten, F. (2015). 'Do "Good Governance" Codes Enhance Financial Accountability? Evidence from Managerial Pay in Dutch Charities', *Financial Accountability & Management*, 31(3): 316–44.

Shaoul, J., Stafford, A., and Stapleton, P. (2012). 'Accountability and Corporate Governance of Public Private Partnerships', *Critical Perspectives on Accounting*, 23(3): 213–29.

Steiner, R., Raess Brenner, K., and Saxenhofer, A. (2014). 'Effects of Public Corporate Governance Guidelines at the Subnational Level in Switzerland', *Yearbook of Swiss Administrative Sciences*, 5(1): 139–61.

Thynne, I. (2011). 'Ownership as an Instrument of Policy and Understanding in the Public Sphere: Trends and Research Agenda', *Policy Studies*, 32(3): 183–97.

Thynne, I (1994). 'The Incorporated Company as an Instrument of Government: A Quest for a Comparative Understanding', *Governance: An International Journal of Public Administration*, 7(1): 59–82.

Van Slyke, D. M. (2006). 'Agents or Stewards: Using Theory to Understand the Government-Nonprofit Social Service Contracting Relationship', *Journal of Public Administration Research and Theory*, 17(2): 157–87.

Van Thiel, S. (2012). 'Comparing Agencies across Countries', in K. Verhoest, S. Van Thiel, G. Bouckaert, and P. Lægreid (eds.), *Government Agencies*. Hampshire, UK: Palgrave Macmillan, 18–26.

Verhoest, K., Van Thiel, S., Bouckaert, G., and Lœgreid, P. (2012). 'Lessons and Recommendations for the Practice of Agencification', in K. Verhoest, S. Van Thiel, G. Bouckaert, and P. Lægreid (eds.), *Government Agencies*. Hampshire, UK: Palgrave Macmillan, 413–39.

Voorn, B., van Genugten, M., and van Thiel, S. (2017). 'The Efficiency and Effectiveness of Municipally Owned Corporations: A Systematic Review', *Local Government Studies*, 43(5): 820–41.

Whincop, M. J. (2005). *Corporate Governance in Government Corporations*. Ashgate: Aldershot.

Wright, D., Siegel, D., Keasey, K., and Filatotchev, I. (2013). *The Oxford Handbook of Corporate Governance*. Oxford, UK: Oxford University Press.

World Bank (2014). *Corporate Governance of State-Owned Enterprises: A Toolkit*. Washington, DC: World Bank.

11

Media or Corporations? Social Media Governance Between Public and Commercial Rationales

Daniela Stockmann

In 2013 the photo-sharing platform Flickr launched—without warning—a completely redesigned website, initiating an outburst of user complaints. Comments expressed distrust of Yahoo, the company that owned Flickr, due to the sudden changes that had not considered user preferences as well as an adjustment to the business model that offered ad-free accounts only at an annual price of US$400. Prior to this change, users had been able to sign up for free accounts without receiving advertisement (Bagust 2014).

The industry largely associated these modifications with a change in Yahoo's business model. Former Flickr co-founder Derek Powazek explained, 'Ad driven companies have different priorities than member driven ones' (Bagust 2014: 91). While the prior business model created incentives to build community, Powazek suggested, Flickr would now mine the data trails and demographic information of individuals to make Flickr more profitable.

Flickr is, of course, not the only case in which the commercial rationales of IT companies have been strongly criticised. In China, for example, Baidu was investigated in 2016 for possibly distorting information about cancer treatments on the company's search engine after public outcry over the death of a student, Wei Zixi, who underwent experimental cancer treatment in a hospital that had appeared at the top of search results as an advertisement. After the story went viral, regulatory authorities launched an investigation asking Baidu to take on more responsibility when promoting advertisements (Liu 2016). The investigation follows an earlier scandal in January 2016 when Baidu admitted that it allows healthcare companies to pay for the right to moderate online health information forums on its social media platform Tieba (Tian 2016).

Daniela Stockmann, *Media or Corporations? Social Media Governance Between Public and Commercial Rationales*
In: *Advances in Corporate Governance: Comparative Perspectives*. Edited by: Helmut K. Anheier and Theodor Baums, Oxford University Press (2020). © Hertie School.
DOI: 10.1093/oso/9780198866367.003.0011

More recently, in March 2018, Facebook came under fire for policies that made it possible for political consulting firm Cambridge Analytica to obtain data from an estimated 87 million users—in the vast majority of cases via users' friend networks without their consent—and use it to develop psychometrically targeted political ads for the Trump campaign during the 2016 United States presidential election (Rosenberg et al. 2018). Facebook's stock lost nearly 20 per cent of its value in the two weeks following the revelations (La Monica 2018), and a movement urging users to 'delete Facebook' gained support from a number of prominent figures in entertainment and technology (Mazza 2018). The scandal also attracted the attention of government regulators, with Facebook Chief Executive Officer Mark Zuckerberg called to testify before the US Congress in April and the European Parliament in May (Zuckerberg 2018). Taking things a step further, the United Kingdom Information Commissioner's Office announced in July 2018 that it would be levying a 500,000 GBP fine on the company, the highest allowable by the law applicable at the time, for breaching the country's Data Protection Act (UKICO 2018a). The European Union's General Data Protection Regulation (GDPR), which came into force after the violations occurred, permits even larger fines for such breaches at up to 4 per cent of a company's annual revenue, the largest to date being Google France at EUR 50 million in January 2019 (Satariano 2019).

Massive online backlash as in the case of Flickr, Baidu, and Facebook often erupts when the commercial and public rationales built into business models of social media companies clash. While users are aware that social media constitute private corporations collecting and selling personal data, they primarily turn to the platform for public service. Users are often outraged when the profit orientation of companies becomes evident.

Here, I elaborate on the tensions between these commercial and public rationales of social media corporations as an entry point into a broader discussion about governance of social media corporations. In the discussion on governance of social media platforms, large corporations, such as Google, Facebook, and Twitter, are often first and foremost seen as providers of information and medium. Surprisingly, these companies have rarely been examined from the perspective of corporate governance, which emphasises internal structures and processes that guide the management of corporations. Therefore, principal–agent theory, transaction cost theory, stewardship theory, and managerial hegemony have not been applied to studies on social media. Clearly, much is to be learned from lessons of other corporations that also deal with public interest, as in the case of social media corporations.

The aim of this chapter is to provide an overview of the discussion that is based on the tension between the public and commercial rationales built into social media platforms and that lacks insights from corporate governance. The chapter opens with the perspective of treating social media primarily as information providers, i.e. as a medium with a public interest, followed by an explanation of the commercial rationales that are built into business models of social media platforms, whereby social media are regarded as corporations with a commercial interest. Next I lay out industry-specific frameworks that govern the social media industry. Over time, the trend has moved away from self-regulation towards a strengthening of national-level and EU-level regulations, that is, from soft to hard law. These industry-specific approaches towards governing social media have not relied on insights from corporate governance in dealing with the challenge of how to combine public and commercial interests. The chapter ends with critique of the current industry-specific regulatory framework and raises potential policy alternatives.

Social Media as Web 2.0 Technology

Social media and Web 2.0 are often discussed synonymously. However, according to Kaplan and Haenlein (2010), 'Web 2.0' refers to a broad set of collaborative, user-generated practices on the internet, while 'social media' are specific internet platforms built using Web 2.0 frameworks. Web 2.0 is thus the 'ideological and technical foundation' of social media (Kaplan and Haenlein 2010: 61).

While some early attempts to define social media focused on features of its technological surface structure (e.g. boyd and Ellison 2007), later definitions have crystallised around the functions of social media, variously referred to as social media 'uses and gratifications' (Whiting and Williams 2013), 'affordances' (Hogan and Quan-Haase 2010), or 'logics' (van Dijck and Poell 2013; Klinger and Svensson 2015). Two core features common to most functional definitions of social media are (1) networked relationships among users; and (2) collaborative, user-led content generation, also known as interactivity (cf. Hogan and Quan-Haase 2010; Kaplan and Haenlein 2010; Kietzmann et al. 2011; Klinger and Svensson 2015; van Dijck 2013; van Dijck and Poell 2013). From these core features flow other phenomena frequently associated with social media, such as self-disclosure (Bazarova and Choi 2014; Hollenbaugh and Ferris 2014; Kietzmann et al. 2011) or content 'going viral' (Blommaert and Varis 2015; Mills 2012; Nahon and Hemsley 2013; van Dijck and Poell 2013). Moreover, most communication scholars claim that it is these features which differentiate social media from more traditional mass media such as newspapers and television (e.g., Hogan and Quan-Haase 2010; Klinger and Svensson 2015). Nevertheless, a few dissenting voices (e.g., Manovich 2009) have highlighted continuities between new and old media, noting that only a relatively small share of users actually produce social media content and that much user-generated content imitates the forms and conventions of traditional mass media.

Obviously, social media differ from most traditional media in that they have been designed and run by private corporations. In Anglo-Saxon and European media systems, newspapers and television have historically been at least partially publicly owned; this is one common thread uniting the three unique media systems within the region identified by Hallin and Mancini (2004), although the exact role of government differs across countries. Even in the Anglo-Saxon model, many broadcasting stations receive some degree of public funding. Moreover, state involvement in media institutions, for example in the form of press subsidies (e.g. Murschetz 2013) and public service broadcasting (e.g. Mendel 2011; Allern and Blach-Ørsten 2011), remains a defining feature of the European and Anglo-American traditional media landscape today, despite increasing commercialisation. This stands in marked contrast to the situation for social media platforms, which have primarily been developed by private sector companies with little to no state involvement. The next section explains the commercial rationales built into business models of social media platforms, taking the perspective of social media as corporations.

Social Media as Registered Private Companies

Social media platforms are (almost all) run by private sector companies and often aim to operate globally. Many of the world's most popular and influential social media companies, including Facebook (which owns Instagram and WhatsApp in addition to its core platform), Twitter, and Alphabet (parent company of YouTube and the now-defunct Google+), are incorporated in the US, and specifically in the state of Delaware, which is known for its corporate-friendly policies and home to more than half of all US publicly traded companies (Carney, Shepherd, and Bailey 2012).

Facebook's business model centres around selling advertisements, which are embedded in users' newsfeeds and targeted according to user profiles the company develops on the basis of Facebook activity, other online activity, and data from offline marketers (Dewey 2016). Of the company's US$13 billion in revenue in 2017, 98 per cent came from the sale of ads (Facebook 2018b). YouTube, part of Google's corporate parent Alphabet, also has an advertising-driven business model: content creators on the platform can elect to run advertising on their channels once they have received a certain number of views and subscribers, with YouTube curating the advertisements shown and receiving a 45 per cent share of the revenue (Matsakis 2018). Chinese social media service WeChat, owned by the internet conglomerate Tencent, is more diversified, with significant revenue streams from online gaming and e-payments in addition to advertising (The Economist 2016).

However, other social media companies have struggled to convert their platforms' popularity into profitability. For example, Twitter did not achieve a profitable quarter until the end of 2017, after several rounds of cost-cutting (Twitter 2018), while Berlin-based music streaming service SoundCloud barely managed to avoid shuttering its doors in mid-2017 after struggling to find advertisers or convince its users to pay a subscription fee (Ram 2017).

Business models of Web 2.0 companies aim to generate income by attracting a large, growing, and active user base. Users are paying for the service provided on the platform in terms of information-sharing and social interaction by providing the company with their data created by the use of the service. These data directly translate into commercial income for the company, as they can be sold for profit to target advertising or sell services to their users (Michaelis, Lenhard, and Hunke 2017; Rohn 2015). The greater the data set of users and the more active the users, the larger the income and potential profit of the company.

The commercial and public rationales of social media platforms often clash when citizens are reminded of the profit-making goals of the companies behind these platforms. While people are aware that social media constitute private corporations collecting and selling personal data, they primarily turn to the platform for public service, and many users grow a strong attachment to the platform. Because platforms are associated with public and personal use, netizens are often outraged when companies abruptly change the design or product provided on the platform or when the extent to which the selling of private data becomes known to the broader public.

In order to deal with these tensions, over time there has been a trend away from industry self-regulation towards a strengthening of national-level and EU-level regulations, that is, from soft to hard law. The next section lays out how this trend developed under industry-specific frameworks governing the social media industry.

Industry-specific Governance Frameworks

The private and global nature of social media challenged existing frameworks of media governance, which leaned heavily on the state as central actor (see, for example, Siebert, Peterson, and Schramm 1973 [1956]; Hallin and Mancini 2004, 2011). In the beginning this required shifts from national towards supra- and international regulation as well as from state to self-regulation in which business and societal organisations became more actively involved in regulation (Latzer et al. 2003: 128). The United Nations Working Group on Internet Governance (WGIG) recognised this as early as 2005, when it proposed its now-classic definition of internet governance as cooperation among governments, the private sector, and civil society in developing 'shared principles, norms, rules, decision-making procedures, and programmes that shape the evolution and use of the Internet'—not just the harmonisation of technical standards, but also security, safety, privacy, and the protection of fundamental rights (WGIG 2005: 4). In this formulation, while governments are tasked with policy-making and implementation, coordination, and over-sight, industry players are expected to self-regulate, develop best practices, and participate in the government policy-making process, and civil society organi-sations raise awareness of key issues, mobilise citizens, and encourage social responsibility, particularly with respect to marginalised groups (WGIG 2005). Taking a similar perspective, Hofmann et al. (2016) define internet governance as 'reflexive coordination', not just governmental regulations targeting internet policy issues, but also unintended outcomes and bottom-up user actions that likewise play a role in shaping and ordering the internet.

Within this broader framework, governance of social media includes four elements: rules of operation, laws, terms of use, and social norms (Almeida et al. 2016). Rules of operation refers to technical factors that are built into the design of social media platforms. The term includes code but also encom-passes interfaces, back ends, data modelling, and other technological infra-structure (Almeida et al. 2016). A platform's rules of operations are usually optimised towards one core function that is built into the design of platforms (Stockmann and Luo 2017). Although much research exists on individual social media platforms, such as Twitter or Facebook, scholars have only recently moved towards systematically comparing the technological design of platforms and understanding differences in rules of operations (see, for example, Poell 2014; Valenzuela, Arriagada, and Scherman 2014).

Laws and regulations vary significantly among countries, thus causing problems for a unique platform to adapt to all of them. For example, Tencent's popular instant messenger WeChat differentiates between users who are holders of a People's Republic of China (PRC) passport and users who enter the territory of the PRC in order to adhere to cross-national differences in content regulation (Stockmann, Garten, and Luo 2020). The entry into force of the EU's revised GDPR in May 2018 similarly posed challenges for internationally active social media companies, who were required to take additional precautions when handling the data of users within the EU (Tikkinen-Piri, Rohunen, and Markkula 2018).

In addition to legal regulations, terms of use are standards, practices, and norms that the company has integrated in contractual agreements between social media users and corporations. For example, Facebook's Community Standards are aimed at keeping users safe, encouraging respectful behaviour, keeping private information secure, and protecting intellectual property.[1] One main issue is that the clauses in the terms of use are often not freely negotiated between parties (Almeida et al. 2016); users also often do not read user agreements (Bakos, Marotta-Wurgler, and Trossen 2014).

As social media enable interactive communication between social networks, norms among users may also govern how social media operate. Social norms or codes of conduct can impose sanctions for those who do not comply with the group's standard or can promote certain behaviour. For example, perceived norms on social media have been found to have a significant effect on the privacy settings individual users adopt (Lewis et al. 2008; Utz and Krämer 2009) and the type of content they share (Kang and Shuett 2013; Rousseau 2012). Going even further, China's social credit score system experiments with making a person's score partially dependent on scores of members in the social network, therefore potentially using social pressure to promote self-censorship (Liang et al. 2018).

In recent years, national governments have increasingly placed corporations that operate the most popular social media sites (Facebook, Twitter, YouTube) under pressure to take stronger responsibility as owners of private data and as content providers, as shown in the EU's 2016 GDPR, revised in 2018, and the German Network Enforcement Act adopted in 2018. As of February 2018, Singapore's Ministry of Communications and Information and Ministry of Law had submitted a Green Paper to Parliament citing the German law as a positive step towards removing illegal online content, while parliaments in Russia and the Philippines were debating draft laws similar to the German act (Human Rights Watch 2018). A Freedom House report (Kelly

---

[1] See https://www.facebook.com/communitystandards, accessed 26 March 2018.

et al. 2016) reveals that these initiatives are part of a larger trend strengthening national-level legislation.[2] In this way, governments are moving beyond general corporate governance codes, which primarily deal with firms' corporate structure and relations with their shareholders (cf. OECD 2015), in their interactions with social media companies. Instead, governments are imposing more targeted regulations that recognise these firms' profound societal importance and wide-reaching influence, similar to those already in place for traditional media firms and often analysed from a media governance perspective (e.g. Siebert, Peterson, and Schramm 1973 [1956]; Hallin and Mancini 2004, 2011).

These initiatives have received mixed reactions on the side of the industry and civil society. For example, the German Network Enforcement Act has been criticised for turning social media companies into arbitrators of 'legal' vs 'illegal' content, a function arguably better served by the courts, which are required to comply with due process guarantees (Knight 2018; Oltermann 2018; Rohleder 2018). Relatedly, there are concerns that the German law might make companies overly cautious, leading them to suppress some lawful content—as has been the case with several satirists and political activists whose posts have been deleted since the law came into effect in January 2018 (Human Rights Watch 2018; European Federation of Journalists 2018).

Self-regulatory Initiatives

As an alternative to strengthening national regulation, companies tend to stress self-regulatory frameworks. Companies often have an interest in proposing solutions themselves in order for policy-makers to develop policies that entail low costs for the company. Existing efforts in this regard have primarily focused on the issues of hate speech, disinformation, and privacy—mirroring and responding to the areas in which regulatory interest has been greatest.

With regard to hate speech, in 2016, Facebook, Twitter, YouTube, and Microsoft signed onto the European Commission's Code of Conduct on Countering Illegal Hate Speech Online, committing to take measures to monitor and remove illegal postings in a timely manner. This came on the heels of a national effort by Germany in 2015, in which the Federal Ministry

---

[2] Governments in fourteen of sixty-five countries passed new laws to increase surveillance in 2015. Twenty-four countries restricted access to social media platforms and communication tools between 1 June 2015 and 31 May 2016, according to the report—up from the fifteen countries that Freedom House identified the previous year. See Kelly et al. (2016).

of Justice and Consumer Protection created a joint task force with Google, Facebook, and Twitter to improve the reporting and removal of illegal hate speech. Assessments of the success of such self-regulatory efforts have yielded mixed results. Annual evaluations by the European Commission indicate that the four companies participating in the European Code of Conduct removed 70 per cent of reported instances of online hate speech by the end of 2017, up from only 28 per cent in 2016 (European Commission 2018b). However, a study of hate speech removal in Germany commissioned by the Federal Ministries of Family Affairs, Senior Citizens, Women and Youth and Justice and Consumer Protection found vast divergences among platforms: while YouTube removed 90 per cent of a sample of user-reported instances of hate speech within one week, this was true for only 39 per cent of user-reported Facebook posts and 1 per cent of user-reported Twitter posts (Jugendschutz 2017). This failure of at least some popular platforms to remove illegal content in a timely manner was an important impetus for Germany's abandonment of the self-regulatory approach and passage of the Network Enforcement Act in mid-2017 (Holznagel 2017). Nevertheless, there seems to be continued interest in self-regulation of hate speech on the European level, with Instagram, Snapchat, (now-defunct) Google+, and Dailymotion all signing on to the European Code of Conduct over the course of 2018, followed by Jeuxvideo in 2019 and TikTok in June 2020.

Companies have also recently become active in combatting political disinformation and 'fake news'. For example, in 2016, Google began collaborating with leading fact-checking organisations to include a 'fact check' rating for certain articles in its News and Search applications, while Facebook has begun testing 'trust scores' for online content based on user surveys and demoting the placement of disinformation in user newsfeeds. With regard to advertising, Twitter has banned political advertising worldwide, while Google has banned microtargeting for political advertising campaigns as of November 2019 (for more information on these and other examples, see European Commission 2018a, 2019). However, it remains to be seen whether such efforts will be enough to counter the disinformation that has become rampant on social media platforms and that independent evaluations have found to have influenced the 2017 parliamentary election in Germany (Neudert 2017) and the 2016 Brexit vote in the UK (UKICO 2018b).

Finally, social media companies' efforts concerning privacy protection have largely focused on responses to government surveillance and information requests (DeNardis 2014; Global Network Initiative 2017a). Thus, members of the Global Network Initiative, including Facebook, Google, Microsoft, and

LinkedIn, have committed themselves to completing 'human rights impact assessments' of their activities and informing users of government information requests with which they have complied (Global Network Initiative 2017b).

On the other hand, social media companies have been much less active in combatting privacy risks stemming from their own data practices, as the Cambridge Analytica scandal in which Facebook was embroiled for much of 2018 illustrates. Prior to 2014, the company permitted third-party app developers to harvest vast troves of user data—not just from the app's actual users, who had (knowingly or not) consented to such use, but also from these users' friends, from whom consent was never secured—with little oversight (Davies 2015). One such app developer then sold the database it had generated, comprising information about 87 million Facebook users, to Cambridge Analytica, a political consulting firm that used it to develop psychometrically targeted political ads that ran on Facebook during the 2016 US presidential election (Rosenberg et al. 2018). Facebook was slow to respond to these developments, even after *The Guardian* reported on Cambridge Analytica's possession of a duplicitously acquired database containing data from millions of Facebook users in December 2015 (Davies 2015).

It was only in March 2018, when the full extent of Cambridge Analytica's actions and influence on the 2016 presidential election became known, and pressure by users and policy-makers began to build, that Facebook rolled out changes to better protect users' data. Specifically, the company banned Cambridge Analytica and its parent company from its platform and announced that it would do the same for any other third-party developers who had collected large troves of user data and refused to submit to a Facebook audit or were found to have misused users' personal data (Facebook 2018a). In the future, third-party developers will require more stringent approval from Facebook before collecting any information beyond a user's name, profile picture, and email address, and will lose access to a user's data if he or she does not access the app for three months (Facebook 2018a). Facebook also changed its user interface to make existing privacy control settings easier for users to find and manage (Facebook 2018c) and ended its partnerships with providers of third-party marketing databases (Hatmaker 2018). However, the extent to which these measures represent self-regulation on the part of Facebook is up for debate; many seem to have already been in the pipeline to ensure Facebook's compliance with the EU's GDPR (Lomas 2018).

Critics of such approaches question the extent to which self-regulation can effectively address the issues raised. Specifically, given that social media companies' business models depend upon having access to vast troves of user data in order to better target advertising, they are arguably in a poor position to address data privacy concerns (Bennett and Raab 2006; Fuchs 2017). Moreover, companies' attempts to curate content in order to address hate speech and disinformation have been criticised for bias and double standards (Chin 2013; McNamee 2013; Tangen 2018), as the rationale for deleting one post but allowing another to remain online is often unclear.

Possible Alternatives

Critics argue that the regulatory framework underlying Web 2.0 needs to be revised, with many proposals revolving around changing the ownership structure of the data that forms the core of social media companies' business models. For example, Greenwood et al. (2014) call for a 'New Deal on Data' in which individual citizens are given ownership rights over their data, even when it is stored and deployed by third-party actors, just as individuals maintain ownership over their money when it is deposited in a bank. Similarly, Wilbanks (2014) envisions a marketplace for data where individuals can sell their personal information to outside organisations or invest it in data analytics projects in the hopes of obtaining a return. Morozov (2015) takes a more collectivist perspective, proposing the creation of government-managed databases of citizens' personal information as part of the provision of basic technology services (e.g. email); these public databases can then be used by government to improve services or be licensed out to private companies seeking to provide more high-end technology services (e.g. purchasing recommendations) on the free market.

However, such proposals are not without their own critics. Scholars such as Ohm (2014), Strandburg (2014), and Janssen and van den Hoven (2015) argue that governments should not be trusted as fiduciaries of individuals' personal data, and that existing barriers between data sets in the possession of various public and private sector entities be preserved in order to safeguard privacy protections. As a first step in this direction, Keen (2018) proposes that national and regional competition authorities take companies' data assets into account when evaluating mergers in order to avoid the further consolidation of data in the hands of a small number of companies. In another critique, Koops and Leenes (2014) discuss how 'hard-coding' privacy protections into data is in many instances technically impossible and can itself compromise privacy by necessitating the inclusion of additional pieces of meta-data unrelated to the purpose of collecting the data in the first place.

An alternative solution draws upon the stakeholder theory of corporate governance (Donaldson and Preston 1995; Friedman and Miles 2002), which advocates expanding the focus of managerial decision-making beyond a narrow consideration of impacts on the firm's shareholders to include a wider range of stakeholders, including consumers of the firm's products (here, social media users), government, and society at large. At an institutional level, this could be facilitated by including representatives of various stakeholder groups on companies' boards of directors (Ayuso and Argandoña 2007; Hillman, Keim, and Luce 2001; Luoma and Goodstein 1999). Several prominent social media companies have taken steps in this direction. For example, Twitter's board currently includes former Nigerian and US government officials, as well as the president of a UK-based non-governmental organisation focused on leveraging technological progress to support democracy. Facebook's board includes several former US government officials, former university presidents, and the current president of the Gates Foundation. However, other major social media companies are unable to implement this strategy because they are subsidiaries of larger technology conglomerates, and thus do not have separate boards (e.g. YouTube is a subsidiary of Alphabet, and China's popular messaging app Wechat is a subsidiary of Tencent). Moreover, in the US, where many of the world's largest social media companies are incorporated, there are several legal and practical barriers to greater outside stakeholder representation on corporate boards. For example, ethics rules prohibit most current high-ranking government officials from serving on corporate boards, although as the examples above illustrate, there is an ample 'revolving door' of former politicians with (often highly lucrative) seats on corporate boards (for more on this topic, see Palmer and Schneer 2016). In addition, corporate boards' own conflict of interest policies tend to require members to recuse themselves from any board business in which they might be viewed as having a conflict of interest (e.g. OECD 2015), complicating efforts to involve stakeholders with a vested interest in the corporation's decisions.

As of 2020, fundamental changes to legal regulations underlying business models do not seem to be in the planning. Public discourse on governance of social media concentrates on the question of how digitalisation can be steered in a direction that improves public well-being while at the same time reshaping its benefits. What the 'right' mix between government, business, and society is in the governance of social media remains a crucial question that requires much further investigation.

Acknowledgements

The research leading to these results has received funding from the European Research Council under the European Union's Seventh Framework Programme (FP/2007-2013)/ ERC Grant Agreement no. [338478]. The Hertie School of Governance and Leiden University are both beneficiaries of the grant. For more information on this project, entitled 'Authoritarianism 2.0: The Internet, Political Discussion, and Authoritarian Rule in China', see www.authoritarianism.net. For superb research assistance I would like to thank Keri Hartman, Hanyu Jiang, and Paxia Ksatryo.

References

Allern, S. and Blach-Ørsten, M. (2011). 'The News Media as a Political Institution: A Scandinavian Perspective', *Journalism Studies*, 12(1): 92–105.

Almeida, V., Doneda, D., and Cordova Y. (2016). 'Whither Social Media Governance?', *IEEE Internet Computing*, 20(2): 82–4.

Ayuso, S. and Argandoña, A. (2007). 'Responsible Corporate Governance: Towards a Stakeholder Board of Directors?', IESE Business School Working Paper No. 701. Barcelona: IESE Business School—University of Navarra.

Bagust, P. (2014). '"Honey, They Stole My Flickr!" Social Network Typologies, Online Trust and Dissent, and the Monetization of Immaterial Labor', *Media International Australia*, 151(1): 89–96.

Bakos, Y., Marotta-Wurgler, F., and Trossen, D. R. (2014). 'Does Anyone Read the Fine Print? Consumer Attention to Standard-Form Contracts', *The Journal of Legal Studies*, 43(1): 1–35.

Bazarova, N. N. and Choi, Y. H. (2014). 'Self-Disclosure in Social Media: Extending the Functional Approach to Disclosure Motivations and Characteristics on Social Network Sites', *Journal of Communication*, 64(4): 635–57.

Blommaert, J. and Varis, P. (2015). 'Conviviality and Collectives on Social Media: Virality, Memes, and New Social Structures', *Multilingual Margins*, 2(1): 31–45.

Bennett, C. J. and Raab, C. (2006). *The Governance of Privacy: Policy Instruments in Global Perspective*. Cambridge: MIT Press.

boyd, d. m. and Ellison, N. B. (2007). 'Social Network Sites: Definitions, History, and Scholarship', *Journal of Computer-Mediated Communication*, 13(1): 210–30.

Carney, W. J., Shepherd, G. B., and Bailey, J. S. (2012). 'Lawyers, Ignorance, and the Dominance of Delaware Corporate Law', *Harvard Business Law Review*, 2: 123–45.

Chin, Y. C. (2013). 'Regulating Social Media: Regulating Life (and Lives)', *Rhodes Journalism Review*, 2013(33): 76–9. Retrieved from https://www.academia.

edu/25901348/Regulating_social_media_regulating_life_and_lives_A_report_on_the_workshop_Social_Media_Regulation_and_Freedom_of_Expression_in_May_at_Hong_Kong_Baptist_University (accessed 20 March 2018).

Davies, H. (2015). 'Ted Cruz Using Firm that Harvested Data on Millions of Unwitting Facebook Users', *The Guardian*, 11 December. Retrieved from https://www.theguardian.com/us-news/2015/dec/11/senator-ted-cruz-president-campaign-facebook-user-data (accessed 16 October 2018).

DeNardis, L. (2014). *The Global War for Internet Governance*. New Haven: Yale University Press.

Dewey, C. (2016). '98 Personal Data Points that Facebook Uses to Target Ads to You', *Washington Post*, 19 August. Retrieved from https://www.washingtonpost.com/news/the-intersect/wp/2016/08/19/98-personal-data-points-that-facebook-uses-to-target-ads-to-you/?utm_term=.11207accbcf6 (accessed 18 March 2018).

Donaldson, T., and Preston, L. E. (1995). 'The Stakeholder Theory of the Corporation: Concepts, Evidence, and Implications', *Academy of Management Review*, 20(1): 65–91.

European Commission (2019). 'Code of Practice on Disinformation: First Annual Reports', European Commission. Retrieved from https://ec.europa.eu/newsroom/dae/document.cfm?doc_id=62698 (accessed 26 June 2020).

European Commission (2018a). *A Multi-dimensional Approach to Disinformation: Report of the Independent High Level Group on Fake News and Online Disinformation, EU Document No. KK-01-18-221-EN-C*. Luxembourg: Publications Office of the European Union.

European Commission (2018b). 'Code of Conduct on Countering Illegal Hate Speech Online: Results of the Third Monitoring Exercise', European Commission. Retrieved from http://ec.europa.eu/newsroom/just/item-detail.cfm?item_id=612086 (accessed 17 March 2018).

European Federation of Journalists (2018). 'Germany: Repeal NetzDG Bill, Deletion is Not the Answer', 9 January. Retrieved from https://europeanjournalists.org/blog/2018/01/09/germany-repeal-netzdg-bill-deletion-is-not-the-answer/ (accessed 10 April 2018).

Facebook (2018a). 'Cracking Down on Platform Abuse', 21 March. Retrieved from https://newsroom.fb.com/news/2018/03/cracking-down-on-platform-abuse/ (accessed 16 October 2018).

Facebook (2018b). 'Facebook Reports Fourth Quarter and Full Year 2017 Results', 31 January. Retrieved from https://investor.fb.com/investor-news/press-release-details/2018/Facebook-Reports-Fourth-Quarter-and-Full-Year-2017-Results/default.aspx (accessed 17 March 2018).

Facebook (2018c). 'It's Time to Make our Privacy Tools Easier to Find', 28 March. Retrieved from https://newsroom.fb.com/news/2018/03/privacy-shortcuts/ (accessed 16 October 2018).

Friedman, A. L. and Miles, S. (2002). 'Developing Stakeholder Theory', *Journal of Management Studies*, 39(1): 1–21.

Fuchs, C. (2017). *Social Media: A Critical Introduction* (2nd ed.). Los Angeles: Sage.

Global Network Initiative (2017a). 'Global Principles on Freedom of Expression and Privacy'. Retrieved from https://globalnetworkinitiative.org/gni-principles/ (accessed 17 March 2018).

Global Network Initiative (2017b). 'Implementation Guidelines for the Principles on Freedom of Expression and Privacy'. Retrieved from https://globalnetworkinitiative.org/implementation-guidelines/ (accessed 17 March 2018).

Greenwood, D., Stopczynski, A., Sweatt, B., Hardjono, T., and Pentland, A. (2014). 'The New Deal on Data: A Framework for Institutional Controls', in J. Lane, V. Stodden, S. Bender, and H. Nissenbaum (eds.), *Privacy, Big Data, and the Public Good: Frameworks for Engagement*. Cambridge: Cambridge University Press, 192–210.

Hallin, D. C. and Mancini, P. (2011). *Comparing Media Systems Beyond the Western World*. Cambridge: Cambridge University Press.

Hallin, D. C. and Mancini, P. (2004). *Comparing Media Systems: Three Models of Media and Politics*. Cambridge: Cambridge University Press.

Hatmaker, T. (2018). 'Facebook Will Cut Off Access to Third Party Data for Ad Targeting', *TechCrunch*, 28 March. Retrieved from https://techcrunch.com/2018/03/28/facebook-will-cut-off-access-to-third-party-data-for-ad-targeting/ (accessed 16 October 2018).

Hillman, A. J., Keim, G. D., and Luce, R. A. (2001). 'Board Composition and Stakeholder Performance: Do Stakeholder Directors Make a Difference?', *Business and Society*, 40(3): 295–314.

Hofmann, J., Katzenbach, C., and Gollatz, K. (2016). 'Between Coordination and Regulation: Finding the Governance in Internet Governance', *New Media and Society*, 19(9): 1406–23.

Hogan, B. and Quan-Haase, A. (2010). 'Persistence and Change in Social Media', *Bulletin of Science, Technology and Society*, 30(5): 309–15.

Hollenbaugh, E. E. and Ferris, A. L. (2014). 'Facebook Self-disclosure: Examining the Role of Traits, Social cohesion, and Motives', *Computers in Human Behavior*, 30: 50–58.

Holznagel, B. (2017). *Legal Review of the Draft law on Better Law Enforcement in Social Networks*. Vienna: OSCE Representative on Freedom of the Media.

Human Rights Watch (2018). 'Germany: Flawed Social Media Law', 14 February. Retrieved from https://www.hrw.org/news/2018/02/14/germany-flawed-social-media-law (accessed 27 March 2018).

Janssen, M. and van den Hoven, J. (2015). 'Big and Open Linked Data (BOLD) in Government: A Challenge to Transparency and Privacy?', *Government Information Quarterly*, 32: 363–68.

Jugendschutz (2017). 'Löschung rechtswidriger Hassbeiträge bei Facebook, YouTube, and Twitter' [Deletion of illegal hate postings on Facebook, YouTube, and Twitter], Federal Ministry of Justice and Consumer Protection. Retrieved from https://www.fair-im-netz.de/WebS/NHS/SharedDocs/Downloads/DE/03142017_Monitoring_jugendschutz.net.pdf?__blob=publicationFileandv=3 (accessed 15 October 2018).

Kang, M. and Schuett, M. A. (2013). 'Determinants of Sharing Travel Experiences in Social Media', *Journal of Travel and Tourism Marketing*, 30(1–2): 93–107.

Kaplan, A. M. and Haenlein, M. (2010). 'Users of the World, Unite! The Challenges and Opportunities of Social Media', *Business Horizons*, 53(1): 59–68.

Keen, A. (2018). *How to Fix the Future*. New York: Grove Atlantic.

Kelly, S., Truong, M., Shahbaz, A., and Earp, M. (2016). *Freedom on the Net 2016: Silencing the Messenger: Communication Apps under Pressure*. Washington, DC: Freedom House.

Kietzmann, J. H., Hermkens, K., McCarthy, I. P., and Silvestre, B. S. (2011). 'Social Media? Get Serious! Understanding the Functional Building Blocks of Social Media', *Business Horizons*, 54(3): 241–51.

Klinger, U. and Svensson, J. (2015). 'The Emergence of Network Media Logic in Political Communication: A Theoretical Approach', *New Media and Society*, 17(8): 1241–57.

Knight, B. (2018). 'Germany Implements New Internet Hate Speech Crackdown', Deutsche Welle, 1 January. Retrieved from http://www.dw.com/en/germany-implements-new-internet-hate-speech-crackdown/a-41991590 (accessed 10 April 2018).

Koops, B. J. and Leenes, R. (2014). 'Privacy Regulation Cannot Be Hardcoded: A Critical Comment on the "Privacy by Design" Provision in Data-Protection Law', *International Review of Law, Computers and Technology*, 28(2): 159–71.

La Monica, P. R. (2018). 'Facebook Has Lost $80 Billion in Value Since its Data Scandal', *CNN Money*, 27 March. Retrieved from http://money.cnn.com/2018/03/27/news/companies/facebook-stock-zuckerberg/index.html (accessed 10 April 2018).

Latzer, M., Just, N., Saurwein, F., and Slominski, P. (2003). 'Regulation Remixed: Institutional Change Through Self and Co-Regulation in the Mediamatics Sector', *Communications and Strategies*, 50(2): 127–57.

Lewis, K., Kaufman, J., and Christakis, N. (2008). 'The Taste for Privacy: An Analysis of College Student Privacy Settings in an Online Social Network', *Journal of Computer-Mediated Communication*, 14(1): 79–100.

Liang, F., Das, V., Kostyuk, N., and Hussain, M. (2018). 'Constructing a Harmonious Data-Driven Society: China's Social Credit System as a State Surveillance Infrastructure', *Policy & Internet*, 10(4): 415–53.

Liu, X. (2016). 'The Joint Investigation Team for Weizexi Event Requires Baidu Rectify Commercial Advertisements', *Sina*, 10 May. Retrieved from http://finance.sina.com.cn/sf/news/2016-05-10/090429635.html (accessed 29 April 2019).

Lomas, N. (2018). 'How Facebook Has Reacted Since the Data Misuse Scandal Broke', TechCrunch, 10 April. Retrieved from https://techcrunch.com/2018/04/10/how-facebook-has-reacted-since-the-data-misuse-scandal-broke/ (accessed 16 October 2018).

Luoma, P. and Goodstein, J. (1999). 'Stakeholders and Corporate Boards: Institutional Influences on Board Composition and Structure', *Academy of Management Journal*, 42(5): 553–63.

Manovich, L. (2009). 'The Practice of Everyday (Media) Life: From Mass Consumption to Mass Cultural Production?', *Critical Inquiry*, 35(2): 319–31.

Matsakis, L. (2018). 'YouTube's Latest Shake-up is Bigger than Just Ads', *Wired*, 18 January. Retrieved from https://www.wired.com/story/youtube-monetization-creators-ads/ (accessed 18 March 2018).

Mazza, E. (2018). 'Apple Co-Founder Steve Wozniak Ditches Facebook After Data Scandal', *Huffington Post*, 9 April. Retrieved from https://www.huffington-post.com/entry/steve-wozniak-quits-facebook_us_5acaf56ee4b09d0a119529bf (accessed 10 April 2018).

McNamee, J. (2013). 'Self-regulation of Content by the Online Industry', in A. Hulin and M. Stone (eds.), *The Online Media Self-Regulation Handbook*. Vienna: OSCE, 44–58.

Mendel, T. (2011). *Public Service Broadcasting: A Comparative Legal Survey (2nd ed.)*. Paris: UNESCO.

Michaelis, D., Lenhard, E., and Hunke, N. (2017). 'Media Companies Must Reimagine Their Data for a Digital World', Boston Consulting Group. Retrieved from https://www.bcg.com/publications/2017/advanced-analytics-media-companies-reimagine-data-digital-world.aspx (accessed 20 March 2018).

Mills, A. J. (2012). 'Virality in Social Media: the SPIN Framework', *Journal of Public Affairs*, 12(2): 162–9.

Morozov, E. (2015). 'Out of the Clouds: The Case for Making Digital Identity a Public Good', *The Berlin Journal*, 28: 14–17.

Murschetz, P. (ed.) (2013). *State Aid for Newspapers: Theories, Cases, Actions*. Berlin: Springer.

Nahon, K. and Hemsley, J. (2013). *Going Viral*. Cambridge: Polity Press.

Neudert, L.-M. N. (2017). 'Computational Propaganda in Germany: A Cautionary Tale', Computational Propaganda Research Project Working Paper No. 2017/7. Oxford: University of Oxford.

OECD (Organisation for Economic Co-operation and Development) (2015). *G20/OECD Principles of Corporate Governance*. Paris: OECD Publishing.

Ohm, P. (2014). 'Changing the Rules: General Principles for Data Use and Analysis', in J. Lane, V. Stodden, S. Bender, and H. Nissenbaum (eds.), *Privacy, Big Data, and the Public Good: Frameworks for Engagement*. Cambridge: Cambridge University Press, 96–111.

Oltermann, P. (2018). 'Tough New German Law Puts Tech Firms and Free speech in Spotlight', *The Guardian*, 5 January. Retrieved from https://www.theguardian.com/world/2018/jan/05/tough-new-german-law-puts-tech-firms-and-free-speech-in-spotlight (accessed 10 April 2018).

Palmer, M. and Schneer, B. (2016). 'Capitol Gains: The Returns to Elected Office from Corporate Board Directorships', *The Journal of Politics*, 78(1): 181–96.

Poell, T. (2014). 'Social Media and the Transformation of Activist Communication: Exploring the Social Media Ecology of the 2010 Toronto G20 Protests', *Information, Communication and Society*, 17(6): 716–31.

Ram, A. (2017). 'SoundCloud Struggles to Turn Fandom Into Hard Cash', *Financial Times*, 16 August. Retrieved from https://www.ft.com/content/23cd9d9a-80c7-11e7-94e2-c5b903247afd (accessed 18 March 2018).

Rohleder, B. (2018). 'Germany Set Out to Delete Hate Speech Online. Instead, It Made Things Worse', *Washington Post*, 20 February. Retrieved from https://www.washingtonpost.com/news/theworldpost/wp/2018/02/20/netzdg/?utm_term=.f310bd86ce3f (accessed 10 April 2018).

Rohn, U. (2015). 'Social Media Business Models', in R. Mansell et al. (eds.), *The International Encyclopedia of Digital Communication and Society*. Hoboken: Wiley-Blackwell.

Rosenberg, M., Confessore, N., and Cadwalladr, C. (2018). 'Firm that Assisted Trump Exploited Data of Millions', *New York Times*, 17 March.

Rousseau, S. (2012). *Food and Social Media: You are What you Tweet*. New York: Altamira.

Satariano, A. (2019). 'Google Is Fined $57 Million Under Europe's Data Privacy Law', *The New York Times*, 21 January, sec. Technology. Retrieved from https://www.nytimes.com/2019/01/21/technology/google-europe-gdpr-fine.html (accessed 26 June 2020).

Siebert, F. S., Peterson, T., and Schramm, W. (1973 [1956]). *Four Theories of the Press: The Authoritarian, Libertarian, Social Responsibility, and Soviet Communist Concepts of What the Press Should Be and Do*. Freeport: Books for Libraries Press.

Stockmann, D., Garten, F., and Luo, T. (2020). 'Who is a PRC User? Comparing Chinese Social Media User Agremeents', First Monday, 25(8).

Stockmann, D. and Luo, T. (2017). 'Which Social Media Facilitate Online Public Opinion in China?', *Problems of Post-Communism*, 64(3–4): 189–202.

Strandburg, K. J. (2014). 'Monitoring, Datafication, and Consent: Legal Approaches to Privacy in the Big Data Context)', in J. Lane, V. Stodden, S. Bender, and H. Nissenbaum (eds.), *Privacy, Big Data, and the Public Good: Frameworks for Engagement*. Cambridge: Cambridge University Press, 5–43.

Tangen, O. (2018). 'The Politics of Deleting Online Hate Speech', Deutsche Welle, 8 January. Retrieved from http://www.dw.com/en/the-politics-of-deleting-online-hate-speech/a-42030848 (accessed 20 March 2018).

Tian, X. (2016). 'Baidu Medical Tieba Chaos: Millions of Yuan Every Year for Selling' [original in Chinese], Sohu Business, 31 January. Retrieved from http://business.sohu.com/20160113/n434345434.shtml (accessed 29 April 2019).

Tikkinen-Piri, C., Rohunen, A., and Markkula, J. (2018). 'EU General Data Protection Regulation: Changes and Implications for Personal Data Collecting Companies', *Computer Law and Security Review*, 34(1): 134–53.

The Economist (2016). 'WeChat's World', *The Economist*, 6 August. Retrieved from https://www.economist.com/news/business/21703428-chinas-wechat-shows-way-social-medias-future-wechats-world (accessed 18 March 2018).

Twitter (2018). 'Twitter Q4 and FY 2017 Earnings Report Presentation'. Retrieved from https://investor.twitterinc.com/financial-information/default.aspx (accessed 18 March 2018).

UKICO (United Kingdom Information Commissioner's Office) (2018a). *Democracy Disrupted: Personal Information and Political Influence*. London: Information Commissioner's Office.

UKICO (United Kingdom Information Commissioner's Office) (2018b). 'Findings, Recommendations and Actions from ICO Investigation into Data Analytics in Political Campaigns', 10 July. Retrieved from https://ico.org.uk/about-the-ico/news-and-events/news-and-blogs/2018/07/findings-recommendations-and-actions-from-ico-investigation-into-data-analytics-in-political-campaigns/ (accessed 13 October 2018).

Utz, S. and Krämer, N. C. (2009). 'The Privacy Paradox on Social Network Sites Revisited: The Role of Individual Characteristics and Group Norms', *Cyberpsychology: Journal of Psychosocial Research on Cyberspace*, 3(2): article 2.

Valenzuela, S., Arriagada, A., and Scherman, A. (2014). 'Facebook, Twitter, and Youth Engagement: A Quasi-experimental Study of Social Media Use and Protest Behavior Using Propensity Score Matching', *International Journal of Communication* 8: 2046–70.

Van Dijck, J. (2013). *The Culture of Connectivity: A Critical History of Social Media*. Oxford: Oxford University Press.

Van Dijck, J. and Poell, T. (2013). 'Understanding Social Media Logic', *Media and Communication*, 1(1): 2–14.

Whiting, A. and Williams, D. (2013). 'Why People Use Social Media: A Uses and Gratifications Approach,' *Qualitative Market Research: An International Journal*, 16(4): 362–69.

Wilbanks, J. (2014). 'Portable Approaches to Informed Consent and Open Data', in J. Lane, V. Stodden, S. Bender, and H. Nissenbaum (eds.), *Privacy, Big Data, and the Public Good: Frameworks for Engagement*. Cambridge: Cambridge University Press, 234–52.

WGIG (Working Group on Internet Governance) (2005). *Report of the Working Group on Internet Governance*. Château de Bossey: Working Group on Internet Governance.

Zuckerberg, M. (2018). Testimony before the United States House of Representatives Committee on Energy and Commerce. Washington, DC: U.S. House of Representatives. Retrieved from http://docs.house.gov/meetings/ IF/IF00/20180411/108090/HHRG-115-IF00-Wstate-ZuckerbergM-20180411.pdf (accessed 11 April 2018).

12

Behavioural Economics, Neuroeconomics, and Corporate Law

Julia Redenius-Hövermann

The corporate governance debate shows no signs of abating; on the contrary, it is omnipresent, given the numerous recent scandals, be it 'Dieselgate', the discussion concerning excessive compensation of members of the board of directors, or the revolving door at management levels mainly in public listed companies. At the same time, this issue raises questions about the substantive continued development of corporate governance and corporate law. Closely linked to that are questions as to what extent corporate law has widened, or still must become more open, and what are the findings from neighbouring sciences and extra-legal arguments, particularly behavioural research in the form of behavioural economics and neuroeconomics.

Consequently, it is necessary—with the aid of various examples—to depict the potential use of the findings of behavioural science for the interpretation and application of standards, such as for German, French, and United Kingdom (UK) corporate law. Here, it is not necessarily a matter of taking up the discussion concerning the incorporation of extra-legal arguments with respect to the continued development of corporate law, but rather it is assumed that extra-legal arguments that correspond to the standards of the respective science can be integrated in corporate law (Redenius-Hövermann 2019). Also, the question of whether the findings of behavioural economics and neuroeconomics justify regulatory intervention concerning the 'correction of bias' ought not be delved into. In this regard, the normative demand for legal intervention due to a present bias is neither prescribed nor compulsory: on the one hand, a justification theory based on real-behaviour-oriented assumptions already exists, and, on the other hand, even with the presence of a (behavioural-) economic justification theory, a conclusive decision to intervene belongs in the realm of legal or economic policy (Redenius-Hövermann 2019). Another question is which regulatory instruments can be used to correct systematic deviations from rational behaviour.

Julia Redenius-Hövermann, *Behavioural Economics, Neuroeconomics, and Corporate Law* In: *Advances in Corporate Governance: Comparative Perspectives.* Edited by: Helmut K. Anheier and Theodor Baums, Oxford University Press (2020). © Hertie School.
DOI: 10.1093/oso/9780198866367.003.0012

Thus, the question of how (adjustment can take place) is at the centre of consideration of the continued development of corporate governance and of German, French, and UK corporate law on the basis of the findings of behavioural science. As the corporate governance debate mainly affects public listed companies and the effects can be best measured in this type of company, this chapter will focus on the corporate law of public listed companies. For this purpose, various kinds of bias (hindsight bias, peer-group effect, groupthink, and denial effect) are presented and are depicted where they have come into or could come into effect in German, French, and UK corporate law. The chapter also explores how law-makers *de lege lata* (the law as it exists) have reacted or *de lege ferenda* (what the law ought to be) could react to it. In so doing, it will be ascertained that in the act of regulating, the insights of behavioural science are a decisive guide. That applies both to the content of the regulation as well as to the selection of the appropriate regulatory instruments that direct behaviour. The chapter begins however with an overview of the fundamentals of behavioural economics and neuroeconomics.

Fundamentals of Behavioural Economics and Neuroeconomics

Fundamentals of Behavioural Economics

Behavioural economics regards itself as critique of the behavioural model of the *homo oeconomicus*. Based on insights obtained in laboratory tests of game theory and in neuroscientific research, it questions the classical model. Undoubtedly, behavioural economics plays a role in all organisational forms, namely, whenever human behaviour is affected. Here, however, the chapter only deals with the potential use of behavioural findings in corporate law; other applications would go beyond this chapter's scope.

Starting Point: The Rational-Theoretical Behavioural Model of *Homo Oeconomicus*
In the view of the standard economic model—depicted in a highly simplified manner—individual actors find themselves in a position of scarcity and therefore must make a rational choice from among multiple options (Kirchgässner 2008). In so doing, the rational choice is affected by individual preferences, which, in turn, are configured such that the actors select that option that promises them the highest expected benefit. For the actors, in the concept of the model of the *homo oeconomicus*, it involves a purely selfish

maximisation of utility (Kirchgässner 2008). Here, other actors influence solely the room for manoeuvring, but do not play any role in the attainment of the objective itself.

Summarised, the economic model proceeds from the assumption of autonomous decisions of the respective actors (Kirchgässner 2008). Certainly, human beings typically neither have all the subordinate dispositions and necessary information at their disposal, nor can they use the necessary capacities to completely process this information (Lüdemann 2007). Nor, therefore, can they act in a completely rational manner with the objective of maximising their own self-interest. In light of this deficit, the neoinstitutional model assumes that human beings conduct themselves with limited rationality and act rationally, maximising utility, solely within the framework of the information and capacities available to them (Kirchgässner 2008).

Thus, the neoinstitutional behaviour model, in contrast to the neoclassical variation, takes into account the fact that human beings do not regularly assess all possible opportunities for action and therefore also cannot completely survey and evaluate them. It also considers that human beings do not always have information available at no cost and do not process such information with unlimited speed (Kirchgässner 2008). The neoinstitutional model does not displace the neoclassical one but rather complements it in the sense that both limited information and limited capacities constitute restrictions, and exceeding them is ultimately associated with expense. Now, if the expenses associated with this excess are greater than the expected utility that would be gained from a greater use of information and capacities, then the rejection of this greater use must be assessed as rational behaviour within the meaning of the neoclassical theory.

The concept of restricted rationality is therefore nothing new, but rather makes the concept taken as a basis for the neoclassical theorem concrete and more realistic. Equally, it acts with the concept of restricted utility maximisation: human beings do not exclusively seek the maximisation of their own benefit, but rather are content with the satisfaction of their needs. For this reason, they do not seek the very best opportunity, but rather a sufficiently good one, which makes it possible for them, under the given circumstances and restrictions, to actually maximise their subjectively imagined benefit. Here too, it can—within the meaning of the neoclassical assumption—be utility-maximising to renounce the better opportunity, because this is associated with overly high expenses.

Ultimately, it is to be noted that the rational-theoretical behavioural model constitutes the basis of the assessment and evaluation of human behaviour in the economic context.

The Behavioural Economic Model

With the aid of behavioural economics, the limits of the rational-theoretical behavioural model are exhibited, in that the assumptions of the *homo oeconomicus* model require modifications. The statements resulting therefrom must be refined by behavioural science and neurosciences using empirical data about deviating human conduct, but without making any pretence of replacing the initial model (Kelman 1998).

For this purpose, a convincing criticism of the behavioural model of *homo oeconomicus* must prove that the prediction of rational choice is wrong in the typical case, i.e. for the majority of all individuals, and that these deviations are essential for institutional design (Englerth and Towfigh 2017). In this respect, behavioural economics is directed against the rational-theoretical standard model because it critically scrutinises the rational capability and preference formation ascribed to human beings in decision-making situations.

From the perspective of behavioural economics, the departure from the strictly rational theorem does not mean that human beings act completely irrationally and without any predictability; rather, the empirically demonstrable deviations are of a systematic nature and are thus subject to a certain forecasting certainty. Consequently, these deviations are designated in behavioural economics as 'quasi-rational' (Thaler 1992) or as 'bias' (Arrow 1982; Kahneman 2003). The bias revealed by behavioural economics offers alternatives to the rational-theoretical standard theory, in that it allows predictions about systematic deviations from the forecasts of the *homo oeconomicus*.

Due to the uncertainties remaining, it can be concluded that behavioural economics can neither topple nor replace the rational-theoretical foundation. Nevertheless, the integration of the insights of the systematic foundational research into human behaviour in modern psychology, neurology, and behavioural economics into corporate law makes it possible for the latter to continue to develop.

At this point of the discussion, it should also be taken into account that legal scientists, as users of the findings of behavioural economics, must look critically at their results, but their task is not to verify them. Criticism regarding replication and the so-called replication crisis must therefore be taken into account, but it cannot lead to the point that the results cannot be used anymore (for discussion concerning the replication crisis and how to handle it, see Camerer et al. 2016 and Camerer et al. 2018).

Fundamentals of Neuroeconomics

Neuroeconomics is the superordinate branch of science that seeks to describe and explain human behaviour in situations of economic judgement and decision-making, combining the methods of economics, psychology, and neuroscience (cf. also, Glimcher 2011). For Camerer, 'the neuroeconomic theory of the individual replaces the (perennially useful) fiction of a utility-maximising individual which has a single goal, with a more detailed account of how components of the individual—brain regions, cognitive control, and neural circuits—interact and communicate to determine individual behaviour' (Camerer 2007: C28).

Consequently, the objective is an enhanced understanding of the human brain, symbolically described as a 'black box', to grasp the cognitive processes in their entirety and to make them fruitful for economic research. McClure et al.'s study (2004), frequently described as the 'cola experiment', is considered to be the cornerstone of the cooperation between the neurosciences and economics in the 1970s. Neuroscientific studies contribute to reassessing the previous economic way of thinking and expanding the classic picture of *homo oeconomicus* by adding an emotional dimension. In addition, through neuroeconomics, behavioural economics can be buttressed by neuroscientific, including neurological, insights (for a detailed description, including the fundamentals of neuroanatomy and of the neuroscientific methods, e.g., in the form of electroencephalography or the positron emissions tomography, see Redenius-Hövermann 2019).

More generally, neuroscientific studies investigate quite differentiated influencing factors and aspects of human decision-making behaviour, and, by extension, contribute to the improved understanding of cognitive processes and human behaviour (Langenbucher 2019). Even if physiological investigations of the brain do not enable any causal statements in the sense that immediately translatable results are generated, they do nevertheless open up the possibility of correlations (Redenius-Hövermann 2019).

Integration of Behavioural Economics and Neuroeconomics Findings in Corporate Law

The following depicts the various forms of bias which have an effect in corporate governance and in corporate law and how lawmakers have reacted *de lege lata* or could react *de lege ferenda*. In the process, the German, French, and UK perspectives will be used as an application example. *In concreto* the most relevant biases that could affect the behaviour of different groups (management board, supervisory board, and shareholder/stakeholder) in listed companies were chosen: hindsight bias, the reference point effect, group behaviour and groupthink, and the denial effect.

Hindsight Bias

Hindsight bias qualifies the so-called hindsight error due to which, simply put, the likelihood of occurrence of an event appears greater than that of alternative courses because the event actually did occur (Fischhoff 1975). Hindsight bias is a subspecies of the availability heuristic, a sort of mental shortcut according to which information that contradicts personal attitudes is not taken into consideration (Tversky and Kahneman 1973).

Experts and courts are also prone to hindsight bias (Guthrie, Rachlinski, and Wistrich 2001). For companies and especially their boards of directors, this carries the danger that due to the hindsight bias, governing-body fault-based liability will become strict liability, since the question of whether the conduct of the board was contrary to its duty is assessed by the judge only after the damage has occurred. Thus, in assessing the board's conduct, the judge already knows the outcome of the decision made.

In order to address the dangers of hindsight bias, German lawmakers have responded by following the American example, with the business judgement rule, in § 93 of the *Aktiengesetz* (the Corporation Act, the '*AktG*') (cf. Fleischer 2019, Recital 62 *et seqq.*). In accordance therewith, members of the board of directors, when making corporate decisions, i.e. those not bound by law, should not be impeded by the Damocles sword of liability risk, provided that they have been able to make reasonable assumptions on the basis of adequate information so as to act for the company's benefit (Fleischer 2004). Thus, it is considered that, if the members of the board of directors are able to substantiate that the decision-making heeded the aforementioned preconditions in the law governing publicly traded companies, then the court will not conduct any review of the duty of care. In this manner, members of the board of directors are granted a 'safe harbour', in that they are not also liable for decisions which subsequently result in losses. In the final analysis, the willingness of the members of the board of directors to undertake risks for the benefit of the company should, with the aid of the business judgement rule, be maintained.

Similar rules exist in UK and French law. In the UK, the codification of a British business judgement rule was set aside on the occasion of the introduction of the Companies Act 2006 as legislators did not see a need to introduce a special safe harbour rule regarding the undeclared practice. As in US jurisprudence, courts in the UK will not review the business decisions of directors who performed their duties in good faith with the care that an ordinarily prudent person in a like position would exercise under similar circumstances and in a manner the directors reasonably believe to be in the best interests of the corporation (Cahn and Donald 2010).

Though there is no codified business judgement rule in France, there are at least equivalent principles. Indeed, there is no mention of fiduciary duties of the board members, but article L. 225–51 *Code de commerce* (French commercial code) provides that the directors can be liable in case of 'mismanagement, violation of the law or violation of statutes'. The fault of management (*faute de gestion*) is not defined in the commercial code and therefore falls under the sovereign assessment of the judges. The jurisprudence has adopted a rather broad interpretation of this concept. This fault is inferred from the conduct of the board members in comparison to what would have been the behaviour of a normally competent board member placed in the same situation (concept of 'the reasonable man' in the US). The French jurisprudence also recognises the failure of supervision or diligence, reckless decisions, and serious errors of assessment (for example, the taking of financial risks, Tribunal de commerce de Paris, 23 November 1992). If the judicial assessment of the fault of management is quite broad, the bad results of a decision are however not sufficient to characterise it as a fault (Redenius-Hövermann 2010).

In the course of the *de lege ferenda* discussion, the question is whether a legal judgement rule is also required, i.e. a legal privilege in terms of liability granted in analogy to the business judgement rule for legally bound decisions, including duties of loyalty, informational duties, and other general breaches of laws and by-laws. For even in the case of legally bound decisions, the board of directors finds itself in a similarly difficult trade-off situation as with the business judgement rule, because a legal assessment can be just as error-prone as a business decision. In this manner, in the event of an ex ante legal question, multiple viewpoints can be reasonable.

The legal judgement rule, however, should not be judged as discretionary, as it would be deprived of any judicial control. Rather, it is effective to make a strict separation between breach of duty and culpability. In this way, a board of director's decision turning out to be a faulty legal assessment could be assessed by the court as a breach of duty. However, the faulty legal assessment is to be accounted for at the level of culpability, such that culpability is to be negated if the board of directors takes the trouble to investigate the legal situation and, upon this basis, carefully formed a reasonable legal position (Laufersweiler and Redenius-Hövermann 2017). Thus, the hindsight bias of the court can be countered even without establishing a legal judgement rule in legislation.

Reference Point Effect/Peer-group Effect

According to the rational-theoretical model, there cannot be any reference point effect, i.e. comparing behaviour with other persons who, from their vantage point, belong to the same social group (Redenius-Hövermann 2019). This reference point effect, however, can be identified within a core topic of corporate governance, namely board members' compensation, in that members of boards of directors and supervisory boards compare their compensation with other reference persons. In so doing, it is demonstrably applicable that, contrary to what is assumed by the rational-theoretical model, what is decisive for the agents is not the absolute income level, but rather its relation to others (Clark and Oswald 1996). Hence, test subjects prefer a low salary, which, however, is distinctly higher than that of their colleagues, versus a high salary that does not diverge or only slightly diverges from the rates of compensation granted on the marketplace.

These insights are undergirded by research results in neuroscience, e.g., concerning the money illusion (Dohmen et al. 2009). Hence, the degree of satisfaction with one's individual income does not increase in a linear fashion with one's purchasing power, but rather depends to a much stronger extent upon comparison with earlier earnings or with the compensation of similarly situated peers (Clark and Oswald 1996).

In this way, the factors of happiness and satisfaction are based more strongly upon nominal than upon real monetary value, because it is more simply processed cognitively. Even the members of the supervisory board are influenced by this effect, in that, when setting the compensation of members of the board of directors, they base their decision on what they themselves earn or have earned (on the relation between CEO compensation and social capital, see Belliveau, O'Reilly, and Wade 1996).

In order to counter this peer-group effect, lawmakers have responded in numerous ways. Hence, in German law the compensation of the board of directors is to be set forth by the plenary supervisory board and not by a committee (§§ 87, 87a, 107 AktG).

In French law, a differentiation has to be made between the one-tier and the two-tier models. In the two-tier *société anonyme* (SA), the remuneration of the members of the board of directors is fixed, as in German law, by the supervisory board (art. L. 225–63 Code de commerce (French commercial code, C. com.)). In the one-tier SA the executive members of the *conseil d'administration* have their *'jetons de presence'* fixed by the general meeting of shareholders (art. L. 225–45 C. com.), and, if they are also directors, the remuneration is fixed by the *conseil d'administration* (art. L. 225–47 para. 1 C. com., art. L. 225–53 para. 3 C. com.) (Germain and Magnier 2017).

According to Sec. D.2.1 of the UK Corporate Governance Code the board should establish a remuneration committee of at least three, or in the case of smaller companies two, independent non-executive directors. In addition, the company chair may also be a member of, but not chair, the committee if they were considered independent on appointment as chair. The remuneration committee should make available its terms of reference, explaining its role and the authority delegated to it by the board.

Moreover, the supervisory board is, in German law as contemplated by § 116(3) *AktG*, libale to the company in the event that inappropriate compensation is established for the board of directors. Although there is no explicit liability in French law regarding inappropriate compensation, the supervisory board can be held liable on the basis of a *faute de gestion* due to inappropriate remuneration (Germain and Magnier 2017).

Also, the compensation of the board of directors is generally to be disclosed individually:

- As contemplated by §§ 286, 315 of the *Handelsgesetzbuch* (German Commercial Code, *HGB*) unless a qualified three-quarters majority of the general meeting of the shareholders of the base capital present for passing a resolution votes for an opt-out in the form of the aggregated publication duty (Spindler 2005);
- By art. L. 225-102-1 para. 3 C. com., as the compensation of the board members of French public listed companies has to be published individually (Redenius-Hövermann 2010);
- By sec. 412 et seq. and sec. 420 et seq. Companies Act 2006 as the remuneration of the directors has to be reported and published (see also Sec. D.1.2. UK Corporate Governance Code 2016 according to which, 'where

a company releases an executive director to serve as a non-executive director elsewhere, the remuneration report should include a statement as to whether or not the director will retain such earnings and, if so, what the remuneration is'; Provision 41. UK Corporate Governance Code 2018).

In addition, the general shareholders meeting can, in the way of 'say-on-pay', take a vote on the system of board of director's compensation that at least allows it to monitor behaviour. While this rule is not binding in German law (Para. 120a AktG), it is binding in French (see Loi n° 2016–1691 du 9 décembre 2016 relative à la transparence, à la lutte contre la corruption et à la modernisation de la vie économique, 'Sapin 2') and UK Law (Sec. 226b Companies Act 2006).

It is questionable whether *de lege ferenda* requires further reforms in order to curb the peer-group effect. Looking at German law, a binding vote by the general shareholders meeting is conceivable; along with that, however, there must also be an abolition of the supervisory board's liability for compensatory damages, should a positive vote be held. Furthermore, it is being discussed in Germany whether a maximal limit to board members' compensation is needed under the law governing public listed companies (see G1 DCGK). This discussion is made analogous to the standards of the banking oversight law.

As contemplated by § 25a para. 5 of the *Kreditwesengesetz* (the German Banking Act, the '*KWG*') or art. L. 511-41-1 C *Code monétaire et financier* (the French Financial Market Act), the variable compensation for board members must not exceed the fixed compensation or, with the consent of the main shareholders meeting, may not represent more than twice the amount. The consequence of the regulation can, however, be an increase in the fixed compensation, taking into consideration the principle of reasonableness, so that the overall compensation, including variable compensation, remains at the previous level. To ensure reasonableness, a contractually established limitation is required, on which the general shareholders meeting votes. Ultimately, such a dynamic limitation regulation can, if at all, constitute only one element in the statutory capping rules. Even an absolute limit to a certain amount, such as in § 5 para. 2 no. 4a of the *Finanzmarktstabilisierungsfondsgesetz* (the German Financial Market Stabilization Fund Act), appears to make little sense, because the circumstances in corporations are too variegated and the compensation, in part, must also be measured in accordance with the size of the company. It is questionable whether lawmakers would be able to establish a fair price. A summary cap would also have as a consequence that up to the set amount, the compensation would have to be qualified as reasonable.

In addition, it is to be presumed that the 'elevator effect' would be triggered, because boards of directors that up to now have been compensated distinctly under the cap would seek to align their compensation with the maximal limit. In the final analysis, a statutorily established, absolute maximal limit to board members' compensation is inadvisable (see also Baums 2004). Not only is freedom of contract being restricted, but instead the control function of the price mechanism on the labour markets is deleteriously impaired (Redenius-Hövermann 2015). Also, the cap opens up room for manipulation. Furthermore, from the vantage point of behavioural science it is entirely unclear from which absolute limit the compensation will no longer lead to improved performance (Pepper, Gore, and Crossman 2013).

Finally, a statutorily configured cap of board members' compensation can also lead to the upper limit's metamorphosis into a minimum wage for board members. Also, the constitutional objections ought to be taken into consideration, under which a statutory maximal limit can be deemed as disproportionate with regard, for example, to Art. 12(1)(2) of the German *Grundgesetz* (the German Constitution). In conclusion, it is to be noted that absolute upper limits, be they established in the law governing publicly traded companies or by corporate governance codes,[1] are 'methodologically unsuitable' (Kort 2015: Recital 394) for the purpose of making the reasonableness standard concrete, and are therefore to be rejected (Redenius-Hövermann 2019).

The situation is different when, within a company, maximal limits for compensation are set that should be established either by agreement or under the by-laws. However, it is to be taken into consideration that (i) having the supervisory board establish an upper limit can elicit misconduct, e.g. groupthink, and that (ii) the upper limit established by the general shareholders meeting pursuant to the by-laws is very inflexible, due to the rigid minimum quorums. For this reason, it has been proposed to have the upper limit set by the supervisory board but to have the general shareholders meeting cast a vote over it within the framework of the vote on compensation (Redenius-Hövermann 2019).

In the one-tier public listed company as in the UK, the shareholder general meeting should decide about the different matters of remuneration, as for

---

[1] Deutscher Corporate Governance Kodex, the German Corporate Governance Code, the 'DCGK', the UK Corporate Governance Code 2018 (the 2018 code applies to accounting periods beginning on or after 1 January 2019), or the French ADEF/MEDEF Code de gouvernement d'entreprise. See Baums, Chapter 3 in this volume, for more on corporate governance codes.

example it is intended in LR 9.4.4. FCA Listings Rule.[2] Other reform proposals are also being discussed (Department for Business, Energy and Industrial Strategy 2016). In conclusion, behavioural science insights can find their way into corporate law, but necessitate translation and implementation from corporate lawyers (Redenius-Hövermann 2019).

Group Behaviour and Groupthink

An additional bias that influences corporate law consists of group behaviour and groupthink (Redenius-Hövermann 2019). What is understood as 'groupthink' and 'group behaviour' from a behavioural science vantage point? Research has shown that homogenously composed groups develop strong cohesion sooner than do heterogeneously composed ones (Whyte 1961). There is an apparent correlation between cohesion and conformity in that the more attractive a group is for its members, the more likely it is that the group's members adjust their opinions, objectives, and norms amongst themselves (Vroom 1964). Cohesive groups in general are inclined to accept in their midst only such persons who meet the objectives, norms, and standards of the group; members who do not conduct themselves with sufficient conformity are rejected by the group as a consequence.

Closely associated with group behaviour is groupthink. The pioneer in exploring groupthink was Irving Janis (1972), who researched the decision-making behaviour of groups and the collective dynamic that determined it. In accordance with the generally applicable understanding, groupthink is a process in which a group of knowledgeable people makes poor or unrealistic decisions because each person adjusts his or her own opinion to the putative opinion of the group. Out of this behaviour, situations can arise in which the group consents to actions or decisions which each individual group member would reject (Rost and Osterloh 2008).

Cohesive groups also tend to hastily create harmony and suppress contrary opinions (Leahy 1992). The result is stereotyping. Janis conceives of this as the behaviour of the group whereby it pervasively perceives enemies and outsiders in a negative fashion and deems it superfluous to engage in serious discussions with them (Janis 1972).

---

[2] 'A listed company must not, without the prior approval by an ordinary resolution of the shareholders of the listed company in a general meeting, grant the option, warrant, or other right if the price per share payable on the exercise of the option, warrant or other similar right to subscribe is less than whichever of the following is used to calculate the exercise price.'

Furthermore, it has been shown that groupthink is augmented by strong persons in leadership positions and by time pressure (Moorhead, Ference, and Neck 1991). The hazard of groupthink, consequently, consists in its marked rigidity and in the irrational behaviour of the group's members. In order to achieve the greatest possible conformity, individuals who deviate from the group standard are excluded. Group members concomitantly conform their own views and their behaviour to the group. Hence, group-think constitutes a great systematic risk for the enterprise (Rost and Osterloh 2008).

Neuroscientific studies concerning herd behaviour and conformity pressure in groups offer insights pertaining to activities, above all, within the limbic system and especially the amygdala, i.e. regions that are connected with processing fear and uncertainty. Such studies have shown that a patently false majority opinion is enforced against the opinion of the minority, and that the minority occasionally will assume the attitude of the majority. In so doing, an activation of the amygdala is ascertainable (Bürger and Weber 2011).

Now, after briefly sketching how groupthink and group behaviour are defined, the question is where these biases can become relevant in corporate law (Redenius-Hövermann 2019).

A first example is compensation of members of the board of directors. Pursuant to §§ 87, 87a AktG, board members' compensation is in German law to be fixed by the supervisory board in a reasonable manner, whereby the supervisory board, without doubt, is making decisions regarding the use of other people's money, viz., the money of the company and, by extension, indirectly that of the principal in the form of the shareholders. As already shown, behavioural economics recognises the danger that both of the agents—the board of directors and the supervisory board—could act in accordance with group behaviour against the primary principal. Thus, it has been shown that board members' compensation increases in the event of marked authority of the chairperson, but, however, not absolutely in the event of the chairperson's continuity (Entorf et al. 2009).

Lawmakers have, in part, recognised these problems. Thus, and pursuant to § 107 AktG, board members' compensation is to be fixed by the plenary supervisory board in its entirety, and not by a committee of the supervisory board or, as in French and UK Law, by the general shareholder meeting. Even though the plenary body is less susceptible to group behaviour than a committee, staffing the supervisory board with independent members can help to make the group more heterogeneous and to counteract group behaviour and group thinking (Redenius-Hövermann 2019).

The independence characteristic, whether in German, French, or English discussion, should be applied *de lege ferenda* with still greater force, be it through a more precise formulation of the meaning of independence or a greater reduction of the upper limit or of the maximal duration of the mandates (Redenius-Hövermann 2019; Redenius-Hövermann and Schmidt 2018). Furthermore, 'say-on-pay' makes it possible to respond to the aforementioned bias. Even though this instrument does not constitute a panacea, it does contribute to critical review of the compensation structures, particularly in cases of high rejection rates.

In concreto, German corporate law, in § 120a AktG, provides that the general shareholders meeting of the exchange-listed company can pass a resolution governing the approval of the remuneration policy and the report concerning board members' compensation, whereby the vote has only an advisory character and, as a result, contains neither rights nor duties; in particular, this article leaves untouched the obligations of the supervisory board under § 87 AktG. If the general shareholders meeting has not approved the remuneration policy, the supervisory board has to submit a revised remuneration policy in the following general shareholders meeting.

Even though a binding vote, as provided by Sec. 439 UK Companies Act 2006 and the Loi Sapin 2, entails immediate behaviour-controlling consequences, an advisory vote does not signify that it has no behaviour-controlling effect; rather, a strong public effect, not to be underestimated, is to be attributed to it as well, and moreover it displays a self-executing effect (Fleischer and Bedkowski 2009). An effective instrument to render the various flawed behaviours less harmful and, in the optimal case, to completely halt them is the disclosure of the board members' compensation. Thus, by way of the duty of accountability, which is imposed upon the board of directors and the supervisory board with respect to the compensation issued, group behaviour can be curbed (Redenius-Hövermann 2019).

In corporate law, as has already been briefly outlined, the compensation of each member of the board of director must, as a fundamental principle, be disclosed. Moreover, an additional cornerstone for confining the bias set forth therein is that the chair of the supervisory board or board of directors (in the one-tier model) would have to evaluate the appropriateness of the salaries drawn by the board of directors and the company's compensation policy in his or her report to the general shareholders meeting (Baums 2004). As a final element at this juncture, consideration is also to be given to any compensatory damages claims and the assertion thereof, which is problematic given that the qualification of the actual damages can be challenging (Redenius-Hövermann 2019).

A second example to be cited of an influence of group behaviour and groupthink in the corporate law context is the distribution of mandates in the board of directors and the supervisory board. The mandates in the board of directors and the supervisory board will typically be assigned so as to remain as homogeneous as possible, although this does not categorically correspond to good corporate governance. The influence of group behaviour and of groupthink can be illustrated, in particular, with the example of filling the board of directors and supervisory board with female members because women, in proportion to their share of the population as well as in company workforces, are under represented at the higher leadership levels.

For the UK Lord Davies recommends in his report that UK listed companies in the FTSE 100 should be aiming for a minimum of 25 per cent female board member representation by 2015 (Davies 2011; see also Principles J, L and Provision 23 of the UK Corporate Governance Code 2018). Also he claims that quoted companies should be required to disclose each year the proportion of women on the board, women in senior executive positions, and female employees in the whole organisation (inserted in UK Corporate Governance Code 2016, Sec. 2.4). Even if a legal fixed quota was rejected by the Davies report, the proportion of women in the boards has risen considerably in a short timespan (Döll 2018).

A different set-up can be found in France, where legal fixed quotas of 20 per cent were introduced by a 2011 law (art. L. 225-17, L. 225-20, L. 225-24, L. 225-18-1, L. 225-69-1 Commercial code). Since 2017 a quota of 40 per cent has to be achieved in public listed companies; otherwise, among other sanctions, the board's remuneration will be 'frozen' until the quotas are reached (Redenius-Hövermann and Weber-Rey 2011).

German lawmakers have recently responded to this issue with a quota provision because, despite a recommendation in the German Corporate Governance Code (DCGK), no appropriate legal steps had been taken to enhance the underrepresentation of women on supervisory boards and boards of directors. Since 1 January 2016, pursuant to § 96 para. 2 AktG, the applicable law requires for all new elections that the supervisory board of publicly traded corporations that are equally represented with co-determination (*paritätisch mitbestimmt*) fulfil a quota of 30 per cent women's participation. For capital corporations that are publicly traded or that are subject to the co-determination duty, targets must be established for the supervisory board, the board of directors, and the management of a limited liability company (GmbH), as well as both management levels under the board of directors. In so doing, it must be taken into consideration that minimising groupthink requires bringing persons on the board and supervisory board who have professional experiences and qualifications that are proportionately of equal value. Otherwise, groupthink could even be reinforced by a quota provision. Furthermore, a quota provision displays a behaviour-controlling effect only if it is supported by appropriate control mechanisms; hence, sanctioning instruments and disclosure also play an important role here (Redenius-Hövermann 2019).

Denial Effect

The denial effect, i.e. when unpleasant facts are denied or dismissed out of hand, is rooted in Freud's displacement theory, which is again being debated today. Some psychologists are convinced that there is experimental evidence of displacement (Erdelyi 2006), while others believe that whether the human being displaces unconsciously cannot be tested experimentally. However, the discussion is all about the question of whether the denial is unconscious or not, and not about whether the denial effect exists.

In a business crisis, this effect is to be found both within the offensive forms of reaction, especially with excessive optimism and with excessive inclination to take risks, and within the defensive forms, above all in the phase of wishful thinking, because boards of directors dismiss a business crisis in order to pursue their objectives further (see Redenius-Hövermann 2019). Fink, Beak, and Taddeo (1971) show that in times of business crisis, 'reality is avoided or denied' by the board.

How lawmakers are trying to forestall this effect in corporate law is disputable. According to German law § 91 para. 2 AktG, the board of directors is obligated to set up a system for early recognition and monitoring (see here Redenius-Hövermann 2019). The board of directors, therefore, must establish measures for recognising early on developments that jeopardise the continued existence of the company, in order to be able to respond promptly to them (Baums 2011). Closely associated with the duty to set up an early warning system is the organisational and monitoring duty of the board of directors (Redenius-Hövermann 2019). Furthermore, the internal reporting duty of the board of directors vis-à-vis the supervisory board pursuant to § 90 AktG, as well as the disclosure duties, can also serve as a means of attenuating the denial effect, because the board of directors is obligated to report on the company's situation. It is precisely here that the periodicity of the reporting duty is a consideration, in order not to, in turn, promote other biases, e.g., the availability heuristic discussed earlier. In terms of the law governing publicly traded companies, the introduction of an emergency system is not obligatory, as is provided by insurance or bank oversight laws (see Chiu, Chapter 4 in this volume for more on governance of financial corporations).

In UK law, the Companies Act 2006 does not state anything concerning information duties, as it does not differentiate between executive and non-executive directors. A similar rule to the German duty might be seen in Principle F of the Corporate Governance Code 2018 where it is stated that: '[...] the chair [...] ensures that directors receive accurate, timely and clear information.'

De lege ferenda, the board of directors ought to be obligated to create an emergency plan as it is the case in Banking Supervision Law (§ 25a KWG, MaRisk AT 7.3 for German Law; 2.1. et seqq., 2.5, 2.5., 5.1. PRA Handbook General Organisation Requirements for UK Law; art. L. 511-64 Code moné-taire et financier for French Law). Such a plan would establish measures that guarantee the continuation of company processes in time-critical stages, par-ticularly those which serve to stabilise the company. Also, the appropriateness and effectiveness of the emergency plan ought to be reviewed at regular inter-vals. With such an obligation, the insights of behavioural science would find their way into the law governing publicly traded companies, as the board of directors creates a preventive instrument which will help to lead it in a crisis and can counteract misconduct such as the denial effect (Redenius-Hövermann 2019). An additional possibility for, *inter alia*, restricting the denial effect in a business crisis could consist of setting up a crisis committee. This crisis committee could be envisaged as a supervisory board committee, but its independence must be maintained. External consultants could partici-pate in the committee, in order to discern any misconduct in the board of directors, disclose it, and thus also restrict and counteract it (see in detail Redenius-Hövermann 2019).

An additional example of the occurrence of the denial effect in corporate law can be identified in the context of the discussion about the independence of supervisory or non-executive board members. Here, this effect can be manifested in belonging to a committee for a very long time because the per-son concerned, in a certain manner, becomes 'routine-blinded' and no longer confronts the activity on the supervisory board in a sufficiently critical man-ner (see Redenius-Hövermann 2019).

Thus far, there are no studies showing at which point in time this effect actually occurs. For the discussion of corporate law, the lack of evidence does not mean that this aspect can be dismissed. Thus, C.3 DCGK recommends that the length of membership on the supervisory board should be published. According to C.7 DCGK, a member of the supervisory board is no longer considered to be independent after twelve years of membership in the same supervisory board. Thus, twenty-four of the thirty DAX companies introduced a limit to the membership duration of supervisory board members in 2018: nineteen companies limit terms of office to between twelve and nineteen years, some even twenty to twenty-five years (von Werder and Danilov 2018). Looking at the denial effect, these timespans appear to be very long, however, and it is debatable whether these control limits need to be lowered. One proposal, which fits well with current comparative legal discussion, recommends a maximum of ten years, beyond which the director is not seen as independent (Redenius-Hövermann and Schmidt 2018).

According to Sec. 8.5.6 of the French MEDEF/AFEP-Code from June 2018 a board member is not independent anymore when he or she has been a director of the company for more than twelve years. The UK Corporate Governance Code is even more strict: according to sec. 2–10, independence has to be denied if a director has served on the board for more than nine years from the date of their first appointment (Redenius-Hövermann and Schmidt 2018).

Summary

Summarising, behavioural science insights provide refined forecasting tools for the corporate governance debate, in order to determine the reaction of the board members, the stewards, or the stakeholders to legal provisions. These insights thus contribute to fulfilling the task of legislative doctrine, whereby the interconnections, conditions, causes, and effects of the legislation are incorporated.

The contribution of behavioural economics and of neuroeconomics to corporate law lies in the enrichment of the search for legal provisions that will lead to the reduction of bias by improving the ability to evaluate actual human behaviour through the results of the neighbouring sciences. A complete, distilled solution cannot be expected from the behavioural sciences, and implementation remains a task that is genuinely one for jurisprudence.

Linear transplantations from behavioural science insights to compulsory implications in corporate law discourse are to be strictly rejected. It cannot and must not be the task of behavioural economics and neuroeconomics to determine the binding material content of provisions. However, to the extent that such insights enrich the corporate law discourse, they should be taken up.

The task of carving out normative implications by aligning actual behaviour with the predefined regulatory objective is ascribed to and reserved for the corporate law expert (Redenius-Hövermann 2019).

In addition, through various regulatory instruments, the correction of systematic deviations from the rational-theoretical model can be achieved, in that the regulation's degree of commitment can range from a compulsory legal standard to framework legislation or a by-laws requirement, all the way to the recommendation of the code. Baums (Chapter 3 in this volume) shows under which circumstances a certain type of regulatory instrument should be preferred: whenever public interest requires a binding rule that does not allow any deviation, rules must be enacted by hard law, i.e. statute. If that is not the case, and company-specific circumstances demand a more flexible approach in the sense of 'comply or explain', regulations should be set up as soft law, e.g. in the form of corporate governance codes. Some argue that the findings of behavioural insights should be incorporated into corporate law via soft law (Binder 2019). According to this view, soft law can ensure that there is no hasty application of behavioural insights, which are partly uncertain, contested, and even contradictory. This line of reasoning, which at first glance appears reasonable, must ultimately be rejected because it would establish a causality between the behavioural insights and normativity. Such causality is just not given. Corporate law is not bound by any model consistency. In addition, soft law should not be a 'catch-up solution', in the sense of a test run for the incorporation of behavioural insights into corporate law. The choice between soft and hard law has to be made in relation to the purpose of protection—whether public interest should be secured by statute—and not on the, especially not yet measurable, intensity of the behavioural deviation of the rational theory model (Redenius-Hövermann 2019). Behavioural insights can, however, support the formulation of corporate governance codes by pointing out behavioural inconsistencies that might occur if corporations are granted more flexibility. Thus, in the future the inclusion of the insights of behavioural science will become indispensable in the continuing development of corporate governance (Langenbucher 2019). More still: these insights will have to be included ever more strongly by way of a critical interdisciplinary exchange of ideas.

References

Arrow, K. J. (1982). 'Risk Perception in Psychology and Economics', *Economic Inquiry*, 20(1): 1–9.

Baums, T. (2004). 'Vorschlag eines Gesetzes zur Verbesserung der Transparenz von Vorstandsvergütungen', *ZIP—Zeitschrift für Wirtschaftsrecht*, 40: 1877–932.

Baums, T. (2011). 'Risiko und Risikosteuerung im Aktienrecht', *Zeitschrift für Unternehmens- und Gesellschaftsrecht*, 40(3): 218–74.

Belliveau, M. A., O'Reilly, C. A., and Wade, J. B. (1996). 'Social Capital at the Top: Effects of Social Similarity and Status on CEO Compensation', *Academy of Management Journal*, 39(6): 1568–93.

Binder, J.-H. (2019). 'Regelsetzung im Gesellschaftsrecht', in F. Möslein (ed.), *Regelsetzung im Privatrecht*. Tübingen: Mohr Siebeck, 373–96.

Bürger, C. and Weber, B. (2011). 'Neurofinance—Geldverarbeitung im Gehirn', in M. Reimann and B. Weber (eds.), *Neuroökonomie: Grundlagen—Methoden—Anwendungen*. Wiesbaden: Gabler, 219–80.

Cahn, A. and Donald, D. C. (2010). *Comparative Company Law*. Cambridge: Cambridge University Press.

Camerer, C. F. (2007). 'Neuroeconomics: Using Neuroscience to Make Economic Predictions', *Economic Journal*, 117(519): C26–C42.

Camerer, C. F., Dreber, A., Forsell, E., Ho, T.-H., Huber, J., Johannesson, M., Kirchler, M., Almenberg, J., Altmejd, A., Chan, T., Heikensten, E., Holzmeister, F., Imai, T., Isaksson, S., Nave, G., Pfeiffer, T., Razen, M., and Wu, H. (2016), 'Evaluating Replicability of Laboratory Experiments in Economics', *Science*, 351(6280): 1433–36.

Camerer, C. F., Dreber, A., Holzmeister, F., Ho, T.-H., Huber, J., Johannesson, M., Kirchler, M., Nave, G., Nosek, B. A., Pfeiffer, T., Altmejd, A., Buttrick, N., Chan, T., Chen, Y., Forsell, E., Gampa, A., Heikensten, E., Hummer, L., Imai, T., Isaksson, S., Manfredi, D., Rose, J., Wagenmakers, E.-J., and Wu, H. (2018). 'Evaluating the Replicability of Social Science Experiments in *Nature* and *Science* between 2010 and 2015', *Nature Human Behaviour*, 2: 637–44.

Clark, A. E. and Oswald, A. J. (1996). 'Satisfaction and Comparison Income', *Journal of Public Economics*, 61(3): 359–81.

Davies, E. M. (2011). *Women on Boards: Review*. London: Department of Business, Innovation and Skills. Retrieved from https://www.gov.uk/government/publications/women-on-boards-review (accessed 20 December 2019).

Department for Business, Energy and Industrial Strategy (2016). *Corporate Governance Reform: Green Paper*. Retrieved from https://www.gov.uk/government/consultations/corporate-governance-reform (accessed 10 January 2020).

Döll, M. (2018). *Aktienrecht und Codes of Best Practices*. Berlin: Duncker & Humblot.

Dohmen, T., Falk, A., Huffman, D., Sunde, U., Schupp, J., and Wagner, G. G. (2009). 'Individual Risk Attitudes: Measurement, Determinants and Behavioural Consequences', *Journal of the European Economic Association*, 9(3): 522–50.

Englerth, M. and Towfigh, E. V. (2017). '§7 Verhaltensökonomie', in E. V. Towfigh and N. Petersen (eds.), *Ökonomische Methoden im Recht: Eine Einführung für Juristen*, 2nd edition. Tübingen: Mohr Siebeck, 165–200.

Entorf, H., Gattung, F., Möbert, J., and Pahlke, I. (2009). 'Aufsichtsratsverflechtungen und ihr Einfluss auf die Vorstandsbezüge von DAX-Unternehmen', *Zeitschrift für Betriebswirtschaft*, 79: 1131–41.

Erdelyi, M. H. (2006). 'The Unified Theory of Repression', *Behavioral and Brain Sciences*, 29(5): 499–511.

Fink, S. L., Beak, J., and Taddeo, K. (1971). 'Organizational Crisis and Change', *Journal of Applied Behavioral Science*, 7(1): 15–37.

Fischhoff, B. (1975). 'Hindsight ≠ Foresight: The Effect of Outcome Knowledge on Judgement Under Uncertainty', *Journal of Experimental Psychology: Human Perception and Performance*, 1(3): 288–99.

Fleischer, H. (2004). 'Gesetz und Vertrag als alternative Problemlösungsmodelle im Gesellschaftsrecht—Prolegomena zu einer Theorie gesellschaftsrechtlicher Regelsetzung', *ZHR—Zeitschrift für das ges. Handelsrecht & Wirtschaftsrecht*, 168(06): 673–707.

Fleischer, H. (2019). 'Kommentierung zu § 93 AktG', in G. Spindler and E. Stilz (eds.), *Kommentar zum Aktiengesetz*, Band 1, 4th edition. München: C.H. Beck.

Fleischer, H. and Bedkowski, D. (2009). ' "Say on Pay" im deutschen Aktienrecht: Das neue Vergütungsvotum der Hauptversammlung nach § 120 Abs. 4 AktG', *Die Aktiengesellschaft*, 60: 677–86.

Germain, M. and Magnier, V. (2017). *Traité de droit commercial. Les sociétés commerciales*, Vol. 2, 22nd edition, Paris: L.G.D.J. Lextenso.

Glimcher, P. W. (2011). *Foundations of Neuroeconomics Analysis*. Oxford: Oxford University Press.

Guthrie, C., Rachlinski, J. L., and Wistrich, A. J. (2001). 'Inside the Judicial Mind', *Cornell Law Review*, 86: 777–830.

Janis, I. L. (1972). *Victims of Groupthink: A Psychological Study of Foreign-policy Decisions and Fiascoes*. Boston: Houghton Mifflin.

Kahneman, D. H. (2003). 'A Psychological Perspective on Economics', *American Economic Review*, 93(2): 162–68.

Kelman, M. (1998). 'Behavioral Economics as Part of a Rhetorical Duet: A Response to Jolls, Sunstein and Thaler', *Stanford Law Review*, 50(5): 1577–91.

Kirchgässner, G. (2008). *Homo oeconomicus: Das ökonomische Modell individuellen Verhaltens und seine Anwendung in den Wirtschafts- und Sozialwissenschaften*, 3rd edition, Tübingen: Mohr Siebeck.

Kort, M. (2015). 'Kommentierung zu § 87', in K. Hopt and M. Wiedemann (eds.), *Großkommentar zum Aktiengesetz*, 5th edition. Berlin: de Gryuter.

Langenbucher, K. (2019). 'Interdisziplinäre Forschung im Unternehmensrecht—auf dem Weg zu einer cognitive Corporate Governance?', *Zeitschrift für Unternehmens- und Gesellschaftsrecht*, 48(5): 717–59.

Laufersweiler, J. and Redenius-Hövermann, J. (2017). 'Brauchen wir eine Legal Judgment Rule?', *Berufsverband Compliance Manager*. Retrieved from https://www.bvdcm.de/sites/default/files/compliance_kommentar_nr.3.pdf (accessed 20 December 2019).

Leahy, R. L. (1992). 'Cognitive Therapy on Wall Street: Schemas and Scripts of Invulnerability', *Journal of Cognitive Psychotherapy*, 6(4): 245–58.

Lüdemann, J. (2007). *Netzwerke, Öffentliches Recht und Rezeptionstheorie*, Preprints of the Max Planck Institute for Research on Collective Goods No. 7. Bonn: Max Planck Institute for Research on Collective Goods.

McClure, S. M., Laibson, D. I., Loewenstein, G., and Cohen, J. D. (2004). 'Separate Neural Systems Value Immediate and Delayed Monetary Rewards', *Science*, 306: 503–7.

Moorhead, G., Ference, R., and Neck, C. P. (1991). 'Group Decision Fiascoes Continue: Space Shuttle Challenger and a Revised Groupthink Framework', *Journal of Human Relations*, 44(6): 539–50.

Pepper, A., Gore, J., and Crossman, A. (2013). 'Are Long-term Incentive Plans an Effective and Efficient Way of Motivating Senior Executives?', *Human Resource Management Journal*, 23(1): 36–51.

Redenius-Hövermann, J. (2010). *La responsabilité des dirigeants dans les sociétés anonymes en droits français et allemande*. Paris: L.G.D.J.

Redenius-Hövermann, J. (2015). 'De la rémunération des dirigeants en droit allemand', in J.-J. Ansault et al. (eds.), *Mélanges en l'honneur du Professeur Michel Germain*, Paris: Lextenso, 729ff.

Redenius-Hövermann, J. (2019). *Verhalten im Unternehmensrecht—Über die realverhaltensorientierte Fortentwicklung des Unternehmensrechts anhand ausgewählter Anwendungsbeispiele*. Tübingen: Mohr Siebeck.

Redenius-Hövermann, J. and Schmidt, H. (2018). 'Zur Unabhängigkeit von Aufsichtsratsmitgliedern', *Zeitschrift für Corporate Governance*, 5: 218–24.

Redenius-Hövermann, J. and Weber-Rey, D. (2011). 'La représentation des femmes dans les conseils d'administration et de surveillance en France et en Allemagne', *Revue des sociétés*, 4: 203–11.

Rost, K. and Osterloh, M. (2008). 'You Pay a Fee for Strong Beliefs: Homogeneity as a Driver of Corporate Governance Failure', CREMA Working Paper No. 28. Zürich: Center for Research in Economics, Management and the Arts (CREMA).

Spindler, G. (2005). 'Das Gesetz über die Offenlegung von Vorstandsvergütungen—VorstOG', *Neue Zeitschrift für Gesellschaftsrecht*, 17: 689–91.

Thaler, R. H. (1992). *Quasi-Rational Economics*. New York: Russell Sage Foundation.

Tversky, A. and Kahneman, D. H. (1973). 'Availability: A Heuristic for Judging Frequency and Probability', *Cognitive Psychology*, 5(2): 207–32.

von Werder, A. and Danilov, K. (2018). 'Corporate Governance Report 2018: Kodexakzeptanz und Kodexanwendung', *Der Betrieb*, 34: 1997–2008.

Vroom, V. H. (1964). *Work and Motivation*. New York: Wiley.

Whyte, W. (1961). *Men at Work*. Homewood: Dorsey Press.

13

Advances in Corporate Governance: Conclusion and Implications

Helmut K. Anheier and Christoph M. Abels

The preceding chapters covered the governance of a wide range of corporate forms. They were motivated by our attempt to balance the emphasis on listed corporations in much of the governance literature by bringing in other private as well as public corporate forms. The chapters also addressed the key issues which we identified and introduced in Chapter 2, and did so from cross-national and interdisciplinary perspectives.

What, then, are the results and implications for corporate governance research and policy? This is best answered by returning to the three questions we posed in Chapter 1: what are the applicability and usefulness of competing approaches for understanding governance behaviour from a theoretical perspective? How does corporate governance differ across organisational forms? And what implications for policy-makers, regulators, and corporate leaders come to mind? We will address each in turn.

Do We Have the Right Theories?

On 15 September 2008 Lehman Brothers, the fourth largest investment bank in the United States, collapsed. Lehman's bankruptcy marked the beginning of the global financial crisis, regarded as the worst financial crisis since the Great Depression of the 1930s. Unsurprisingly, the global financial crisis was soon connected to large-scale failures of corporate management across many corporations, financial and others. Many failed because they did not fulfil basic governance duties: monitor corporate performance, establish adequate remuneration schemes, and implement effective risk management (OECD 2009).

Although there are many advocates for the corporate governance failure hypothesis, others argue that boards and management did exactly what they

Helmut K. Anheier and Christoph M. Abels, *Advances in Corporate Governance: Conclusion and Implications* In: *Advances in Corporate Governance: Comparative Perspectives.* Edited by: Helmut K. Anheier and Theodor Baums, Oxford University Press (2020). © Hertie School.
DOI: 10.1093/oso/9780198866367.003.0013

were supposed to do according to principal–agent theory: they aligned the interests of shareholders and managers. Banks with shareholder-friendly boards were associated with worse financial performance, exposing their banks to larger losses (Beltratti and Stulz 2009). The problem, it seems, is not the failure to follow through on monitoring duties, but lies with the model itself. Indeed, financial institutions are hardly the only type of organisation that raises questions about the appropriateness of the principal–agent model. For social media corporations as well, current corporate governance regimes have not prevented some corporations from causing major scandals—with Facebook leading the pack with at least twenty-one scandals in 2018 alone (Lapowsky 2018).

These examples and others described in this volume refer to a fundamental question: Should principal–agent theory still be the most relevant paradigm for researchers and policy-makers? Even if the approach may still apply to listed corporations, there are other corporate forms to which the theory has limited relevance. As we have seen in this volume, the universe of organisational forms is diverse: from non-profit organisations, to social enterprises and philanthropic foundations, to public and international organisations. The range of organisational forms may well be as broad as that of their governance models. Moreover, the economy is more than the sum of publicly traded corporations. In other words, one theoretical approach such as principal–agent does not capture the governance requirements of all organisational forms.

In the case of social enterprises, for example, the premise of agency theory does not hold in the face of managers primarily driven by intrinsic motivation and the will to contribute to the organisation's success, sometimes even at the expense of their own interests (Mair, Wolf, and Ioan, Chapter 8 in this volume). The same is true for non-profit organisations, where application of traditional approaches to corporate governance might even hurt the organisation, since agency approach-based governance systems do not account for differences in upward and downward accountability—both to funders and beneficiaries (Donnelly-Cox, Meyer, and Wijkström, Chapter 7 in this volume).

The shifting sources of financial support for international organisations also calls into question the basic premises of agency theory. While in the past, member states acted as principals which funded and mandated international organisations as their agents, contributions from non-state actors have dramatically increased. Member state funding for the World Health Organization, for example, has dropped from 100 to 22 per cent, making private actors such as foundations and trust funds the de facto principals (Cannon and Biersteker, Chapter 9 in this volume). For social media corporations, with their increasing relevance as a forum for public debate and opinion, it is so far unclear whether principal–agent approaches apply (Stockmann, Chapter 11 in this volume); but in this case, given the prevalence of co-production, the role of the customer remains unsettled for corporate governance.

Corporate Governance and Organisational Forms

In general, the needs for corporate governance vary across organisational forms, and so do models and approaches.

Financial institutions are a prototypical case for misguided corporate governance approaches: adherence to conventional standards has repeatedly failed to serve shareholders and, even more importantly, the public interest, thus creating financial instability. High-profile failures of financial institutions during the financial crisis, e.g. AIG, Lehman Brothers, and Bear Stearns, provide prominent examples of the influence these corporations have and highlight why they differ from regular listed corporations. This distinction has been at the centre of Chiu's argument (Chapter 4 in this volume), pointing out that shareholder-centred corporate governance regimes can have deleterious effects on financial corporations, and thereby the economy as a whole. However, regulatory intervention might not always benefit shareholders and other stakeholders, such as bondholders, equally (Mülbert 2010). Decision-making that aims at securing financial stability, for example, does not necessarily increase shareholder wealth. Therefore, the corporate governance of financial institutions differs in many respects from that of listed corporations.

In non-profit organisations, governance approaches and codes serve a different purpose, especially given their frequently pronounced value base and the presence of multiple stakeholders. Here, such codes are primarily seen as a way to create external legitimacy or to strengthen internal legitimacy and board members' perception that the board is well governed (Walters and Tacon 2018). In many cases, 'comply or explain' approaches are furthermore implemented as certification marks and quality regulations for charities that compete for donations.

In social enterprises, governance is said to support organisational goals by providing a mechanism to cope with different institutional logics that make social enterprises vulnerable to mission drift, meaning that they lose sight of their social mission when responding to market and political pressure (Cornforth 2014; Ebrahim, Battilana, and Mair 2014). Corporate governance can therefore help social enterprises to fulfil multiple goals and attend multiple stakeholders, and thereby 'stay hybrid' (Mair, Mayer, and Lutz 2015).

With their specific structure as being asset-based and purpose-driven without owners and shareholders, corporate governance in foundations serves other purposes. Foundations suffer from what Anheier and Leat (2019) describe as the benign fallibility syndrome. The dual independence of foundations from market and electoral oversight means weaker incentives for managers to perform and weaker signals to managers to guide and correct their performance. Therefore, without clear roles for principals and agents, traditional corporate governance recommendations may not be suitable for foundations. Anheier and Leat (2019) argue that knowledge diversity of board members in combination with an active involvement of other stakeholders in identifying opportunities and best strategies are crucial for helping foundations achieve their goals.

For international organisations, corporate governance is different from other organisational forms discussed in this volume. International organisations are composed of individual sovereign member states which delegate authority and operations to a secretariat, which then often establishes executive boards to advise member states and to oversee the secretariat's operations (Saz Carranza, Federo, Marin, and Losada 2016).

History is full of examples highlighting the need to overcome biases that undermine effective management and problem solving. In his seminal article, Janis (1972a: 84) pointed to the Bay of Pigs invasion, where a group of what he calls 'the greatest array of intellectual talent in the history of American Government' did not anticipate the disaster the invasion might eventually become. Roughly a decade later, the failed launch of the Challenger space shuttle, which exploded 73 seconds after take-off, raised further concerns about flawed decision-making (Hirokawa, Gouran, and Martz 1988). Both examples were said to be caused by groupthink, which Janis (1972b: 9) defines as 'a mode of thinking that people engage in when they are deeply involved in a cohesive in-group, when the members' strivings for unanimity override their motivation to realistically appraise alternative courses of action.' These incidents were especially prominent as they involved highly respected agencies, the US Central Intelligence Agency and the National Aeronautics and Space Administration.

It demands little imagination to depict how these decisions could have happened in other organisations as well. A sound corporate governance regime, informed by behavioural science, can help protect organisations against such developments. Janis (1991) argues that an insulated group, a lack of impartial leadership, missing norms demanding methodical procedures, and social as well as ideological homogeneity of group members are structural flaws of an organisation that can make a group of decision-makers, such as members of an executive board, more prone to groupthink.

Therefore, as Redenius-Hövermann argues in Chapter 12 of this volume, corporate governance codes should also consider the findings of the behavioural sciences when designing recommendations. Even beyond the boards and managements of listed corporations, organisations can profit from behaviourally informed policies.

Implications

Overall, all authors included in this volume have pointed to future research needs. In more traditional realms of corporate governance, such as listed corporations and financial institutions, the debate focuses on the question of whether mandatory or voluntary regulation should be applied. It remains open how these tensions should be approached: is regulation policy the suitable approach, or should policy-makers aim for voluntary regulations, such as 'comply or explain'? In Chapter 3 of this volume, Baums argues that a company's specific circumstances should be considered when discussing regulatory approaches, since corporations might need the flexibility of 'comply or explain' mechanisms. If deviation from corporate governance principles is not in the public interest, governance rules should be enacted by statute.

In other organisational forms, the debate is quite different. Gabrielsson, Huse, and Åberg (Chapter 5 in this volume) stress the importance of a balanced theoretical perspective to account for the characteristics of small and medium enterprises (SMEs), since SME is a highly diverse category, ranging from small companies that intend to grow as fast as possible to those that intend to stay small. In contrast to large listed corporations, SMEs often have a concentrated ownership and a mixture of corporate governance roles among shareholders, board members, and managers. Above all, SMEs are important actors: they account for 75 per cent of European GDP (European Confederation of Directors' Associations (ecoDa) 2010).

Mair, Wolf, and Ioan (Chapter 8 in this volume) argue that an umbrella mechanism should be established to address the hybrid needs of social enterprises. A mechanism like this could work for both for-profit and non-profit legal forms, improving the regulation of using legal forms for legitimacy reasons. The authors furthermore suggest formalising structures to involve beneficiaries in organisational governance. However, more empirical research on social enterprises is needed that investigates actual governance experience and practices.

With new global and transnational problems emerging, Cannon and Biersteker (Chapter 9 in this volume) question governance driven by the principal–agent relationship among member states, secretariats, and executive boards. In the face of hybrid governance arrangements which encounter considerable competition in the marketplace for global governance authority, they suggest changing the way we traditionally think about international organisations and their governance.

Stockmann (Chapter 11 in this volume) describes the inclusion of representatives of different stakeholder groups in the board of directors. Twitter and Facebook are already using this approach. However, other companies such as YouTube and WeChat do not have their own boards, as they are subsidiaries of larger conglomerates and therefore unable to directly appoint directors. In some countries, like the US, the legal environment poses additional barriers to implementing such strategies. Corporate boards' conflict of interest policies furthermore complicate the inclusion of stakeholder representatives.

Although the empirical basis for this approach is limited thus far, and the right mix between government, business, and society in the governance of social media has not yet been determined, policy-makers should foster intersectoral exchange. Facebook, for example, is already using non-governmental organisations and journalists to fact-check content and flag wrong or misleading information (Facebook 2018). However, these collaborations appeared to be of varying success (Levin 2018), and policy-makers should create frameworks in which these joint ventures could succeed.

Chiu (Chapter 4 in this volume) questions the suitability of shareholder-centred approaches to the governance of financial institutions. As the financial crisis has shown, the focus on shareholder value of some institutions has led to worse financial performance (Beltratti and Stulz 2009). These shareholder-friendly boards have ignored their responsibility to other stakeholders. As a response to these shortcomings, Hopt (2017) suggests creditor governance that includes creditors, especially depositors and bondholders, as another stakeholder group. Creditor governance would establish improved risk management, as creditors would demand higher interest rates for companies known for their excessive risk-taking (Kokkinis 2014). Especially bondholders have fundamentally different interests compared to shareholders, as corporate failure would cause bondholders to lose their entire investment, while improved corporate performance does not increase their gains. As risk-taking was identified as one of the major causes of failures that led to the global financial crisis (Kirkpatrick 2009; Larosière et al. 2009), creditor governance appears to be a well-suited approach to prevent excessive risk-taking in the future. In her chapter, Chiu furthermore points out that UK policy-makers already started to look into problematic corporate behaviour and impose regulation on financial institutions, which reaches risk management and corporate culture. The next crisis will tell whether these developments could serve as a blueprint for future improvements of the governance of financial institutions.

The research presented in this volume highlights the necessity to rethink how corporate governance is approached in different corporations. In particular, it has become apparent that corporate governance regimes have to be tailored to the corporate form to fulfil their intended purpose. Applying a one-size-fits-all approach can have devastating consequences, as seen during the financial crisis. On a theoretical level, the comparison of various corporate forms has shown that agency theory, while being useful for listed corporations, does not fit all corporate forms. Other theoretical approaches discussed in this volume, such as multiple agency, stewardship, or stakeholder theory, are better suited to cope with company-specific circumstances and the demands of various stakeholders beyond shareholder. These theories can help to design corporate governance mechanisms that support the corporation to reach its goals, without being just an administrative burden.

Approaching corporate governance from a comparative perspective can help analysts and policy-makers to develop better corporate governance regimes. Still, a substantial need for further research remains, as listed corporations and agency theory have been the main focus of many scholars. And even in these areas, many fundamental questions, for example, how corporate governance regimes relate to corporate performance, remain largely unanswered. We are confident that comparative research can help to increase our understanding of governance across corporate forms and inform the design of more effective corporate governance regimes.

References

Anheier, H. and Leat, D. (2019). *The Ambiguity of Success: On the Performance of Philanthropic Foundations*. London: Routledge.

Beltratti, A. and Stulz, R. M. (2009). 'Why Did Some Banks Perform Better during the Credit Crisis? A Cross-Country Study of the Impact of Governance and

Regulation', ECGI Working Paper Series in Finance No. 254. Brussels: European Corporate Governance Institute (ECGI).

Cornforth, C. (2014). 'Understanding and Combating Mission Drift in Social Enterprises', *Social Enterprise Journal*, 10(1): 3–20. https://doi.org/10.1108/SEJ-09-2013-0036

Ebrahim, A., Battilana, J., and Mair, J. (2014). 'The Governance of Social Enterprises: Mission Drift and Accountability Challenges in Hybrid Organizations', *Research in Organizational Behavior*, 34: 81–100. https://doi.org/10.1016/j.riob.2014.09.001

European Confederation of Directors' Associations (ecoDa) (2010). *Corporate Governance Guidelines and Principles for Unlisted Companies in Europe*. Brussels: ecoDa.

Facebook (2018). 'Third-party Fact-checking on Facebook', Facebook. Retrieved from https://en-gb.facebook.com/help/publisher/182222309230722 (accessed 3 January 2019).

Hirokawa, R. Y., Gouran, D. S., and Martz, A. E. (1988). 'Understanding the Sources of Faulty Group Decision Making', *Small Group Behavior*, 19(4): 411–33. https://doi.org/10.1177/104649648801900401

Hopt, K. J. (2017). 'Corporate Governance von Finanzinstituten', *Zeitschrift für Unternehmens- und Gesellschaftsrecht*, 46(4): 438–59. https://doi.org/10.1515/zgr-2017-0018

Janis, I. (1991). 'Groupthink', in E. Griffin (ed.), *A First Look at Communication Theory*. New York: McGrawHill, 235–27.

Janis, I. L. (1972a). 'Groupthink', *Psychology Today*, 84–9.

Janis, I. L. (1972b). *Victims of Groupthink*. Boston: Houghton Mifflin Company.

Kirkpatrick, G. (2009). 'The Corporate Governance Lessons from the Financial Crisis', *OECD Journal: Financial Market Trends*, (1): 61–87. https://doi.org/10.1787/fmt-v2009-art3-en

Kokkinis, A. (2014). 'A Primer on Corporate Governance in Banks and Financial Institutions: Are Banks Special?', in I. H-Y. Chiu, M. McKee, A. P. Donovan, R. Edmunds, A. Kokkinis, J. Lowry, M. T. Moore, and A. Reisberg (eds.), *The Law on Corporate Governance in Banks*. Cheltenham: Edward Elgar Publishing, 1–41.

Lapowsky, I. (2018). 'The 21 (and Counting) Biggest Facebook Scandals of 2018', *Wired*, 28 December. Retrieved from https://www.wired.com/story/facebook-scandals-2018/ (accessed 23 August 2019).

Larosière, J. De, Balcerowicz, L., Issing, O., Masera, R., McCarthy, C., Nyberg, L.,...Ruding, O. (2009). *The High-Level Group on Financial Supervision in the EU*. Brussels: European Commission.

Levin, S. (2018). '"They Don't Care": Facebook Factchecking in Disarray as Journalists Push to Cut Ties', *The Guardian*, 10 November. Retrieved from https://www.theguardian.com/technology/2018/dec/13/they-dont-care-facebook-fact-checking-in-disarray-as-journalists-push-to-cut-ties (accessed 23 August 2019).

Mair, J., Mayer, J., and Lutz, E. (2015). 'Navigating Institutional Plurality: Organizational Governance in Hybrid Organizations', *Organization Studies*, 36(6): 713–39. https://doi.org/10.1177/0170840615580007

Mülbert, P. O. (2010). 'Corporate Governance of Banks after the Financial Crisis—Theory, Evidence, Reforms', ECGI Working Paper Series in Law No. 151. Brussels: European Corporate Governance Institute (ECGI).

OECD (2009). *Corporate Governance and the Financial Crisis: Key Findings and Main Messages. OECD Steering Group on Corporate Governance*. Paris: OECD.

Saz Carranza, A., Federo, R., Marin, X. F., and Losada, C. (2016). 'The Boards of International Governmental Organizations: Resource Providers or Delegated Controllers?', paper for the 9th Annual Conference on Political Economy in International Organizations, Salt Lake City, 7–9 January 2016. Salt Lake City: INOMICS.

Walters, G. and Tacon, R. (2018). 'The 'Codification' of Governance in the Non-profit Sport Sector in the UK', *European Sport Management Quarterly*, 18(4): 482–500. https://doi.org/10.1080/16184742.2017.1418405

Index